Corporate law and economic analysis

Corporate law and economic analysis

Edited by

LUCIAN ARYE BEBCHUK
Harvard Law School

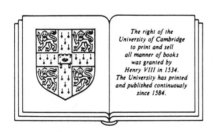

The right of the
University of Cambridge
to print and sell
all manner of books
was granted by
Henry VIII in 1534.
The University has printed
and published continuously
since 1584.

CAMBRIDGE UNIVERSITY PRESS
Cambridge
New York   Port Chester   Melbourne   Sydney

Published by the Press Syndicate of the University of Cambridge
The Pitt Building, Trumpington Street, Cambridge CB2 1RP
40 West 20th Street, New York, NY 10011, USA
10 Stamford Road, Oakleigh, Melbourne 3166, Australia

First published 1990

Printed in Canada

Library of Congress Cataloging-in-Publication Data
Corporate law and economic analysis / edited by Lucian Arye Bebchuk.
p. cm.
Papers from a conference held at Harvard Law School, Nov. 1986,
and sponsored by the Harvard Law School Program in Law and
Economics.
Includes index.
ISBN 0-521-36054-4
1. Consolidation and merger of corporations – United States –
Congresses.   2. Corporate reorganizations – United States –
Congresses.   3. Corporation law – Economic aspects – United States –
Congresses.   I. Bebchuk, Lucian A.   II. Harvard Law School.
Program in Law and Economics.
KF1477.A75C644   1989
346.73'06626–dc20
[347.3066626]   89-32997
                                                                      CIP

British Library Cataloguing in Publication Data
Corporate law and economic analysis.

1. Companies. Law
I. Bebchuk, Lucian Arye
342.6'66

ISBN 0-521-36054-4 hard covers

Contents

List of contributors   *page* vii
Introduction   ix
Acknowledgments   xiv

1   Mergers, acquisitions, and leveraged buyouts: an
    efficiency assessment   1
    Oliver E. Williamson

2   Discounted share prices as a source of acquisition gains   29
    Reinier Kraakman

3   Ties that bond: dual class common stock and the
    problem of shareholder choice   74
    Jeffrey N. Gordon

4   Property rights in assets and resistance to tender offers   118
    *David D. Haddock, Jonathan R. Macey, and Fred S.
    McChesney*

5   A new approach to corporate reorganizations   150
    Lucian Arye Bebchuk

6   The corporate contract   182
    Frank H. Easterbrook and Daniel R. Fischel

7   The state competition debate in corporate law   216
    Roberta Romano

8   The positive role of tax law in corporate and capital
    markets   255
    Saul Levmore

9   Ownership of the firm   281
    Henry Hansmann

    Index   315

Contributors

Lucian Arye Bebchuk Professor of Law, Harvard Law School

Frank H. Easterbrook Judge, United States Court of Appeals for the Seventh Circuit, and Senior Lecturer, The Law School, University of Chicago

Daniel R. Fischel Professor of Law and Finance, The Law School and Graduate School of Business, University of Chicago

Jeffrey N. Gordon Professor of Law, Columbia Law School

David D. Haddock Professor of Law, Northwestern University

Henry Hansmann Professor of Law, Yale Law School

Reinier Kraakman Professor of Law, Harvard Law School

Saul Levmore Professor of Law, University of Virginia Law School

Fred S. McChesney Robert T. Thompson Professor of Law and Professor of Economics, Emory University

Jonathan R. Macey Professor of Law, Cornell Law School

Roberta Romano Professor of Law, Yale Law School and Yale School of Organization and Management

Oliver E. Williamson Transamerica Professor of Business, Economics, and Law, University of California, Berkeley

Introduction

Drafts of all the articles in this volume were presented in a conference at Harvard Law School in November 1986. The conference was sponsored by the Harvard Law School Program in Law and Economics. I wish to thank the John M. Olin Foundation which, through its generous grant to the Law and Economics Program, made possible the organization of the conference and the preparation of this volume.

The purpose of the conference and of this volume has been to put together research work at the frontier of the economic analysis of corporate law, especially work on the main policy questions now confronting this area of the law. The last decade has brought certain corporate transactions and arrangements to the forefront of public attention and public debate. At the same time, the last decade has been one in which a new mode of corporate law analysis has developed – one that uses the tools of economics to study the consequences and desirable features of corporate rules and regulations. The present collection should provide readers with a good sense of the power, current state, and future direction of work in economic analysis of law.

The first five articles in the volume focus directly on those transactions in corporate control and structure that have attracted much interest and controversy in the past decade – corporate takeovers, buyouts, recapitalizations, and reorganizations. These transactions have had great impact on the way in which capital markets – and the public companies traded in them – operate. The first two articles consider the economic motives and forces that underlie these transactions, whereas the following three articles discuss important policy issues raised by these transactions.

In Chapter 1, Oliver E. Williamson uses his well-known approach to the study of economic organization to explain the motives for the main corporate control transactions. Williamson's approach focuses on examining which economic structures can best minimize the transaction costs involved in the functioning of complex economic organizations. From this perspective, Williamson analyzes the potential motives that underlie mergers, takeovers, and buyouts. He suggests that cost savings from horizontal mergers, if any, take the form of economies of scale, whereas those associated with vertical mergers usually take the form of transaction costs economies. He shows that conglomerate mergers can be interpreted from an internal capital markets perspective. The appearance of takeovers, he argues, is an outgrowth of earlier developments of which the conglomerate is a part. Finally, he seeks to explain leveraged buyouts as motivated by the opportunity for a more efficient use of financial instruments: Because the rational use of debt and equity depends on the characteristics of the firm's assets, a leveraged buyout can create efficiency gains in those cases in which the use of equity financing has become "excessive."

Reinier Kraakman offers, in Chapter 2, a different perspective on the motives for corporate acquisitions and restructuring. He explores the implications of the conjecture that discounted share prices are an acquisition motive for an important subset of recent takeovers. Share prices are discounted if they fall below reliable appraisals of the net present value of cash flows that target assets are expected to generate. Kraakman presents evidence of share discounts in closed-end funds, natural resource firms, and recent targets of acquisitions, buyouts, and recapitalizations. He proposes that share discounts can survive in today's acquisition market, that they are a plausible source of large premia paid to target shareholders, and that they can explain much financial restructuring among American firms. Two broad hypotheses, he suggests, might explain how share discounts arise. One is that investors rationally expect the managers of discounted firms to misinvest future corporate cash flows. The other is that share prices themselves are noisy or skewed. Kraakman suggests that the two hypotheses have divergent policy implications. He argues, however, that existing evidence does not enable selecting between these two accounts of discounting behavior.

In Chapter 3, Jeffrey Gordon examines the policy issues involved in dual class recapitalizations. Such recapitalizations, which produce classes of common stock with different voting rights, have become very important in recent years, as companies have sought to use them in defense against the takeover threat. Gordon argues that, as a theoretical and empirical matter, it seems likely that dual class recapitalizations reduce the wealth of public shareholders. Collective action and strategic choice problems in shareholder voting, he points out, may nevertheless lead to approval of proposals for such recapitalizations. He suggests that the traditional NYSE one share–one vote rule offered a unique and suitable bond against opportunistic renegotiation of the firm's capital structure that would lower the cost of capital. He therefore recommends that the SEC adopt rules that protect the NYSE's ability to offer this bond. Specifically, he argues that the SEC should bar the Amex and the NASDAC from listing the stock of a firm delisted by the NYSE for violating its traditional one share–one vote rule.

The volume's fourth chapter is by David D. Haddock, Jonathan R. Macey, and Fred S. McChesney. They argue that resistance to tender offers – even when such resistance is unlikely to facilitate an auction – may be beneficial to shareholders. Defensive tactics by target managements are likened by the authors to bargaining by agents for the owners of other assets that are traded in thin markets. Haddock, Macey, and McChesney argue that, under such circumstances, resistance enables sellers of assets to garner a greater share of the gains from exchange and thereby provides assets' owners with greater initial incentives to make value-enhancing investments with their assets. Finally, they take issue with the argument that, even if defensive tactics enhance the value of the firms that employ them, such tactics should be banned because they impose external costs on other firms by reducing the monitoring done by potential bidders.

In the volume's fifth chapter, I discuss the policy problems involved in Chapter 11 reorganizations and put forward a new method for dividing the reorganization pie among participants in reorganizations. Corporate reorganizations have always been the main way for handling insolvency problems of large corporations. The reorganization process, however, as thus far practiced, involves substantial efficiency and fairness problems: It produces substantial delay and transactions costs; it often results in an inefficient capital structure; and it frequently produces substantial deviations from participants' contractual entitlements. I then propose a method for addressing these problems: Participants in a reorganization would receive a set of rights with respect to the reorganized company's securities; these rights would be designed so that, whatever the reorganization value is, the participants would not have a basis for complaining that they are receiving less than the value to which they are entitled. Although the method is put forward as a basis for law reform, I show that it also can be used under the existing reorganization rules.

The next two articles expand the scope of analysis by considering not some particular corporate transactions, however important, but rather the market forces that shape such corporate arrangements in general. In Chapter 6, Frank H. Easterbrook and Daniel R. Fischel focus on the corporate arrangements established by corporate charters. A fundamental question in corporate law concerns the extent to which companies should be free to shape the corporate arrangements governing them. To answer this question, Easterbrook and Fischel consider the various market forces and incentives that affect the decisions of those who design and change corporate charters. Their analysis leads them to adopt a "contractualist" position. Under this view, corporate law should not impose mandatory terms restricting the choice available to private parties; it should only facilitate the process of private contracting.

In Chapter 7, Roberta Romano considers the market forces that shape state corporate law. States compete over incorporating companies, and many of the rules governing companies are provided by the state in which the company is incorporated. A perennial issue in corporate law reform has been whether the competition among states has been a race to the top or a race to the bottom. Romano offers a synthesis of the existing learning on this competition. After summarizing the traditional positions on the issue, she puts forward her own approach, which is based on a transaction-cost explanation for Delaware's success in the competition among states. She then examines a controversial subset of state laws – antitakeover statutes – whose problematic place in corporation codes muddies the debate. She next reviews the findings of the empirical studies that have sought to arbitrate the state competition debate by employing financial econometric techniques. She concludes by discussing the implications for public policy of the new learning on state competition.

The last two articles further expand, in different ways, the scope of the volume's analysis. Whereas preceding articles in the volume examine how corporate behavior is affected by corporate-law rules, Chapter 8 by Saul Levmore discusses the effect of tax rules on corporate behavior. Taxes are usually viewed as distorting the "real" decisions of companies. Although Levmore agrees that taxes often have such distortionary effect, he attempts to show that there are instances in which the presence of taxes has a surprisingly "positive" effect on the operation of corporations. He first explores this positive role of tax law in the context of financing decisions, or the capital structure, of the firm. He suggests that the tax rules concerning the issue and distribution of debt and preferred stock discourage the very sort of managerial behavior that ought to be discouraged according to corporate finance theory. He then considers the positive role of tax rules with respect to large stock purchases by corporate acquirers. Here, the strategy picked up by the Internal Revenue Code can be understood, he argues, as designed to interfere as little as possible with the decision making of a target's shareholders in the face of a tender offer.

Whereas all the preceding articles concern traditional corporations in which ownership is given to the investors of capital, the last article (Chapter 9), by Henry Hansmann, expands the discussion by exploring the forces shaping the ownership of firms in general. Hansmann examines the considerations that determine whether ownership of a firm is assigned to investors of capital or, alternatively, to some other group of persons, such as consumers of the firm's products or suppliers to the firm of a factor of production other than capital. He argues that ownership is generally assigned in a manner that tends to minimize total transaction costs for all persons who transact with the firm. This involves minimizing the sum of (a) the costs of market transactions for those who are not owners and (b) the costs of ownership for the class of persons who have ownership rights. The most significant costs of market transactions are generally those associated with monopoly and asymmetric information. The most significant costs of control are the costs of exercising effective oversight, the losses from managerial slack in the absence of effective oversight, the costs of collective decision making when owners' objectives are diverse, and the costs of risk bearing. After presenting his theory, Hansmann illustrates its usefulness by applying it to several specific alternative patterns of ownership: conventional investor-owned business firms; customer-owned retail, wholesale, and supply cooperatives; mutual life insurance companies; and worker-owned firms.

Lucian Arye Bebchuk

Acknowledgments

Bebchuk, Lucian Arye, "A New Approach to Corporate Reorganizations," *Harvard Law Review* 101: 775 (1988).

Easterbrook, Frank H., and Daniel R. Fischel, "The Corporate Contract," *Columbia Law Review* 89: 1416 (1989). Copyright © 1989 by the Directors of the Columbia Law Review Association, Inc. All Rights Reserved. Reprinted by permission.

Gordon, Jeffrey, "Ties that Bond: Dual Class Common Stock and the Problem of Shareholder Choice," *California Law Review,* 75: 1(1988). Reprinted by permission.

Haddock, David D., Fred S. McChesney, and Jonathan R. Macey, "Property Rights in Assets and Resistance to Tender Offers," *Virginia Law Review* 73: 701(1987). Reprinted by permission of Virginia Law Review Association and Fred B. Rothman & Co.

Hansmann, Henry, "The Ownership of Enterprise," *Journal of Law, Economics and Organization* 4: 267 (1988). Reprinted by permission.

Kraakman, Reinier, "Taking Discounts Seriously: The Implications of 'Discounted' Share Prices as an Acquisition Motive," *Columbia Law Review* 88: 891(1988). Copyright © 1988 by the Directors of the Columbia Law Review Association, Inc. All Rights Reserved. Reprinted by permission.

Levmore, Saul, "The Positive Role of Tax Law in Corporate and Capital Markets," *Journal of Corporation Law,* 12: 483 (1987). Reprinted by permission.

Romano, Roberta, "The State Competition Debate in Corporate Law," *Cardoza Law Review* 8: 709 (1987). Copyright © *Cardoza Law Review.* Reprinted by permission.

Williamson, Oliver E. "Mergers, Acquisitions, and Leveraged Buyouts: An Efficiency Assessment" in Gary D. Libecap, ed., *Corporate Reorganization Through Mergers, Acquisitions and Leveraged Buyouts,* Supplement 1 to *Advances in the Study of Entrepreneurship, Innovation, and Economic Growth.* Greenwich, Conn: JAI Press, 1988. Reprinted by permission.

CHAPTER 1

Mergers, acquisitions, and leveraged buyouts: an efficiency assessment

Oliver E. Williamson

> ... men in general, and within limits, wish to behave economically, to make their activities *and their organization* "efficient" rather than wasteful. This fact does deserve the utmost emphasis; and an adequate definition of the science of economics ... might well make it explicit that the main relevance of the discussion is found in its relation to social policy, assumed to be directed toward the end indicated, of increasing economic efficiency, of reducing waste.
>
> (Knight, 1941; emphasis added)

The implications of mergers, acquisitions, and leveraged buyouts are herein examined with reference to the efficiency purposes to which Frank Knight refers above. That Knight, or any other economist, should refer favorably to efficiency is hardly novel. But there is much more to the statement than a mere affirmation of efficiency. Contrary to the main tradition, Knight asserts that the manner in which economic activity is organized really matters. He furthermore treats organizational efficiency in very primitive terms: the reduction of waste.

The prevailing opinion – at the time Knight advanced these views and over the next thirty years – was that technology was largely determinative of economic organization. It was therefore customary to characterize business firms, whatever their size and configuration, as production functions. The considerable merits of this framework notwithstanding, it was also responsible for serious omissions: "How easy it is for an inefficient manager to dissipate the differentials on which profitability rests, and that it is possible, *with the same techni-*

A similar version of this paper appears in Gary D. Libecap, ed., *Corporate Reorganization Through Mergers, Acquisitions and Leveraged Buyouts*, Supplement I to *Advances in the Study of Entrepreneurship, Innovation, and Economic Growth*. Greenwich, Conn: JAI Press, 1988.

cal facilities, to produce with a great variety of costs, are among the commonplaces of business experience which do not seem to be equally familiar in the study of the economist" (Hayek, 1945, p. 523; emphasis added).

The possibility that the internal organization of the firm – hierarchical structure, incentive and control apparatus – had a significant bearing on economic efficiency was ignored or dismissed. Hybrid forms of organization (tie-ins, joint ventures, reciprocity, franchising, and the like) were regarded mainly as efforts to acquire and perfect monopoly. The alternative point of view to which Ronald Coase (1972) forcefully referred and that I adopt here is that the internal organization of firms and recourse to hybrid forms of organization can and often do have significant efficiency ramifications.

To be sure, economic organization is sometimes deflected from efficiency and/or serves other purposes. The study of complex systems is nonetheless facilitated by distinguishing primary or main purposes from secondary or ancillary purposes. Knight maintains that efficiency is the core purpose. This article embraces that view.

Efficiency analysis can take several forms. Knight proposes that a very primitive form of efficiency be examined: the reduction of waste. This contemplates movement toward, rather than along, an efficiency frontier. Comparative analysis, rather than optimality analysis, thereby suffices. Coase's remarks on choice among alternative forms of organization are plainly in this spirit (1964, p. 195; emphasis added):

Contemplation of an optimal system may suggest ways of improving the system, it may provide techniques of analysis that would otherwise have been missed, and, in special cases, it may go far to providing a solution. But in general its effect has been pernicious. It has directed economists' attention away from the main question, *which is how alternative arrangements will actually work in practice*. It has led economists to derive conclusions for economic policy from a study of an abstract model of a market situation. . . . Until we realize that we are choosing between social arrangements which are all more or less failures, we are not likely to make much headway.

Section I considers horizontal and vertical mergers from the efficiency perspective. Acquisition issues are addressed in the context of organization form in Section II. The efficiency ramifications of leveraged buyouts are examined in Section III. Leading organizational innovators in each of the above respects are briefly discussed in Section IV. Qualifications to the main case are sketched in Section V. Concluding remarks follow.

I   Horizontal and vertical mergers

Possible efficiency benefits of horizontal and vertical mergers and some of the little noted bureaucratic costs of internal organization are discussed here. Conglomerate mergers are treated under the heading of acquisitions in Section II.

A   *Horizontal mergers*

The theory of the firm-as-production-function makes express provision for economies of scale. Orthodox analysis has thus always conceded the possibility that scale economies might be realized by combining two firms that are producing the same good or service. It was once widely believed, however, that mergers that simultaneously yielded economies and market power would preponderately lead to an adverse social outcomes. To suggest that economies might justify a merger of large firms was dismissed with the observation that even small adverse market power effects would normally swamp any possible efficiency benefits.

That intuition, when processed through the basic partial equilibrium apparatus of applied welfare economics,[1] turned out to be incorrect. What I have referred to as the "naive tradeoff model" disclosed that large market power effects were needed to offset the welfare benefits of small cost savings (Williamson, 1968, 1977).

To be sure, there are a number of qualifications to that result (Williamson, 1968, 1977; Fisher and Lande, 1983). The main point, however, to which I want to call attention is that a dramatic reversal in efficiency thinking has progressively developed over the past twenty years. Not only are real economies of all kinds now affirmatively valued by the antitrust enforcement agencies, but the possibility of using economies as an antitrust defense has actually been introduced into the Antitrust Merger Guidelines.[2] The earlier disdain[3] if not hostility for efficiency and efficiency reasoning has thus been reversed.

---

1 The basic postulates of partial equilibrium welfare economics are set out in Arnold Harberger (1971, p. 785) see also Williamson (1977, pp. 703–4).

2 The 1984 Merger Guidelines of the Department of Justice state that "some mergers that the Department otherwise might challenge may be reasonably necessary to achieve significant net efficiencies. If the parties to the merger establish by clear and convincing evidence that a merger will achieve such efficiencies, the Department will consider those efficiencies in deciding to challenge the merger" (U.S. Department of Justice 1984 Merger Guidelines, Sec. 3.5). I think this appropriate at an administrative level but have grave reservations that a full-blown economies defense should be permitted in a

B   Vertical mergers

That horizontal mergers might sometimes be justified by cost savings was granted reluctantly. But since no such economies of scale could be ascribed to vertical combinations, the prevailing antitrust skepticism for the merits of these was thought to be soundly based. Vertical mergers were thus widely regarded as overreaching and driven by monopoly purpose.[4]

To be sure, the applied price theory tradition made provision for exceptions. But these were narrow and limited. The principal exceptions were these: (1) vertical integration might be justified as a way by which to correct factor proportions distortions that occur when a monopolized input is sold to a downstream variable proportions production technology, and (2) vertical integration is sometimes a source of cost savings when successive production stages are tightly linked by a "physical or technical aspect." The first of these was argued by Lionel McKenzie (1951) and has been elaborated and qualified since (Blair and Kaserman, 1983). The second was argued by Joe Bain (1968, p. 381):

> ... the cases of clear economies of integration generally involve a physical or technical integration of the processes in a single plant. A classic case is that of integrating iron-making and steel-making to effect a saving in fuel costs by eliminating a reheating of iron before it is fed to a steel furnace. Where integration does not have this physical or technical aspect – as it does not, for example, in integrating the production of assorted components with the assembly of those components – the case for cost savings from integration is generally much less clear.

Vertical integration unattended by such special physical or technical conditions was thus thought to be of dubious merit (e.g., a device to evade sales taxes) if not outright anticompetitive.

Coase had long resisted an applied price theory approach to industrial organization in favor of a broader view. Rather than invoke a monopoly explanation upon observing a nonstandard organizational form or unfamiliar business practice, he counseled that scholars and others should "inquire whether it may not be the case whether the practice in question is a necessary element in bringing about a competitive situation. If this

court if the department decides to challenge a merger and the case is brought to trial. (Permitting the respondent to present economies to the court as a part of its rationale for a merger could, however, have salutary effects [Williamson, 1968, pp. 113–14; 1977, pp. 727–29].)

3 For pertinent statements of the earlier tradition, see Williamson (1985, pp. 286–87, 366–69).

4 See Williamson (1986) for references to the ruling opinions.

were done, I suspect that a good deal of supposed monopoly would disappear" (Coase, 1972, p. 68).

An effort to reformulate the vertical integration issue along the transaction cost lines that Coase had much earlier advanced (1973) was even then taking shape (Williamson, 1971). That technology was the proximate cause for vertical integration was disputed by adopting a comparative contracting approach to economic organization. Why not use *autonomous* contracting to replicate the *very same* efficient factor proportions that McKenzie associated with unified ownership? Bain's characterization of vertical integration in technological terms was likewise subjected to reexamination: Why not neutralize the "technical or physical aspects" on which Bain relied by locating successive *autonomous* stages in cheek-by-jowl relation to each other and thereafter mediating the supply of molten ingot by interfirm contract? The superiority, or not, of intrafirm as compared with interfirm contracting thus became the object of analysis.

Not only did this comparative contracting approach to economic organization go beyond the particulars to which McKenzie and Bain referred, but it had general application to backward, lateral, and forward integration. Subsequent research revealed, moreover, that the key features of economic organization – in intermediate product markets, labor markets, capital markets, regulation, and the like – were variations on the very same underlying transaction-cost economizing theme. The basic strategy for deriving refutable implications was this: Assign transactions (which differ in their attributes) to governance structures (the costs and competencies of which differ) in a discriminating (mainly transaction-cost economizing) way. A very different rationale for vertical integration and other nonstandard or unfamiliar business practices emerged.

These matters are dealt with in detail elsewhere. Suffice it to observe here that

1. the most important single attribute that is responsible for bilateral dependency, which is the contracting condition that is fundamentally responsible for vertical integration, is the condition of asset specificity (Williamson, 1971, 1975, 1985; Klein, Crawford, and Alchian, 1978);
2. the predictions of the transaction cost approach to firm and market organization are broadly consonant with the data;[5] and

---

5 See Williamson (1985, Chapter 5) for a review of the evidence. Also see David Levy (1985). The evidence supports the following: (a) vertical integration out of manufacturing into distribution is *selective* and reflects transaction-cost economizing principles; (b) the same is true of backward vertical integration into raw materials and lateral

3. antitrust enforcement regarding vertical integration has been progressively reshaped and now reflects transaction-cost economizing principles.[6]

That vertical and horizontal mergers are sometimes supported by a broader efficiency rationale than was previously admitted does not, however, imply that all such mergers are unproblematic. Vigilance with respect to the strategic purposes sometimes served by such mergers – whereby actual and potential entrants are disadvantaged without redeeming social benefits – is needed.[7] Strategic purposes are viable, however, only if severe structural preconditions (mainly high concentration coupled with high hurdles to entry) are satisfied. The upshot is that efficiency reasoning, of which transaction-cost economics is a part, plays a much more prominent role in industrial organization than was the case ten or twenty years ago – when the technology/monopoly predispositions were ruling. Regarding efficiency, rather than monopoly or technology, as the "main case" has played a major role in this transformation.

C   *The costs of bureaucracy*

Although it is widely agreed that vertical integration is sometimes mistaken, there is nevertheless a deep puzzle as to why integration should ever be the source of added costs. Thus if a buyer acquires a supplier, simply instruct the (now integrated) supply stage to repeat all of the good things that it had been doing in the preacquisition condition. Only on those few occasions when autonomous trading gives rise to conflict is the authority that inheres in unified ownership exercised to effect a superior outcome. The integrated firm can thus everywhere do as well as the nonintegrated (by replicating), and it sometimes does better (by selective intervention). According to this scenario, integrated firms can do everything that nonintegrated firms can do and more.

Unpacking the puzzle "Why is not all production carried out in one

---

integration into components; (c) the premise that more integration is always superior to less is mistaken.

6 Both the Merger Guidelines and merger enforcement have been reshaped during the past twenty years. Thus whereas the 1968 Vertical Merger Guidelines were very restrictive, the current guidelines have been relaxed and substantially reflect transaction-cost reasoning (Williamson, 1986). Also, whereas there were 441 preliminary investigations of vertical mergers in 1968 (and only fifty-one horizontal merger investigations) under the then prevailing inhospitality orientation, in 1984 there were but seven preliminary investigations of vertical mergers (and 108 horizontal) (Johnson and Smith, 1968, p. 16).

7 See Williamson (1985, Chapter 14) for a discussion.

big firm?" (Coase, 1937, p. 340) requires that the *added* costs of internal organization be discovered. These added costs take several forms, of which the following are the most important:[8] (1) replicating marketlike incentives within internal organization (a) gives rise to asset malutilization and (b) is incomplete because it is predictably degraded by accounting manipulation; (2) internal organization is subject to a series of bureaucratic distortions; and (3) internal organization supports politicking, especially at investment renewal intervals. The upshot is that "selective intervention" is a fiction. The coordination benefits of internal organization are unavoidably attended by offsetting costs. Only, therefore, in circumstances where nontrivial benefits from integration are in prospect is a decision to take a transaction out of the market and organize it internally warranted.

Transaction cost reasoning is thus symmetrical in that it serves to display the leading costs as well as the leading benefits that accrue to vertical integration. Although much more needs to be done before the bureaucratic failure literature can be thought to operate on a parity with the market failure literature, where the latter has been in progress for thirty and more years, a start has been made to redress this condition.

II   Acquisitions

Albeit arbitrary, I treat mergers as voluntary and reserve the term *acquisitions* for efforts to secure control over a corporation that have an imposed or involuntary character.[9] What are the instruments for bringing about involuntary transfers of control? In order of historical appearance, these are (1) the proxy contest, (2) the takeover contest, and (3) the leveraged buyout. The first two will be examined here. Section 3 deals with leveraged buyouts.[10]

Although, in principle, all three of these techniques for effecting a change of control were continuously available – in that there were no

8 These are elaborated in Williamson (1985, Chapter 6). For a discussion in which ownership differences are more strongly featured, see Sanford Grossman and Oliver Hart (1986).
9 To be sure, some mergers are agreed to "voluntarily" only because target managements perceive that a refusal to merge will result in a contest for control that they wish to avoid (often because they expect to lose it). Accordingly, the target firm management strikes a deal and decides to "cooperate." Many acquisitions that are not publicly contested are more appropriately assigned to the involuntary category as a result.
10 The leveraged buyout need not be used as a takeover technique. It may merely be a form of changing (rationalizing) the capital structure – by substituting debt for equity and concentrating control in the process. With or without a challenge to incumbent management, the leveraged buyout is a recent financial innovation.

8   Oliver E. Williamson

legal impediments to any, and none required any technological innovation – the last two appeared only in the past quarter of a century.
Prior to the appearance of these, the proxy contest was the only instrument for challenging incumbent managements.

The proxy contest is akin to a political campaign. The incumbents
have their slate of candidates for the board of directors. The insurgents
offer a rival slate. The insurgents claim that the incumbents have botched
the job and "promise" to do better. The incumbents claim that they
have done well, especially in view of trying economic circumstances,
and state that the insurgents' promises are not to be believed.

Proxy contests are costly. Given the difficulties of evaluating claims
of incompetence and the fact that promises of superior performance
upon award of control are not backed by credible commitments, few
proxy contests were ever waged, and, of these, few were won.[11] In the
colorful language of Oswald Knauth, incumbent managements had to
"fail obviously and even ignominiously before the dispersed forces of
criticism [became] mobilized for action" (1948, p. 45). The Berle and
Means query "have we any justification for assuming that those in control of a modern corporation will also choose to operate it in the interests
of the stockholders?" (1932, p. 121) was thus poignant.

Many economists evidently believe, however, that it is unrewarding
to entertain the hypothesis of managerial discretion.[12] If investors part
with their money voluntarily, then wherein can it ever be said that they
are "victimized" by abuses of managerial discretion?[13] To maintain,
however, that "pricing out" supports unrestrained laissez-faire is a
"triumph of [free market] ideology over theory and fact" (Stiglitz, 1985,
p. 134).

A curious schizophrenia characterizes much of the antimanagerialist
literature. Focusing on any given time, enthusiasts of laissez-faire capitalism deny that managerial discretion is a problem. Over time, however, they point with pride to the development of new techniques that
have brought managerial discretion under more effective control.[14]

To be sure, the earlier condition may have been irremediable: The
corrective instruments to which investors earlier had access could have
been, indeed arguably were, fully deployed. But it is inconsistent to

11 During the period 1956–60, only nine out of twenty-eight proxy contests for control
were fully successful (Hayes and Taussig, 1967, p. 137).
12 Many of the main papers in the 1982 conference Corporations and Private Property,
which papers are published in the June 1983 issue of the *Journal of Law and Economics*,
view the Berle and Means query as misguided if not absurd.
13 This appears to be Robert Hessen's criterion (1983, p. 288).
14 This material is taken from Williamson (1985, pp. 320–21).

employ the *very same* neoclassical model – whereby the firm is characterized as a production function to which unrestricted profit maximization is continuously ascribed – at both the earlier and later dates. A conception of the firm in which opportunities for managerial discretion are expressed as a function of the control instruments is needed instead. Such a conception leads to greater respect for successive organizational innovations that have superior control properties and that attenuate managerial discretion.

Managerial discretion can take numerous forms, some very subtle. Individual managers may run slack operations; they may pursue subgoals that are at variance with corporate purposes; they can engage in self-dealing. Such distortions become more severe where there is logrolling. These and other manifestations of managerial discretion were well-known to Berle and Means, Edward Mason (1959), and other observers of the corporate scene. What went unnoticed, however, was the vast transformation of the corporate form between 1930 and 1960 and the consequences that had on managerial discretion. The earlier, centralized, functionally organized, unitary (or U-form) structure of the corporation was progressively supplanted by the multidivisional (or M-form) structure.

The M-form innovation had several effects on corporate performance (Williamson, 1985, Chapter 11). For one thing, the shift from a functional to a divisional form served to rationalize decision making. The confusion of purposes that characterized the U-form firm, where causality and responsibility were difficult to trace, was supplanted by a divisionalized structure where separability among quasi-autonomous parts was emphasized. Sharper definition of purpose and economies of informational cost resulted.

Disengaging the general office from operating affairs also improved incentives. What had been short-run, partisan involvements by the top executives who had previously been heads of functional activities (e.g., manufacturing, marketing, finance) gave way to longer-run, strategic decision making. Not only did the general office give greater weight to overall enterprise objectives in relation to functional subgoals, but a competence to monitor the performance of the divisions, allocate resources to higher-valued uses, and use internal incentives and controls in a more discriminating way was successively perfected. The M-form organization thereby attenuated managerial discretion in what had previously been U-form firms.

These internal checks on managerial discretion do not, however, imply its elimination. Rather, the argument is comparative. Albeit in reduced and deflected degree, managerial discretion can be expected to continue. Interestingly, however, the M-form innovation had unanticipated systems consequences that served further to attenuate managerial discretion. These additional checks on managerial discretion operated through competition in the capital market.[15]

It has often been noted that tender offers increasingly replaced proxy contests as a takeover technique beginning in the late 1950s.[16] What explains this? Gregg Jarrell and Michael Bradley contend that the costs of proxy contests were increased by new regulations.[17] Takeovers are thus explained as the response to a regulation-induced change in the relative price of the methods for gaining control.

That is an interesting hypothesis, but it would be more compelling if proxy contests actually had been widely and successfully used to challenge incumbent managements before those rule changes. As noted above, however, proxy contests were never numerous and were usually unsuccessful. Moreover, although the regulation of proxy contests could encourage greater reliance on a takeover, why should a switch to this (previously inferior) device be associated with a larger number of contests for corporate control and a greater degree of success?

In principle, takeover by tender offer was always feasible. I submit that the reason why it was not employed earlier is that a corporate structure conducive to takeover was not yet in place. Specifically, reorganization of the corporation from a functionally departmentalized to a divisionalized structure had profound consequences for corporate control. Conceiving of the firm as a governance structure rather than as a production function is the key to understanding the phenomenon of takeover by tender offer.

The main advantage of an M-form firm over a U-form enterprise in takeover respects is the ability of an M-form acquirer to "digest" its acquisition. The acquired firm is normally assigned profit center status and thereafter becomes subject to the corporation's internal incentive, control, and resource-allocation processes. The firm does not attempt to integrate comprehensively the new assets with the old. Inasmuch as

15 Henry Manne's classic treatment (1965) of the market for corporate control is germane.
16 As Greg Jarrell and Michael Bradley observe, "Cash takeover bids were very rare in the United States prior to the 1960's, but they burst onto the financial scene in the mid-1960's, a period of much corporate conglomeration" (1980, p. 371, n. 1).
17 They cite the work of Peter Dodd, who "associated the sudden emergence of cash tender offers as a takeover device with the successive expansions in 1955 and 1964 (Securities Acts Amendment) by the SEC of its rules governing proxy contests. . . . These changes in proxy rules increased insurgents' costs of assuming corporate control via the proxy and, therefore, increased usage of the cash tender offer to achieve a change in management" (Jarrell and Bradley, 1980, p. 371, n. 1).

M-form firms separate operating from strategic decision making, the general office neither seeks nor requires the same familiarity with the operating parts that managers in U-form firms must have. The greater competence of the large M-form firm to manage extant assets thus applies to the management of acquired assets as well.

Activating the market for corporate control, thereby better to check managerial discretion, is an outcome that most economists regard favorably. These benefits, however, need to be evaluated in relation to the costs of takeover – which some students of the corporation believe have been very high. Some of these concerns are addressed in Section V. Suffice it to observe here that

1. Although some takeovers turn out to be "mistaken," in that the winner thereafter has ex post regrets, this does not necessarily imply ex ante error. The overall process, rather than individual outcomes, needs to be assessed.
2. Subsequent divestment of an earlier acquired activity does not necessarily signal failure. There may have been an initial period during which net gains are realized. After the benefits have been exhausted and the net gains turn negative, however, divestment is a rational course of action.
3. An uncounted or "invisible" benefit of takeover is that potential targets are induced to take self-corrective actions, thereby to deter the likelihood of takeover.
4. Whereas continuous scrutiny and concern over the workings of the market for corporate control are warranted, public policy should intervene only upon a showing of *remediable* failure – where remediability implies expected net gains.[18]

The upshot is that managerial discretion has arguably been brought under more effective control as the proxy contest has given way to takeover as the principal capital market control device.

III   Leveraged buyouts

Leveraged buyouts are a particular form of transfer of control for which grave skepticism has recently been expressed. To be sure, owners have sold their businesses and accepted secured debt as partial payment for centuries. It was not until the early 1970s, however, that *publicly* held firms were taken private in significant numbers. Louis Lowenstein associates this development with the precipitous stock market decline (by

18 See the quotation from Coase near the beginning of this chapter.

almost one half) that occurred in 1974. Since the stocks of a "substantial number of small public companies . . . sold at particularly depressed prices . . . , [many managements] decided to reverse the public offering of a few years earlier" and take the company private (Lowenstein, 1985, p. 733). Although a premium over current market price was being paid in these going-private transactions, the way in which management orchestrated the deal was troublesome: "The management of the firm used the resources of the firm, the credit of the firm, and, when necessary, the proxy machinery of the firm to eliminate the public ownership of the firm – an ownership that the management had only recently offered to the public, often at much higher [offering] prices" (Lowenstein, 1985, p. 734).

As it turned out, this was the tip of the iceberg: "The $3 million [declining market] buyout of the mid-1970s has been replaced by the $1 billion buyout [in the rising market] of the mid-1980s" (Lowenstein, 1985, p. 735). It is widely believed that something radically wrong is going on here.

Without disputing that leveraged buyouts can and sometimes do pose public policy problems, I submit that many leveraged buyouts satisfy an underlying transaction-cost economics rationale. The resulting economies, if any, are appropriately taken into account in reaching a net social assessment.

A   *The rational uses of debt and equity*

The Modigliani-Miller theorem that the cost of capital in a firm was independent of the proportion of debt and equity revolutionized modern corporate finance. It gave rise to an extensive literature in which a special rationale for debt in an otherwise equity-financed firm was sought. The first of these, unsurprisingly, was that debt had tax advantages over equity. But this was scarcely adequate. Further and more subtle reasons why debt would be used in preference to equity even in a tax-neutral world were also advanced. The leading rationales were these: (1) debt could be used as a signal of differential business prospects (Ross, 1977); (2) debt could be used by entrepreneurs with limited resources who were faced with new investment opportunities and did not want to dilute their equity position, thereby to avoid sacrifice of incentive intensity (Stiglitz, 1974; Jensen and Meckling, 1976); and (3) debt could serve as an incentive bonding device (Grossman and Hart, 1982).

I have examined each of these elsewhere and advance a different explanation for the rational use of debt and equity based on transaction-cost considerations (Williamson, 1988). Rather than regard the firm as

Table 1.1

Governance feature	Financial instrument	
	Debt	Equity
Contractual constraints	Numerous	Nil
Security	Preemptive	Residual claimant
Intrusion	Nil	Extensive

a production function, which is the framework out of which Modigliani-Miller and each of the aforementioned operate, I employ the firm-as-governance-structure approach instead. I maintain that the investment attributes of projects and the governance structure features of debt and equity need to be aligned in a discriminating way. The key governance structure differences between debt and equity are shown in Table 1.1.

The transaction-cost approach maintains that some projects are easy to finance by debt and *ought to be financed by debt*. These are projects for which physical asset specificity is low to moderate. As asset specificity becomes great, however, the preemptive claims of the bondholders against the investment afford limited protection – because the assets in question have limited redeployability. Not only does the cost of debt financing therefore increase, but the benefits of closer oversight also grow. The upshot is that equity finance, which affords more intrusive oversight and involvement through the board of directors (and, in publicly held firms, permits share ownership to be concentrated), is the preferred financial instrument for projects where asset specificity is great.

Although this sketch oversimplifies greatly,[19] it nevertheless captures the flavor of the transaction-cost approach to corporate finance and discloses that the capital structure of the firm ought to reflect rational transaction-cost economizing principles.[20] Assuming, arguendo, that the

19 For an elaboration, see Williamson (1986b).
20 The recent paper on financial leverage by Michael Long and Ileen Malitz uses a financial rationale akin to but nonetheless distinguishable from that advanced here. Thus they rely on Steward Myers' (1977) treatment of finance which emphasized debt covenants and *unobservables*. Specifically, Long and Malitz contend that (1985, p. 326) "because intangible, firm-specific, and therefore unobservable growth opportunities reduce the effectiveness of bond covenants, the only way in which owners of firms can [finance such projects is through equity]. . . . The same arguments apply to the asset substitution problem . . . With intangible investments, it is a relatively easy matter for owners to increase firm risk without bondholders' [knowledge]."   [*Continued*]

approach has merit, what are the ramifications, if any, for leveraged buyouts?

B   Applications to LBO[21]

Suppose, as an evolutionary matter, that a firm is originally financed along lines that are consistent with the debt and equity financing principles set out above. Suppose further that the firm is successful and grows through retained earnings. The initial debt–equity ratio thus progressively falls. And suppose finally that many of the assets in this now expanded enterprise are of a kind that could have been financed by debt.

Added value, in such a firm, can be realized by substituting debt for equity. This argument applies, however, selectively. It only applies to firms where the efficient mix of debt and equity has gotten seriously out of alignment. These will be firms that combine (1) a very high ratio of equity to debt with (2) a very high ratio of redeployable to nonredeployable assets.

Interestingly, many of the large leveraged buyouts in the 1980s displayed precisely these qualities. Thus Robert Colman's examination of leveraged buyouts disclosed that "only an existing firm with a small amount of debt is able to support" a leveraged buyout and that a "frequent characteristic of the leveraged buyout company is that the firm has a high proportion of its total assets in tangible property" (1981,

---

Note, however, that my discussion of asset financing does not assume that firm-specific investments are unobservable. To the contrary, the critical feature on which I rely is whether the assets afford security or not. This goes to *redeployability,* not observability issues. Intangible investments, such as research and development and advertising, which Long and Malitz use as proxies for intangibles more generally (1985, pp. 334–35, 345), are apt to be nonredeployable, but the redeployability of many tangible investments is limited also.

Moreover, Long and Malitz make no distinctions of a governance-structure kind, while the crafting of governance structures to support equity is fundamental to the transaction-cost economics approach. Be that as it may, Long and Malitz' treatment of finance and that advanced here are closer to each other than to the conventional finance approach, which works out of composite capital.

Their examination of the evidence supports the proposition that "corporations which invest heavily in intangibles, such as R&D and advertising, have a tighter capital market imposed debt capacity than those investing in tangible assets. Our findings provide direct empirical evidence that the moral hazard problem is important and that investment and financing decisions are not independent" (Long and Malitz, 1985, p. 345). I agree with this conclusion but would emphasize again that the straightforward way to examine transactions and their governance is through redeployability.

21 This subsection is based on Williamson (1988).

p. 531). Although the tangible–intangible distinction is not identical to the redeployability test that I employ, there is plainly a correlation. Lowenstein's observation that many of these firms are in "prosaic businesses – retailing, textiles, and soft drink bottling" (1985, p. 749) – is also consonant with the view that many of the assets in question have a stable, long-term value and hence would afford redeployable security.

Colman furthermore observes that leveraged buyouts are put together with a view toward providing managers with high-powered incentives. This may or may not involve equity investment by the management, but it always involves a significant contingent compensation arrangement (Colman, 1981, pp. 532, 537, 539). The management, moreover, is usually on a tight leash. It ordinarily owns a minority (often less than 15 percent) of the equity, the remainder being concentrated in the hands of the banks, insurance companies, and the investment bankers who package the deal (Mason, 1984). According to Nicholas Wallner, moreover, "The management never gets more than 50 percent of the equity unless the secured lenders are the only other participants in the deal" (1980, p. 20), in which event those outsiders who supply finance are little concerned over inept management because their preemptive claims against redeployable assets provide them with adequate protection.

As earlier remarked, the most interesting feature of leveraged buyouts is the substitution of debt for equity. The following points are pertinent:

1. The major lenders are finance companies and banks and insurance companies. The finance companies specialize in shorter-term inventory and receivable financing, where they have an advantage over the banks in policing the collateral, and will lend up to 85 percent of the liquidation value. Banks and insurance companies specialize in intermediate and longer-term financing, usually at a lower lending percentage of liquidation value (Colman, 1981, p. 539).

2. The cash-flow and asset-based financing approaches are distinguished by the fact that under "the conventional approach, the lender wanted protection primarily via cash flow" whereas under "the asset-based approach . . . the lender ties all or at least part of his loan to the liquid value of the borrower's assets . . . , [and realizes protection by] taking a security interest in the assets . . . , [establishing] a lending formula on the basis of the liquid value, and . . . [obtaining] periodic information on the nature and size of those assets" (Colman, 1981, p. 542).

Plainly, the shift from cash-flow to asset-based financing lines up rather closely with the transaction-cost economics rationale for secure transactions.

The transaction-cost approach to economic organization also has ramifications for whether the incumbent management will participate extensively in a buyout refinancing (thereafter to hold a substantial equity position in the restructured organization) or should be displaced instead. The argument is this: Since employment continuity is the source of added value wherever firm-specific human capital is great, a management buyout is favored by high human asset specificity, ceteris paribus. Thus whereas a substitution of debt for equity is warranted in any firm where redeployable physical assets are equity financed, an informed choice between an outside buyout (attended often by incumbent displacement) and a management buyout (incumbent continuity) requires that the human assets of the managers be assessed. The buyout transaction is therefore influenced by *both* physical and human asset specificity conditions.

C   The free cash-flow hypothesis

Michael Jensen offers a related, albeit distinguishable, hypothesis on the appearance of leveraged buyouts. His explanation relates to the existence of "cash flow in excess of that required to fund all projects that have positive net present values when discounted at the relevant cost of capital" (1986, p. 323). One possibility would be to pay this excess out as dividends. But since promises to make a "permanent" increase in common stock dividends lack credibility, the exchange of debt for equity (which substitutes nondiscretionary interest for discretionary dividends) "enables managers to effectively bond their promise to pay out future cash flows" (Jensen, 1986, p. 324).

The argument is akin to that advanced by Sanford Grossman and Oliver Hart (1982) on the use of debt to bond the management, but Jensen specifically relates it to free cash flows. Both the Grossman and Hart analysis, which works out of composite (undifferentiated) capital, and Jensen's treatment (which deals with cash flows rather than with assets) are different, however, from that advanced here. My argument is that the *characteristics of the assets* are fundamentally implicated in the choice of financial instrument.

In fact, of course, the condition of asset specificity is only one important attribute of an investment project. Among other things, the time profile of expected cash flows also matters. Thus redeployable assets with deferred cash flows require greater equity funding at the outset than those with earlier cash flows, ceteris paribus. More generally, the investment attribute approach to project financing stands in need of elaboration and refinement. I nevertheless conjecture that redeployability will remain the key feature of an extended asset attribute approach to corporate finance.

IV   The Innovators

The main organizational innovations that I examine here are those associated with vertical integration, multidivisionalization, and leveraged buyouts.

A   Vertical integration

Many manufacturing firms had integrated forward from manufacturing into wholesaling or retailing at the turn of the century. The earlier appearance of the railroads (Porter and Livesay, 1971, p. 107), and of telegraph, continuous processing machines, and interchangeable parts manufacture were evidently instrumental (Chandler, 1977). Firms that integrated forward out of manufacturing into distribution include some of the great names of American industry.

Although it is sometimes argued that capitalist corporations seek to extend vertical integration at every opportunity, in the belief that more integration is always better than less (Horvat, 1982, pp. 15–16), transaction-cost economics holds otherwise. It maintains that vertical integration will be selective rather than comprehensive. The data support the selective integration hypothesis.

Four types of forward integration are usefully distinguished: none; forward integration into wholesaling; additional integration into retailing; and mistaken integration. Vertical integration is unneeded where – both presently and prospectively – markets work well. (Indeed, to integrate in these circumstances will commonly entail a sacrifice in the aggregation economies that markets afford, to say nothing of the added bureaucratic costs that internal organization, as compared with markets, incurs.) Some goods and services, however, require careful inventory management. And some require specialized investments at the wholesale stage that independent wholesalers are loath to make.

Inventory management is a special concern for branded goods that can go stale. James Dukes's decision to integrate forward into the wholesaling of cigarettes and Whitman's in candy were evidently undertaken in response to the problems of contract that attended the sale of branded perishables.[22] Gustavus Swift faced similar problems in selling branded meat. The problems of quality control were here compounded, moreover, by the need to build refrigerator cars to transport cattle that had been slaughtered and dressed in the Midwest to markets in the East. Faced with boycotts by local wholesalers, Swift was pressed further to construct a network of branch houses that provided "refrigerated storage space, a sales office, and a sales staff to sell and deliver meat to the retail butchers, grocers, and other food shops" (Chandler, 1977, p. 300). Swift, therefore, not only had to recognize the opportunity but needed to make specialized investments (in refrigeration) and to orchestrate local distribution. This entailed organizational innovation on a grand scale.

Integration into final sales and service represents an even more comprehensive variety of forward integration. Three classes of product can be distinguished: specialized consumer nondurables for which perishability concerns again arise; consumer durables requiring information aids, credit, and follow-on service; and producer durables requiring the same.

George Eastman explained his decision to eliminate independent wholesalers and sell photographic film directly as follows:

The wholesaler or jobber is a detriment to our business because a large proportion of it is in sensitized goods which are perishable. . . . We have organized our distribution facilities so as to get the goods into the hands of the consumer as quickly as possible. Our sensitized goods carry an expiration date. Our own retail houses . . . have been educated to control their stocks very accurately so that the goods are kept moving. Porter and Livesay, 1971 (p. 178)

Upon resolution of the legal contests over sewing machine patents in 1854, patents were released to twenty-four manufacturers. Three integrated forward into retail. Interestingly, only those three firms that integrated thereafter thrived. Firm-specific customer information, credit, and follow-on service were arguably responsible. Isaac Singer was a leading force here.

Producer durables were distributed through two networks. Small, standardized machinery was sold through commission merchants and jobbers. For products that were of special design, technologically complex, and quite expensive and for which installation and repair required

22 Whitman's response to this is especially noteworthy. Whitman sold inexpensive bar and packaged candies through the usual jobber and wholesale grocer network. Highgrade branded candy, however, was "sold directly to retailers so that the company could regulate the flow of the perishable items and avoid alienating customers" (Porter and Livesay, 1977, p. 220).

special expertise, however, integrated marketing systems were developed (Porter and Livesay, 1971, pp. 183–84). Examples include Cyrus McCormick, who pioneered the development of integrated distribution for farm equipment and set the stage for others thereafter to imitate (Livesay, 1979, Chapter 3). Office machines were another case where demonstration, sales, and service required specialized expertise for which franchised dealers were instrumental to success (Porter and Livesay, 1971, pp. 193–94).

That integration is no organizational panacea is revealed by integration mistakes. Unless the objective properties of the product will support added value through integration, the bureaucratic costs of integration counsel against such an effort. (see Section I.C). Integration mistakes are sometimes attributable to the "wish" to realize strategic advantage, unsupported by objective factors (Williamson, 1985, p. 111).

B Multidivisionalization

Chandler identifies nine large firms as ones that (more or less) independently discovered that the multidivisional structure offered prospective organizational economies over the functional or holding company forms of organization. These companies were E. I. Du Pont de Nemours & Co., General Motors, Standard Oil (New Jersey), Sears, United States Rubber, B. F. Goodrich, Union Carbide, Westinghouse, and The Great Atlantic and Pacific Tea Company (Chandler, 1966, pp. 2–3). Of these, Du Pont and General Motors seemed to have worked through the conceptual merits of multidivisionalization most carefully. The two key entrepreneurial figures here were Pierre S. Du Pont and Alfred P. Sloan, Jr. Their organizational genius notwithstanding, other executives – in these two companies and in others – were also instrumental in perfecting the M-form structure (Chandler, 1966).

As I have argued elsewhere, the M-form structure became the basis for two subsequent organizational developments. One of these was to use this structure to support diversification. More and less successful conglomerates appear to be distinguished by the organizational structure employed by each. Royal Little (Textron) was among the innovators that employed M-form organization principles to effect diversification.

The use of the M-form structure to support multinational business organization is a second extension. Effecting technology transfer by contract (licensing) or by ownership (direct foreign investment) is among the key issues here. M-form multinationalization is commonly associated with the successful transfer of leading-edge technologies, whereas more mundane technologies can be successfully transferred by contract. The need to support transfer with specialized human assets is what distinguishes the former.

C   *Leveraged buyouts*

As Lowenstein observes, most of the early management buyouts involved taking small public firms private. Although these occasioned concern within the Securities and Exchange Commission, it was widely believed that small firms constituted the relevant universe for such transactions.

That changed in 1979 when Kohlberg, Kravis, Roberts & Co. put together the first leveraged buyout to exceed $100 million. This was the Houdaille transaction, which was a $390 million deal.[23] Colman observes that large leveraged layouts were pioneered by new firms "started by people who sensed early what was happening and moved while the big investment houses had their attention engaged elsewhere" (1981, p. 534). Although the more established investment banking firms have since become involved, the newcomers who first perceived the opportunity were Kohlberg, Kravis, Roberts & Co. and Gibbons, Green & Rice.

The real innovation here was to recognize the merits of asset financing and to put together an internally consistent "contract" for debt and equity that provided for the financing needs of the transaction in a discriminating way. As discussed above, this is what the LBO accomplishes.

V   **Some caveats**

Mergers, acquisitions, and leveraged buyouts often elicit expressions of dismay and sometimes give rise to alarm. Transaction-cost economics is more sanguine, in large measure because economizing is held to be the main case. Economizing does not, however, exhaust the possibilities. Some of the leading alternative views are briefly examined here, after which I focus on unresolved concerns.

A   *Organizational innovation*

Whereas technological innovation enjoys a generally favorable reputation, organizational innovation is commonly viewed with deep suspicion. Possibly this is because new forms are believed to be "the

23 This transaction is described in Colman (1981).

adventitious result of legal, social, or political forces" (Granovetter, 1985, p. 488). More reprehensibly, the inhospitality tradition in antitrust viewed nonstandard or unfamiliar forms of organization as having pernicious design and effect.[24]

As discussed earlier, vertical integration operated under a cloud. That the conglomerate form of organization was believed to be even more problematic is no surprise. Thus Robert Solo characterized the conglomerate as "a truly dangerous phenomenon . . . produced by financial manipulators making grist for their security mills" (1972, p. 47). And Harlan Blake described the anticompetitive potential of the conglomerate as "so widespread that it might appropriately be described as having an effect upon the economic system as a whole – in every line of commerce in every section of the country" (1975, p. 585).

The leveraged buyouts of the 1980s have elicited similar concern. Thus although Louis Lowenstein concedes "a tendency for lawyers to see devils in the boardroom and in the executive suite" (1985, p. 740), he regards the abuse potential of leveraged buyouts as intensely real (1985, pp. 740, 749).

B   Troublesome concerns

As Friedrich Hayek observed, markets are "marvels" (1945, p. 527). Albeit perhaps in less profound degree, the same is true of many internal and hybrid forms of economic organization. But both markets and other forms of economic organization are also subject to "failures." Although much of what is sometimes thought to be a failure turns out, upon examination, to be irremediable – in that no superior alternative can be crafted – this is not true of all.

I have discussed some of the comparative limitations of horizontal, vertical, and conglomerate mergers elsewhere (Williamson, 1968; 1977; 1985). I merely incorporate these by reference and turn my attention to purported capital market failures.

Victor Brudney's recent examination of the puzzles, if not failures, of capital markets is instructive. Among the more troublesome conditions to which he refers are (1) disequilibrium contracting, (2) antitakeover defenses, (3) other self-dealing, and (4) the losses recorded by the shareholders of acquiring firms in a takeover contest.

---

24 Donald Turner thus remarked "I approach customer and territorial restrictions not hospitably in the common law tradition, but inhospitably in the tradition of antitrust." (The quotation is attributed to Turner by Stanley Robinson, N.Y. State Bar Association Antitrust Symposium, 1968, p. 29.)

Brudney expresses dissatisfaction with the "neutral" nexus of contract view advanced by Michael Jensen, Eugene Fama, and other scholars working out of this tradition. One concern is that so-called independent directors and management may form a coalition to the disadvantage of the stockholders (Brudney, 1985, pp. 1433–35). A separate concern with the neutrality of contracting hypothesis – to which I have referred elsewhere, though Brudney does not – is the possibility of contrived inconsistency among contracts. Implicated as they are in all of the contracts, management is in a position to strike deals that expose some constituencies (labor, customers) to undisclosed and unwanted hazards (Williamson, 1985, pp. 318–19). To dismiss such coalition and multilateral contracting concerns as imaginary because ex post settling-up processes will reliably penalize offenders is to assign inordinate and unwarranted weight to the efficacy of reputation effects (Williamson, 1985, pp. 395–96, 406–7).

As Brudney notes, the elaborate defenses that incumbent managements have devised to forestall takeover smack of protectionism. He further observes that "even dedicated contractarians advocate occasional intervention to curtail management's freedom by imposing a rule of passivity on target management faced with a tender offer" (Brudney, 1985, p. 1432, n. 74). But he goes on to characterize this as schizophrenic: "If it is proper for government to impose a rule of passivity on a target's management, then 'contract' [comprehensive ex post settling up] is not an adequate constrainer of managerial discretion" (Brudney, 1985, p. 1432, n. 74).

Mark Hirschey has since argued that whereas the "strong-form theory of managerial labor market efficiency" ignores important information asymmetries and thus exaggerates the efficacy of ex post settling up (1986, p. 318), a semistrong form version of this theory has merit and indeed justifies the use of takeover defenses (Hirschey, 1986, p. 321):

When the cost of takeover defense covenants falls short of the . . . [uncompensated] value of the management's firm-specific human capital, they will be adopted by the stockholders. . . . [otherwise] they will be rejected by the stockholders. . . . Therefore, [takeover defenses] can be thought of as market mechanisms that permit incumbent managements to obtain a greater share of the rentals accruing to their firm-specific human capital.

Albeit imaginative, Hirschey evidently assumes that stockholders have unbiased estimates of managerial asset specificity. If, however, managers "enjoy valuable inside information concerning managerial performance" (Hirschey, 1986, p. 318), it is difficult to understand why this information advantage does not extend to the display of human asset values. Since Hirshey gives no hint, much less an explicit statement, of the valuation mechanics by which stockholders discriminate between meritorious and protectionist takeover covenants, the deeply troubling and possibly self-serving quality of takeover defenses cannot, without more, be so easily dispelled.

Related self-dealing concerns are posed when management participates significantly in a leveraged buyout. Lowenstein's suggestion that open bidding be mandated to assure stockholders that a "fair" price has been realized (1985, pp. 779–84) runs into the obvious objection that search will thereby be deterred (Schwartz, 1986). Whatever the force of this concern in the context of takeovers, which has been disputed (Bebchuk, 1986), it is presumably less in the case of management buyouts. Thus whereas outsiders have to expend real resources to discover takeover candidates, managers merely self-disclose recapitalization values. To invite outside offers is a deterrent to disclosure nonetheless.[25]

A final puzzle in the corporate control area is that stockholders in acquiring firms experience negative expected returns. The observation that overall returns (to both acquired and acquiring firm stockholders) are positive is reassuring. But it does not explain why a process would be continued when those who initiate it experience expected negative returns. What kinds of biases/myopia are operative here?

Merely to record these concerns does not imply that a remedy can be fashioned. But to dismiss these concerns with a shrug is hardly satisfactory. Confidence in and an appreciation for the marvels of markets is one thing. What Kenneth Arrow has referred to as the "worship of the market" (1974, p. 16) is another.

VI   Concluding remarks

The leading hypotheses for assessing mergers, acquisitions, and leveraged buyouts (and, more generally, nonstandard or unfamiliar forms of economic activity) are (1) monopoly, (2) efficiency, (3) adventitiousness, and (4) financial manipulation. The monopoly hypothesis is plausible only if the structural preconditions for market power are satisfied – which

---

25 For managers to disclose that recapitalization potentially adds value does not necessarily imply that the firm was poorly managed previously – although it may have been, and this is the "natural" interpretation. The contracting process needs to be examined, however, in its entirety. Thus at least two things happen with a leveraged buyout: The firm is recapitalized *and* the management is exposed to closer oversight. This is another illustration of simultaneity: Corporate capitalization and management compensation cannot be determined independently, and both have a bearing on corporate performance (Grossman and Hart, 1982).

conditions obtain only for a small fraction of the mergers and acquisitions that are observed. The monopoly hypothesis makes no contact whatsoever with the leveraged buyout. The hypothesis that economic organization is the resultant of a series of historic accidents is instructive – in that many organizational innovations appear to be the result of trial and error. But the adventitious hypothesis has no power to sort among those innovations that have merit and those which are misguided or mistaken. Without more, the adventitious hypothesis invites ex post rationalization.

The financial manipulation hypothesis is similarly elastic. Any transaction in which the promoters and participants in a deal gain is held to be suspect.[26] But that is not an adequate criterion. Who are the losers in these manipulation exercises? What are the unanticipated events which give rise to manipulative abuses? (Since farsighted investors will make allowance for statistically foreseeable events in striking ex ante bargains, presumably only genuine surprises qualify as manipulative opportunities.)[27] If, moreover, it is only the organizational innovators who realize the big gains, in that afterward these are "handed on" through the competitive process (which is the Schumpeterian view of innovation [1947, p. 155]), then time will restore (more or less) fair returns. Manipulation, according to this view, is a transient phenomenon. Persistent manipulation is presumably explained, therefore, as disequilibrium contracting. Our understanding of this condition is very primitive.

The efficiency approach to mergers, acquisitions, and leveraged buyouts adopts Knight's view that economic organization is largely driven by economizing purposes. Scale and scope economies are obvious candidates. Less obvious, but plainly central to the economics of organi-

---

26 Lowenstein, who has deep suspicions of management buyouts, nonetheless observes that "all of the immediate participants have been winning" (1985, p. 751) – where this includes shareholders, managers, investment bankers, and commercial bankers. He nonetheless expresses "doubts as to whether the gains are sufficient social utility" (1985, p. 751, n. 77). The sufficiency test is obscure. What threshold needs to be crossed? Who are the social losers (expressed in comparative institutional terms)?

27 The extensive literature on decision process biases (much of it associated with Daniel Kahneman and Amos Tversky) to which Brudney refers (1985, p. 1418, n. 35) documents individual decision-process distortions. But this literature does not address the question of organizational responses to these distortions. Plainly, however, systematic losses present opportunities for gain to those who perceive the distortion condition. Why do these potential gain opportunities go unrealized? One leading purpose of "organization" is to concentrate decision making on more informed and less biased parties.

zation, are economies of contracting. Vertical integration is an organizational response to the contracting difficulties that attend intermediate product markets where trades that are supported by transaction specific assets are exposed to hazard.

The conglomerate form of enterprise is associated not with intermediate product markets but with capital markets. The M-form structure is thus regarded as an internal capital market in which depth is traded off against breadth (Alchian and Demsetz, 1972; Williamson, 1970). Takeover, according to this view, supplants the proxy contest as a corporate control device. The M-form needed to be invented and the conglomerate variant perfected before this became feasible. Whether efficiency gains accrue is, however, disputed (Magenheim and Mueller, 1987; Ravenscraft and Scherer, 1987).

Finally, the leveraged buyout is interpreted as an effort to align financial instruments with the attributes of assets in a discriminating (transaction-cost economizing) way. The preliminary data on this appear to be corroborative.

Although there is more to the story of complex organization than efficiency, no alternative hypothesis remotely qualifies for "main case" standing. Nonefficiency theories of economic organization nevertheless flourish in the face of the cumulative evidence that the increase of economic efficiency through the reduction of waste to which Knight referred goes to core issues.[28]

To be sure, excesses of efficiency reasoning need to be checked. Overreaching is not merely a hypothetical possibility but can be documented. But an antiefficiency predisposition – with or without "good intentions" – does not, without more, constitute a viable contender. Those who would register major and minor qualifications to the economizing approach need first to engage in main-case reasoning.

---

28 I would go further and urge that *microanalytic* efficiency reasoning is needed to reach the core issues of economic organization. This is not a unanimous opinion. Other economists who are persuaded that the study of microanalytics has benefits pull up short: "If one wishes to model the behavior of organizations such as firms, then study of the firm as an organization ought to be high on one's agenda. This study is not, strictly speaking, necessary: one can *hope to divine* the correct 'reduced form' for the behavior of the organization without considering the micro-forces within the organization. But the study of organization is likely to help in the design of reduced forms that stress the important variables" (Kreps and Spence, 1985, pp. 374–75; emphasis added). My own view is that the study of organization is absolutely essential. History records that previous efforts to "divine" appropriate reduced forms uninformed by an examination of the underlying microanalytics have often foundered.

26   **Oliver E. Williamson**

REFERENCES

Arrow, Kenneth J. 1974. *The Limits of Organization.* New York: Norton.
Bain, Joe. *Industrial Organization,* 2d ed. New York: Wiley.
Bebchuk, L. 1986. "The Case for Facilitating Competing Tender Offers: A Last
    (?) Reply," *Journal of Law, Economics and Organization,* 2 (Fall).
Berle, Adolph A., and G. C. Means. 1932. *The Modern Corporation and Private
    Property,* New York: Macmillan.
Blair, Roger, and David Kaserman. 1983. *Law and Economics of Vertical In-
    tegration and Control.* New York: Academic Press.
Blake, Harlan M. "Conglomerate Mergers and the Antitrust Laws," *Columbia
    Law Review,* 73 (March 1973): 555–92.
Brudney, V. "Corporate Governance, Agency Costs, and the Rhetoric of Con-
    tract," *Columbia Law Review,* 85 (November): 1403–44.
Chandler, A. D., Jr. 1962. *Strategy and Structure.* Cambridge, Mass.: MIT Press.
    (Reprinted, Garden City, N.Y.: Doubleday, 1966).
Chandler A. D., Jr. 1977. *The Visible Hand: The Managerial Revolution in
    American Business.* Cambridge, Mass.: Harvard University Press.
Coase, Ronald H. 1952. "The Nature of the Firm," *Economica N.S.,* 4 (1937):
    386–405. Reprinted in G. J. Stigler and K. E. Boulding, eds., *Readings
    in Price Theory.* Homewood, Ill.: Richard D. Irwin.
Coase, Ronald H. 1964. "The Regulated Industries: Discussion," *American
    Economic Review,* 54 (May): 194–97.
Coase, Ronald H. 1972. "Industrial Organization: A Proposal for Research."
    In V. R. Fuchs, ed., *Policy Issues and Research Opportunities in Industrial
    Organization.* New York: National Bureau of Economic Research,
    pp. 59–73.
Colman, R. 1981. "Overview of Leveraged Buyouts." In S. Lee and R. Colman,
    eds. *Handbook of Mergers, Acquisitions and Buyouts.* Englewood Cliffs,
    N.J.: Prentice Hall.
Fisher, Alan, and Robert Lande. 1983. "Efficiency Considerations in Merger
    Enforcement," *California Law Review,* 71 (December): 1580–1696.
Grossman, S., and O. Hart. 1982. "Corporate Financial Structure and Mana-
    gerial Incentives." In J. McCall, ed., *The Economics of Information and
    Uncertainty.* Chicago: University of Chicago Press, pp. 107–37.
Grossman, S., and O. Hart. 1986. "The Costs and Benefits of Ownership: A
    Theory of Vertical and Lateral Integration," *Journal of Political Economy,*
    94 (August): 691–719.
Harberger, A. 1971. "Three Basic Postulates for Applied Welfare Economics:
    An Interpretive Essay," *Journal of Economic Literature,* 2 (September):
    785–97.
Hayek, F. 1945. "The Use of Knowledge in Society," *American Economic
    Review,* 35 (September): 519–30.
Hayes, S. L., III, and R. A. Taussig. "Tactics of Cash Takeover Bids," *Harvard
    Business Review,* 46 (March–April): 136–47.
Hessen, R. 1983. "The Modern Corporation and Private Property: A Reap-
    praisal," *Journal of Law and Economics,* 26 (June): 273–90.
Hirschey, M. 1986. "Mergers, Buyouts and Fakeouts," *American Economic
    Review,* 76 (May): 317–22.

Horvat, Bronko. 1982. *The Political Economy of Socialism.* New York: M.E. Sharpe.

Jarrell, Gregg, and Michael Bradley. 1980. "The Economic Effect of Federal and State Regulation of Cash Tender Offers," *Journal of Law and Economics,* 23 (October): 305–60.

Jensen, M. 1986. "Agency Costs of Free Cash Flow, Corporate Finance, and Takeovers," *American Economic Review,* 76 (May): 323–29.

Jensen, M. and W. Meckling. 1976. "Theory of the Firm: Managerial Behavior, Agency Costs, and Capital Structure," *Journal of Financial Economics,* 3 (October): 305–60.

Johnson, R. and D. Smith. 1986. "Antitrust Division Merger Procedures and Policy 1968–1984," Economic Analysis Group, 86–10, Washington, D.C. (June).

Klein, Benjamin, R. A. Crawford, and A. A. Alchian. 1978. "Vertical Integration, Appropriable Rents, and the Competitive Contracting Process," *Journal of Law and Economics,* 21 (October): 297–326.

Knight, Frank H. 1941. "Review of Melville J. Herskovits' 'Economic Anthropology," *Journal of Political Economy,* 49 (April): 246–58.

Kreps, D., and A. Spence. 1985. "Modelling the Role of History in Industrial Organization and Competition," in G. Feiwel, ed., *Issues in Contemporary Microeconomics and Welfare.* London: Macmillan, pp. 340–79.

Levy, D. 1985. "The Transaction Cost Approach to Vertical Integration: An Empirical Examination," *Review of Economics and Statistics,* 67 (August 1985): 438–45.

Long, N., and I. Malitz. 1985. "Investment Patterns and Financial Leverage," in B. Friedman, ed., *Corporate Capital Structures in the United States.* Chicago: University of Chicago Press, pp. 325–48.

Lowenstein, L. 1985. "Management Buyouts," *Columbia Law Review,* 85 (May): 730–84.

McKenzie, L. 1951. "Ideal Output and the Interdependence of Firms," *Economic Journal,* 61 (December 1951): 785–803.

Magenheim, E., and D. Mueller. 1987. "On Measuring the Effect of Acquisitions and Acquiring Firm Shareholders," in J. Coffee, L. Lowenstein, and S. Rose-Ackerman, eds., *Knights, Raiders, and Targets.* New York: Oxford University Press.

Manne, Henry G. 1965. "Mergers and the Market for Corporate Control," *Journal of Political Economy,* 73 (April 1965): 110–20.

Mason, Edward. 1959. *The Corporation in Modern Society.* Cambridge, Mass.: Harvard University Press.

Mason, L. 1984. *Structuring and Financing Management Buyouts.* San Diego, Calif.: Buyout Publications, 1984.

Myers, S. 1977. "Determinants of Corporate Borrowing," *Journal of Financial Economics,* 5:147–75.

Porter, G., and G. C. Livesay. 1971. *Merchants and Manufacturers: Studies in the Changing Structure of Nineteenth Century Marketing.* Baltimore: Johns Hopkins Press.

Ravenscraft, D., and F. Scherer. 1987. "Mergers and Managerial Performance," in J. Coffee, L. Lowenstein, and S. Rose-Ackerman, eds., *Knights, Raiders, and Targets.* New York: Oxford University Press.

Ross, S. 1977. "The Determination of Financial Structure: The Incentive Signaling Approach," *Bell Journal of Economics*, 8 (Spring): 23–40.

Schwartz, Alan. 1976. "Search Theory and the Tender Offer Auction," *Journal of Law, Economics and Organization*, 2 (Fall).

Schumpeter, J. A. 1947. "The Creative Response in Economic History," *Journal of Economic History*, 7 (November): 149–59.

Solo, Robert. 1972. "New maths and old sterilities," *Saturday Review*, January 22, pp. 47–48.

Stiglitz, J. 1974. "Incentives and risk sharing in Sharecropping," *Review of Economic Studies*, 41: 219–57.

Stiglitz, J. 1985. "Credit Markets and the Control of Capital," *Journal of Money, Credit, and Banking*, 17 (May): 133–52.

Tversky, Amos, and Daniel Kahneman. 1974. "Judgment under Uncertainty: Heuristics and Biases," *Science*, 185: 1124–31.

Wallner, N. 1980. "Leveraged Buyouts: A Review of the State of the Art, Part II," *Mergers and Acquisitions* (Winter): 16–26.

Williamson, O. 1968. "Economies as an Antitrust Defense: The Welfare Trade-offs," *American Economic Review*, 58 (March 1968): 18–35.

Williamson, O. 1971. "The Vertical Integration of Production: Market Failure Considerations," *American Economic Review*, 61 (May): 112–23.

Williamson, O. 1975. *Markets and Hierarchies: Analysis and Antitrust Implications*. New York: Free Press.

Williamson, O. 1977. "Economics as an Antitrust Defense Revisited." *University of Pennsylvania Law Review*, 125 (April): 669–736.

Williamson, O. 1985. *The Economic Institutions of Capitalism*. New York: Free Press.

Williamson, O. 1986. "Transforming Merger Policy: The Pound of New Perspectives," *American Economic Review*, 76 (May): 114–19.

Williamson, O. 1988. "Corporate Finance and Corporate Governance," *Journal of Finance*, 43 (July): 567–91.

CHAPTER 2

Discounted share prices as a source of acquisition gains

Reinier Kraakman

If the Acme Oil Company has 100,000 shares of stock trading at $10 per share, no debt, and a proven oil well as its only asset, how much should an identical firm pay to acquire Acme? Businessmen might fail the quiz, but finance students would probably answer: "Not more than $1 million ($10 x 100,000), excluding synergy gains or tax savings."[1]

This answer echoes a common presumption in the finance literature that informed securities prices credibly estimate the underlying value of corporate assets. Firms whose share prices fall below the market value of their assets – for example, many closed-end investment funds, holding companies, or natural resource firms – are frequently tagged as anomalies on the force of this view.[2] But these "anomalous" firms happen to be the only firms whose asset values are readily visible. Here, then, is the rub: The direct evidence, as far as it goes, is more consistent with the conjecture that securities prices *often* "discount" – or underprice – expected cash flows from corporate assets than with the standard pre-

An expanded version of this article appears as "Taking Discounts Seriously: The Implications of 'Discounted' Share Prices as an Acquisition Motive," *Columbia Law Review,* 88: 891–941 (1988). I am indebted for helpful comments on earlier drafts of this paper to William Andrews, Lucian Bebchuk, Bernard Black, Frank Buckley, Robert Clark, John Coffee, Henry Hansmann, Ronald Gilson, Catherine Krupnick, Roberta Romano, Alan Schwartz, Craig Wasserman, and participants in the Harvard Law School Conference and the Yale Faculty Workshop. Needless to say, the generous assistance of these readers does not constitute an endorsement of my views. Craig Wasserman and Jonathan Grunzweig provided valuable research assistance. For financial support, I am grateful to the Harvard Law School Faculty Summer Research Program and the Harvard Program in Law and Economics, which is funded in part by the John M. Olin Foundation.
1 See J. Van Horne, *Financial Management and Policy.* 7th ed. (Englewood Cliffs, N.J., 1986), p. 260, for discussion of acquisition gains.
2 See section II.A for review of "anomalous" firms.

sumption that share prices fully value these assets. If discounts are widespread, however, they may have significant consequences for many areas of corporate behavior, including, above all, acquisitions behavior and the takeover market.

As the Acme hypothetical suggests, the standard presumption that share prices fully value corporate assets carries a basic implication for acquisition premia. If share prices already reflect the value of targets' assets, then takeover premia, which now average over 50 percent of prebid share prices, must reflect something else of value that bidders bring to acquisitions: for example, better management or synergy gains. As astute acquirer would never pay $1,500,000 for Acme's shares unless it could earn at least $500,000, on a present value basis, more than what Acme already expected to earn. By contrast, on the view that share prices may discount asset values, takeover premia have an alternative source in the *existing* value of targets' assets. Acme's acquirer might pay $1,500,000 simply because Acme's oil well is reliably appraised at, say $1,700,000. In this case, the "premium" received by Acme's shareholders might be more accurately described as a "recaptured" discount.

The discount claim conforms to an intuition, deeply rooted in corporate law and business practice, that share prices often diverge from asset values.[3] I will argue that this intuition is plausible for important classes of acquisitions. Nevertheless, the discount claim is an incomplete account of acquisition gains absent an explanation of how share discounts arise in the first instance. Here, at least two familiar but divergent hypotheses are possible. One – the "misinvestment" hypothesis – holds that investors rationally expect managers of target firms to misinvest the future returns on corporate assets, and discount the value of these assets accordingly. The second hypothesis – the "market" hypothesis – asserts that share prices themselves may be noisy or skewed. On this view, market prices simply fail to reflect informed estimates of likely cash flows generated by target firms. Both discount hypotheses predict similar acquisition behavior and carry similar implications for other corporate behavior as well, including the influence of financial policy on share prices. Nevertheless, the distinction between these hypotheses is crucial, since the choice of a discount hypothesis will govern the regulatory implications of the discount claim.

This article seeks to establish the plausibility of the discount claim and assess its implications for the behavior and regulation of the acquisitions market. Section I contrasts traditional and discount hy-

---

3 See, e.g., *Smith* v. *Van Gorkom*, 488 A.2d 858, 875–76 (Del. 1985). Even large premia over market price may undervalue corporate assets.

potheses as accounts of acquisition activity. Section II presents the case for taking discounts seriously by examining their existence for specialized firms and demonstrating their congruence with much recent acquisition behavior. Section III demonstrates how discounts might survive in a competitive takeover market, even though eliminating discounts on potential takeover targets would profit both hostile acquirers and target shareholders. Section IV examines how, despite the relative stability of discounts, they can nonetheless trigger takeovers in conjunction with other sources of acquisition gains or as a result of managerial inattention to rising discount levels. Finally, Section V sketches the divergent implications of the misinvestment and market explanations of discounts for the regulation of hostile takeovers: Acquisitions that are ultimately explained by noisy security prices may impose social costs, while explanations that arise from rational skepticism about managers' investment policies create real social gains.

I   An overview of acquisition gains

Three possibilities might occur to an observer who first learned that acquirers pay large premia over share price for the assets of target firms: (1) Acquirers may be discovering more valuable uses for target assets: (2) share prices may "underprice" these assets; or, finally, (3) acquirers may simply be paying too much. These same possibilities point to a useful typology of current explanations of acquisition gains. A broad class of "traditional" hypotheses presumes that acquirers can create or claim new value to pay for acquisition premia. These explanations accord with the assumption that informed share prices fully reflect asset values, and they include all accounts in which acquirers might expect to increase the net cash flows of targets by, for example, improving management or redeploying assets. A second class of "discount" hypotheses asserts that while acquirers' bid prices reflect real private gains, these gains result because share prices discount the underlying value of target assets. Finally, a third and more troubling class of "overbidding" hypotheses questions whether bid prices and takeover premia reflect real opportunities for acquisition gains at all. Under these theories, managers of acquiring firms misperceive or misvalue targets out of "hubris,"[4] or they may pursue distinctly managerial interests such as corporate growth at great cost to shareholder interests.[5]

4 R. Roll, "The hubris hypothesis of corporate takeovers," *Journal of Business* 59: 197 (1986).
5 See, e.g., O. Williamson, *The Economics of Discretionary Behavior: Managerial Objectives in a Theory of the Firm* (Chicago, 1967).

The extent to which this third class of acquisition hypotheses might explain takeover premia remains a difficult issue. Nevertheless, a prosperous acquisitions market and a large empirical literature both suggest that most acquisitions do generate private gains, at least as measured by their impact on share prices. Target shareholders earn large returns in the form of premia, while shareholders of acquiring firms do not seem to suffer losses and may also register gains.[6] Since a primary role for private gains in motivating takeovers seems likely, inquiry must turn to the traditional and discount hypotheses. The question thus becomes: What mix of opportunities can explain these gains and, in particular, the size of acquisition premia?

A   Traditional gains hypotheses

Most traditional accounts of motives and gains in the acquisitions literature favor active and resourceful acquirers who seek to increase cash flows from target assets through the redeployment or better management of these assets. The reorganization of assets can lead to synergy benefits, while new management may slash operating costs and increase returns in a variety of ways.[7] In either case, acquisitions create both private gains

6 See G. Jarrell, J. Brickley, and J. Netter, "The Market for Corporate Control: The Empirical Evidence Since 1980," *Journal of Economic Perspectives* 2: 49, 53 (1988) and M. Jensen and R. Ruback, "The Market for Corporate Control: The Scientific Evidence, *Journal of Financial Economics* 11:5 (1983), pp. 9–22. Recent studies provide additional evidence of aggregate gains from mergers and takeovers. See, e.g., D. Denis and J. McConnell, Corporate Mergers and Securities Returns, *Journal of Financial Economics* 16: 143 (1986) and P. Malesta and R. Thompson, "Partially Anticipated Events," *Journal of Financial Economics* 14: 237 (1985). Basic ambiguities in the interpretation of these market studies, however, leave the issue of aggregate gains far from closed. See, e.g., E. Magenheim and D. Mueller, Are Acquiring-Firm Shareholders Better Off After an Acquisition Than They Were Before? in *Knights, Raiders, and Targets: The Impact of the Hostile Takeover,* ed. J. Coffee, L. Lowenstein, and S. Rose-Ackerman (New York, 1988), p. 172, and R. Roll, Empirical Evidence on Takeover Activity and Shareholder Wealth," in *Knights, Raiders, and Targets,* p. 241.

7 For overviews of acquisition hypotheses, see note 6, Jarrell, Brickley, and Netter, pp. 54–8; Roll, and Jensen and Ruback, pp. 22–33. The specialized literature on acquisition gains is large. The synergy hypothesis, including gains from vertical integration and economies of scale, is the most strongly supported traditional account; see, e.g., Roll, note 6, pp. 245–6; M. Bradley, A. Desai, and H. Kim, The Rationale Behind Interfirm Tender Offers: Information or Synergy? *Journal of Financial Economics* 11: 183 (1983); and J. McConnell and T. Nantell, "Corporate Combinations and Common Stock Returns: The Case of Joint Ventures," *Journal of Finance* 40: 519 (1985) (extrapolating from joint ventures to merger gains). However, the case for pure "financial synergies," including diversification and coinsurance gains in conglomerate mergers, is

for the participating parties and net social gains. In addition, there are less prominent, if no less traditional, accounts of how acquisitions might create private gains by imposing costs on third parties: for example, by exploiting monopoly power,[8] or by breaching "implicit contracts" between target shareholders and creditors, employees, or incumbent managers.[9]

Two further accounts of acquisition gains straddle the line between traditional and discount hypotheses. One of these is a "private information" theory, which assumes that the market may be uninformed about the real value of target assets. In this case, acquirers who privately learn key information can exploit true discrepancies between share prices and asset values. The possibility of such information is a traditional caveat to the identification of share prices and asset values. Yet, its practical significance seems largely limited to friendly transactions. Short of hiring informers, hostile acquirers lack access to inside information about targets. In addition, evidence that unsuccessful bids fail to increase the share prices of target firms over the long run also suggests that hostile bids do not release key inside information.[10]

not persuasive; see Y. Amihud and B. Lev, "Risk Reduction as a Managerial Motive for Conglomerate Mergers," *Bell Journal of Economics* 12: 605 (1981).

8 Indirect evidence strongly suggests that market power is not an important acquisition motive. See E. Eckbo, "Horizontal Mergers, Collusion, and Stockholder Wealth," *Journal of Financial Economics* 11: 241 (1983).

9 Among the most provocative revisionist accounts of private gains in takeovers are implicit contract theories that locate private gains in the redistribution of surplus from nonshareholder factors of target firms to acquiring firms. Thus, several commentators portray takeovers as a species of shareholder opportunism vis-à-vis incumbent managers, e.g., C. Knoeber, Golden Parachutes, Shark Repellents and Hostile Tender Offers, *American Economic Review* 76: 155 (1986), pp. 159–61, and J. Coffee, "Shareholders Versus Managers: Strains in the Corporate Web," *Michigan Law Review* 85: 1 (1986), p. 24. This view suggests that acquirers profit in part by breaching implicit agreements to pay incumbent managers deferred compensation or to provide other perquisites. Schleifer and Summers generalize the implicit contract perspective to other major corporate factors including employees and creditors (A. Schleifer and L. Summers, "Hostile Takeovers as Breaches of Trust," NBER Working Paper No. 2342, [1987]).

10 See note 7, Bradley, Desai, and Kim (share prices of targets fall to preoffer levels within five years after unsuccessful bids). Share prices would presumably remain at postbid levels if the market believed that hostile bids were based on inside information. For more recent studies replicating the Bradley, Desai, and Kim result, see G. Jarrell, The Wealth Effects of Litigation by Targets: Do Interests Diverge in a Merge? *Journal of Law and Economics* 28:151 (1985); R. Ruback, Do Target Shareholders Lose in Unsuccessful Control Contests, in A. Auerbach, ed., *Mergers and Acquisitions* (Chicago, 1988).

The second of these hypotheses concerns the import of tax savings for acquisition premia. The tax hypothesis can be either a traditional or a discount hypothesis depending on the nature of the asserted tax gain. In most instances, it is a traditional hypothesis that turns on corporate-level tax savings. Acquirers are said to garner significant tax gains by stepping up the basis on target assets, transferring valuable operating loss carryovers (NOLs), or increasing their interest deductions by borrowing against target assets.[11] These forms of the tax hypothesis resemble accounts of creating gains through better management, although here tax management is at issue and the savings are private gains made at the expense of the Treasury.[12] Recent studies suggest that each of these corporate-level tax gains has played some role in acquisitions and, more importantly, in management buyouts.[13] Yet, apart from leveraged buyouts, this role seems to have been modest in the recent past; tax effects seldom appear to have been primary motives for acquisitions.[14]

A more controversial form of the tax hypothesis – the so-called trapped-equity theory – looks to shareholder-level tax savings as a source of acquisition gains.[15] On this view, share prices reflect the expectation that corporate distributions will be taxed at dividend rates to shareholders. Cash acquisitions, then, create value by allowing target shareholders to extract capital from "corporate solution" at more favorable

---

11 See, e.g., R. Gilson, M. Scholes, and M. Wolfson, Taxation and the Dynamics of Corporate Control: The Uncertain Case for Tax Motivated Acquisitions (Stanford Law School Law and Economics Program, Working Paper No. 24, [January 1986] and A. Auerbach and D. Reishus, The Effects of Taxation on the Merger Decision (NBER Working Paper No. 2192 [March 1987]).

12 This point is made most forcefully by considering that alternative transactions would permit target managers to realize most tax gains for shareholders that are ordinarily attributed to acquisitions; see note 11, Gilson, Scholes, and Wolfson.

13 See A. Auerbach and D. Reishus, Taxes and the Merger Decision, in *Knights, Raiders, and Targets* (note 6, Coffee, Lowenstein, and Rose-Ackerman), p. 310 (tax losses and credits potentially important in 20% of mergers but fewer apparent tax benefits from stepping up asset basis or leverage); note 11, A. Auerbach and D. Reishaus, pp. 27–9 (use of tax losses and credits by acquiring companies appears to have "some impact" on merger activity, while interest deductions "could not have been an important factor" during 1968–83). The evidence is more persuasive that tax gains are critical in many management buyouts. See K. Lehn and A. Poulsen, "Sources of Value in Leveraged Buyouts" (Working Paper [February 1987]). L. Lowenstein, "Management Buyouts," *Columbia Law Review* 85: 730 (1985), pp. 759–67.

14 See note 13 (citing sources) and note 6, Roll, pp. 246–8.

15 See, e.g., M. King, "Takeovers, Taxes and the Stock Market" (London School of Economics, 1986); A. Auerbach, "Wealth Maximization and the Cost of Capital," *Quarterly Journal of Economics* 93: 443 (1979).

tax rates, just as shareholders might profit from other unconventional distributions such as share repurchases or liquidations.[16] This mechanism, unlike corporate-level tax gains, is a true discount hypothesis that operates through the medium of the securities market: Acquirers of corporate assets need only observe that share prices discount the asset values of target corporations. Again, however, because recent studies cut against the trapped-equity theory, it is likely to remain a weak form of the tax hypothesis and a poor competitor with other discount hypotheses.[17]

B   Discount hypotheses

True discount hypotheses do not rely on either the private information or the traditional inquiry into how acquirers might extract larger net cash flows from target assets. The discount claim presumes that acquisition premia reflect the existing value of target assets, a value that may be much higher than the market value of target shares. A discount hypothesis must explain why these values differ. In broad terms two explanations are possible, which I term the misinvestment hypothesis and the market hypothesis.

The misinvestment hypothesis comes closest to traditional accounts of takeover gains. This account locates discrepancies between share prices and asset values in a rational mistrust of managers' future investment decisions. As such, it belongs to the broader family of agency cost theories. Unlike accounts of manager-shareholder conflict over slack and perquisites, however, the misinvestment hypothesis follows more recent analyses of manager-shareholder conflict over the distribution of corporate returns.[18] On this view, managers exercise discretionary control over what Professor Jensen terms free cash flows: that is, cash flows exceeding the investment requirements of the firm's ex-

---

16 See note 15, King, pp. 5–9.
17 See R. Harris, J. Franks, and C. Mayer, Means of Payment in Takeovers: The Results for the U.K. and U.S. (NBER Working Paper No. 2456 [1987]), pp. 26–8 (trapped equity theory totally fails to explain tax developments in the United Kingdom), and note 11, Auerbach and Reishus, p. 28 (share repurchase data, although ambiguous, fail to confirm trapped equity theory).
18 See e.g., M. Jensen, "Agency Costs of Free Cash Flows, Corporate Finance, and Takeovers," *American Economic Review* 76: 323 (1986); E. Jacobs, "The Agency Cost of Corporate Control: The Petroleum Industry" (Massachusetts Institute of Technology Center for Energy Policy Research Working Paper 86–021 [1986]); F. Easterbrook, "Two Agency-Cost Explanations of Dividends," *American Economic Review* 74:650 (1984); note 9, Coffee, pp. 16–24.

isting projects. If managers are reluctant to distribute these cash flows and are unable – or unwilling – to discover profitable new investments, shareholders will inevitably price firms at below their asset values.[19]

Although the misinvestment hypothesis is conceptually related to traditional accounts of acquisition gains arising from improvements in the operational management of target firms, there is an important difference. Ongoing mismanagement of targets' assets reduces their cash flows. Thus, low share prices may accurately mirror the value of mismanaged target assets; there may be no discounts. By contrast, the misinvestment hypothesis permits discounts to arise even when targets' assets are already put to their best uses. These discounts, which acquirers can exploit, result from the ongoing or expected misinvestment of surplus cash flows in excess of targets' operating requirements. Acquiring firms can profit, then, merely by purchasing discounted shares at any price up to the full value of targets' assets.

The alternative discount hypothesis – the market hypothesis – fits less easily with standard accounts of the securities market. On this view, share prices may discount asset values for reasons endogenous to the formation of market prices. Financial economics conventionally assumes that share prices are best estimates, given available information, of the present value of expected corporate cash flows available for distribution to shareholders.[20] Thus, share prices should fully capitalize the value of

19 Agency cost analyses focusing on distribution policy build upon evidence that managers often seek to maximize total corporate resources including debt capacity. See G. Donaldson, *Managing Corporate Wealth: The Operation of a Comprehensive Financial Goals System* (New York: 1984). Maximizing resources may lead in turn to investments with a negative net present value. Managerial incentives to misinvest in this fashion are variously attributed to organizational inertia, a desire to increase size (or sales) per se, and the close associations among firm size, managerial career opportunities, and managerial compensation. See note 18, Jensen, p. 323. In addition, misinvestment may follow from managers' relative risk aversion in comparison to that of shareholders. See note 9, Coffee, pp. 16–24.

20 Professor Merton terms this core assumption the "rational market hypothesis." R. Merton, On the Current State of the Stock Market Rationality Hypothesis (M.I.T. Working Paper No. 1717-85, 1 [1985]). The same assumption is sometimes termed "fundamental-valuation" or "allocative" efficiency to distinguish it from the presumptively weaker claim that the markets are "informationally" or "speculatively" efficient; that is, that share prices respond to new information too rapidly to permit arbitrage profits. See, e.g., J. Tobin, On the Efficiency of the Financial System, *Lloyds Bank Review* 5 (July 1984); J. Gordon and L. Kornhauser, Efficient Markets, Costly Information, and Securities Research, *New York University Law Review* 60: 761, 825–830 (1985). Most discussion of the "efficient capital market hypothesis" focuses on the informational efficiency of share prices. See, e.g., R. Gilson and R. Kraakman, The Mechanisms of Market Efficiency, *Virginia Law Review* 70: 549 (1984). Note, however,

corporate assets in the hands of existing managers. In real markets, this assumption is an approximation; it is unlikely to be either precisely correct or, given the sensitivity of share prices to new information, wholly misguided. It is a very good approximation in the standard view. By contrast, the market hypothesis asserts that discounts arise because share prices are sometimes very poor estimates of the expected value of corporate assets.

Modern objections to identifying share prices with asset values typically fall into two classes. The first class includes "valuation" challenges that question whether a single valuation model can apply across the markets for shares and firms, or even within the share market itself. Even if traders in both the asset and share markets value corporate assets similarly, share prices might nonetheless discount asset values simply because assets and shares differ in ways that matter to traders.[21] For example, the share prices of firms holding liquid assets might discount asset values if traders placed an intrinsic value on the right to liquidate firms in the asset market – a right that minority shareholders in these firms would necessarily lack.[22] Alternatively, overlapping clienteles of traders within the securities market might have heterogeneous demands for timing, magnitude, or tax attributes of shareholder distributions.[23] In this case, shares might sell at either a discount or a premium relative to asset values.

The second and more prominent class of objections to equating share prices with asset values challenges the price setting role of informed traders. Thus, there is a growing theoretical literature on "mispricing" behavior, which argues that uninformed traders may introduce persistent

that the distinction between informational and allocative efficiency is cogent only if the standard view, the rational market hypothesis, is suspect.

21 Professors Lowenstein and Shubik vigorously urge this point as part of their broader advocacy of the market hypothesis. See L. Lowenstein, Pruning Deadwood in Hostile Takeovers: A Proposal for Legislation, *Columbia Law Review* 83: 294 (1983); M. Shubik, Corporate Control, Efficient Markets, The Public Good, and Economic Theory and Advice, in *Knights, Raiders, and Targets* (note 6, Coffee, Lowenstein, and Rose-Ackerman). A separate argument is that traders in the asset and share markets systematically differ in their valuations of underlying assets or cash flows; for example, that corporate acquirers have different risk preferences or valuation models from traders in shares. See, e.g., note 20, Gordon and Kornhauser, p. 825.

22 I am grateful to Bernard Black for suggesting a more developed form of this liquidity discount theory in the context of closed-end investment funds.

23 See, e.g., R. Thompson, The Information Content of Discounts and Premiums on Closed-End Fund Shares, *Journal of Financial Economies* 6: 151 (1978), pp. 180–2 (suggesting heterogeneous demand as possible source of discounts on closed-end funds).

biases or cumulative noise into share prices or that speculative trading might lead to positive and negative price "bubbles."[24] Large-scale noise trading – arising from misconceived strategies, erroneous valuation-assumptions, fashion and fads, or simple pleasure in trading[25] – might distort share prices and generate discounts or premia through the sheer pressure of trading. In addition, some commentators suggest that noise trading further distorts share prices by encouraging informed traders to speculate on noise and by imposing "noise trader risk" on all traders in a noisy market.[26] Finally, noise theorists find evidence of mispricing in the long-term price behavior of both individual firms and the entire market.[27]

24 E.g., F. Black, Noise, *Journal of Finance* 41: 529 (1986) (cumulative noise in price following uninformed trading); O. Blanchard and M. Watson, Bubbles, Rational Expectations, and Financial Markets, in *Crises in Economic and Financial Structure*, P. Wachtel, ed., pp. 295–315 (Lexington, Mass.: 1982) (modeling the formation of "rational" bubbles); J. Tirole, On the Possibility of Speculation Under Rational Expectations, *Econometrica* 59: 1163 (1982).
25 Several sources of noise trading have been proposed. See, e.g., note 24, F. Black, p. 531 (noise trading by mistake or because trading yields direct utility); R. Shiller, Fashions, Fads and Bubbles in Financial Markets, in *Knights, Raiders, and Targets* (note 6, Coffee, Lowenstein, and Rose-Ackerman), (fashions and fads); J. Delong, A. Shleifer, L. Summers, and R. Waldmann, The Economic Consequences of Noise Trading (CRSP Working Paper No. 218, 4–5 [September 1987]) (irrational belief or cognitive bias); B. Trueman, A Theory of Noise Trading in Securities Markets, *Journal of Finance* 43: 83 (1988) (rational noise trading by uninformed fund managers to fool investors).
26 For a model addressing both of these effects, see note 25, DeLong, Shleifer, Summers, and Waldmann. In this two-generation, two-period model, some noise traders succeed by unwittingly accepting large risks, and are copied by a second generation of noise traders. These assumptions generate mispricing and "noise trader-created risk," even when there is no uncertainty about the fundamental value of assets. The authors identify noise trader risk as the source of share discounts on closed-end investment funds.
27 Much recent evidence concerns the volatility and mean-reverting behavior of share prices. For example, several studies suggest that share prices overreact to bad news about particular firms. See W. DeBondt and R. Thaler, Does the Stock Market Overreact? *Journal of Finance* 40: 793 (1985); W. DeBondt and R. Thaler, Further Evidence on Investor Overreaction and Stock Market Seasonality, *Journal of Finance* 42: 557 (1987). Additional studies indicate mean-reverting behavior on the level of the market. See note 25, DeLong, Shleifer, Summers, and Waldmann, pp. 21–24 (summarizing studies). The well-known work of Robert Shiller argues that the market as a whole has exhibited too much volatility to accord with plausible models of fundamental value. See, e.g., note 25, Shiller; R. Shiller, Do Stock Prices Move too Much to be Justified by Subsequent Changes in Dividends? *American Economic Review* 71: 421 (1981). Shiller's work and related studies have attracted much methodological criticism. See, e.g., note 20, Merton.

For present purposes, however, the important point is less a particular model of noisy prices than the cumulative uncertainty, generated by a wide range of recent research, about the extent and persistence of mispricing behavior.[28] Few observers would assert that mispricing never occurs, just as few would deny that share prices rapidly reflect information bearing on future corporate prospects. What remains uncertain is how effectively share prices estimate the full present value of corporate cash flows as distinct from predicting near-term share prices, and how large residual mispricing effects are likely to be.[29] The market hypothesis simply asserts that recurrent discrepancies between share prices and asset values can explain major portions of at least some acquisition premia.

Stepping back from the market hypothesis, then, it is apparent that neither this account nor the misinvestment theory of acquisition gains is easily evaluated. Unlike traditional gains hypotheses such as synergy or private information, the discount hypotheses turn on far-reaching and sharply divergent narratives about the securities market. The misinvestment hypothesis implies that prices sensitively anticipate future management decisions, while the dominant market hypothesis holds that prices may be systematically depressed (or inflated) by noise trading. The fact that both hypotheses can be further particularized in diverse ways makes their evaluation even more formidable. Fortunately, however, one task does not require such an evaluation: namely, examining the discount claim in its own right as a motive for acquisitions. Evidence of discounts can support either hypothesis. But equally important, such evidence can also support a unitary account of acquisition behavior that does not immediately force us to choose between discount hypotheses.

II   The case for discounts

In principle, market discounts must satisfy three conditions to be meaningful. First, potential acquirers and market professionals must be able to frame reliable asset or breakup values for the firm "as is"; that is, as its component assets are already managed and deployed. Asset values in this sense are particularly credible where assets can be separated from the functions of top management. Thus, natural resources or established

---

28 See notes 21–27 (citing sources). For additional discussion, see L. Summers, Does the Stock Market Rationally Reflect Fundamental Values? *Journal of Finance* 41: 591 (1986); W. Wang, Some Arguments that the Stock Market is Not Efficient, *University of California at Davis Law Review* 19: 341 (1986).
29 See note 20 (distinguishing speculative from allocative efficiency).

corporate divisions may lend themselves to reliable valuation, while start-up projects or undeveloped investment opportunities might be impossible to value with confidence. Second, of course, share prices must fall significantly below asset values. And third, potential acquirers must accept appraisals within the consensus range as useful – perhaps as minimal – estimates of what target assets may be worth to themselves and competing bidders.

Although these conditions do not invite easy testing, the case for discounts is nonetheless persuasive. Certain specialized firms that hold easily priced assets provide direct evidence of discounting. In addition, pervasive discounting can explain much recent acquisition behavior, including breakup acquisitions,[30] management buyouts, and the sheer size of takeover premia. Finally, support for discounts can be found in many forms of corporate restructuring, including the wave of share repurchases and recapitalizations that swept American corporations during the mid-1980s.[31]

A   Discounts on specialized firms

Specialized firms whose shares clearly trade below the value of their assets provide direct evidence of discounting. Because these firms hold fungible assets that trade in separate markets and require little active management, even casual observers can locate discounts by comparing share prices with asset values. The closed-end investment fund is the best example of such a firm, and discounts on closed-end funds have long been viewed as important anomalies by financial economists.[32] Yet, discounts appear to be common among holding companies and natural resource companies, which are also firms that possess easily accessible and seemingly reliable asset values. Thus, even though reliable appraisals are not widely available for most firms, the suggestion is clear: Since discounts appear wherever they might be detected, we have good reason to suspect that they may be pervasive elsewhere.

Like mutual funds (or open-end funds), closed-end investment funds

---

30 Breakup acquisitions of multidivisional firms rely on the preplanned resale of target divisions to finance premia and generate gains.

31 Coffee provides an illuminating overview of the sweep of the share repurchase and leveraged restructuring phenomenon during the 1980s. See note 9, Coffee, pp. 40–60.

32 See, e.g., B. Malkiel, The Valuation of Closed-End Investment Company Shares, *Journal of Finance* 32: 847, (1977), p. 847, and R. Thompson, The Information Content of Discounts and Premiums on Closed-End Fund Shares, *Journal of Financial Economics* 6: 151 (1978), pp. 151–2.

are investment companies. Like ordinary corporations, however, closed-end funds issue shares that trade publicly but are not redeemable against their issuers.[33] Many closed-end funds hold diversified portfolios of publicly traded stocks and are themselves traded on major stock exchanges. The financial press regularly publishes dual market prices for both the shares of exchange-traded funds and the net asset value (per share) of their securities portfolios. The interesting feature of these dual prices is that they frequently diverge. Compared with the market value of their portfolios, funds often trade at discounts and occasionally trade at premia. While start-up funds generally begin trading at a premium, their share prices subsequently drop relative to their asset values. Thereafter, discounts on seasoned funds of 20 percent or more, persisting for five years or longer, have been common in the recent past.[34] Moreover, sustained discounts of this magnitude also afflict the similar closed-end vehicles of dual purpose funds[35] and investment trust companies in Great Britain.[36]

Although there have been numerous investigations of discounts on closed-end funds,[37] none as yet has satisfactorily accounted for their

33 As public investment companies, closed-end funds are the older and less popular siblings of mutual funds. While mutual funds continuously issue and redeem shares, closed-end funds issue a fixed number of shares at their initial organization and thereafter distribute their portfolio returns to shareholders through the usual corporate devices of dividends and share repurchases.

34 See, e.g., D. Mullins, Managerial Discretion and Corporate Financial Management, Chapter 5, pp. 3–5 (unpublished Ph.D. dissertation, Harvard Business School, July 29, 1983); W. Sharpe and H. Sosin, Closed-End Investment Companies in the United States: Risk and Return, in *European Financial Association 1974 Proceedings*, ed. B. Jacquillat (Amsterdam: 1975), pp. 39–40. Historically, average discounts on closed-end funds have narrowed during long-term bull markets including 1984–1987. But discounts have reopened to historical levels since the October 1987 crash. See T. Herzfeld, Closed-End Funds: Watch that Discount! *Personal Finance*, January 20, 1988, p. 16 (return of 20% to 30% discounts).

35 Dual purpose funds hold diversified portfolios and issue common and preferred shares. Holders of preferred stock receive dividend income from the fund portfolio and a liquidation preference on a preset redemption date. Holders of common stock receive capital appreciation. During the early 1980s, these funds traded at a discount relative to the combined market value of their common and preferred shares, despite fixed redemption dates. See note 28, Wang, pp. 387–9; B. Malkiel, *A Random Walk Down Wall Street*, 4th ed. (1985), pp. 344–5.

36 J. Macleod, Investment Trust Companies, *British Tax Review* 5: 278, 283–4 (1985). The British investment trusts represent 6% of market capitalization on the London Exchange. For the past decade, they have traded at 20% to 30% discounts, or at levels similar to American closed-end funds during the 1950s and 1970s. Up for Grabs? *The Economist*, September 27, 1986, p. 84.

37 See, e.g., J. Brickley and J. Schallheim, Lifting the Lid on Closed-End Investment

origins. Discounts are certainly not due to misinformation about the value of fund assets, nor are they attributable to management expenses or trading costs, which are generally modest.[38] Tax liabilities may explain some discounting behavior, but even this is unclear.[39] Thus, the larger portion of the variance in discounts is fair game for informed conjecture. Not surprisingly, competing explanations divide along the familiar lines of the market-or-manager dichotomy. On the market side, discounts are usually attributed either to gross market inefficiencies or to our failure to understand the true structure of investor returns on closed-end funds.[40] On the manager side, discounts are often ascribed to doubts

Companies: A Case of Abnormal Returns, *Journal of Financial Quantitative Analysis* 20: 107 (1985); G. Brauer, 'Open-Ending' Closed-End Funds, *Journal of Financial Economics* 13: 491 (1984); D. Leonard and N. Noble, Estimation of Time-Varying Systematic Risk and Investment Performance: Closed-End Investment Companies, *Journal of Financial Research* 4: 109 (1981); see note 32, Thompson; R. Thompson, Capital Market Efficiency, Two Parameter Asset Pricing and the Market for Corporate Control: The Implications of Closed-End Investment Company Discounts and Premiums (unpublished Ph.D. dissertation, Graduate School of Management, University of Rochester, 1978); M. Mendelson, Closed-End Fund Discounts Revisited, *Financial Review*, Spring 1978, p. 48; B. Malkiel, The Valuation of Closed-End Investment Company Shares, *Journal of Finance* 32: 847 (1977); R. Roenfeldt and D. Tuttle, An Examination of the Discounts and Premiums of Closed-End Investment Companies, *Journal of Business Research* 1: 129 (1973); K. Boudreaux, Discounts and Premiums on Closed-End Mutual Funds: A Study in Valuation, *Journal of Finance* 28: 515 (1973).

38 See note 37, Mendelson, pp. 53–6, and Thompson, p. 33.

39 Because investors are taxed directly when funds realize capital gains, discounts might arise from tax liability on unrealized capital gains. Malkiel found that unrealized capital gains and distribution policy were among the few variables that correlated with discount levels. Even so, they "explain only a small portion of the discounts that exist." See note 32, Malkiel, p. 857. Most other commentators are similarly skeptical of the tax explanation. See, e.g., note 37, Thompson, pp. 15–24, 99–100, 135–6.

40 Thompson terms the dominant market hypothesis "naive market inefficiency." See note 37, Thompson, p. 46. Pratt is an early proponent: "most closed-end investment companies, as compared with mutual funds, sell at a discount primarily because of a lack of sales effort and public understanding." See Pratt, Myths Associated with Closed-End Investment Company Discounts, *Financial Analysis Journal*, July–August 1986, p. 82. See also note 32, Malkiel, who makes the same point, pp. 857–8. Yet, sponsorship by brokerage firms appears to have little to do with discount levels. See note 37, Mendelson, p. 66. To muddy the waters still more, Thompson finds that it would have been possible to earn cumulative abnormal returns as high as 4%, or as low as −7.9%, per year by investing in funds with exceptionally high or low discounts over a thirty-two-year period. These data are consistent with naive market inefficiency, but Thompson speculates that they may also arise from clientele effects, which introduce heterogeneous demand for closed-end funds. See note 32, Thompson, pp. 180–2.

about future performance, which are usually linked to the investment skills of fund managers[41] but might relate to other risks of misinvestment or expropriation as well. As might be expected, moreover, each genre of discount explanation has significant drawbacks. In particular, the market-based accounts seem to challenge basic hypotheses in financial economics, while agency cost explanations have difficulty explaining why the past performance of funds is only a modest predictor of discounts.[42] If there is a significant risk of agency losses, it has not yet materialized – or at least not since the Great Depression.

Regardless of the origins of discounts on closed-end funds, however, the market demonstrates a rational if uneven response to the existence of large discounts. Discounts rapidly disappear when closed-end funds announce plans to liquidate or merge with mutual funds.[43] In addition, funds with larger discounts are more likely to liquidate or "open" than those with smaller discounts, whether openings occur on management's initiative or in response to threats of proxy contests or takeovers.[44] Thus, discounts are an important stimulus for fund reorganizations and also explain in part the overwhelming market preeminence that mutual funds enjoy over their closed-end competitors. But despite the apparent advantages of the mutual form, many large closed-end funds have weathered years of steep discounts without reorganization, presumably because the costs of proxy contests or hostile takeovers would have exceeded the gains.[45]

For present purposes, the key issue is how far discounting behavior

---

41 See, e.g., note 37, Roenfeldt and Tuttle, p. 129, and Boudreaux, p. 517. Agency-cost explanations emphasize management investment decisions because there is little room for attributing fund discounts to straightforward costs, such as management fees or churning of fund portfolios. See note 37, Thompson p. 33.

42 See note 37, Mendelson, p. 55. In addition, it is difficult to explain why investors might fear that poor managers will systematically pick losing investments in an efficient securities market. See note 37, Thompson, p. 36. Yet, hot new funds often initially sell at premia, apparently because their managers are expected to pick winners. See, e.g., *Forbes,* July 28, 1986, p. 123; *Business Week*, October 13, 1986, p. 150. Beyond this, the fact that heavily discounted funds are more likely to "open," or convert to the mutual form, when their ratios of management expenses to total assets are small also suggests a role for agency costs. See note 37, Brauer, pp. 496–9.

43 See note 37, Brauer, pp. 503–6.

44 Ibid., pp. 493–5.

45 See note 37, Thompson, pp. 136–46. Fund managers often fiercely oppose reorganization efforts that would jeopardize the size and viability of funds. In addition, a free-rider effect works against takeover bids priced below the net asset value of funds. Shareholders who hold out to await reorganization following takeovers can receive nearly the full asset value of their shares. See note 37, Mendelson, p. 67.

extends beyond closed-end funds. Here, there is direct evidence for at least two categories of firms. The first includes holding companies with large investment in marketable securities. Two familiar examples from the late 1970s, Kaiser Industries and the American Manufacturing Company, suggest that these firms behave much like closed-end funds.[46] Shares in both of these large corporations traded at discounts exceeding 40 percent of the total estimated value of their assets, which consisted largely of common stock in publicly traded affiliates.[47] At least in the case of Kaiser Industries, moreover, the announcement of a liquidation and spin-off plan immediately raised the share value of the parent company and eventually eliminated any discount, just as the analogy to closed-end funds would suggest.[48]

The other category of firms that are frequently cited as examples of discounting are natural resource companies. For much of the past decade, oil and timber stocks have traded at less than half of industry appraisal values for their holdings. Even allowing for appraisal errors, such dramatic numbers are difficult to dismiss. They are especially hard to ignore for the oil industry, which witnessed numerous major acquisitions during the same period and accounted for 26 percent of all acquisition activity between 1981 and 1984.[49] In addition, as Professor Jensen has argued, recent event studies strongly suggest that discounts in the oil industry may have been linked to investor disapproval of corporate investments in costly exploration and development projects.[50]

46 A more recent example is Chris-Craft Industries, a holding company with a large stake in Warner Communications. See J. Tinker, *Morgan Stanley Research Comment,* February 10, 1988 (Chris-Craft shares sell for less than value of Warner holdings alone).

47 The chief assets of Kaiser Industries were common stock holdings of 56.3% of Kaiser Steel Corporation, 37.4% of Kaiser Aluminum & Chemical Corporation, and 37.1% of Kaiser Cement & Gypsum Corporation. Umbriac v. Kaiser, 467 F. Supp. 548, 550 (D. Nev. 1979). Immediately prior to Kaiser's liquidation announcement in 1975, Kaiser shares sold at a discount of 40% off the market value of these common stock holdings alone and 55% off the value of its total assets, including its operating companies. See note 34, Mullins, Chapter 6, p. 4. Similarly, American Manufacturing Company, Inc., traded in 1978 at 15% less than the market price of its stock holdings of Eltra Corp. alone, and an estimated 41% less than the total values of all its holdings. M. Whitman and M. Shubik, *The Aggressive Conservative Investor* (New York, 1979), pp. 382–3.

48 W. T. Grimm Co. See note 34, Mullins, Chapter 6, p. 5.

49 W. T. Grimm Co., *Mergerstat Review* 41 (1984), as reported in M. Jensen, The Takeover Controversy: Analysis and Evidence, in *Knights, Raiders, and Targets* (note 6, Coffee, Lowenstein, and Rose-Ackerman); see also note 34, Mullins, Chapter 6, pp. 16–20 (discussing timber appraisals).

50 See note 49, Jensen, pp. 329–30; see J. McConnell and C. Muscarella, Corporate Capital Expenditure Decisions and the Market Value of the Firm, *Journal of Financial*

After natural resource firms, direct evidence of discounts trails off in the absence of reliable appraisals. Estimates of the replacement costs of the tangible assets of public corporations are available and incorporated in Tobin's Q, a widely used ratio of the capitalized market value of firms to the inflation-adjusted replacement costs of their tangible assets.[51] The data on Tobin's Q are suggestive. The total market value of corporate equity and debt has varied from a low of roughly 50 percent of the estimated replacement costs of corporate assets during the late 1940s and mid-1970s to a high of 105 percent during the bull market of the mid-1960s.[52] In addition, there is a well-known empirical literature linking acquisitions to low Q values.[53] Shares of targets in hostile bids tend to be priced well below the replacement cost of their assets; that is, they have significantly lower Q values than either firms in general or the targets of friendly acquisitions.[54] If low Q values reflected share discounts, these findings would suggest that pervasive discounts were cyclic and that deeply discounted firms, like deeply discounted investment funds, were particularly vulnerable to restructuring. Unfortunately, however, the Q data may be interpreted in other ways. Low Q values for all corporations might be fully explained by a troubled economy, while unusually low Q values for individual firms might indicate operational mismanagement or the presence of assets that, although costly to replace, are simply no longer valuable.[55] In short, Tobin's Q is no substitute for observing discounts directly.

Economics 14: 399 (1985) decreases in share prices associated with increases in exploration and development expenditures by oil companies).

51 J. Tobin and W. Brainard, Asset Markets and the Cost of Capital, in *Economic Progress, Private Values, and Public Policy* (Cowles Foundation Paper No. 440 [Amsterdam 1977]), pp. 235, 237–38.

52 D. LeBaron and L. Speidell, Why are the Parts Worth More than the Sum? "Chop Shop": A Corporate Valuation Model, exhibit 2 (Prepared for Federal Reserve Bank of Boston Conference on the Merger Boom [October 12–14, 1987] (summarizing U.S. Treasury data and Batterymarch Financial Management estimates). Casual inspection suggests that changes in Tobin's Q for the economy roughly correlate with changes in average discount levels on closed-end funds since the late 1940s. Compare idem. (Tobin's Q) with note 34, Sharpe and Sosin, pp. 38–40 (average fund discounts).

53 E.g., J. Bartley and C. Boardman, Replacement-Cost-Adjusted Valuation Ratio as a Discriminator Among Takeover Target and Nontarget Firms, *Journal of Economics and Business* 38: 41 (1986).

54 See A. Shleifer, R. Vishny, and R. Morck, Characteristics of Hostile and Friendly Takeover Targets (CRSP Working Paper No. 213 [May 1987]), pp. 17–21.

55 Additional analysis suggesting that the bulk of Q's influence is an industrywide (rather than a firm-specific) effect lead Shleifer, Vishny, and Morck to reject an operational mismanagement hypothesis in favor of an industrywide misinvestment hypothesis to explain the incidence of takeovers among low-Q firms. Ibid., p. 25. If low Q values

Nevertheless, difficulty in observing discounts across all categories of firms does not diminish the significance of their presence on closed-end funds and natural resources firms. These examples create a presumption in favor of the discount claim. They cannot be ignored unless they can be explained or distinguished as anomalous by some still undiscovered characteristic of the securities market. This is a methodological point at bottom, for closed-end funds are corporate oddities only if the dominant conjecture – the norm of "no discounts" – prevails for other firms. In the absence of other data, extrapolating from the evidence at hand seems to be the only defensible course. Again, why suppose that discounts perversely exist only where they can be seen and nowhere else?

B   Acquisition behavior

Given a basic presumption in favor of discounts, the discount claim becomes an intuitively attractive explanation over a broad spectrum of corporate activity. In particular, it accords well with at least two aspects of acquisition behavior where traditional hypotheses falter. One is the sheer size of premia in hostile acquisitions and management buyouts. The other is the recent prominence of breakup acquisitions that exploit perceived differences between the share prices and asset values of conglomerate firms.

Consider first the size of acquisition premia. In recent years, premia have averaged about 50 percent in management buyouts and 50 percent or more in hostile acquisitions.[56] Most studies suggest that acquisitions of all kinds are either zero, or positive, net present value transactions on average.[57] Thus, on the assumption that most acquirers reasonably expect to recover their premia costs, the obvious question is: How can they be so sure? Apart from possible tax gains, which few commentators believe to dominate premia, we are left to choose between market

---

are indeed an industrywide phenomenon, they are unlikely to correlate with the performance of particular managers. They might, however, also arise from industrywide market dynamics.

56 See, e.g., J. Grundfest and B. Black, Stock Market Profits from Takeover Activity Between 1981 and 1986: $167 Billion is a Lot of Money, *SEC News Release*, September 28, 1987, pp. 9–13 (reporting total returns on recent tender offers and mergers of 50.1% and citing similar results from other studies); H. DeAngelo, L. DeAngelo, and E. Rice, Going Private: Minority Freezeouts and Stockholder Wealth, *Journal of Law and Economics* 27: 367, 401 (1984) (total returns 59% in leveraged buyouts and freezeouts).

57 See note 6.

discounts and the usual suspects, including the displacement of inefficient management, synergy gains, or the exploitation of private information.[58] Although these various sources of premia and gain are not
mutually exclusive, this hardly simplifies matters. We must still learn
which sources of gain dominate in which transactions and, in particular,
whether discounts yield significant gains at all. In the absence of better
information, our only handle is the plausibility of the assumptions that
underlie each source of gain.

It is here that the discount claim shows its advantage. Large premia
are easily explained if reliable appraisals of large firms can reveal the
existence of market discounts. Under these circumstances, acquirers can
"see" discounts with standard appraisal techniques and simultaneously
learn, within the limits of appraisal error, that the bulk of their premia
costs are a simple purchase of assets at their existing values. That is,
acquirers learn that their premia costs largely pay for assets that are
worth the price if they merely continue to perform as they have in the
past. By contrast, the synergy and better management hypotheses require acquirers to value novel and still hypothetical changes in targets'
operating assets, while the information hypothesis demands that acquirers routinely discover dramatic good news relative to market expectations about targets.

This comparison becomes more pointed for particular transactions.
In hostile bids for large firms, for example, a purely private information
story is generally weak. Acquirers lack any unique informational edge
over the market, and incumbent managers, who know their firms best,
have every incentive to reduce takeover risks by keeping the market
informed.

In addition, informational disabilities undermine efforts to explain
hostile bids solely in terms of synergy or management gains. Without
detailed information about operating assets, novel management or synergy strategies must often be very obvious or very large to be valued –
or even formulated – with confidence before control changes hands. For
example, risk neutral acquirers who are only 50 percent certain of realizing operational gains from hostile bids must expect gains exceeding
100 percent of target value to justify 50 percent premia.[59] Thus, even
when operating changes might yield generous returns, acquirers who
wish to rely on these changes to justify 50 percent premia may face an
exceptionally difficult challenge. Either they must be able to value hy-

---

58 See notes 7–9 and accompanying text.
59 It may be more realistic to presume that acquirers' managers are risk averse, in which
case expected returns would have to be even larger in this hypothetical.

pothetical changes reliably, or they must discover opportunities so lucrative that the uncertainties of planning and valuing wholesale changes
in target assets simply cease to matter.

The key intuition, then, turns on the informational constraints confronting hostile acquirers. Generally, these acquirers need much less
information to evaluate discounts than to appraise opportunities for
management or synergy gains. Rough appraisals of the value of assets
"as is" may be generated from aggregate financial data, reporting documents, analyst reports, and general familiarity with an industry. By
contrast, valuing operational changes requires familiarity with existing
projects that can only come from close study and internal records. The
exchanges of information and warranties that characterize friendly acquisitions highlight the uncertainties facing hostile acquirers.[60]

Many commentators implicitly recognize the difficulty of valuing hypothetical changes by surmising that the costs of search for opportunities
to extract operating gains is a principal determinant of takeover activity.[61] But this assumption encounters institutional difficulties. Casual
evidence of several kinds suggests that acquirers rely heavily upon routine appraisals of the existing value of target assets rather than farsighted
assessments of their potential value.[62] Investment bankers deploy standard valuation programs in advising their clients, second bidders enter
bidding contests on short notice, and outside analysts offer roughly

60 See J. Freund, *Anatomy of a Merger: Strategies and Techniques for Negotiating Corporate Acquisitions* (1975) (friendly acquisitions). Apart from this informational point,
moreover, operational accounts of takeover premia also face other anomalies. For
example, the better management hypothesis runs afoul of survey data suggesting that
acquirers prefer well-managed targets. See J. Coffee, Regulating the Market for Corporate Control: A Critical Assessment of the Tender Offer's Role in Corporate Governance, *Columbia Law Review* 84: 1145, 1212 (1984). In addition, neither
management efficiencies nor synergy gains can easily explain why tender offers by
controlling shareholders (who lack obvious synergy prospects) should reward target
shareholders as generously as offers from outsiders. See note 6, Roll, pp. 12–13.

61 See, e.g., F. Easterbrook and D. Fischel, Auctions and Sunk Costs in Tender Offers,
Stanford Law Review 35: 1 (1982) and A. Schwartz, Search Theory and the Tender
Offer Auction, *Journal of Law, Economics and Organization* 3: 49 (1986).

62 Like most generalizations, this contrast between the informational requisites for evaluating operational and discount gains should not be overstated. Clearly, large synergy
or operating gains can sometimes be estimated relatively accurately. The question is:
How often – and how much – do they contribute to total premia in hostile takeovers?
Casual empiricism suggests that they are much less important in hostile acquisitions
than in friendly deals. See note 54, Shleifer, Vishny, and Morck, p. 26 (contrasting
likely synergy gains in friendly deals with hostile bids targeted at firms in low-Q
industries).

similar and often accurate predictions of acquisition values as soon as firms are rumored to be "in play."[63] Moreover, the rapid convergence of offer prices in auctions suggests common criteria for estimating value that seem unlikely to result from operating gains.[64] Of course, consensus in the acquisitions market might also follow if first bidders fully revealed common opportunities for exploiting operating gains through their offers. But precisely because operating gains are complex and potentially unique to particular firms, this prospect seems unlikely. By contrast, the discount claim organizes many of the basic features of today's takeover market – large premia, acquirers' "wish lists," rapid decisions, and routine bidding contests – into a comprehensible game. It is a sporty game. Still, it is less risky than premia levels would otherwise suggest if acquirers can rely on market discounts to cover the bulk of their offers, and thus limit their real risks to a fraction of their investments.[65]

Similar considerations suggest that discounts may underlie premia in many management buyouts. Private information is an improbable source of premia in large management buyouts, if only because managers seem unlikely to conceal information able to support 50 percent premia – and then reveal it through buyout proposals.[66] In addition, buyouts often

---

63 Schedule 13E-3 reports, filed with the SEC in going-private transactions, document the standard valuation reports that investment bankers provide clients for pricing purposes.

64 Synergy opportunities arise from unique complementarities between firms. Thus, bidding contests between dissimilar bidders also caution against attributing premia to synergy gains. Presumably tender offers can claim the bulk of any such unique gains for themselves. See D. Leebron, Games Corporations Play: A Theory of Tender Offers, *New York University Law Review* 61: 153, (1986), p. 198.

65 Additional evidence for assigning a major role to discounts as a motive for hostile takeovers comes from several sources. First, repeat acquirers often *say* that they are purchasing discounted assets. See e.g., C. Icahn, Icahn on Icahn, *Fortune*, February 29, 1988, pp. 54, 55 and Lampert, Britons on the Prowl, *N.Y. Times*, Business World. Pt. II, November 29, 1987, pp. 22, 24 (Hanson Trust's Sir Gordon White). Second, targets of hostile bids tend to be asset rich but have significantly lower Q values than firms in general – although not firms in the same industry. See note 54, Shleifer, Vishny, and Morck, pp. 25–6. Finally, the sharp, marketwide drop in share prices since October 1987 appears to have stimulated hostile takeovers. See, e.g., Celis, Low Stock Prices Spur Takeover Flurry, *Wall Street Journal*, March 1, 1988, p. 3 (crash created "bargain atmosphere"). Although the discount claim does not necessarily require an increase in bids following a market crash, the occurrence of such an increase is surely suggestive.

66 See note 13, Lowenstein, p. 743, and A. Shleifer and R. Vishny, Management Buyouts as a Response to Market Pressure 12–13 (paper prepared for the National Bureau of Economic Research Conference on Mergers and Acquisitions [October 7, 1986]). Disclosures to buyout investors and lenders generally become public through Schedule

anticipate or respond to threats of hostile acquisitions, which hints that managers and outsiders may pursue the same sources of gains.

The traditional sources of operating gains also seem unlikely to support buyout premia. Pure management buyouts retain corporate divisions intact, but they neither displace managers nor redeploy assets. Any operating gains, therefore, must arise from the incentive effects of offering managers equity stakes in highly leveraged firms. These effects may be large, but they are highly uncertain. It is difficult to believe that buyout syndicates or unsecured lenders – the real sources of buyout premia – are willing to risk large premia solely on their account. Rather, operating gains are more likely to remain inchoate until after buyouts occur. Thus, the conventional wisdom of the business press may well be correct: Market discounts followed by tax gains account for the bulk of initial buyout premia.[67] The second stage in the life cycle of successful buyouts – when erstwhile targets go public again at well above their initial buyout prices – may be far easier to explain by operating gains or even private information than initial buyout premia.[68]

Finally, the discount claim can help to explain breakup acquisitions. Breakup acquisitions, whether hostile or friendly, present a clear analogy to the liquidation of closed-end investment funds. Where discounted funds hold portfolios of stocks, breakup targets are typically conglomerates holding several divisions that acquirers can resell piecemeal with their managements and markets intact. Although the prima facie likelihood of immediate operating gains from conglomerate breakups is greater than the likelihood of similar gains from management buyouts or the acquisition of natural resource firms, conglomerates would still have to impose enormous costs on their operating divisions for acquirers

---

13E-3 reports and informal circulation. See Lederman, Citron, and Macris, Leveraged Buyouts – An Update, in Fifteenth Annual Institute on Securities Regulation 281, 295–9 (1984) (valuation reports circulate widely).

67 See note 13, Lowenstein systematically develops this position.

68 Typical buyouts are geared to a five-year time horizon. Buyout syndicates, which include key managers as equity participants, take the firm private in a highly leveraged, initial transaction that pays a generous premium to target shareholders. The firm then struggles to pay down its debt. If successful, it is then often resold at a second premium to public investors, private buyers, or a syndicate including a new generation of internal managers. E.g., Many Firms Go Public Within a Few Years of Leveraged Buyout, *Wall Street Journal,* January 2, 1987, p. 1; 'Reverse Buyouts' Bring Riches, *N.Y. Times,* April 2, 1987, p. D1. Operating gains that seem unlikely sources of initial premia are natural sources of second-stage premia paid to buyout syndicates, since at this stage operating changes are already implemented and capable of valuation. For a similar analysis, see note 66, Shleifer and Vishny, pp. 9–10.

to generate 50 percent premia merely by eliminating the conglomerate structure.[69] A more plausible place for operating gains in breakup acquisitions occurs – as in management buyouts – at the point where corporate assets are resold. Acquirers expect profits from the breakup and resale of target divisions, and these profits, in turn, may reflect the synergy or management gains that are available to the third-party purchasers of target assets. Standing alone, however, these resale profits seem unlikely to explain large initial premia paid to target shareholders. Acquirers and their financial backers cannot predict ex ante the synergy and management gains of end purchasers.[70] Once again, operating gains would have to be improbably large to support prepayments of 50 percent premia, particularly since these gains must be divided between acquirers and end-purchasers in negotiated transactions. While breakups may ultimately generate synergy gains, then, the discount claim presents a more compelling account of initial premia.

Discounts are an appealing explanation of breakup acquisitions for another reason as well. The value of discounts to acquirers rests largely upon the reliability of appraisals. The less certain appraisals are, the larger suspected discounts must be if they are to serve as the certainty equivalents of prevailing premia levels. Aside from natural resource firms, large conglomerates may be among the easiest firms to value because random appraisal errors and informational uncertainties wash out when individual divisions are valued separately – by, for example,

---

69 The conglomerate structure does not appear to create wealth for shareholders. See, e.g., note 9, Coffee, pp. 33–5, and R. Gilson, *The Law and Finance of Corporate Acquisitions* (1986), pp. 341–70. In addition, the record of conglomerate acquisitions, as measured by the percentage of acquired firms that are subsequently divested, has been disappointing. See, e.g., F. Scherer, Corporate Takeovers: The Efficiency Arguments, *Journal of Economic Perspectives* 2: 69 (1988), pp. 74–7 (⅓ sell-off rate) and M. Porter, From Competitive Strategy to Corporate Strategy, *Harvard Business Review* 87: 43 (May–June 1987), pp. 50–1 (56.5% sell-off rate). Porter argues that large decision-making costs, revealed by this high divestiture rate, are endemic to the "portfolio" structure of pure conglomerates and explain the steep "conglomerate discount" that share prices impose on conglomerates. See also p. 52. The difficulty with this argument, however, is that conglomerate assets frequently appear discounted relative to their performance within the conglomerate structure – and by amounts that vary by industry class. See note 52, Le Baron and Speidell, pp. 12–13. It is these results that suggest an independent closed-end fund effect associated with multi-industry firms, pp. 15–17
70 Target assets are occasionally "presold" prior to breakup acquisitions. But here, the question is whether end purchasers can guarantee firm prices before obtaining information to value potential operating gains.

looking to line of business financial data.[71] Thus, discounted conglomerates may be especially vulnerable targets partly because their discounts are more accurately estimated than those of other firms.

C   Conversion behavior

After acquisition behavior, the discount claim can also comfortably accommodate a broad class of what might be termed "conversion behavior." The most prominent examples are shareholder distributions financed by debt or the sale of assets, which managers often initiate to raise share prices. Since virtually any form of discounting would imply that these redemptions must indeed raise share prices, their success lends support to the discount claim.

Consider first the intuitive relationship between discounts and distributions to shareholders financed by sales of corporate assets. By hypothesis, shareholders must recapture all discounts net of transaction costs when discounted firms are liquidated at their asset values. It follows that expected distributions from partial liquidations are also likely to raise share prices. If shareholders forecast constant discounts relative to the value of corporate assets before and after partial liquidations, then shareholders will merely expect to recapture discounts on those corporate assets that are actually sold at prices reflecting "true" asset values.[72] On the more plausible assumption that distributions may disproportionately affect discounts, fractional liquidations might even lower discount levels on assets that remain in the hands of discounted firms. This is why, presumably, discounted investment funds often liquidate securities to finance periodic redemptions of limited numbers of shares.[73]

Equally important, however, exactly the same recapture effects should result when managers finance share repurchases by borrowing against the assets of discounted firms. Because lenders look to the cash flows and resale values of assets for repayment, such recapitalizations implicitly arbitrage between the asset and equity markets. Thus, managers should be able to redeem equity with debt – and reduce discounts

---

71 See note 52, LeBaron and Speidell, pp. 6–15 (proposing valuation model).

72 Recall that asset values here are the going concern – or discounted cash flow – values of assets in the hands of incumbent managers. Absent synergies, market imperfections, or unique managerial skills, however, these values should also approximate what third parties will pay for a wide range of proved capital assets.

73 See, e.g., The Japan Fund, Inc., *Notice of Annual Meeting of Stockholders,* March 26, 1987, p. 6.

– until the marginal costs of additional debt exceed marginal increases in the value of equity of discounted firms.[74]

On a more theoretical level, this relationship between equity conversions and discounts follows from both major accounts of how discounts might arise. Recall first the misinvestment hypothesis, which holds that investors discount in the rational expectation that managers may misinvest *future* discretionary cash flows.[75] On this view, all disbursements to shareholders – whether they are financed by divestment, debt, or cash on hand – must reduce discounts by at least as much as they reduce managers' discretion to misinvest. The critical condition here is that disbursements must tie managers' hands; that is, managers must not be able to make the same investment decisions after redeeming shares by resorting to the capital markets to replace lost sources of internal financing. If this condition holds, as the evidence suggests that it does,[76] then disbursements limit the risks of future misinvestments and may also bolster the reputations of suspect managers who voluntarily attend to shareholder interests.

A similar conclusion follows from a market account of discounts. Recall that under the most prominent form of this hypothesis, noise trading by uninformed investors generates share prices that persistently discount informed estimates of asset values.[77] Such discounts, however, are unlikely to survive promises either to redeem equity for cash or to convert equity into low-risk debt. The reason is that these proposed transactions, regardless of how they are structured, are in fact promises to arbitrage between the asset and share markets.

To see why, begin with a promise to redeem equity for cash at a price equaling a pro-rata claim on corporate assets – as, for example, in the announcement of a self-tender offer or a statutory liquidation. In this case, shares become easily valued claims against the firm that shareholders can shortly expect to cash out at full asset value. Shareholders no longer depend on the market for their liquidity. Nothing changes,

---

74 The costs of additional debt include bankruptcy costs and the agency costs of leverage, i.e., of bearing or protecting against shareholder opportunism at the expense of debt holders. See M. Jensen and W. Meckling, Theory of the Firm: Managerial Behavior, Agency Costs and Ownership Structure, *Journal of Financial Economics* 3: 305 (1976).

75 See notes 18–19 and accompanying text (misinvestment hypothesis).

76 See note 19, Donaldson, pp. 42–62. Given a reluctance to seek external financing, cash disbursements, existing debt, and even the soft promise of future dividends tie managers' hands under the misinvestment theory, and thus protect against discretionary misinvestment.

77 See notes 24–7 and accompanying text.

moreover, if the issuer promises to redeem with long-term debt in lieu of cash. Low risk, publicly traded debt is also an easily valued claim against the firm that leaves little leeway for noise trading, because its market value will depend chiefly on interest rates rather than on the firm's long-term business prospects. Finally, consider the more common case in which a discounted firm promises to repurchase, using either cash or debt, its own equity at market price rather than asset value. Here, we return to the simple arithmetic of arbitrage. As the firm buys discounted shares, the pro-rata asset value, and hence the market price, of all remaining shares must increase. Indeed, market price should anticipate this effect as soon as a share repurchase program is announced. In addition, under the market hypothesis, price might increase for another reason as well: Share repurchases turn the issuer into a buyer of last resort, and thus introduce limited insurance against mispricing by noise traders.[78]

Given that equity redemptions can increase the share prices of discounted firms under both the market and the mismanagement hypotheses, many aspects of corporate behavior fall into place. Some of these still await exploration in the literature; for example, the puzzle of why transfers of corporate assets to limited partnerships might increase the share prices of corporations even when most partnership units remain in corporate hands.[79] But at least two forms of conversion activity have prompted extensive comment: the growing use of financial restructuring as a takeover defense, and a broad pattern of empirical results suggesting that share redemptions and exchanges of equity for debt generally tend to increase share prices.[80] In both cases, the evidence is consistent with the discount claim.

Equity conversions financed by cash, debt, or divestitures are now

78 For a discussion combining these features of the market hypothesis and the misinvestment hypotheses into a single justification of share repurchases, see investor Warren Buffett's 1984 annual report to the shareholders of his investment vehicle. Berkshire Hathaway Inc., *Annual Report to the Stockholders* (1984), pp. 15–17.
79 E. Freier, Master Limited Partnerships: A Phenomenon in the Enhancement of Corporate Value (March 1986 draft). As misinvestment theorists note, a variety of corporate restructurings besides equity redemptions raise share prices for apparently similar reasons. Thus, positive returns from divestitures, royalty trusts, and master limited partnerships might be explained by the constraints that these ownership changes impose on managers' discretion over free cash flows. See note 49, Jensen, pp. 319–22 and note 18, Jacobs, pp. 22–5. However, this result is also consistent with the market hypothesis, since these restructurings tend to fix payouts and reduce shareholder dependence on the market.
80 See, e.g., note 9, Coffee, p. 5 (financial restructuring) and note 49, Jensen, pp. 323–7 (empirical results).

routine takeover defenses. The most dramatic illustrations are self-tenders or recapitalizations made in direct response to hostile tender offers. Prominent examples include the recent recapitalization announcements of Union Carbide, CBS, Phillips Petroleum, Gencorp, Caesar's World, and Harcourt Brace Jovanovich.[81] In each instance, a recapitalization plan yielded gains to shareholders that approached or exceeded the value of outside offers. In effect, these targets bid for their own assets and won through what amounts to a leveraged buyout of much of their own outstanding equity. In addition, other firms have earned comparable returns from recapitalizations even without the threat of a takeover.[82]

Like premia in management buyouts, shareholders' premia in leveraged recapitalizations invite explanation in terms of the discount claim. Tax savings may account for some recapitalization gains, but the case for operating gains or returns from private information seems weak. Long-run operating gains are possible, since heavy borrowing to finance shareholder distributions may ultimately force novel cost-cutting measures on managers. Yet, leeway for belt tightening is uncertain at the outset, and neither lenders nor shareholders can anticipate its results when recapitalization plans are proposed.[83] The private information hypothesis is also unpersuasive for much the same reason that it fails to explain premia in management buyouts. Recapitalization gains comparable to acquisition premia are simply too large to attribute to the signaling or disclosure effects of recapitalization plans, particularly when these plans are announced in response to hostile bids. Beyond this, the fact that recapitalizations often respond to hostile outsiders – and presumably tap the same gains that outsiders seek – undercuts the plausibility of a private information account.[84]

Leveraged recapitalizations, moreover, are only the most dramatic examples of equity conversions. Many more firms have repurchased

---

81 See note 49, M. Jensen, pp. 332–6 (Phillips Petroleum, CBS, and other examples); The New Way to Halt Raiders, *N.Y. Times,* May 29, 1987, p. D1.

82 See, e.g., Cowan, *N.Y. Times,* May 29, 1987, p. D4 (Metromedia recapitalization prompted by controlling family's desire for partial liquidation).

83 Ibid. Like management buyouts, leveraged recapitalizations might be analyzed in two steps. After initial distributions to shareholders – analogous to buyout premia – public shareholders in recapitalized firms retain the equity "stubs," or highly levered residual claims. The initial distributions may reflect share discounts. Later appreciation in the price of equity stubs, which has generally been substantial, may reflect operating gains.

84 To the extent that both recapitalizations and management buyouts are prompted by takeover threats, a private information hypothesis must also confront the evidence against information effects in hostile takeovers generally. See note 10 and accompanying text.

equity on a modest scale for what appear to be preemptive reasons. As Professor Coffee observes, the great wave of recent share repurchases and divestitures has followed a sharp increase in takeovers and, equally important, a dramatic expansion of the range of potential takeover targets.[85] Thus, much of this redemption activity is likely to reflect the desire of incumbent managers to reduce acquisition risks by raising share prices. For this purpose, managers have not needed to understand exactly how equity redemptions might work, only that redemptions do work to raise share prices.

A recent empirical literature confirms the price effects of these conversion policies in ways that accord well with the discount claim.[86] Event studies have found that announcements of share repurchases and equity conversions yield large positive abnormal returns to shareholders (averaging 16 percent for repurchases and as high as 21.9 percent for conversions[87]); that conversions of debt to equity generate large negative returns (averaging −9.9 percent[88]); that new issues of equity or convertible debt also decrease share prices (by roughly −3 percent and −2 percent respectively for industrial firms[89]); and that announcements of new debt without equity features has little effect on share prices.[90] The apparent pattern, then, is that redemptions or conversions of equity tend to increase share prices, while new issues of equity or equitylike

---

85 See note 9, Coffee, pp. 40–4 and note 66, Shleifer and Vishny, p. 4–7 (also attributing acquisition activity and equity conversions to inflation-induced decline in real debt and to improved financing techniques).

86 See note 49, Jensen, pp. 323–8 (surveying studies); Smith, Investment Banking and the Capital Acquisition Process, *Journal of Financial Economics 15:* 3, 4–14 (same).

87 See note 86, Smith, pp. 8 (Table 2) and 12 (Table 3). Smith aggregates four event studies of share repurchases to yield a two-day abnormal return of 16.2%. Positive returns of 21.9% are associated with self-tenders financed by new debt (idem). See also R. Masulis, Stock Repurchases by Tender Offer: An Analysis of the Causes of Common Stock Price Changes, *Journal of Finance* 35: 305 (1980). Direct exchange offers of debt for common stock yield a lower two-day positive return of 14%. R. Masulis, The Impact of Capital Structure Change on Firm Value: Some Estimates, *Journal of Finance* 38: 107 (1983). Moreover, even the exchange of preferred stock, which lacks the tax advantages of debt, for common stock generates a positive return of 8%.

88 See note 86 Smith, p. 12 (citing Masulis' analysis of exchange offers of common stock for debt). Common stock issued to finance the retirement of debt generates smaller negative returns of −4.2%.

89 Ibid. p. 5; P. Asquith and D. Mullins, Equity Issues and Offering Dilution, *Journal of Financial Economics* 15: 61 (1986).

90 See note 86, Smith, p. 5, and E. Eckbo, Valuation Effects of Corporate Debt Offerings, *Journal of Financial Economics* 15: 119 (1986). Issues of convertible debt, unlike "straight" debt, are associated with negative shareholder returns on the order of −2%.

securities decrease share prices. This is just what we might expect if share discounts were widespread, and discounted firms opted for equity conversions and against new issues of equity in disproportionate numbers. Moreover, the fact that new debt alone has little influence on share prices suggests that the price effects of equity conversions and redemptions do not result primarily from leverage-related phenomena such as tax shields created by corporate debt.[91]

As with other evidence of discounts, these results are not conclusive. A competing interpretation of market responses to financing decisions looks (once again) to investor inferences about managers' private information, or what is more commonly styled as the "asymmetric information" problem.[92] Thus, investors might infer that managers who know that shares are overvalued issue new equity, while those who know that shares are undervalued redeem old equity.[93] Indeed, such information effects might operate simultaneously with discounts to produce an aggregate association between market returns and equity redemptions. As between these two explanations, however, there is much to recommend the discount claim. It reliably predicts the direction of price responses over the entire spectrum of financing decisions, and it easily extends to defensive recapitalizations where the difference between pre- and post-announcement prices seems too large to attribute to information effects

---

91 Positive returns are also associated with exchanges of preferred for common stock, which cannot be explained by tax savings. See note 18, Jensen, pp. 327–8.

92 Information asymmetries refer to informational disparities between shareholders and managers. Several information-based accounts of capital structure have been advanced. Managers may actively signal information about firm prospects through financing decisions. See S. Ross, The Determination of Financial Structure: The Incentive-Signalling Approach, *Bell Journal of Economics* 8: 23 (1977). Alternatively, investors may draw inferences about internal cash flows from managers' external financing decisions. See M. Miller and K. Rock, Dividend Policy Under Asymmetric Information, *Journal of Finance* 40:1031 (1985), p. 1038. Or, finally, investors may infer the quality of corporate projects from financing decisions if managers only issue equity when there is no danger of diluting returns to existing shareholders. See S. Myers and N. Majluf, Corporate Financing and Investment Decisions When Firms Have Information That Investors Do Not Have, *Journal of Financial Economics* 13: 187 (1984). These models, and particularly the Myers and Majluf hypothesis, dominate recent empirical literature on financing decisions. Yet, as Jensen demonstrates, note 49, pp. 320–33, the data are equally consistent with a misinvestment account of share discounts – and, as I would add, with a market account of discounts. Indeed, the weight placed on seemingly fragile information effects by researchers on financial policy seems troublesome from the acquisitions perspective. Why, for example, should investors trust managers to value future prospects reliably, much less to reveal their appraisals obliquely through financing decisions?

93 See note 92, Myers and Majluf, p. 209.

alone. In addition, to return to a familiar puzzle, share repurchases are favorite devices for reducing discounts on closed-end funds, and these repurchase effects cannot stem from the release of information about asset values.[94]

III   Why discounts persist

Once large discounts are plausible, the inquiry shifts to their implications for acquisition activity. Here, paradoxically, the threshold question is how large discounts can simultaneously penalize shareholders, tempt acquirers, and still survive in an active acquisitions market. The evidence from specialized firms and the acquisitions market generally favors persistent or evolving discounts over rapid price shifts that trigger immediate takeovers.[95] But under this scenario, why don't incipient discounts instantly attract acquirers, or at least prompt managers of discounted firms to limit damage to shareholders by redeeming equity for debt or cash?[96] To survive, then, discounts must coexist with managers and evade acquirers.

On closer inspection, however, neither of these conditions seems difficult to meet below a critical discount level. Regardless of how discounts arise, managers may not attempt to eliminate discounts voluntarily because large redemptions of equity – the only certain method of reducing discounts – can impose costs on managers, limit growth, and may even appear to injure the interests of long-term shareholders. Below a certain threshold, moreover, acquirers will not intervene to claim discounts. Discounts must be large to prompt hostile takeovers because target shareholders rather than acquirers are likely to recapture most of the gains from discounts as takeover premia.

With respect to target managers, the key point that I develop in a parallel article[97] is that managers will be reluctant to reduce discounts regardless of how discounts arise. This point is obvious under a misin-

---

94 See notes 33–38 (asset values of closed-end funds are public).
95 See notes 34–6, 43–5, and accompanying text (persistent discounts on closed-end funds). While many investigations of target share prices indicate negative abnormal returns over one to three year periods prior to takeovers, the declines are gradual and substantially smaller than takeover premia. See note 69, Gilson, pp. 337–83 (summarizing empirical results). Discounts on closed-end funds, however, can widen rapidly under exceptional circumstances such as the October 1987 crash. See note 34 (post-crash discounts of 20% to 30%).
96 See notes 72–80 and accompanying text controlling discounts through equity redemptions).
97 *Columbia Law Review* 88: 891 (1988).

vestment hypothesis, in which discounts result from managerial self-interest or error. It is only slightly less so under a market theory of discounts. On this view, managers are likely to perceive that the market misvalues discounted firms. Shareholders, then, will lack a homogeneous interest in immediate liquidation. Short-term shareholders may prefer to cash out immediately at the pro-rata asset value of their shares. If managers perceive profitable opportunities for reinvestment, however, their compensation incentives are likely to incline them toward the interests of long-term shareholders who would prefer reinvestment in profitable corporate projects – knowing full well that a decision to liquidate the firm can be made at any time.

The key point with respect to would-be acquirers, which I also develop in a parallel article,[98] is that competitive auctions and unconstrained defensive tactics allow target managers to deprive first bidders of virtually all discount gains other than gains secured by prebid, open-market purchases. Thus, hostile bidders act on the basis of discount gains alone only if their bidding costs are more than offset by the fractional gains that they expect to win from their open market purchases. Put differently, first bidders can expect to earn a "commission" – a small percentage – of total discount gains because they will be compelled to pay out the full asset values of discounted shares in their tender offers. They will only bid if their bidding costs are well below their expected earnings, which in turn will be far less than aggregate discount gains.

IV   Discounts as an acquisition motive

Given that discounts are sufficiently stable to survive in an active acquisitions market, the inquiry moves to how they might nonetheless prompt takeovers. Thus far, I have portrayed a world of stable discounts policed by vigilant managers. On the one hand, managers resist outsiders' attempts to recapture discounts through takeovers; on the other hand, managers themselves may be forced to limit discount levels through shareholder distributions in order to control acquisition risks. But this world is only relatively stable. Widespread discounts on target firms might still trigger takeovers by either combining with other sources of acquisition gains or outpacing managers' efforts to control acquisition risks.[99]

---

98 Ibid.
99 In addition, the possibility that discounts on potential *acquirers* might either encourage or deter acquisitions deserves scrutiny, although the evidence thus far does not seem to indicate either of these incentive effects. I explore this possibility in a parallel article. See *Columbia Law Review* 88: 891 (1988), pp. 930–2.

A   Joint gains

The most important way in which discounts can prompt takeovers is in combination with other sources of acquisition gains such as operating gains or private information. Only large discounts can trigger takeovers in isolation if, as I have argued, target shareholders ordinarily capture most of the value of discounts. Nevertheless, small gains from other sources might transform firms with modest discounts into attractive targets, provided that these ancillary gains are – unlike discounts – uniquely available to particular acquirers. The key assumption here is that acquirers are able to capture most unique gains for their own accounts. Like prebid purchases on the open market, such gains give first bidders a strategic edge. They are unavailable to rival bidders, and they are likely to be invisible or at least difficult to value for defending managers or the market at large.[100]

A simple example can clarify how such appropriable gains might affect acquisition decisions on the margin. Suppose that a target trades at a 30 percent discount below its asset value of $500 million, and that an acquirer can purchase 10 percent of the target's stock at the discounted price. In addition, assume that a tender offer for the remaining 90 percent must be priced at the target's pro-rata asset value in order to discourage management resistance, including the solicitation of rival bids.[101] In this case, a potential bidder would anticipate a gross return of $15 million (0.10 x 0.30 x $500,000,000) from the target's discount. Thus, if the expected costs of a successful bid – including professional fees, financing and solicitation costs, contingent liabilities, defensive tactics, and transition expenses – totaled to, say, $20 million, no acquirer would bid on the basis of the target's discount alone. If, however, an acquirer expected even minor synergy gains (on the order of $10 million) in addition to discount gains, a hostile bid would become an attractive proposition.

As this example illustrates, existing discounts can create a "fund" to

100 Although in theory resistance by target managers might force first bidders to relinquish all gains, in practice management resistance is likely to diminish as bid prices approach consensus appraisals of target values.
101 Of course, when discounts are large, first bidders might deliberately plan to induce second bids or extract greenmail. The raider's strategy in a world of discounts is to capture gains by inducing managers to pay full price for discounted shares or, alternatively, to force managers to disclose additional gains opportunities to second bidders. Contrast this with the raider's role as information producer. See R. Gilson, Seeking Competitive Bids Versus Pure Passivity in Tender Offer Defense, *Stanford Law Review* 35: 51 (1982), pp. 59–62.

defray premium and acquisition costs when even modest operating gains are at stake. First bidders who expect unique operating gains or who have informational advantages may succeed in releasing large premia – stemming from preexisting discounts – to target shareholders. This observation helps to explain the two-stage progression that characterizes many management buyouts, breakup acquisitions, and leveraged recapitalizations.[102] In each case, potential operating gains are unlikely to support 50 percent premia to shareholders, if only because the information needed to value such gains is unavailable at the initial stage of the transaction. But if large discounts can offset premia and subsidize first-stage transactions costs, even uncertain synergies or management gains might suffice to motivate buyout syndicates or breakup acquirers. Thus, the joint-gains hypothesis can accommodate conflicting evidence about the "real" motives behind these transactions and explain one of their most puzzling features: Why buyers pay "second premia" when breakup assets are resold, buyout targets go public, or residual shares in recapitalized firms appreciate in the market. Second premia on this account are merely the rewards of forecasting previously uncertain operating gains.[103]

The joint-gains hypothesis also bears on possible efforts to test the discount claim. First, it suggests that discount levels alone cannot reliably predict takeovers. Given a distribution of acquirers' opportunities to exploit unique gains, takeovers might occur at all discount levels. The discount claim is probabilistic; larger discounts only increase the likelihood of acquisitions. But second, and more promising, the joint-gains model predicts that average takeover premia may vary *inversely* with synergies or other acquirer-specific gains. The reason is that without acquirer-specific gains, only large discounts – which, by hypothesis, yield large premia – are likely to trigger takeovers. Put differently, acquirers who locate opportunities for large, unique gains do not need to bid for heavily discounted targets that command large premia. Thus, the discount claim might be tested by exploring whether breakup takeovers, for example, yield larger premia on average than acquisitions aimed at obvious synergy gains.[104] The same principle may help to explain the

---

102 Typically, premia are paid at each stage. At stage two, third-party acquirers pay a second round of premia to first-stage acquirers. See notes 68–70, 83, and accompanying text.

103 Alternatively, managers in buyouts and recapitalizations may sense opportunities for operating gains from the outset, just as breakup acquirers may research resale possibilities before bidding. See note 70.

104 Such synergies are likely in intraindustry takeovers where significant economies of

lower levels of shareholder returns in negotiated mergers, where synergy and management gains are likely to be visible from the outset.[105]

B   *Changing acquisition risks*

The second occasion for takeovers in a world of discounts stems from management failure to respond to changing acquisitions risks. Major financial restructurings are costly and time consuming. Last-minute defensive tactics often crumble under shareholder pressure when the bidder's price is right.[106] In addition, although managers may "see" discounts, they cannot see takeover risks directly. Only the acquisitions market can reveal how growing discounts or declining acquisitions costs alter the risks of hostile offers. Thus, takeovers may occur before targets learn to adapt to exogenous events that modify the economics of take-overs by inflating discounts or lowering takeover costs.

The prime example of such a window of opportunity for acquirers is the most recent wave of takeovers (extending from 1981 to the present) and the even larger wave of corporate restructurings that these takeovers seem to have triggered.[107] Commentators agree on at least two under-lying causes of this dramatic increase in takeovers. One is the rapid expansion of institutional supports for takeovers, including a specialized capital market.[108] The second is the joint impact of severe inflation during the 1970s and sustained economic expansion in the 1980s.[109] Both factors profoundly altered acquisition risks. A maturing acquisitions market dramatically lowered takeover costs, while rising nominal – and real – asset values raised discount levels by upsetting existing relation-ships among corporate cash flows, debt obligations, and distribution

scale, scope, or vertical integration are available. See note 69, Gilson, pp. 400–430 (sources of synergy gains).
105 See note 6 Jensen and Ruback, p. 7 (mergers average abnormal returns of 20%, and tender offers 30%, for target shareholders). Opportunities for information exchange and planning make operating gains more visible in negotiated deals.
106 See, e.g., The Office of the Chief Economist of the Securities and Exchange Com-mission, *The Effect of Poison Pills on the Wealth of Target Shareholders*, October 23, 1986, pp. 25–26 (while poison pills defeated fourteen of thirty hostile offers, only 20% targets deploying older tactics remained independent).
107 See M. Salter and W. Weinhold, Corporate Takeovers: A View from the "Buy Side," in *Knights, Raiders, and Targets* (note 6, Coffee, Lowenstein, and Rose-Ackerman), pp. 135–7 (accelerating wave of offers since 1979); note 9, Coffee, pp. 3–5 (reviewing sources).
108 See, e.g., note 9, Coffee, pp. 4–5 ("junk bonds"); note 66, A. Shleifer and Vishny, p. 5.
109 Note 66, Shleifer and Vishny, pp. 3–4.

policies.[110] The predictable consequence was a burst of takeover activity that persists today as managers continue to adapt financial policies to the new acquisitions climate.

A subsidiary question is precisely how rising asset values act to increase discount levels under both the discount and the misinvestment hypotheses. First, consider Michael Jensen's application of the misinvestment hypothesis to the energy industry. In his view, a sharp increase in oil prices coincided with a sharp decrease in the marginal productivity of new investment in the energy industry during the late 1970s.[111] Rather than reflect the declining profitability of new investment, however, investment spending rose to match the rising cash flows generated by higher prices. The result could only have been a dramatic increase in discount levels for oil firms.

Although Jensen describes this conjuncture as unusual in its dimensions,[112] the misinvestment hypothesis suggests that the same result must occur whenever exogenous events increase the asset values of discounted firms. Without offsetting changes in the investment and distribution policies of such firms, larger discretionary cash flows can only mean more misinvestment and lower returns on total equity. Share prices, then, must always lag behind the revaluation of assets until managers can credibly limit their investment discretion by, inter alia, converting equity into debt.[113]

The market hypothesis dictates much the same result. On this view, shares trade at depressed prices due to uninformed trading or speculative biases. Informed traders must look partly to existing prices and disbursement policies to anticipate price changes. Disbursement policies, in turn, influence prices by "focusing" investors on either the asset values of discounted firms or the easily valued terms of debt securities.[114] Thus,

---

110 Ibid., p. 5. Professors Shleifer and Vishny, who focus on management buyouts, stress tax savings and discount opportunities arising from the larger net asset values that result when inflation reduces debt obligations and increases firms' free cash flows. For a market hypothesis of how inflation might introduce bias directly into share prices, see F. Modigliani and R. Cohn, Inflation, Rational Valuation, and the Market, *Financial Analysis Journal* 35 (March/April 1979), p. 24.

111 See note 49, Jensen, pp. 329–32; see also note 18, Jacobs, 30 (elaborating Jensen's analysis).

112 See note 49, Jensen, pp. 330–1.

113 Put differently, the misinvestment account does not necessarily require declining returns on new investment, as in Jensen's model of the energy industry, for discounts to increase. Discounts will rise whenever growth opportunities are limited and free cash flows increase, as when inflation devalues debt and increases net asset values for shareholders.

114 Recall that under the market hypothesis, discounts originate in the remote or un-

share prices cannot fully – or even proportionately – reflect increases in asset values without offsetting changes in disbursement expectations. Exogenous events may increase the free cash flows of discounted firms, but share prices failed to reflect the asset values of these firms even *before* their reappraisals. Unless the market revises its expectations about the distribution policies of these firms – after, for example, announcements of share repurchases or higher dividends – savvy traders must expect even larger discounts when discounted assets are revalued.

In sum, almost any theory that builds financial policy into the formation of share prices implies that these prices must be "sticky" with respect to changes in asset values. This prediction accords well with the behavior of discounts on closed-end investment funds. At the outset of bull markets, discounts have tended to increase as funds' portfolio values have risen faster than their share prices; while at the outset of bear markets, discounts have tended to decrease as portfolio values have fallen faster than share values.[115] Furthermore, countercyclical changes in discount levels are also consistent with the recent wave of breakup takeovers and the broader association between acquisitions and rising stock markets.[116] Although takeover motives other than discounts also link acquisitions to prosperity, none places as much weight on changes in asset values or so easily explains the parallel behavior of investment funds.

V   Implications for takeover regulation

Thus far I have argued that the discount claim is a useful framework for exploring important elements of acquisition behavior regardless of

certain payout of common stock, which permits noise trading and imposes market risks on informed traders. See notes 23–9 and 77–8 and accompanying text. Settled payout expectations in the form of dividends, repurchases, or debt exchanges limit noise trading in this view.

115 See note 32, Malkiel, pp. 856–7. Note, however, that discounts decline at the peak of bull markets. See note 34. Moreover, the October 1987 crash, unlike sustained bear markets, triggered an immediate and large increase in discount levels.

116 See R. Brealey and S. Myers, *Principles of Corporate Finance*. 2d ed. (New York, 1984), p. 722. If rising stock markets reflect underlying increases in asset values, then stock prices and discounts might increase simultaneously, just as they have done for closed-end funds. Of course, the value of acquisition gains other than discounts – for example, operating or tax gains – is also likely to be greater during boom periods, leaving the relationship between market peaks and takeovers overdetermined. Yet, the discount claim, at least in its market form, can also provide a ready explanation for increases in takeovers after sharp drops in the market, such as the October 1987 crash. See note 65 (crash-induced takeovers). Larger discounts can be triggered by declines in share prices as well as by increases in asset values.

how discounts arise. As an acquisition motive, discounts lead to similar behavior regardless of how they are explained. Both the misinvestment and market hypotheses can account for this behavior because both permit share prices to diverge from asset values and both allow managers to influence discount levels through identical financial policies. On the misinvestment account, financial policies that restrict investment discretion or distribute cash flows also limit losses from future investments. On the market account, the same policies focus traders on asset values or on the easily valued terms of debt securities. Together, then, the misinvestment and market stories support a single acquisition motive – the opportunity to capture discounts – that compares with other motives including opportunities to exploit operating gains or private information.[117]

Yet, discount hypotheses part company abruptly at the level of policy analysis. The misinvestment hypothesis views takeovers favorably. Given this view, regulatory debate is likely to center on the design and justification of a statutory auction period. By contrast, the market hypothesis counsels against takeovers triggered by discounts. From this perspective, policy discussion is likely to focus on the merits of selectively deterring discount-driven takeovers.

A   The misinvestment hypothesis and the auction debate

Under the misinvestment hypothesis, discounts reflect the risk that managers will misallocate capital in the future. This implies that share prices for well-managed firms should always equal or exceed corporate asset values. Individual takeovers may or may not shift assets to higher valuing users,[118] but at least they shift share prices in the right direction. More importantly, the risk of acquisition prompts suspect managers to reduce discounts by tying their own hands, and so allows the market a weak veto over investment policy. It follows that legal rules should lean toward increasing acquirers' net returns, which in turn will increase in the risk of takeovers, force more hands-tying on discounted managers, raise the quality of corporate investments, and assure that share prices more

---

117 Beyond supporting the same acquisition motive, the misinvestment and market accounts also suggest similar motives for other types of corporate behavior. Under the misinvestment hypothesis, for example, spin-offs, divestitures, conversions to limited partnerships – and even, ironically, visible commitments to particular capital projects – might raise share prices by limiting management investment discretion. Under the market hypothesis, the same range of devices might also raise prices by influencing traders' disbursement expectations or focusing investors on underlying asset values.

118 Recall that acquirers may also be discounted.

closely reflect asset values. On this view, auction periods that invite defensive tactics by incumbent managers or rival bids by white knights are suspect.

The Williams Act[119] structures a de facto auction period for tender offers pursuant to its broad purpose of safeguarding target shareholders from coerced or poorly informed decisions. The act requires, inter alia, that bidders report open market purchases after accumulating 5 percent of a target's voting securities,[120] and allow a minimum of twenty business days following tender offers during which shareholders may tender or withdraw their shares.[121] The first provision limits possible gains on prebid purchases of target shares, while the second allows twenty days for rival acquirers to initiate offers and for defending managers to "shop" the target or pursue defensive strategies ranging from harassing litigation to poison pills and recapitalization plans. The effect of these provisions appears to have been a dramatic increase in takeover premia since the passage of the Williams Act.[122]

Since larger premia are presumed to reflect increased misinvestment costs, the misinvestment hypothesis strongly supports reform of the operative provisions of the Williams Act. The primary issue is whether the entire act works to inflate takeover premia or only one of its features has this consequence: the window for defensive tactics and friendly deals that the act creates. Thus, the misinvestment hypothesis leads to the familiar debate over auction periods by a new route.[123] Repealing the Williams Act in toto would obviously lower the threshold at which discounts could persist in the acquisitions market without attracting suitors. But repealing the act would also eliminate any auction period, with the consequence that acquirers might be able to capture most

---

119 Pub. L. No. 90–439, 82 Stat. 454 (1968) (codified as amended at 15 U.S.C Sec. 78n [d]–[f] [1982]).
120 15 U.S.C. Sec. 78n(d) (1) (1982).
121 17 C.F.R. Sec. 240.14e–1 (a) (1987) (offers must remain open at least twenty business days); 17 C.F.R. Sec. 240.14d–7 (a) (1987) (tendered securities may be withdrawn any time during the period the offer remains open).
122 See G. Jarrell and M. Bradley, The Economic Effects of Federal and State Regulations of Cash Tender Offers, *Journal of Law and Economics,* 23: 371, 389 (1980) (target shareholder abnormal returns increased from 22% to 40% while bidder returns dropped form 9% to 6%, after passage of the Williams Act).
123 Chief defenders of auctions include L. Bebchuk, The Case for Facilitating Competing Tender Offers: A Reply and Extension, *Stanford Law Review* 35: 23 (1982); R. Gilson, Seeking Competitive Bids Versus Pure Passivity in Tender Offers, *Stanford Law Review* 35: 51 (1982); and Coffee, note 60. For opponents of auctions, see note 61. Easterbrook and Fischel, and Schwartz.

available discount gains by resorting to high-pressure, "take it or leave it" offers.[124]

Allowing acquirers to capture the lion's share of large discounts would be regrettable for at least two reasons. First, it would needlessly cloud the inchoate claim of target shareholders to the going concern value of their firms. Discounted shares underprice the value of expected cash flows from existing corporate projects. Implicitly, both the Williams Act and evolving state corporation law seem to recognize this value as the appropriate measure of shareholders' claims.[125] Second, quite apart from existing claims, there is a plausible efficiency argument for permitting shareholders to recapture discounts: Redistributing cash flows from target shareholders to acquirers may increase the costs of capital for all corporate projects by jeopardizing the claim of shareholders to future returns on their investments.[126]

Given these concerns, an auction period that limits acquirers and protects target shareholders is clearly attractive, as long as it does not raise acquisition premia and insulate discounts by deterring first bidders. But why must auctions deter first bids in a world of discounts? In fact, first bids are likely to deter *rival* bids if the only gains available to all bidders are discount gains. A first bidder's sunk costs, including its prebid stock purchases, give a strategic edge that potential rivals are unlikely to challenge absent a low first offer or a helping hand from target managers. Conversely, rival bidders threaten first bidders chiefly when they can exploit large gains that are foreclosed to first bidders, gains that are most likely to arise from the defensive tactics or private information of target managers. Regulators, then, can neutralize the effects of auctions on discount levels by barring target managers from

---

124 Repeal of the Williams Act auction period would reintroduce "Saturday Night Specials," or twenty-four- to forty-eight-hour take-it-or-leave-it offers, that would undoubtedly exploit shareholders' vulnerabilities far more than strategic bidding behavior still permitted by the Williams Act. See A. Schwartz, The Fairness of Tender Offer Prices in Utilitarian Theory, *Journal of Legal Studies* 17: 165 (1988), pp. 175–9; see note 122, Bradley and Jarrell, p. 376.

125 The Williams Act does so merely by attempting to assure that shareholders can make an informed tender decision. State corporate law does so by according shareholders appraisal rights in corporate mergers and employing asset values to determine fair prices when firms are sold.

126 Bebchuk first introduced this argument in the context of synergy gains. Without auctions to guarantee their returns in the event of a takeover, potential targets might avoid projects that could create synergy opportunities for acquirers. See, e.g., note 123, Bebchuk, pp. 42–44. The argument extends easily to discounts, since all corporate projects might be vulnerable to discounting.

any favoritism or defensive tactics, limiting auction periods, and permitting acquirers to make generous prebid share purchases – or by
adopting all three measures.[127]

The same point can be made about shareholder resistance to first
bids. Without the prospect of second bidders or support from incumbent
managers, target shareholders have every incentive to accept first bids
that approximate consensus asset values net of transactions costs and
normal returns to acquirers. Indeed, given the risks to continuing shareholders who fail to tender their shares under present law, target shareholders may be inclined to accept a good deal less than this.[128]

In sum, moderate proponents of the misinvestment hypothesis would
be likely to prescribe (1) a ban on target defensive tactics, (2) a limited
auction period, (3) a generous opportunity for prebid open market purchases, and (4) a rule of informational parity among rival bidders. The
implications of the misinvestment hypothesis for efforts to alleviate dis-
torted tender choices by target shareholders are less clear, although such
reforms would not necessarily be precluded.[129]

B   The market hypothesis and management discretion

In contrast to the misinvestment hypothesis, the market hypothesis pulls
in a very different direction. On this view, many takeovers occur in
response to trading dynamics in the securities market that have no correlation with the management of real assets or the investment of corporate cash flows. Yet, the chief danger may not even be that discounts
generate socially wasteful takeovers; over time, discounted managers
can adjust discounts through equity conversions to mitigate their acquisition risks. Rather, the primary danger may be that this adjustment
is itself exorbitantly costly in real terms because it forces inefficient

127 In particular, strictly limited auction periods preclude rival bidders from closely valuing opportunities for unique acquisition gains, such as operating synergies. See note
60 and accompanying text. Thus, limited auctions would focus bidding on discount
gains, which is precisely what misinvestment analysts should wish in order to dissipate
discounts.
128 See L. Bebchuk, Toward Undistorted Choice and Equal Treatment in Corporate
Takeovers, *Harvard Law Review* 98: 1695 (1985) pp. 1722–3 (pressure to tender).
129 See ibid., pp. 1738–9 (right to tender disapprovingly as device for overcoming shareholders' collective action problem). As discount levels decline, it becomes critical in
the misinvestment view that shareholders do not exploit first bidders' sunk costs by
demanding premia equivalent to gross asset values of discounted targets. The import
of this problem is unclear, however, given shareholder uncertainty about the magnitude of these costs and the likelihood that shareholders would be worse off if bids
failed.

capital rationing on firms and biases managers toward short-term projects and excessive distributions to shareholders. Presumably these real losses dwarf any secondary benefits of discount-induced takeovers, including efficiencies from more accurate pricing in the securities market.[130]

Given the costs of skewing corporate investment policies, the key problem from the market perspective is when to permit hostile acquisitions at all. Here, too, there is a simple solution akin to repealing the Williams Act under the misinvestment hypothesis, namely, a flat ban on hostile takeovers. Indeed, this would be the only sensible reform if managers reliably attended to shareholder interests, and discounts were the sole motive for takeovers. After all, who but the firms' managers should balance a firm's investment prospects against its acquisition price or the heterogeneous values that shareholders might place on investments and distributions in a noisy securities market?

Yet, there are important difficulties with a ban on hostile acquisitions, even under the market hypothesis. First, it fails to weigh shareholders' liquidity and risk preferences. By assumption, share prices are subject to arbitrary discounting. Since shareholders cannot exercise redemption rights against corporations at will, the values of their claims are inevitably reduced by the unpredictable, and potentially unrestricted, volatility of share prices. Second, discounts may not be the only source of acquisition gains. Insofar as takeovers may also tap synergies or management gains, a ban on hostile offers would deprive shareholders of valuable opportunities. Further, the assumption that share prices are untrustworthy hardly implies the converse proposition that managers are reliable agents of shareholder interests in acquisition decisions.

Thus, lawmakers who accept a market analysis are likely to prefer specific deterrents to discount-driven bids over a global ban on hostile acquisitions. Several deterrent strategies are possible. One is to bar or discourage acquisitions that clearly arbitrage between share prices and asset values, such as breakup acquisitions or takeovers financed by leveraging against targets' assets. Recent New York State takeover legislation moves in this direction.[131] A second alternative is to neutralize

---

130 On the market hypothesis, takeovers arbitrage between the asset and securities markets, and thus "correct" discounted share prices. This price effect reduces market risk for investors, and lowers the cost of capital.

131 New York prohibits state corporations from entering into a "business combination" with a 20% stockholder for five years after the 20% threshold is crossed, unless the target's board of directors has approved the combination before the 20% acquisition. N.Y. Bus. Corp. Law Sec. 912 (b) (McKinney 1986). Inter alia, this requirement limits the easy sale or leveraging of target assets to finance takeovers. In addition,

discounts as motives for takeovers by assuring that all discounts gains go to target shareholders. This effort would simply invert the prescriptions of the misinvestment hypothesis by, for example, barring bidders from any open-market purchases or mandating lengthy auction periods to aid searches for second bidders with unique gains. Recent proposals for amending the Williams Act as well as the extended waiting periods mandated by some state takeover statutes move in this direction.[132] Finally, market-oriented lawmakers might follow a strategy of restricting the voting rights of "short-term" shareholders. Such a strategy would entrust the tender decision to "loyal" shareholders who invest for long-term gains at the cost of eliminating the arbitrageurs' role in facilitating hostile bids. This strategy is presaged by the recent wave of charter amendments that attempt to shift voting power to long-term investors and corporate insiders.[133]

These examples illustrate how far the policy implications of the market and misinvestment hypotheses are likely to diverge. There are, to be sure, considerations within each perspective that might temper reform proposals. Thus, within the market framework, large discounts impose market risks and agency costs on shareholders that would persist even if mispricing were the sole source of discounts; within the misinvestment framework, some managers might be forced to sacrifice profitable investments if market forecasts were – as seems inevitable – often noisy or wrong.[134] But these secondary considerations do not alter the policy

proposed congressional legislation has also sought to regulate tender offer financing and the issuance of junk bonds. See e.g., H.R. 685, 100th Cong., 1st Sess. (1987) (Representative Richardson) (one-year moratorium on junk bond financing).

132 On the federal level, several recent bills propose restricting the 5% reporting threshold, extending the mandatory offer period, or both. See, e.g., S. 678, 100th Cong., 1st Sess. (1987) (Senator Metzenbaum) (reduces reporting threshold to 3%, reduces reporting window to one day, and extends offer period to sixty days). In addition, many state statutes effectively increase offer periods. See, e.g., Indiana control shares acquisition statute, Ind. Code Ann. Secs. 23–1–42 (Burns Supp. 1987) (increasing offer period to fifty days or more in practice). See note 21, Lowenstein, pp. 317–18, proposes a far more dramatic six-month open offer period.

133 See Pamepinto, *Dual Class Common Stock and Unequal Voting Rights* (Investor Responsibility Research Center Corporate Governance Service [January 1987]); see also note 21, Shubik, p. 47 (voting constraints from the perspective of the market hypothesis).

134 Market forecasts of future management policies and opportunities are necessarily uncertain. It follows that managers may often be erroneously discounted, even when discounts are rational in the aggregate. This risk imposes costs on investors akin to the costs imposed by biased share prices under the market hypothesis. First, talented managers who are erroneously discounted may abandon profitable investment opportunities. Second, there are "excess deterrence" costs. See note 60, Coffee, p. 1238.

thrust of either hypothesis. The basic dilemma remains: Both hypotheses give credible and internally consistent accounts of acquisition behavior; nevertheless, they lead to very different and mutually incompatible prescriptions.

VI   Concluding remarks

I will not attempt to resolve the dilemma of choosing between discount hypotheses in this paper. For the most part, analytical arguments that might seem to decide the issue are illusory. The misinvestment hypothesis always retains some plausibility when managers exercise discretion over investment policy. Without direct insight into the expectations of securities traders, the fact that discounts may seem to have been unjustified ex post can never fully answer the claim that they were indeed rationally related to investors' ex ante expectations.

At first glance, the market hypothesis might seem to be more vulnerable. For example, one might argue that it is discredited by the mere existence of hostile takeovers. Takeovers seem to create a puzzle for the market hypothesis. If mispricing creates discounts, why would acquirers ever initiate tender offers and displace incumbent managers in lieu of simply investing in discounted firms? Under the market hypothesis, passive investors eventually receive a pro-rata portion of a discounted firm's expected cash flows. Thus, it may seem that acquirers should become rentiers rather than sharks. They should collect their return as dividends, or wait for price swings in the market, rather than sharing discounts with target shareholders by paying out acquisition premia.[135]

There are several responses to this argument. One is that many large investors, including some well-known acquirers, sometimes *do* invest

For example, if all managers risk displacement as a result of "mistaken" discounting, even talented managers may invest to minimize acquisition risks rather than to maximize shareholder returns. If compensation incentives (such as golden parachutes) cannot offset these investment biases, shareholders might prefer to insulate modest discounts from takeover bids in order to avoid incentive problems, even under the misinvestment hypothesis.

135 Thus, rather than make a single acquisition, an acquirer might purchase, say, 10% blocks in ten equally discounted targets. If these investments only marginally affected share prices, the long-term returns from this strategy should, on the market hypothesis, exceed the returns from a single acquisition. The acquirer would purchase the same aggregate claim on future cash flows at a lower cost because it would not pay an acquisition premium. By hypothesis, acquisition premia reflect share discounts. See notes 56–65 and accompanying text. I am grateful to Henry Hansmann and Bob Clark for independently suggesting this objection to the market hypothesis.

passively in firms they consider undervalued.[136] A second is that acquirers may seek joint gains that are available only upon assuming
control of discounted targets. A third response is that acquirers may not
know why firms are discounted. They may thus blame target managers
for discounts even when these managers merely fail to reduce discounts.[137] But the most basic response to the question "Why takeovers?"
arises from the market hypothesis itself. Passive investors have no assurance that discounts will ever disappear. To be sure, perpetual discounts need not matter to very long-term investors. For corporate
investors, however, investing passively in discounted firms is to risk
becoming a holding company subject to precisely the same discounts
that afflict closed-end investment funds. In effect, passive investment
invites double discounting for corporate investors.[138] Under the market
hypothesis, only transactions that redeem shares for asset values can
eliminate discounts with any certainty.

While there may be other analytical challenges to the market hypothesis, they are unlikely to succeed without new empirical support.
Both the market and the misinvestment hypothesis are defensible on
the basis of existing literature.[139] Paradoxically, the empirical case for
accepting discounts as an acquisition motive is more persuasive than the
case for selecting either account of how discounts arise. This conclusion

136 See, e.g., Icahn on Icahn, *Fortune,* February 29, 1988, pp. 54, 55 (strategy of asset
   arbitrage does not necessarily involve displacing management); see note 78 (Warren
   Buffett's strategy of passive investment).
137 Acquirers face an easier valuation task than passive investors: They need not decide
   how discounts arise. If there is any uncertainty on this point, the only safe course
   may be to displace incumbent managers.
138 See notes 46–8 and accompanying text (holding companies). Investment analysts
   commonly assert that such double discounts exist. E.g., note 46, J. Tinker (double
   discount on Warner Communication shares held by Chris-Craft Industries).
139 See notes 19–29 and accompanying text. I prefer the misinvestment hypothesis for
   its simplicity and fit with the dominant paradigm of share prices in corporate finance.
   Recent analyses of the energy industry, moreover, serve as cogent models of how
   the misinvestment hypothesis might be elaborated more generally. See note 49, Jensen; see note 19, Jacobs and cf. note 54, Shleifer, Vishny, and Morck (generalizing
   free cash flow explanation to low-Q industries). Nevertheless, the growing literature
   on noise trading, the October 1987 market crash, and the puzzling behavior of closed-
   end investment funds are useful reminders of how far we remain from understanding
   securities prices. The simplicity of the misinvestment hypothesis falls short of providing a definitive basis for conviction. Rational market theory, which underlies the
   misinvestment hypothesis, remains, in Robert Merton's words, a "hot issue" whose
   resolution is likely to structure the research agenda of corporate finance for some
   time. See note 20, Merton, p. 37. If forced to speculate further, I would guess that
   both the market and the misinvestment hypotheses may contribute to understanding
   discounts.

should not disappoint. If discounts are indeed as persuasive as I have suggested, the discount claim successfully organizes broad elements of otherwise puzzling corporate behavior. In lieu of selecting discount hypotheses, however, I offer a final observation that has been implicit in my discussion thus far.

A basic shift in legal argument follows from the introduction of financial economics into corporate law. The choice between discount hypothesis is not the only example, even in the acquisitions literature, of the difficulty of choosing between broad narratives about market behavior.[140] This difficulty is pervasive, and it accounts for much of the peculiarly deep divisions among commentators over takeover policy. For the most part, these divisions are about market behavior rather than competing norms or interests. In the case of share discounts, the divisions are likely to be resolved eventually as more powerful evidence accumulates on the mechanisms of share pricing. But until they are resolved, different systemic frameworks confront lawmakers with a difficult challenge. Lawmakers, who lack vocational experience in what might be termed the exploratory acceptance of powerful models, must offer justifications for policy decisions today. The temptation to choose between explanatory frameworks is particularly insistent, moreover, because a single framework will often offer precisely the kind of rationale that legal rules require. Norms and interests can be cogently "balanced," but differing narratives of how markets might function are much harder to integrate within the context of a single prescriptive argument.[141] Nevertheless, the analysis of share discounts suggests that a balancing approach, or at least a tolerance for ambiguity on the level of basic explanation, is precisely what is required. This, then, is also a plea to proceed slowly with legal innovations based on a single account of acquisition gains, which in today's climate can only mean the legislative agenda of the critics of takeovers and the rationality of share prices.

---

140 The conflict between implicit contract and better management hypotheses is another example. See note 9.

141 The Williams Act itself is pervasively informed by interest-balancing. See *CTS Corp. v. Dynamics Corp. of America*, 107 S. Ct. 1637, 1645 (1987) (Williams Act strikes "a careful balance between the interests of offerers and target companies"). A more systematic approach to market behavior may change the form of balancing more than its fundamental wisdom.

CHAPTER 3

Ties that bond: dual class common stock and the problem of shareholder choice

Jeffrey N. Gordon

Introduction

For Berle and Means in the 1930s the "separation of ownership and control" was a realpolitik account of the relationship between management and the widely dispersed shareholders of the public corporation.[1] In the 1980s the Berle–Means metaphor may become a structural fact for many major public firms. Over the past five years, and at an accelerating pace, more than eighty public firms have adopted, or proposed to adopt, capital structures with two classes of common stock. One class, intended principally for public shareholders, carries limited voting rights; the second class, intended principally for management and its associates, carries enhanced, or "super," voting rights. Although proposals for dual class common stock vary in their details, their effect would be significantly to unbundle corporate governance from economic participation. Overall, the move toward dual class common stock portends the most important shift in the underlying structure of corporate

I am grateful to Steve Brams, Victor Goldberg, Lewis Kornhauser, Homer Kripke, David Leebron, John Pound, Mark Ramseyer, Ricky Revesz, Roberta Romano, Helen Scott, Stanley Siegel, Jack Slain, and the participants at the Harvard Conference on the Economics of Corporate and Capital Markets Law for comments on an earlier draft and to Charles Kamimura, Karen Weidmann, and Eric Wright for very able research assistance. The Filomen d'Agostino and Max E. Greenberg Research Fund of New York University Law School provided generous financial support for which I am grateful.

Because of space limitations, references to backup materials have been omitted in many cases and some of the argument has been abridged. A fuller version will be found in *California Law Review* 75: 1–85 (1988). This chapter reflects developments through December, 31, 1987. In particular, it does not discuss the SEC's adoption in July 1988 of Rule 19c–4 that purports to address the problems raised herein.

1 See A. Berle and G. Means, *The Modern Corporation and Private Property* (New York, 1932).

governance since the rise of institutional stock ownership in the 1960s and 1970s.

Firms capitalized with dual, or even multiple, classes of common stock have been a well-known feature of the corporate landscape. Closely held corporations and public firms with significant dynastic family voices have frequently used the dual class common device. However, the dual class common has typically been part of these firm's capital structure since their initial public offerings (IPOs). It is no secret that the current popularity of dual class common among public firms is a response to the recent wave of hostile takeovers. Even the largest firms have become possible takeover targets because of the development of leveraged acquisition strategies that rely on "junk bond" financing. The current repertoire of defensive tactics – "poison pills," "shark repellant" charter amendments, assorted partial liquidation schemes, and defensive litigation – pale in effectiveness when compared to dual class common. For if management and its allies hold the voting stock necessary to elect directors, a hostile bid becomes practically impossible.[2] One crucial difference for firms now seeking to adopt the dual class common structure is that the required corporate action is a recapitalization, rather than an initial public offering. In ways that will bear subsequent analysis, existing public shareholders must be induced to part with their voting stock in order for the scheme to work.

Different stock exchange policies on dual class common stock have complicated matters. The New York Stock Exchange (NYSE), which historically has forbidden dual class common, has the most restrictive policy. The National Association of Securities Dealers (NASD), overseer of the over-the-counter market (OTC), places no limitations on the use of multiple classes of common stock. The American Stock Exchange (Amex) has permitted firms to issue multiple classes of common stock, but lists only those classes that have the right to elect at least 25 percent of the board of directors.

---

2 Whether managers–directors with voting control are free to turn down any bid for the firm, no matter how lucrative, is an interesting fiduciary duty question. The traditional view that a shareholder may vote (or sell shares) as he pleases was questioned in the recent battle for control over Resorts International. There Donald Trump had acquired most of the supervoting stock and had made an offer to acquire the remaining limited voting stock as well. Merv Griffin countered with a higher bid for the limited voting stock and claimed in litigation that the directors had an obligation to allow shareholders to sell their shares at the higher price by issuing additional supervoting stock to dilute Trump's control. The matter apparently was settled through a division of the company's assets between Griffin and Trump. See "Griffin Wins Resorts in Deal with Trump," *New York Times,* April 15, 1988, D1.

The weakening competitive position of the NYSE in the provision of stock transaction services has put pressure on the exchange to abandon its single class common rule. Formerly, the NYSE could insist on its rule because of the perceived benefits of an NYSE listing. The liquidity and market-making functions provided by the NYSE arguably lowered the firm's cost of capital. A listing also carried prestige that probably entailed pecuniary benefits for the firm and gratification for its principals. In recent years, however, advances in communications technology and the regulatory efforts to create a "national market system" have dramatically enhanced the competitive position of the OTC market. Recent empirical work has underscored the narrowing advantage of an NYSE listing. Thus NYSE firms that desire to establish dual class common capital structures are able credibly to threaten a shift from the NYSE to the Amex or the OTC.

This threat has triggered an extraordinary series of actions. Rather than lose listings, listing fees, and commission revenue for its broker-dealer membership, the NYSE Board of Governors proposed a substantial dilution of its single class common rule.[3] As overseer of the self-regulatory organizations, the SEC was required to approve the NYSE rule change. Because of great interest in the matter, the SEC held public hearings in December 1986. For several months thereafter the SEC attempted to broker an agreement on a uniform voting rights rule among the NYSE, the Amex, and the NASD. However, these negotiations broke down, largely because of the Amex's strategic insistence on a uniform one share–one vote standard.

In June 1987, after these negotiations failed, the SEC proposed a rule drawn somewhat more narrowly than the voluntary rule nearly agreed upon. Proposed Rule 19c-4 would prohibit the exchanges and the NASD from listing the stock of a firm "that issues any class of a security or takes other corporate action that would have the effect of nullifying, restricting, or disparately reducing the per share voting rights of holders" of stock registered under the 1934 Act.[4] The proposed rule would permit firms on all exchanges, including the NYSE, to issue limited voting common stock but would prohibit dual class recapitalizations that diminished the power of present shareholders. However,

---

3 The history of the NYSE rule is described in J. Seligman, Equal Protection in Shareholder Voting Rights: The One Common Share, One Vote Controversy, *George Washington Law Review* 54: 687–724 (1986).

4 Exchange Act Release No. 24,623, Voting Rights Listing Standards – Proposed Disenfranchisement Rule, 52 Fed. Reg. 23,665 (1987), reprinted in (1987 Transfer Binder) Fed. Sec. L. Rep. (CCH) par. 84,143. This release and Exchange Act Release No. 34-23803, 51 Fed. Reg. 41715 (1986) are the sources of many of the details in the text.

even if the SEC adopts this rule, the matter may not end, since Congress is considering legislation that would impose a uniform one share–one vote rule.

If the proposed SEC rule is adopted, the NYSE single class common rule will not be preserved because the competitive pressure that triggered the initial NYSE proposal is likely to persist. Hence, the rule could facilitate a dramatic change in the ownership structure of large public firms.

This article presents a framework for analysis of the dual class common issue that focuses on problems of shareholder choice and management opportunism in the large publicly held corporation. Dual class recapitalizations present these problems in a very powerful way because the triggering decision must be put to a shareholder vote.

Section I of this chapter argues that dual class recapitalizations are likely to turn out badly for public shareholders. This claim is based on a critique of the purported benefits of these recapitalizations and is supported by empirical data that strongly suggest that the recapitalizations diminish public shareholder welfare.

In Section II, I argue that managers can exploit a series of collective action and strategic choice problems faced by public shareholders to win approval of even welfare-reducing proposals. Firms that propose recapitalizations are likely to have an insider-dominated ownership structure that exacerbates collective action problems. The assertion that recapitalization is necessary to permit the exploitation of profitable investment projects sets up a strategic choice game, a variant of "chicken," that managers are well-situated to win.

Section III argues that because many of these problems are foreseeable ex ante, the costs of such potential managerial opportunism will fall on the insiders when they try to sell their stock. In particular, insiders who seek to lower the cost of capital will find it valuable to bond a promise that the firm's single class capital structure will not be renegotiated. The parties may agree that the defects of shareholder voting are so severe that voting should not be used to make certain decisions. The NYSE's traditional one share–one vote rule should be understood as a means of bonding that agreement. The rule provides what I call a "bonded nonrenegotiation right." Given present institutional arrangements, the NYSE rule is the only secure bond available for such a promise.

Section III goes on to contend that the competition among the exchanges that has undermined the NYSE rule is more likely a race to the bottom than to the top. The limited number of exchanges and the high entry barriers belie the claim that the permissive rule that emerges from competition is necessarily the most efficient. Thus the basis for SEC intervention becomes clear. With such intervention, but not otherwise, parties can bond agreements that lower the cost of capital.

The argument then turns in Section IV to policy prescription. Two types of rules are possible. One type of rule permits nonuniform standards but offers competitive protection to an exchange adopting a shareholder-protective corporate governance regime. The second type of rule prescribes uniform voting rights standards across exchanges.

The essential element of a nonuniform rule is a restriction on migration by firms among exchanges to escape provisions that protect shareholders. On this approach, the SEC would require the Amex and the NASD to adopt a rule to prohibit the listing of any firm that has been delisted by the NYSE, voluntarily or involuntarily, because of a dual class recapitalization. This restriction on the other exchanges would permit the NYSE to maintain its rule.

Proposed Rule 19c-4 is a uniform rule that permits a dual class recapitalization on any exchange so long as the limited voting stock is issued through an initial public offering and existing shareholder voting rights are not diminished. It has the virtue of offering greater protection for shareholders of Amex or NASDAQ firms than is provided by the rules of those exchanges. Given the competition among exchanges, however, such a rule would make it very difficult for the NYSE to maintain its single class common rule. I argue that limited voting common stock imposes certain economic costs on public shareholders. The bond provided by the NYSE single class common rule thus has value to the firm and its elimination imposes a cost.

I therefore recommend the addition of a nonmigration clause to the proposed SEC rule to prohibit a firm that moves between exchanges from adopting a voting rights structure that is prohibited by the exchange it is leaving. This approach has the additional virtue of setting in motion an experiment with limited voting common by Amex and NASDAQ firms that does not alter the governance structure of the largest firms, which will remain within the NYSE's one share–one vote regime.

I   The implausible case for dual class recapitalizations

A   The purported justifications

The intended effect of dual class common stock usually is to give management and its associates voting power disproportionate to their equity in the firm, that is, disproportionate to their claim on residual cash flows. Indeed, the usual intention is to give management majority voting

power. Several explanations have been offered as to why management
values ownership of voting rights and why management's objectives are
not inconsistent with the maximization of shareholder wealth.[5] The problem with these explanations is that while they may account for initial
public offerings of dual class common, they are unlikely to justify a dual
class common recapitalization. A dual class IPO does not require justification on shareholder wealth maximization grounds because the purchasing shareholders will be compensated for the costs associated with
a dual class structure by an appropriate discount on the share price
(assuming adequate disclosure and a reasonably efficient market). In
contrast, a dual class recapitalization ordinarily does require a shareholder wealth maximization justification. Otherwise, how are we to
explain why public shareholders would vote for it? But, as shall be
developed, such justifications conflict in the most basic way with the
arguments on behalf of the market for corporate control. In short,
recapitalization justifications must be defended as stories about market
failure.

The common justifications fall into five categories: (1) protection
against shareholder misjudgments because of inferior information; (2)
protection of shareholders against predatory takeover tactics; (3) avoidance of shareholder opportunism with respect to deferred compensation
and firm-specific human capital investment; (4) protection of bargained-
for management perquisites; and (5) compensation for greater firm specific risk. The first three justifications are arguably applicable to any
firm; the last two seem applicable only to firms in which there is a
dominant shareholder group at the time of the proposed recapitalization.
Let us consider these justifications in turn.

(1) Inferior shareholder information. Because of its inside position,
management frequently will have better information about the firm than
shareholders. The resulting information asymmetry is the basis for a
bundle of shareholder wealth-maximizing justifications for dual class
recapitalizations. In particular, managers may fear that shareholders
will sell control of the firm to a hostile bidder because of mistaken beliefs,
or misinformation, about management performance and the firm's prospects. Alternatively, the fear of such shareholder mistake may distort
management decisions. For example, managers may not make investments that, although profit maximizing, are difficult to explain to a
relatively uninformed shareholder body, that require substantial secrecy

5 See H. DeAngelo and L. DeAngelo, Managerial Ownership of Voting Rights, *Journal
of Financial Economics* 14: 33–70 (1985).

for competitive reasons, or that are expected to show a profit only in the long term. Similarly, management may be constrained in financing decisions by the optimistic or pessimistic signals that such choice transmit. Another variant is that the need to explain decisions to uninformed shareholders diverts management from its mission of maximizing profits. Use of dual class common to give management voting control obviously avoids these problems. Thus, runs the argument, a dual class recapitalization may maximize shareholder wealth.

This justification for dual class common obviously proves too much, for it would validate a wide range of antitakeover devices for virtually every kind of firm. The information asymmetry rationale for management control, a form of management paternalism, gives insufficient weight to the risks of management opportunism. The rationale is fundamentally at odds with any belief in allocatively efficient capital markets, which depend upon the ability of outsiders to assess accurately firm performance and potential. There is no evidence that shareholders make systematic mistakes in selling to third party bidders, or that acquirers are able to buy control at bargain prices. If anything, the evidence suggests that acquirers overpay.[6] In other words, this justification is based on an unstated and unproved assumption of widespread failure in the market for corporate control that most observers would reject.

(2) Predatory takeover tactics. In struggles for corporate control acquirers may use "predatory" tactics that arguably decrease shareholder welfare. Examples include two-tier, front-loaded tender offers that coerce tenders at less than the optimum price, toehold acquisitions by "greenmailers" who threaten disruption unless paid to go away, and defensive countertender offers by a target (known as a Pac Man defense) that may thwart a desirable acquisition. All of these tactics can be avoided by lodging voting control with management. In the case of a third party bid, management can coordinate negotiations on behalf of shareholders to obtain the highest price. Greenmail and the Pac Man defense become ineffective. Thus, the argument once again concludes that dual class common recapitalizations increase shareholder wealth.

This kind of argument is very frequently made in the management proxy statements of firms proposing recapitalizations. It is not very persuasive in light of alternatives that protect shareholder interests with-

6 See generally G. Jarrell, J. Brickley and J. Netter, The Market for Corporate Control: The Empirical Evidence Since 1980, *Journal of Economic Perspectives* 2: 49–68 (1988) (citing studies). The evidence is that target shareholders do extraordinarily well, with average gains between 30% and 60%.

out granting management voting control. Assorted "shark repellant" charter and by-law provisions are available to block many predatory practices. For example, "fair price" provisions can assure that shareholders on the back end of a two-tier offer receive equivalent compensation. Other provisions can bar the payment of greenmail or prescribe shareholder meeting and voting rules that take the bite out of a Pac Man defense. Moreover, management already has ample discretionary measures, including the issuance of "poison pill" stock or rights and the initiation of defensive litigation, to protect shareholders against a predatory takeover. The virtual disappearance of the hostile two-tier bid over the past few years suggests the effectiveness of these devices. Nor is there any reason to believe that a dual class recapitalization is a cheaper defensive tactic than others in the management arsenal. Finally, too much management coordination and negotiation is not necessarily a good thing for the shareholders. There is ample evidence that premiums for target shareholders are higher in hostile takeovers than in negotiated mergers.

(3) Shareholder opportunism. It may be that the gains to target shareholders in a hostile takeover partially derive from breach of an implicit contract to pay deferred compensation to managers. On this view, vesting managers with power to block a hostile bid will avoid (a) explicit compensation contracts that are more expensive for shareholders or (b) a derogation in managers' willingness to make firm-specific human capital investments that would also reduce the value of the firm. Thus goes this argument, dual class recapitalization may increase shareholder wealth.

(a) Managerial compensation. The deferred compensation problem arises in managerial contracts because of the difficulties in linking management compensation to managerial performance, in particular the difficulty in determining actual performance against the background of unpredictable events that affect the firm. It will be easier to gauge performance over time, since positive and negative events will tend to wash out. Thus compensation contracts will often have a significant component of deferred compensation, which represents a "settling up" for previous managerial effort. Such contracts need not be explicit. Indeed, since the amount is determinable only sometime after performance and is not directly tied to the firm's performance, writing an explicit ex ante deferred compensation contract may be impossible. Compensation may take the form of a cash bonus, a promotion, greater

pension benefits, or even the retention of a now ineffective but once diligent manager.

As long as the firm remains in business, concern about its reputation will lead it to honor such implicit deferred compensation contracts. Welshing will make it more costly to retain and recruit managers. A hostile takeover, however, removes the constraints on shareholder opportunism. In particular, shareholders can sell the firm to an acquirer free of any implicit contractual obligations. As long as the acquirer observes implicit contracts with its own managers, it will not suffer significant reputation effects. It reaps the rewards of the unpaid deferred compensation claims of target managers, which it may share with target shareholders.

The potential for this expropriation will lead to the reformulation of managerial compensation contracts. The golden parachute, for example, in which top management receives special severance pay following a shift of corporate control, may be seen as an explicit contractual means of averting shareholder opportunism.[7] Golden parachutes are costly for shareholders, however. If the payment exceeds the discounted present value of the deferred compensation claim, managers will have an incentive to induce a hostile bid by, for example, poor performance that reduces the value of the firm. Similarly, once the takeover attempt is underway, the parachute may reduce management's incentive to obtain the highest price for the shareholders. Thus, insofar as dual class common stock will prevent takeover-related shareholder opportunism, it will eliminate costly contracting alternatives and thereby enhance shareholder wealth.

This argument is not persuasive. Let us assume that the only effect of dual class common is to route all decisions in respect of a bid for the firm through management (because a tender offer for nonvoting shares cannot obtain control). The moral hazard problems associated with golden parachutes return: In negotiating to protect its deferred compensation claim, management can obtain excessive side payments from the acquirer and trade a reduced share price for increased side payments. In the heat of battle, such trade-offs may be harder to detect than abuse of the golden parachute. But our starting assumption is, of course, too limited. Dual class common gives rise to agency problems not only in merger negotiations but in the management of the firm generally. The negative consequences for shareholder wealth of such ongoing management insulation from shareholder control are likely to exceed the one

---

7 A formal model of a similar idea is found in C. Knoeber, Golden Parachutes, Shark Repellents, and Hostile Tender Offers, *American Economic Review* 76: 155–67 (1986).

time parachute costs or alternative compensation arrangements that may arise.

(b) Firm-specific human capital. Shareholders need to induce managers to make the optimal investment in firm-specific human capital. There are two distinct labor markets: the labor market within the firm, the "internal market," and the labor market across all firms, the "external market." Specialization by task or skill that brings rewards in the internal labor market may not lead to increased value in the external market. Thus the situation resembles the shareholder opportunism problem discussed above. Many firm-specific human capital investments pay off only over time and thus entail a significant element of deferred compensation. Reputation effects induce firms to honor implicit contractual obligations to reward and protect with tenure those who make such human capital investments. As before, a takeover gives shareholders the chance to behave opportunistically with respect to such obligations.

Once again the wheel continues to turn: Managers will demand increased current compensation or will reduce their investment in firm-specific human capital. In more homely terms, loyalty suffers. Managers may prefer to undertake projects that increase their external labor market value. These projects may not necessarily be the best projects for the firm, or those that would best advance the managers' careers within the firm. By this reasoning, a dual class recapitalization that eliminates the possibility of an opportunistic takeover will improve shareholder welfare.

One powerful argument against this scenario is that it fails to address the underlying agency problem: If managers can freely avoid shareholder wealth-maximizing activity when there *is* a threat of a hostile takeover, what will prevent even greater opportunism when that threat ends? Proponents of dual class recapitalizations must argue that eliminating the hostile takeover threat *reduces* agency costs because of a better alignment of management and shareholder interests. Such an argument might go as follows: Projects associated with firm-specific human capital investments ordinarily have a higher return to the firm than projects associated with general human capital investments. Thus, we can ordinarily expect managers to act to maximize their value on the internal labor market by pursuing projects that are shareholder wealth-maximizing projects. Returns to managers, however, consist of current and expected future compensation. The advantage to managers in making firm-specific human capital investment ordinarily derives from the expectation of higher future compensation. The prevalence of takeovers raises managers' discount rate for such future compensation and thus reverses the managers' ordinary ranking of firm-specific versus general human capital investment projects.

But notice where this argument goes: to the claim that takeovers are not the solution to managerial underperformance but frequently its cause. The fear of takeovers leads managers systematically to prefer projects that produce immediate compensation or that increase their value in the external labor market, rather than projects that maximize the value of the firm. Such a conclusion radically contradicts the basic premises of the market in corporate control. It leaves unexplained why acquirers began to undertake takeovers in the first place and is contradicted by the empirical evidence that shows significant gains to shareholders from takeovers. In short, the human capital argument seems unlikely to supply a shareholder wealth-maximizing justification for dual class recapitalizations.

(4) Protection of bargained-for management perquisites. A traditional explanation for a dual class IPO is the protection of management perquisites implicitly provided for in the initial management/shareholder contract. For example, the firm's founders may wish to assure continued family dominance, including the ability to employ and pay family members preferentially and to enjoy other economic and noneconomic perquisites. These factors are presumably reflected in the price that outsiders pay for shares. It would be difficult to spell out such management perquisites by specific contract, so a dual class common capital structure may serve this purpose.

But this justification for a dual class IPO does not justify a dual class *recapitalization*. Public shareholders are asked to bear costs which by assumption they have not been compensated for. A major problem for public shareholders in a family-dominated firm is the risk that insiders will divert a disproportionate share of firm cash flow. With a single class of stock, continued family control requires a relatively large equity stake, which at least partially bonds against discrimination against public shareholders. In a dual class IPO public shareholders will presumably demand a significant discount to compensate for the risks of exploitation, including the risk that the family may reduce its equity stake while retaining control. Given a single class IPO, public shareholders would ordinarily refuse to consent to a dual class recapitalization that exposes them to these risks.

(5) Compensation for firm-specific risk. Most of the recent dual class common recapitalization proposals were made by firms in which family–management groups hold large blocks of stock. Such investments indicate that the holders are not diversifying, but rather choose to bear considerable firm-specific risk.

Thus dual class capital structures can then be seen as securing extra compensation for such risk bearing. This compensation can take different forms: assurance of continued exercise of what is believed to be a. comparative advantage in managing the firm; or pecuniary and non-pecuniary benefits as discussed above, including some diversion of firm cash flow. Such an account explains dual class IPOs but does not immediately suggest a benefit to public shareholders from dual class re-capitalization. In what way could public shareholders benefit? One possibility is that continued concentration of ownership benefits public shareholders, who free-ride on monitoring by dominant shareholders. That is, assuming that diversion of cash flow is held within reasonable bounds, public shareholders benefit from the intense involvement of a dominant shareholder group, which has its fortune and reputation tied to the performance of the firm. Indeed, this is presumably a reason public shareholders buy shares in such firms. These benefits will be lost without dual class common, it is argued, because without compensation for risk-bearing, the dominant shareholders will sell some of their shares. The threat posed by dominant shareholders is, in effect, this: Unless we are guaranteed control, we will diversify our holdings, and you will lose the benefit of our intense efforts on behalf of the firm, including our monitoring of managers.

This justification seems implausible. A recapitalization that assures the family–management group such control raises tremendous agency problems, including the possibility of an increasing diversion of cash flow, against which public shareholders would have little defense. These problems probably explain why the firm was initially capitalized with single class common. It seems unlikely that a controlling shareholder group would reduce its equity stake merely because it was not *assured* of control. This would only jeopardize control further. Indeed, once given such assurance through dual class common, the group would find it feasible to *reduce* its equity stake in the firm. Moreover, management's continuing belief in its comparative advantage in controlling the firm is not necessarily warranted. Presumably only when that belief is incorrect could a hostile bidder attract support from public shareholders.

In sum, a canvass of five common justifications for dual class recapitalizations suggests that the case is highly implausible. There may be reasons why the joint welfare of insiders and public shareholders is maximized in an initial public offering of dual class common stock. But it is very difficult to believe that the wealth of public shareholders is likely to be increased by a transaction in which their voting participation is dramatically reduced, generally without compensation. What is the bearing of the empirical evidence on this theory? To that evidence we now turn.

B   *The empirical evidence*

The most comprehensive empirical tests strongly suggest that dual class recapitalizations give rise to economically significant negative effects on shareholder wealth, perhaps as large as −3 percent. There is also reason to believe that if anything, these empirical tests *understate* the negative impact. Thus the empirical evidence supports the theoretical arguments that dual class recapitalizations will work out badly for public shareholders.

(1) The studies summarized. Researchers have conducted a series of empirical studies of dual class recapitalizations. The results of the tests vary considerably depending upon the endpoints. A study by Prof. M. Megan Partch that covers forty-four recapitalizing firms from 1962 through 1984 shows in general no statistically significant wealth effects.[8] A study that I conducted that covered nineteen recapitalizing NYSE firms from 1984 through 1986 is generally consistent with Partch's results.[9]

Particularly revealing, however, are two studies recently conducted by the SEC's Office of Chief Economist. The first study covers sixty-three recapitalizations from 1976 through May 1986 and finds no wealth effects.[10] The second study covers ninety-seven firms starting with 1976 but with a later end point, May 1987.[11] This second study shows negative wealth effects of −1 percent for the entire sample. The inference is inescapable that later-recapitalizing firms experienced negative wealth effects of −3 percent. Apparently no distinctions among the firms, such as size of the insiders' initial block of stock, accounts for the difference. The most compelling explanation is the existence of a learning process in which shareholders have come to realize the negative impact of a recapitalization over time.

8 M. Partch, The Creation of a Class of Limited Voting Common Stock and Shareholder Wealth, *Journal of Financial Economics* 18: 313–39.
9 See J. Gordon, *California Law Review* 75: 1–85 (1988), pp. 26–30. This article also elaborates on the empirical studies described in the text.
10 SEC Office of the Chief Economist, *The Effects of Dual Class Recapitalizations on the Wealth of Shareholders* (June 1, 1987).
11 SEC Office of the Chief Economist, Update – *The Effects of Dual Class Recapitalizations on Shareholder Wealth: Including Evidence from 1986 and 1987* (July 16, 1987).

These empirical studies use an "event study" methodology that focuses on the effect of a particular event on share prices for a sample of firms undergoing the same event. In other words, the technique records investor expectations about the effect of the event on the firm. It is assumed that across a broad sample of firms, investor expectations will be rational, that is, investors will correctly assess the impact of the event. Sometimes investors can be wrong, particularly in the short term, but will eventually learn the true effects. The two OCE studies provide an interesting window on this learning process. Investors' experience with the earlier dual recapitalizations condition new expectations about the effect of recapitalizations generally. Thus the -3 percent wealth effect for the most recent subsample may be a better measure of the impact than the average across the whole sample.

(2) Limits of the empirical research. The studies by the SEC Office of Chief Economist, the most comprehensive studies available, offer important evidence that dual class recapitalizations reduce public shareholder welfare. Nevertheless, even if the empirical evidence had not revealed negative wealth effects, this would not disprove their existence. This is because other factors may obscure a negative impact from these recapitalizations.

First, one common characteristic of firms that have undergone a dual class recapitalization is a large family–management bloc. Given this prior ownership distribution, public shareholders would already have discounted the stock price to reflect the improbability of gains from a near-term takeover bid or losses from any near-term increase in agency costs. The negative consequences of the recapitalization in such cases are more likely to be felt in the future; therefore, the effects, when discounted to present value, may not measurably register on current prices.

Even more importantly, the immediate negative effects of a recapitalization are likely to be washed out by a positive signal carried by the recapitalization proposal, namely, that the firm has profitable investment opportunities to exploit. Recapitalizing firms typically link the dual class proposal to the desire to pursue new investment opportunities through the issuance of equity but in a way that will not dilute the control position of the dominant family–management bloc. Thus it would not be surprising that an event study of recapitalization proposals shows no negative shareholder wealth effects. The good news is entangled with the bad.[12]

12 Recent empirical evidence suggests in other contexts that announcements of equity offerings are associated with *negative* effects on shareholder wealth, because they are

In sum, the empirical evidence suggests that dual class common recapitalizations decrease shareholder wealth across a broad range of
firms. The OCE studies show that negative wealth effects might be quite
large. Moreover, the studies also show that despite announcement of
desirable investment opportunities, firms that concurrently undertake a
dual class recapitalization do not experience an increase in value. This
suggests that the recapitalization is an offsetting negative factor. In any
event, the empirical work and its interpretation certainly offer little
comfort to the competing claim, that shareholders are better off.

The puzzle, of course, is that firms nonetheless make such proposals
and shareholders adopt them. How can it be that shareholders will
approve proposals that do not increase, and may reduce, shareholder
wealth? To that problem we now turn.

II   The problem of shareholder choice

This article contends that shareholder approval of a dual class common
recapitalization – even by a majority of public shareholders – does not
necessarily support a belief that these actions increase shareholder
wealth. Indeed, such approval can be elicited even if the recapitalization
almost certainly reduces shareholder wealth. This is true because of
collective action and strategic choice problems associated with shareholder voting. In order to understand this claim, it is first necessary to
examine the recapitalization mechanisms that firms propose and their
impact on shareholder choice.

A   *Recapitalization mechanisms*

Most of the firms that have recently recapitalized have used one of three
mechanisms: exchange offers, special distributions, and alteration of
voting rights. It is useful to consider each in turn.

(1) Exchange offers. In the typical exchange offer recapitalization,
shareholders must first approve a charter amendment that authorizes
the issuance of a new class of common stock carrying several votes per
share, most frequently ten. In most cases this supervoting stock receives

taken as reflecting management's belief that the firm's stock is overpriced. For dual
class firms, which tend to be very conservatively leveraged, managers may be unwilling
to issue debt to raise capital because of the threat to control through restrictive covenants or the risk of default. For these managers, the choice is not between equity
and debt, but between equity and no investment. Thus the decision to issue equity
sends a different signal.

reduced dividends, most commonly, 10 percent less than is paid to limited-voting stock. In almost all cases the supervoting stock may not be transferred, other than to family members or trusts of the beneficial owner. An impermissible transfer works an automatic conversion from supervoting common to ordinary common.[13] After the new class of common is authorized, the firm conducts a one-time exchange offer, in which shareholders may exchange their ordinary common for the supervoting common, typically on a one-for-one ratio. For reasons explained below, public shareholders are very unlikely to make this exchange where the ordinary common is given any dividend preference.

Supervoting common fortifies the position of a management bloc in at least three ways. First, the supervoting common votes with the ordinary common in the election of directors and other matters, such as merger proposals, that come before the common shareholders.[14] Thus if no public shareholders exchange their stock, an insiders' bloc of 9.091 percent of the firm's common equity could incontrovertibly control the firm. Second, even if public shareholders did exchange, the transfer restrictions mean that such supervoting shares could not be transferred to a hostile acquirer. The only risk to management's control is a proxy battle mounted by the exchanging shareholders. This limited possibility is cut back further by transfer restrictions that are often written so broadly as to suggest that the formation of a dissident shareholder group would trigger an automatic conversion of their supervoting common. Third, the recapitalization terms typically provide for stock dividends and stock splits by class. This provides an easy avenue to repeatedly fortifying the supervoting class. Thus no matter how much ordinary common the firm subsequently issues, it should be possible to maintain the control of the holders of supervoting common.

(2) Special distributions. In the typical special distribution recapitalization, shareholders must first approve a charter amendment that authorizes the issuance of a new class of common stock carrying several votes per share, most frequently ten. The supervoting stock usually takes no dividend reduction. In most cases it may be transferred only to family members or trusts, and the stock automatically converts to ordinary common upon an impermissible transfer. After authorization of the new

---

13 The firm will convert the supervoting stock to ordinary common for disposition. Upon an unauthorized transfer, the supervoting stock automatically converts into ordinary common.

14 This is the usual pattern. In some cases the limited voting class is entitled to a minimum percentage of directors.

class of common, the firm distributes the supervoting common, most frequently on a one-for-one ratio.

The distribution does not itself alter the relative voting power of public shareholders and the management bloc. Thus it differs from the exchange offer, where any public shareholder preference for the superior dividends of the ordinary common stock immediately shifts voting power to management. Nevertheless, the overall entrenchment effect is similar. As public shareholders begin to adjust their portfolios and dispose of stock, management's voting percentage will increase. Most importantly, the transfer restriction is protection against a hostile takeover. The possibility of a proxy battle by public shareholders may last longer in a distribution recapitalization because, unlike an exchange offer recapitalization, all public shareholders automatically receive supervoting shares. Given a substantial family–management bloc, however, this threat is limited. Moreover, as noted above, broadly written transfer restrictions may discourage the formation of a dissident shareholder group.

(3) Voting rights alterations. The third mechanism is not, strictly speaking, a recapitalization. Rather, shareholders must approve a charter amendment that simply alters the voting rights of the firm's outstanding common to give multiple votes (typically ten) to "long-term shares" while retaining one vote for "short-term shares." Long-term shares are those shares acquired before the amendment date and held continuously thereafter, or subsequently acquired shares, held continuously for a particular period, typically forty-eight months. Because all shares are of the same class, they participate equally in dividends. Shares are freely transferrable, but any transfer will divest them of their supervotes. A narrowly drawn exception is generally made for transfers to family members.

This voting rights alteration enhances the voting power of a management bloc even more powerfully than a distribution of supervoting shares. Any portfolio adjustment by a public shareholder – not just a decision to dispose of supervoting shares – reduces the voting power of public shareholders as a group. Like a direct transfer restriction, the voting rights alteration makes a hostile acquisition virtually impossible. Similarly, proxy battles by public shareholders, even long-term holders, may be chilled by the concern that formation of a dissident shareholder group would itself trigger the voting rights alteration.

B   Collective action and strategic choice problems

The effect of each of these recapitalization mechanisms on the balance of power between public shareholders and insiders is apparent. The proxy statements issued by the firms make relatively candid disclosures that the proposals will tend to entrench the management bloc and, in particular, will make a hostile takeover bid at a premium price very difficult. Despite this candor, these plans apparently have been adopted whenever proposed. Further scrutiny, however, reveals two sorts of problems – concerning collective action and strategic choice – that undermine the claim that shareholders approve these plans in the belief that they will produce an increase in shareholder wealth.

(1) Collective action problems. The reliability of shareholder voting as a decision mechanism for the public corporation has come under sharp attack on the grounds that widely dispersed shareholders face severe "collective action" problems in dealing with managers who control the proxy machinery. There are two main elements to the attack. First, shareholders are likely to be "rationally apathetic." The cost of informing oneself sufficiently to cast an intelligent vote on a management proposal frequently exceeds the expected payoff, even assuming one's vote will be determinative. Thus the shareholder compliantly returns the management proxy. Second, even where some shareholders have determined that a particular proposal will reduce shareholder wealth, "free rider" problems will discourage their organizing an opposition. Each shareholder may gain from opposition, but each will gain even more if other shareholders bear the costs. Because no compulsory cost-sharing mechanism exists in these circumstances and because no single shareholder can capture the whole gain to shareholders generally from the proposal's defeat, there will be insufficient incentive to organize opposition.[15] If a shareholder's stake is large and the expected negative impact is high, then her expected payoff from opposition may warrant some expenditure against the proposal, but not the optimum amount.

These collective action problems that pertain generally are exacerbated by the distribution of share ownership in the firms that have proposed dual class recapitalization. In a recent survey of recapitalizing NYSE firms, I found a significant family–management bloc, on average 30 percent (the median). In only one case was the family–management bloc smaller than 10 percent. In virtually all cases, the vote for recap-

---

15 These free-rider problems arise from two corporate law norms. First, the rules regarding reimbursement of proxy expenses, which could operate as a compulsory cost-sharing mechanism, permit reimbursement of insurgents only upon board action. A battle against a management proposal, even if successful, leaves in place the incumbent directors, who are unlikely to respond to a defeat (or a victory) with magnanimity. Second, the benefit of defeating the proposal flow equally to all shareholders on a per share basis. No opposing shareholder can capture disproportionate gains, except by buying more shares prior to the battle.

italization required by state law and the firm's charter was a simple majority of outstanding stock. Thus, in most cases, approval of the recapitalization required affirmative votes of less than a majority of the stock held by public shareholders. Moreover, only a handful of the surveyed firms reported significant stock ownership positions (blocs of 5 percent or more) held by particular institutions or by individuals not allied with the management group.

These conditions give rise to severe collective action problems. The only concentrated stock ownership is that of a family–management bloc; the remaining shares are widely dispersed. In light of the insiders' position, defeat of the proposal would require negative votes by a very large proportion of the public shareholders, so even significant public shareholder opposition has no effect on outcome. In these circumstances the payoff to public shareholders for informing themselves about the proposal will rarely be positive. Thus the typical public shareholder facing a proposal exhibits rational apathy and votes with management.

The pattern of share ownership heightens the free-rider problem in a number of ways. First, the size of the family–management bloc, and the resulting need to obtain a very high percentage of public shareholder votes, sharply reduces the probability of a successful battle and thus lowers the expected payoff. Second, the absence of public shareholders with large stakes has a number of consequences. Costs of opposition increase, because communicating with and coordinating actions among a dispersed group are more expensive than in a more concentrated group. Efforts to share costs are more difficult, because free-riding in large groups is harder to overcome than in small groups. It is less likely that a single shareholder would reasonably expect to benefit by an amount sufficient to cover the organizational costs of even less than the optimal amount of opposition. Thus, even if defeat of the proposal would increase public shareholder welfare, these free-rider problems make opposition unlikely.

The pattern of proposed recapitalizations – almost exclusively by firms with a significant family–management ownership bloc and without reportable institutional ownership – undercuts the asserted shareholder wealth maximization rationales. If such recapitalizations produce the most efficient contractual terms with respect to shareholder opportunism, to cite one rationale with at least surface plausibility, we would expect to see such proposals in firms where managers are most exposed – that is, where their ownership stake is smallest – not the reverse. As discussed above, the motivations for recapitalization by managers with large stock positions, such as protection of bargained-for perquisites, or compensation for firm-specific risk, are unlikely to be associated with increasing the wealth of public shareholders.

Moreover, if dual class recapitalizations increased shareholder wealth, we would not see the evident reluctance to make such proposals in firms with reportable institutional holdings. Institutions are presumably easier to persuade of the sophisticated arguments that support the wealth increase claim than would be dispersed, and perhaps unsophisticated, public shareholders. Institutions have a large enough stake and sufficient staff to take these complex arguments seriously. The pattern of recapitalization proposals suggests instead that firms are attempting to exploit the collective action problems of dispersed shareholders with measures they know would likely be rejected by institutional shareholders.

(2) Strategic choice problems. Management control of the structure and timing of a dual class recapitalization proposal permits strategic behavior vis-à-vis public shareholders. First, management can bundle the recapitalization with a "sweetener," an unrelated proposal that shareholders may independently desire. In addition, management can play "chicken" by credibly threatening to pursue less than optimum strategies for the firm if the recapitalization proposal is defeated. Finally, management can exploit defects in the regulatory process to increase the likelihood of approval. All of these elements enhance management's ability to obtain shareholder approval of measures that may reduce shareholder wealth.

(a) Sweeteners. Management can "sweeten" a proposal that decreases shareholder wealth by bundling it with an unrelated proposal that increases wealth. For example, many firms announce plans to increase cash payouts to shareholders if the recapitalization is adopted but not otherwise. These plans include substantially higher dividends and even open market repurchases of stock. Exchange offer recapitalizations offer the possibility of a dividend preference upon exchange for limited voting shares. Even if the recapitalization reduces shareholder wealth, these sweeteners produce offsetting gains for public shareholders. Where distributions are increased, the gain includes not only the cash payout but also the reduced agency costs associated with a reduction in free cash flow.[16]

Adding a sweetener to the recapitalization proposal complicates the

---

16 See M. Jensen, Agency Costs of Free Cash Flow, Corporate Finance, and Takeovers, *American Economic Review* 76: 323–9 (1986). Jensen defines "free cash flow" as cash flow "in excess of that required to fund all projects that have positive net present values when discounted at the relevant cost of capital." When a firm generates free cash flow, there is often a conflict between shareholder desire for payouts and management desires for growth, even if uneconomic, and for noneconomic consumption.

shareholder choice problem considerably and in the end distorts the choice in management's favor. First, as a matter of mechanics or law, nothing about a dual class recapitalization requires an increased cash payout or a dividend preference, or provides a financial reason to reconsider the firm's payout policy. Yet the increased payout is conditioned on approval of the recapitalization. If the recapitalization itself served shareholder interests, presumably a simple shareholder vote would suffice.

Second, public shareholders may find it difficult to value the sweetener. The value of increased dividends depends upon their expected duration and the likelihood of a further increase. But management is not obligated to continue a particular level of dividend payments. Within the bounds of fraud, its ultimate intentions are hidden at the time of the shareholder vote. After approval of the recapitalization proposal, management could presumably lower the dividend with impunity.

At this point an objection might be raised: Approval of a sweetened recapitalization proposal means only that management and public shareholders have engaged in a mutually beneficial trade that reflects a decision that the recapitalization package is mutually worthwhile, even assuming that the recapitalization alone would reduce shareholder wealth. This view of the transaction ignores the context. In particular, it ignores the impact of a significant insider bloc in a context in which only a simple majority vote is required and in which calculation is difficult.

Ordinarily when public shareholders evaluate a management proposal, there will be a distribution of predictions as to its effect. Shareholders may disagree on the effect, as to the amount and even as to whether it will be positive or negative; disagreement widens if calculation is difficult. If the median point of the distribution is negative – that is, if holders of a majority of shares believe that the proposal decreases shareholder welfare – then the proposal will be defeated even if a substantial number of shareholders "get it wrong." Insider control of a significant block of stock radically changes this scenario. In order to prevail in a simple majority vote regime, the insiders need to obtain the votes of only a minority of public shareholders. Thus even if the median belief of public shareholders is negative, the proposal is likely to pass. The addition of a sweetener to the recapitalization proposal makes a calculation of its effect on shareholder wealth more difficult. This increases the likelihood that a sufficiently large minority will believe the package is wealth increasing even if the median shareholder belief is otherwise. In this way, a sweetener operates less as a basis for a trade and more as a means for distorting shareholder choice.

(b) Strategic games. Management asserts in most cases that the dual class recapitalization proposal stems from a desire to issue equity to pursue profitable projects without diluting management's control. If the projects are pursued, public shareholders benefit, but so does management, because it has large holdings. Conversely, if the projects are not pursued, managers and public shareholders will lose. This set of outcomes makes recapitalization a variant of the game "chicken." In the stylized game two parties face each other on a collision course. If one party yields, the other party is better off, but if neither party yields, both are worse off.

In the recapitalization context, management can employ a combination of incentives, credible threats, and bluffs to increase its chances of winning the game. It may be that the value of the firm increases because of profitable projects pursued upon the issuance of limited voting common. Nevertheless, public shareholders may be worse off in comparison to a scenario in which the recapitalization had not been permitted. Thus even without strong collective action problems, approval of a recapitalization can be driven by strategic considerations that distort shareholder choice rather than by a collective judgment that approval is optimal for public shareholders.

This point can best be illustrated by an example of the game structure. Let us begin with the following assumptions:

1. Management holds a significant block of stock.
2. The firm has profitable investment projects (which may include acquisitions) for which financing is required.
3. The value of the firm will be maximized if the projects are financed by additional equity rather than by debt.
4. The firm's charter permits the issuance of additional single-class common.
5. Management consumption of perquisites will not increase if the recapitalization is approved.[17]
6. Management consumption of perquisites will be reduced if its control position is diluted.[18]

---

17 This is an assumption highly favorable to management. In effect, it provides that the recapitalization will not increase agency costs. This is unlikely, as I have argued strenuously above, both as a matter of theory and in light of the empirical evidence. The point of this example, however, is to demonstrate that management strategic behavior is a problem even when shareholder wealth is not necessarily reduced.

18 This might result when dilution of control would make management more vulnerable to a hostile takeover bid.

7. Recapitalization will lock management in control; i.e., it will assure management's ability to consume perquisites throughout the existence of the firm and will virtually eliminate possible gains to public shareholders from a hostile takeover bid.[19]

8. Disapproval of the recapitalization proposal will demonstrate public shareholder willingness and ability to oppose management; that is, it is effectively a "no confidence" motion. This will enhance the possibility of a proxy battle or a hostile takeover and thus is assumed to increase the wealth of public shareholders.

An illustration with particular numerical assumptions may be instructive, although it is possible to generalize the results more formally. Therefore let us make these further assumptions:

9. Management (M) owns 25 percent of the stock; the public shareholders (S) own 75 percent.

10. The value of the new investment projects to the existing shareholders (including management in its role as shareholder) is $100.

11. Management consumption of economic perquisites stemming from its control position (both before and after recapitalization) is valued at $15.[20]

12. The consequence of assured management control is identically valued by M and S at $10.

13. The consequence of a vote of no confidence is identically valued by M and S at $5.

The game is not a simultaneous game; rather, there are two sequential moves. First, the shareholders vote on the recapitalization. Then, management decides whether to issue equity: limited voting common if the proposal is approved, ordinary common if it is not.

The payoff structure is shown in Table 3.1. The explanation for this payoff structure is as follows:

Cell (1). Shareholders approve the recapitalization, and management issues new limited voting equity to finance new projects or an acquisition. This produces a $100 gain for the firm, which is allocated among public shareholders and managers in accordance with their stock ownership percentages; thus shareholders gain $75 and managers gain $25. The assurance of management control benefits managers by $10 and produces

19 A merger might occur with management approval, but side payments to managers would reduce shareholder gain.
20 This is consistent with assumption 5 above.

Table 3.1

	Public shareholders	
Management	Approve	Not approve
Issue equity	(1) 35/65	(2) 5/95
Not issue equity	(4) 5/ − 25	(3) − 10/ − 10

a $10 loss for public shareholders. The net result is that public shareholders gain $65 and management gains $35.[21]

Cell (2). Shareholders disapprove the recapitalization but management nonetheless issues equity (single class common) to finance new projects or an acquisition. This produces a $100 gain for the firm, which generates a $75 gain for the public shareholders and a $25 gain for the managers. The dilution of management's control position by the issuance of additional common stock eliminates its ability to consume perquisites. This results in a wealth transfer from managers to public shareholders. Public shareholders gain $15, and managers lose $15. The rejection of the proposal is a vote of no confidence, which increases the likelihood of a hostile takeover bid and results in a gain to public shareholders of $5 and a loss to managers of $5. The net result is that public shareholders gain $95 and management gains $5.[22]

Cell (3). Shareholders disapprove the recapitalization, and management does not issue equity to finance the investment. The value of the firm declines because future expected growth will be lower due to the need to finance investments with internally generated funds, or with debt, which is not optimal by hypothesis. We will assume that this produces a loss to the firm of $20. On the basis of allocation of share ownership, this results in a loss to public shareholders of $15 and a loss to management of $5. The rejection of the proposal is a vote of no confidence, which results in a gain to public shareholders of $5 and a

---

21 It would be easy to visualize a scenario in which the payoff to public shareholders in Cell (1) was negative. It need only be the case that the projects to be financed by new equity are relatively small, and that contrary to assumption 5, management consumption of perquisites and other agency costs will increase significantly.

22 The actual numbers are not crucial. To make the point it is necessary only that public shareholders are relatively better off in Cell (2) (disapproving, if management then issues single class equity) than in Cell (1) (approving, if management then issues limited-voting equity), and vice versa for managers.

loss to managers of $5. The net result is that public shareholders lose $10 and management loses $10.

Cell (4). Shareholders approve the recapitalization but management does not issue new equity. The value of the firm declines because of either the suggestion of management incompetence or deception of public shareholders in order to assure management control. If we assume this results in a loss to the firm of $20, public shareholders will lose $15 and managers, $5. The assurance of management control produces a gain to managers of $10 and a loss to public shareholders of $10. The net result is that public shareholders lose $25 and management gains $5.[23]

Assuming that all parties are rational, have identical beliefs as to the payoff structure, and are not subject to collective action problems, this game has a simple solution.[24] Shareholders will always disapprove the recapitalization proposal, because they realize that management does best by then issuing single class common (which has a payoff to management of $5) rather than by refusing to issue any equity (which has a payoff to management of −$10). Yet public shareholders invariably approve the recapitalization proposals. One reason apart from collective action problems is that management can take steps to change the payoff structure.

The most potent change is an attempt to eliminate Cell (2), issuance of ordinary common following shareholder disapproval. In that case, the best outcome for shareholders would be approval, Cell (1). Management can explicitly or implicitly threaten not to issue ordinary common. To make such a threat credible, management might make a hands-tying declaration in a liability-creating document. Several of the surveyed firms explicitly asserted in recapitalization proposal proxy statements that the dominant family groups valued control so highly that they would not permit dilution through the issuance of additional ordinary common, even for profitable investments. The threat gains force

---

23 Once again the actual numbers are less important than the magnitudes. Both managers and public shareholders are worse off in Cell (3), because profitable projects have been forgone. In terms of the classic formulation of Chicken – two teenagers headed toward one another in their cars – this is the cell where they crash. Public shareholders are worst off in Cell (4), because managers have used the ruse of potential projects to obtain assured control.

24 Management and public shareholders may have different beliefs about the payoff structure. For example, management may have much less faith that profitable projects exist and thus will assign a much lower value of its payoff in Cell (1), conceivably below its payoff in Cell (4). Adding asymmetric beliefs obviously would make the game very complex.

from *Mills* v. *Electric Auto-Lite Co.*,[25] in which the U.S. Supreme Court held that liability for misrepresentation in a proxy statement did not turn on damage to shareholders caused thereby. Thus a proxy violation could be found in such a case even if the firm *benefited* from management's subsequent issuance of ordinary equity.

The payoff structure described above assigns no value to the noneconomic perquisites of control. Yet management may value such perquisites highly, perhaps more than the potential gains from future investment projects. In the illustration above, if shareholders believe that management assigns a value of more than $15 to such perquisites, then the outcome of the game shifts dramatically. Shareholders will realize that upon disapproval of the proposal, management will choose not to issue equity, Cell (3).[26] In this case, the optimal shareholder strategy will be approval followed by management issue of new equity, Cell (1).[27] Management will promote this result by fostering the belief that it does indeed value noneconomic perquisites highly. Several of the surveyed firms made especially strong claims of this sort in proxy statements, for example: the importance of the legacy of the founder and his family, the obligation to protect the integrity of the news media, and the unique responsibilities of a charitable trust.

Note that both in the case of the threat not to issue ordinary common and in the case of noneconomic perquisites, management has powerful incentives to bluff. The bluff can succeed even if it does not convince most public shareholders in firms where management controls a substantial block of stock and only a simple majority is required for approval.

Another important factor bearing on the payoff structure is the effect of a no-confidence vote. Because the recapitalization proposal becomes a test of management's control, public shareholders know it will be costly for management to issue ordinary common (and thereby risk dilution) if the proposal is defeated. The no-confidence phenomenon makes approval more likely because it adds credibility to management's threat that it will not issue ordinary common if the proposal is disapproved. Management thus partially bootstraps its way to shareholder approval.

This can be illustrated in terms of the payoff structure. Let us assume that management places a value of more than $15 on noneconomic

---

25 396 U.S. 375 (1970).

26 This is because the management payoff in Cell (2) falls from +$5 to less than −$10 (gain of $5 minus loss of noneconomic perquisites that exceeds $15), and thus Cell (3) becomes more desirable to management than Cell (2); management will not issue the stock and will instead forgo the new projects.

27 This is true even if Cell (1) provided a negative payoff to public shareholders, as long as this payoff is a smaller loss than −10, the payoff in Cell (3).

perquisites of control. Then, if shareholders disapprove the recapitalization, the effect of the no-confidence vote (a $5 loss for management) will make the refusal to issue ordinary common, Cell (3), a better choice for management than an issuance, Cell (2). This follows because the Cell (2) management payoff will fall from $5 to less than − $10 because of the loss of noneconomic perquisites while the Cell (3) management payoff remains unchanged at − $10. Perceiving this, shareholders will vote to approve, leading to the inferior outcome for them of Cell (1). Thus, as throughout these strategic choice problems, management's ability to set the agenda and to affect the pay-off structure can radically alter the public shareholders' decisions.

(c) Supplementary approval requirements. A third important factor bearing on the shareholder choice problem is the whipsaw effect of supplementary approval requirements that attempt to address these issues. The best example is the rule proposed by the NYSE, which would have conditioned continued listing upon approval of a recapitalization by a majority of the public shareholders, which means that management's votes would not count.

The problem is that the NYSE rule would have supplemented, not supervened, state regulation in a way that would have only exacerbated the shareholder choice problem. In most cases, state law requires only a simple majority of outstanding shares to approve the charter amendment that triggers recapitalization. Management might announce that continuation of the firm's NYSE listing requires a special supermajority vote but that it will go forward with the recapitalization even if only a simple majority approves. If the public shareholder believes that simple majority approval is likely and that management is not bluffing, she faces a Hobson's choice: A vote *against* the recapitalization may further reduce her wealth by causing delisting. The strategy that minimizes loss is to vote for the recapitalization. Thus the supplementary NYSE requirement will increase the likelihood of *simple* majority approval, because the shareholder might have incorrectly calculated the likelihood of majority approval or failed to realize that management was bluffing. Moreover, this whipsaw effect reduces the value of a public shareholder vote as a reliable measure of support for the proposal. In these circumstances, a majority vote does not necessarily mean that public shareholders have been persuaded that the recapitalization is in their collective welfare.

(3) Post-approval collective action problems. Some might argue that even if collective action and strategic choice problems elicit approval of the recapitalization, the result is not necessarily to the detriment of individual shareholders. The issue is put most acutely in the case of an exchange offer recapitalization, in which shareholders may choose between supervoting shares and ordinary common shares with a 10 percent dividend differential. Even if a majority of shareholders can impose the recapitalization on dissenters, each shareholder independently chooses whether to exchange. Why doesn't the outcome of this choice simply reflect shareholder judgment about the value of the vote in a particular firm? Or, otherwise put, why isn't the shareholder choice a fair comparison of the possibility of increased agency costs and diminished takeover gains versus the discounted present value of an increased dividend stream?

The reason is that the public shareholder choice is not a free vote on wealth maximization but rather a game in which the dominant strategy will be to refuse the exchange. In other words, there is a free-rider problem: Each public shareholder would be better off if enough shareholders chose to exchange for supervoting stock to prevent management entrenchment. Each public shareholder individually, however, is even better off exchanging a vote for a dividend preference and letting other shareholders bear the burden of preventing management entrenchment. Given the absence of coordination among public shareholders, this problem predictably leads to a general refusal to exchange and thus to management entrenchment.

This argument can be usefully illustrated with another game matrix. Let the percentage of family–management shares equal x, all of which will be exchanged for supervoting shares in accordance with the intention expressed in the proxy statements. The percentage of remaining shares, the public shareholder shares, equals $100 - x$. Let us assume that the transfer restrictions on supervoting shares are unenforceable (i.e., a favorable assumption for shareholders). If the exchange by public shareholders (PE) equals or exceeds x (PE $\geq x$), public shareholders end up with a majority of votes and management is constrained. Agency costs will be no greater than before and the possibility of takeover gains will be no less. The game is presented by Table 3.2, where payoffs are changes in relative welfare.

Assuming that no single public shareholder believes that she can change the outcome and that public shareholders cannot coordinate their response, the game reveals that the dominant strategy is to refuse to exchange (Not E). If the individual shareholder believes that enough public shareholders will exchange such that management is constrained (PE $\geq x$), then she is better off refusing the exchange and taking the 10 percent dividend differential (Not E). This restates the free-rider

Table 3.2

Result of choices of other public shareholders	Public shareholder strategies	
	E	Not E
PE $\geq x$	0	10%
PE $< x$	<0	<10%

problem: Every public shareholder would be better off if management were constrained, but each would be best off if others bore the burden. On the other hand, if the individual shareholder believes that too few public shareholders will exchange (PE $< x$), she is again better off refusing the exchange (Not E). Increased agency costs and reduced takeover possibilities may reduce the value of her shares, but at least she receives a 10 percent dividend preference.

The model also points to other important factors. If the management bloc is greater than 50 percent prior to the exchange offer, then public shareholders can never hold more votes than management (i.e., PE $>$ x can never be satisfied) and public shareholders should always refuse the exchange. In that case, nothing can be gained by forgoing the dividend differential. If institutional holdings were significant, shareholder coordination might be possible; nevertheless, since public shareholders can always convert from supervoting common to ordinary common (but not the reverse), cheating would make an agreement very hard to sustain. Reversing the assumption that the limitation in transferability will be held void virtually precludes coordination agreements, since all will know that normal portfolio adjustment decisions will reduce the number of public supervoting shares (PE). Thus, even assuming some ability to coordinate, public shareholders will not delay receipt of the 10 percent dividend differential if management is likely to attain a majority within a short time.

It is also apparent that the 10 percent differential in no way corresponds to the actual decrease in public shareholder welfare, that is, to the "value of the vote." This should be no surprise. It would be an amazing coincidence if a *ten*fold increase in votes could be recompensed by a *10* percent reduction in dividends. It would be even more extraordinary were the compensatory amount identical across differently situated firms. The absence of any real economic rationale for the 10 percent differential confirms that it is merely a sweetener that triggers the dynamic described above. In other words, the differential is not primarily a compensatory measure designed to elicit public shareholder approval of the recapitalization proposal. Approval flows instead from the collective action and strategic choice problems described above. The differential is designed to elicit the choice of limited voting common.[28]

The model also provides some insight into the motivation of an exchange offer recapitalization, which imposes on management the cost of the dividend differential. The exchange offer provides greater speed and certainty to management's entrenchment. If public shareholders do not opt for the supervoting stock in the one-time exchange, management has an immediate voting majority. In addition to sure control, this allows management immediately to reduce its holdings in the firm in order to diversify. A reduction in firm-specific risk would at least partially compensate management for the dividend differential. By contrast, the special distribution and the voting rights alteration give management its majority only over time, as shareholders sell their positions. Although the firm is immediately safe from a tender offer because of the transferability restrictions, a proxy battle remains possible for a long period. Thus to assure control, management must retain its holdings during this period.

Perhaps more important, these two mechanisms would be undone by a judicial determination that restrictions on the transfer of common stock are unenforceable. By contrast, in an exchange offer recapitalization, most public shareholders will never have held supervoting shares, because of the game dynamic discussed above. Thus management retains its majority even if the transfer restriction is voided. Finally, the downside of an exchange offer for management, the dividend preference in favor of public shareholders, may be only a temporary cost. Once entrenched, management will have a freer hand to divert cash flow.

All of these factors, then, strongly suggest that approval of dual class recapitalization does not necessarily reflect the considered judgment of public shareholders that such an action serves their collective interests. Collective action and strategic choice problems could readily explain such approvals in many recent recapitalizations. In light of the inherent implausibility of dual class recapitalization as a device to increase shareholder welfare, the negative wealth effects suggested by the empirical evidence, and shareholder choice problems, the recent wave of recapitalizations appears abusive.

---

28 For an elaboration of the shareholder choice problem in an exchange offer, see R. Ruback, Coercive Dual-Class Exchange Offers, *Journal of Financial Economics* 20: 153–73 (1988).

III   Bonded nonrenegotiation rights

The previous section has presented some of the defects of shareholder voting as a means of expressing collective shareholder judgment. Opportunistic managers can exploit these defects to obtain approval of plans that may reduce or fail to maximize shareholder wealth. These problems, however, are foreseeable to a significant extent at the time a firm issues stock. At that time shareholders and managers may make mutually beneficial agreements concerning the possibilities of management opportunism. Shareholders may demand a premium, in the form of a discount on the stock price, for bearing the risk of certain forms of opportunism. To reduce this premium, management may accept certain constraints on its subsequent behavior. The supervisory authority of a board of directors elected by shareholders can be understood as one sort of constraint. An undertaking to maintain a capital structure with a single class of common can be understood as another.

The problem for the firm is this: Given the flaws of shareholder voting, how can the firm provide convincing assurances that specific constraints, such as single class common, will have continuing effect? In this context, the NYSE one share–one vote rule may be understood as a way of bonding the firm's promise to maintain the single class capital structure without renegotiation. The ultimate argument of this section is that, given present institutional arrangements, the NYSE rule continues to provide the most secure bond of that promise.[29]

A   Nonrenegotiation rights

Let us develop these arguments. Assume a family–management group has established a firm and is contemplating a public offering. If they create a dual class capital structure, in which the public can purchase only limited voting stock, the group would reasonably anticipate that investors will demand a discount on the stock price. A dual class ownership structure will ordinarily signal lower expected returns and higher risk. Expected returns will be lower, all other things being equal, because of management perquisites and other agency costs. Risks will be higher, all other things being equal, because a poorly performing management team will be more difficult to oust except through an internal coup.

---

29 The argument draws from O. Hart and B. Holmstrom, The Theory of Contracts, in T. Beatley, ed., *Advances in Economic Theory: Fifth World Congress* (1987); M. Jensen and W. Meckling, Theory of the Firm Managerial Behavior, Agency Costs, and Capital Structure, *Journal of Financial Economics* 3: 305–360 (1976).

Another way of characterizing the resulting discount in share price is to say that the firm's cost of capital will be higher. The costs associated with a dual class structure will undoubtedly vary depending on the particular firm, the firm's history, and its management.

As discussed in Section I, the family–management group that controls the firm at the time of the public offering may have various reasons to bear these costs rather than dilute its control. On the other hand, it may have different preferences. The increased cost of capital may limit the firm's ability to undertake investments it regards as desirable. The discount on the shares may be objectionable to family members who wish to cash out some of their holdings. A capital structure with only a single class of common stock will avoid these costs. The problem for both the firm and the prospective public shareholder is how to provide assurances that the firm will not undergo a welfare-reducing dual class recapitalization at some future time. In other words, unless public shareholders can be protected against an opportunistic dual class recapitalization in the future, they will demand a discount on the purchase of the firm's single class common in the present.

In this regard it is helpful to think of the firm's capital structure as part of a long-term contract between managers and shareholders. A recapitalization is a renegotiation of certain contractual terms. Where opportunistic renegotiation is possible, the parties to a long-term contract may be better off ex ante if they can agree that particular terms may not be renegotiated. This gives the exposed party what I call a nonrenegotiation right.[30]

B Bonding a nonrenegotiation right

On the argument thus far, a nonrenegotiation right with respect to a single class capital structure is desirable because it lowers the cost of capital to the firm. The problem is how to bond, or guarantee, such a right. A nonrenegotiation term that is itself subject to change or renegotiation does not have the desired effect. Thus, for example, a management declaration at the time of a public offering that it has no intention ever to propose a dual class recapitalization is not an effective bond: Intentions change. Four mechanisms of establishing a bond are worth considering in the recapitalization case: the firm's charter, state law, federal law, and a stock exchange rule. In present institutional

---

30 A nonrenegotiation right would eliminate many of the strategic choice problems in the game described in the previous section, for example, the no-confidence vote that tilts the payoff structure against the issuance of single class common.

circumstances, the only satisfactory bond is provided by the last mechanism, and then only if supported by a federal rule against migration.

(1) Corporate charters. The traditional means of setting forth the relationship between managers and shareholders is a firm's charter. Under state enabling regimes of corporate law, customized charters may be seen as permitting, but not requiring, managers and shareholders to bargain for provisions that will lower the firm's cost of capital. Charters, however, do not offer very secure bonds for such provisions. As a contract, a charter may be changed by mutual consent of the parties.[31] Even a provision barring the renegotiation of an element of the firm's capital structure can be renegotiated.[32] Under the corporate law of most states, including Delaware, charter amendments ordinarily require the approval of only a simple majority of the outstanding common shares, and dissenters have no appraisal rights.

Special charter provisions that require a supermajority vote for amendment are no solution to the bonding problem, however. A supermajority requirement that applies to all charter amendments must be relatively low, to avoid giving a veto to an obstreperous minority over many significant actions that might be taken by the firm. However, a low supermajority requirement (67%, for example) may not offer a sufficient check to management prerogative because of collective action and strategic choice problems.

Even a high supermajority requirement (90%, for example) targeted at a nonrenegotiation right regarding the firm's capital structure does not provide a secure bond. Strategic choice problems persist. More importantly, the firm can avoid this constraint by reorganizing, typically through a reorganization such as a holding company merger. In such a transaction shareholders receive shares of a firm with a new charter that can provide for dual class common. Yet it would be very unlikely that the charter would subject such a reorganization to a high supermajority requirement. Such transactions serve many useful corporate purposes, including, for example, the creation of a limited liability shield as the corporation expands into new lines of business. Allowing a small minority to veto such transactions creates the potential for costly holdup problems. On balance, such a provision is unlikely to improve share-

---

31 See, e.g., H. Henn and J. Alexander, *Laws of Corporations*, 3d ed. (1983), sec. 345.
32 Delaware law, for example, contemplates the possibility that a shareholder protective provision could be amended through normal means. The only exception is for a provision requiring a supermajority vote for certain transactions. In that case, an affirmative vote of the same supermajority is needed to amend the required percentage. Del. Code Ann. tit. 8, sec. 242 (b) (4) (1987).

holder welfare because the costs of an effective bond will outweigh its benefits. In light of the variety of possible corporate maneuvers,[33] charter provisions may be unable to produce a bond against a dual class recapitalization without costly substantial overbreadth.

(2) State law. If external constraint is necessary for a satisfactory bond, a possible source is state law. By incorporating in a state with a particular prescriptive rule, the firm could attempt to bond against opportunistic changes as to matters covered by the rule. The states, however, are not well suited to provide a bond against dual class recapitalizations. At present virtually all states permit dual class common stock,[34] and most states where large firms typically incorporate permit such recapitalizations. To those who would rely on a market in corporate law, this is not a problem. If the NYSE single class common rule has significant value, upon its abandonment by the NYSE, some state will adopt it to attract incorporations.

Several difficulties attend such an argument, however. First, since the goal is not to prohibit dual class common altogether, but to bond a nonrenegotiation right, the rule of a single legal regime may be an inherently unsatisfactory tool. More simply, if the state prohibits dual class common, then many corporations that use such a capital structure in a legitimate way will incorporate elsewhere. If the state does not prohibit this capital structure, then the possibility of corporate maneuvers, such as the holding company reorganization discussed above, will significantly reduce the security of the bond. More generally, this suggests that the interests of flexibility and certainty – separately desirable but often incompatible – are best served through multiple levels of legal regimes. This point is developed more fully below.

A second problem is that a corporation can avoid the effect of a particular state's law simply by reincorporating in a state without the restriction. Such a reincorporation can be effected through a holding company merger, in which the holding company is incorporated in the new state. A statute that attempts the problematic distinction between "legitimate" recapitalizations and dual class recapitalizations would be ineffective against interstate evasion. This is because the Commerce Clause is likely to forbid state restrictions on the ability of a firm to

---

33 The history of corporate law is filled with examples of corporate maneuvers that eliminate apparent contract claims, much to the surprise of common shareholders, preferred shareholders, and bondholders. See note 9, Gordon, p. 63 n. 191.

34 A few state statutes and constitutions restrict the use of nonvoting stock, see note 31, Henn and Alexander, sec. 189, n. 33, but would not apply to the recapitalization plans here, which use limited voting stock.

migrate to another state.[35] In other words, a state law regime is an inadequate bond because the firm can simply slip away from its constraints.

(3) Federal law. The reflexive response to the interstate migration problem is a federal rule. Although a federal rule on dual class common would bond against the firm's ability to shift jurisdictions, ultimately it may not solve the problem. As with the rule of a particular state, a federal rule faces the problems of flexibility and certainty. A federal rule that banned dual class common would surely bond against such recapitalizations, but only by denying dual class structures to those firms in which it is mutually advantageous to management and shareholders. If the goal is only to bond a nonrenegotiation right, such a rule is clearly overbroad. A more narrowly tailored federal rule that barred "illegitimate" recapitalizations, however, would have severe design and application difficulties that would reduce its effectiveness as a bond.

(4) Stock exchange rule. We now are in a position to understand the virtues of a stock exchange rule on the dual class common issue, and in particular, of the NYSE single class common rule. The existence of a stock exchange rule that prohibits dual class common stock will permit, but does not require, a firm to select a legal regime, an external rule, that bars recapitalization. The availability of multiple levels of legal regimes allows the firm to decide, first, if it wants dual class common, immediately or as an option, and second, whether it is prepared to bond its choice of single class common against a subsequent renegotiation. This serves the interests of flexibility, in that different firms can organize in different ways, and certainty, in that a particular firm can opt for a legal regime with an absolute prohibition and thus a secure bond.

The virtues of the NYSE rule are conditional, of course, on the inability of firms to migrate to exchanges with less strict rules. Otherwise the NYSE rule will have no more effect than the law of a particular state. Until recently, marketplace forces made such migration highly

---

35 The statement in the text could have been offered with greater assurance before the recent Supreme Court case of *CTS Corp.* v. *Dynamics Corp. of America,* 107 S. Ct. 1637 (1987), which sustained an Indiana antitakeover statute. But even after *CTS,* a state's ban on interstate corporate migration seems unlikely to prevail. The key factor for the *CTS* court was that the Indiana statute, which set the conditions on which an acquirer of a large bloc of the corporation's stock could vote those shares, was simply state regulation of a corporation's "internal affairs." A state statute that prohibits any transaction, such as a merger or a sale of assets that has the effect of moving the corporation's state of incorporation, is more blatant economic protectionism.

unlikely. As noted above, an NYSE listing once provided unique liquidity and reputational benefits. Sacrificing these benefits entailed very significant costs for the firm, both in terms of subsequent efforts to raise capital and in the loss of the pecuniary and nonpecuniary rewards of being an NYSE firm. These costs, borne by management both as shareholders and as beneficiaries of the firm's prestige, were sufficiently great to bond the firm's choice of the NYSE corporate governance requirements and, in particular, the rule against dual class common. Indeed, the costs to shareholders of delisting were thought so great as to provide a basis for judicial intervention against action that put the NYSE listing at risk.[36]

The success of NASDAQ's National Market System (NMS) has obviously changed this situation. The costs of losing an NYSE listing have diminished to the point that they are no longer sufficient to bond the choice of single class common. This allows managers to behave opportunistically with regard to public shareholders. The importance of the SEC's backstop for the NYSE rule therefore becomes clear. Market forces have eroded the ability of any exchange to bond a nonrenegotiation right against dual class common. Yet such a bond previously existed and presumably had value. An SEC rule that barred the listing by the Amex or the NASD of a firm delisted by the NYSE because of a dual class recapitalization would simply provide a different mechanism for a bond that previously existed. Put otherwise, a federal rule aimed at migration between exchanges is one effective way that a firm could be given both the opportunity to choose its capital structure and the ability to bond its promise to maintain single class common stock.

C   Stock exchange competition and shareholder welfare

The claim thus far has been that a secure bond for a nonrenegotiation right as to dual class common has value to a firm because the bond can lower the firm's cost of capital. A change in the NYSE rule would thus have three negative effects on public shareholder wealth. First, shareholders of NYSE firms would bear a greater risk of opportunistic recapitalizations by management. They paid for security, and now it is gone. Second, shareholders of those NYSE firms would lose because the inability to bond the firm's capital structure makes subsequent trips to the public equity markets more costly. Third, and perhaps most seriously, founders and shareholders of new enterprises face an in-

---

36 See, e.g., *Norlin Corp.* v. *Rooney, Pace Inc.*, 744 F.2d 255, 267–9 (2d Cir. 1984) (citing cases).

creased cost of capital. Even before listing on the NYSE, such firms could hold themselves out as on a trajectory that would lead them quickly to the NYSE, and thus offer a "bridge" bond against recapitalization. The first effect is arguably only a wealth transfer between shareholders and managers. The latter two consequences would have negative GNP effects: As the cost of capital increases, marginal projects will not be funded.

These negative effects would be difficult to demonstrate by the empirical evidence that financial economists commonly examine. The first shareholder wealth effect probably could not be tied to any specific event, since the possibility of a change in the NYSE rule and its implications have emerged over an extended period of time. Nor are conventional econometric methods well suited to discern systematic effects, effects that cut across almost all firms. The second shareholder wealth effect (and perhaps the third) could conceivably be discerned by comparing the cost of equity capital for NYSE firms and new ventures well before intimations of the possibility of the rule changes and the costs that prevail currently. Unfortunately, such effects are likely to be swamped by much more basic economic factors – interest rates, inflationary expectations, etc. One possible test might compare the cost of equity capital for NYSE, Amex, and NASDAQ–NMS firms before and after the possibility of rule changes arose. A relative increase in the cost of capital for NYSE firms would arguably demonstrate the wealth effect suggested here.

A critic of these ideas about bonded nonrenegotiation rights would respond that there already is a test, a market test, that demonstrates that the alleged bond has minimal value. Exchanges, it is said, will compete in the offering of transaction and other services that investors demand:

Exchanges do not compete for listings per se, but rather seek to maximize the volume of trade, which is a function of the number of listings and the amount of trading in listed securities. . . . If an exchange allows managers of some firms to exploit investors, investors will lose confidence in the exchange, as a whole, causing *all* firms on the exchange to face higher costs of capital. This in turn will decrease the amount of listings in the future and thus also will reduce the amount of trade.[37]

In effect, we have a repetition of the "race to the top" argument, applied here to exchanges rather than states; that is, that the optimal

37 Fischel, *Organized Exchanges and the Regulation of Dual Class Common Stock* (March 1985) p. 12; revised version, *University of Chicago Law Review* 54: 119–52 (1987), pp. 127–30.

rule of law will emerge from competition. Whatever the validity of the argument in the state competition context, it has no validity for exchanges. There are too few national exchanges – three – for effective competition and the barriers to entry are simply too high to make potential competition a real threat. Moreover, the argument fails to address the fact that migration among exchanges makes it simply impossible for any exchange to offer a secure bond.

There is a further reason to believe that abandonment of the NYSE rule is not the happy result of a race to the top. Let us assume that the NYSE holds fast to its rule against dual class common and that the SEC does not forbid migration. We can then assume further that some firms will migrate to other exchanges for recapitalizations, because managers prefer secure jobs to the lowest cost of capital. The decrease in listings is bound to hurt the NYSE, if only because of the loss in listing fees and the lost commissions to members. The NYSE may also believe that a significant loss of listings over time will undermine its position in the center of the securities markets. It is not credible that investors will refuse to trade in the securities of firms whose managements behaved opportunistically, or on the exchanges that harbor such malefactors. The price may be lower, but the volume will be the same, and this volume will be lost to the NYSE.

Now let us assume that the NYSE abandons its dual class common prohibition. Presumably no firm would leave the NYSE. Firms that wish to pursue recapitalizations would have no need to do so. But firms that prefer a bonded, nonrenegotiation right as to a single class capital structure would have no choice but to remain. The expense of starting an exchange makes such an alternative quite unlikely. More importantly, even a new exchange could not offer the bond, because of the ever-present possibility that firms would simply return to the NYSE. The point is that, at least in the exchange context, in the absence of a marketplace or rule-based barrier to migration, the competition seems to push toward the bottom.

IV   Policy responses

A   Nonuniform rules

The previous section has explained the evolution and current function of the NYSE one share–one vote rule as a bond of a promise by firms to maintain single class capital structures. Two policy responses to the argument above are apparent. The first is a rule that permits nonuniform standards across exchanges but protects one exchange's continued capacity to bond the single class promise. The second establishes uniform voting rights standards across all exchanges.

Thus one response to the current problem is a federal rule, presumably authored by the SEC, that permits the NYSE to continue to offer such a bond. This rule should restrict the capacity of firms to migrate among exchanges. In particular, this minimal rule should require the Amex and the NASD to adopt rules to prohibit the listing of any firm that has been delisted by the NYSE, voluntarily or involuntarily, because of a dual class common recapitalization.[38]

A minimum proposal should also include an exception for dual class recapitalizations in the case of certain arm's-length mergers that present little reason for concern. These are mergers in which the limited voting common pays dividends that are substantially linked to the performance of assets acquired in the merger, and where the equity represented by all limited voting stock issued by the firm does not represent more than 25 percent of the firm's total equity (as measured by market value). In this limited case, the NYSE should be permitted to list all classes of the firm's stock.[39]

B   Uniform rules

The recently proposed SEC Rule 19c-4 would require the NYSE, Amex, and NASD to bar the continued listing of any firm that "issues securities or takes other corporate action that would have the effect of nullifying, restricting or disparately reducing the voting rights" of holders of the firm's common stock.[40] The rule, according to the SEC's gloss, would not allow any of the three dual class recapitalization mechanisms that have been recently employed. On the other hand, the rule would permit a firm to recapitalize by issuing limited voting stock on initial public offering, on the grounds that willing purchasers will buy with knowledge of the limitations while present shareholders will not be disenfranchised.

This is obviously a uniform federal rule that purports to distinguish between "good" and "bad" recapitalizations. As argued above, such a rule will inevitably face problems of design and application. In the accompanying release, the SEC begins a process of exegesis, elaboration,

---

38 More technically, the rule should prohibit the NASD from authorizing trading of the firm's stock on the NASDAQ National Market System. Only NASDAQ's National Market System offers sufficient over-the-counter liquidity to compete with the NYSE or Amex.

39 For a detailed justification of this limited exception for arm's-length mergers, and the 25% cap, see note 9, Gordon, pp. 71–72.

40 See note 4, Exchange Release No. 24,623, 52 Fed. Reg. 23,665.

and loophole-plugging that will undoubtedly continue if the rule is adopted. Although the exchanges presumably are responsible for applying the rule in first instance, the competition for listings will generate erosive pressure, the "'disintegrating' erosion' of particular exceptions."[41] The SEC should anticipate long-term involvement in the production of no-action letters if it wishes to protect the policy behind the rule. But the need for regulatory vigilance is simply a cost, not necessarily a dispositive objection.

Proposed Rule 19c-4 applies both to exchanges that had no prior one share–one vote policy and to the NYSE, which did. Thus consideration of its merits divides into two branches.

(1) Application to NYSE firms. As to "abusive" recapitalizations of NYSE firms, in which present shareholders suffer a diminution in voting rights, Proposed Rule 19c-4 is consistent with the bonding theory developed in this article. The proposed rule sustains the bond provided by the NYSE against such management opportunism by subjecting the firm to an identical rule on any other exchange. The firm gains nothing from migration. On the other hand, the bond is not complete, because the SEC rule would permit the firm to issue limited voting stock in initial public offerings.

The SEC's justification for permitting limited voting IPO's is that new purchasers are not harmed because they get what they pay for. The bonding perspective leads us to ask, Is there harm to current public shareholders? I want to suggest that there may be harm and that therefore the capacity of the NYSE to bond against any deviation from a single class structure has value. The principal focus of the proposed Rule 19c-4 has been on the dilution of voting participation; the proposal is aimed directly at that problem. But the proposed rule does not address another harm to public shareholders from the issuance of limited voting common – the costly dilution of economic participation. This harm follows from the market's insistence on compensation for the additional risk associated with the inferior status of limited voting common. Such stock couples a residual economic claim with a limited governance role. This means vulnerability to opportunistic behavior by the regular voting common shareholders, especially in recapitalizations and in sales of control. Presumably purchasers of such stock will demand compensation for such risk in the form of higher expected returns, either through a dividend preference or a discount, that is, a lower price for an equivalent participation in expected returns.

41 *Meinhard* v. *Salmon*, 249 N.Y. 458, 464, 164 N.E. 545, 546 (1928) (Cardozo, J.).

In other words, to raise a given amount of capital the firm will have to sell a larger number of limited voting common shares than ordinary common or give limited voting common greater than pro-rata dividends. But there is no reason to think that the costs of this economic dilution will fall equally on the inside and the public shareholders of the firm. Indeed, one can predict that the insiders will use this financing tool only where the increased value of control, through diversion of cash flow and otherwise, exceeds the costs of economic dilution of their stock. But public shareholders receive no such compensation for their economic dilution costs. In short, where insiders control the firm, it seems likely that they will attempt to recoup the dilution costs of issuing limited voting common at the expense of public shareholders.[42]

A firm that is making a single class common IPO may wish to assure prospective purchasers against the possibility of this scenario. Eliminating such risk will lower the cost of capital. The consequence, however, of Proposed Rule 19c-4, in light of the competition for listings, is likely to be the end of a securely bonded single class common promise. The SEC's efforts to create a uniform standard will make it impossible for any exchange to maintain a one share–one vote standard, even though an exchange might desire to do so and even though this standard may serve shareholder interests.

The nub of the problem is the ability of firms to migrate among exchanges in search of the least restrictive corporate governance standards. Ideally we would like to bar both the most abusive recapitalizations for all firms, which Proposed Rule 19c-4 should accomplish, while at the same time making it possible for a particular exchange to maintain a more stringent rule. Proposed Rule 19c-4 sets a floor. We need a way to avoid its becoming a ceiling as well.

The general approach I recommend is an addition to Proposed Rule 19c-4 that would prohibit a firm that switches its listing from adopting a capital structure that is prohibited by the exchange it is leaving. More

42 An objection to this argument is the possible implications for the firm's issuance of preferred stock and debt: How are those nonvoting securities different from limited-voting common stock? There are several answers. First, debt and preferred stock to a lesser degree have fixed contractual claims on firm cash flows, not residual claims, and are less risky. The greater safety of these securities is reflected in a lower rate of expected return. Thus, contrary to limited voting common, preferred stock and debt should not be a higher cost way of raising capital for the firm, i.e., there will not be economic dilution costs for the insiders to shift onto existing public shareholders. Second, existing outsiders will benefit from the way that financial and operational covenants in senior securities reduce agency costs. The potential loss of control brings pressure on management with respect to its diversion of firm cash flows.

technically, the rule would prohibit an exchange (or the NASD for the NASDAQ–NMS) from listing a firm that does so. This addition could be tailored to focus on capital structure elements that bear specifically on shareholder voting, or could be made subject to a time period. Observe that such an approach would not mandate one share–one vote but would merely permit the NYSE to maintain a rule it desires to maintain.

(2) Application to Amex and NASD firms. Application of Proposed Rule 19c-4 to the Amex and the NASD may trouble born-again contractarians. From the ex ante perspective, shareholders of such firms could foresee at the time of their purchase the possibility of a dual class recapitalization, the possibilities of collective action and strategic choice problems, and the resulting possibility that some recapitalizations might result from management opportunism. Nevertheless, the terms agreed upon between managers and shareholders did not include any promise or any bond to maintain a single class structure. Thus the proposed rule is an ex post adjustment that ignores the parties' earlier optimal bargain.

The questions raised by such arguments, first, how much could the parties possibly have foreseen, and, second, what is the appropriate background rule where foresight is limited and information asymmetries may favor managers: Is it caveat shareholder or caveat manager? The variables bearing on an opportunistic recapitalization may be very hard to predict when the firm's stock is first offered. Collective action problems are a function of the distribution of the firm's stock. Public shareholders are unlikely to have any reliable projection of whether the management bloc will remain stable and cohesive or the extent of future institutional ownership. Nor is any projection about the range of strategic carrots and sticks available to management at any given time likely to be close to the mark. Moreover, from the shareholder perspective, one could argue that the likelihood of a regulatory response to opportunistic recapitalizations was also part of the parties' ex ante bargain. In these circumstances, it would be consistent with contractual norms to require managers, as the drafters of the contract with shareholders, to bear the burden of uncertainty.

The more important issue, however, is whether caveat manager is a more efficient rule than caveat shareholder. Caveat manager has this to recommend it: It will discourage investment in ingenious methods of cheating and will thus reduce a systematic risk of investment.

All of this argues in favor of the application of the SEC proposal to the Amex and the NASD. The collective action problems are severe; the likelihood of negative shareholder wealth effects is substantial. Intervention to bar abusive recapitalizations therefore seems appropriate. On the other hand, there seems to be little basis to argue that shareholders in such firms should also be entitled to protection against the IPO issuances of limited voting stock.

In sum, if Proposed Rule 19c-4 is the basis for addressing the dual class recapitalization problem, it should be modified to prohibit a firm from migrating among exchanges in search of the most permissive rule. This modification solves a number of problems. It permits, but does not require, the NYSE to maintain its single class common rule and thus its bond. It will set in motion an experiment with limited voting common by Amex and NASDAQ firms. The experiment will answer a number of important questions: How difficult is it to administer a rule that attempts to distinguish between "good" and "bad" issuances of limited voting common? Is limited voting stock, stripped of managerial entrenchment effects, a useful financing tool? Will Rule 19c-4 serve only as an invitation to investment bankers and corporate lawyers to devise entrenchment schemes that thread the rule? Such an experiment will provide additional data and time for a consensus to emerge without risking a major alteration in the governance structure of the most significant firms.[43]

Conclusion

It is tempting at this point to refer the reader to the introduction and say, "I have done what I set out to do" and end. But a few things further should be said. First, this article is based on what some may regard as a narrow assumption – the importance of the shareholder wealth-maximization criterion. This is not because I think that value exhausts the field in the regulation of large publicly held corporations, but because I think it is the value with which there is greatest agreement. If a set of transactions does not maximize shareholder wealth, this is cause for greatest suspicion.

But one may be troubled by a gathering wave of dual class recapitalizations out of legitimacy concerns as well. The formal unbundling of corporate governance from residual economic participation claims may create the fact or appearance of a selfperpetuating managerial elite wielding unaccountable authority over tremendous economic resources. Legitimacy concerns, of course, have their instrumental side. For ex-

43 The SEC proposal owes much to the analysis developed in R. Gilson, Evaluating Dual Class Common Stock: The Relevance of Substitutes, *Virginia Law Review* 73: 807–44 (1987). For a critique of that analysis, see note 9, Gordon, pp. 77–8 n. 224.

ample, a populist backlash, such as that triggered by the first appearance of dual class common stock in large public firms in the 1920s, could conceivably lead to enormous reductions in managerial authority. In another example, courts could alter the business judgment rule if managers are no longer perceived as accountable to shareholders. In this sense, firms' forbearance with regard to dual class common may be seen as a kind of public good that the NYSE rule supports. But I believe the legitimacy point has normative weight. Even if "shareholder democracy" is more illusory than real, the notion that high corporate office is earned and retained on the sufferance of marketplace scrutiny is a comforting one. We need no corporate princes here.

CHAPTER 4

Property rights in assets and resistance to tender offers

David D. Haddock, Jonathan R. Macey, and
Fred S. McChesney

The recent spate of highly publicized hostile tender offers has prompted questions about the proper reaction of target firm management to takeover bids. Traditionally, the law has not constrained management's ability to resist acquisition. To the contrary, courts recognize not just "a large reservoir of authority" in management to respond to takeover bids, but "an obligation to determine whether the offer is in the best interests of the corporation and its shareholders," and to resist if it is not.[1]

Particularly since the publication of an important article on the issue by Frank Easterbrook and Daniel Fischel,[2] however, the wisdom of allowing managerial resistance has been challenged. All else being equal, resistance by any target firm reduces the bidder's net expected returns. Consequently, it is argued, other potential targets would face a greater likelihood of an advantageous takeover, and all firms would receive greater monitoring, if resistance were impermissible.[3] In addition, it is

We received valuable comments from Henry Butler, William Carney, Louis De Alessi. Frank Easterbrook, Daniel Fischel, David Friedman, Charles Goetz, Clifford Holderness, Roger Meiners, Richard Posner. David Schap, and Alan Schwartz; from the participants in presentations made at the University of Chicago, Cornell University, and Emory University; and from participants in presentations made at the 1986 Western Economic Association meetings and the Conference on the Economics of Corporate and Capital Markets Law at Harvard University.

An expanded version of this chapter appeared in the *Virginia Law Review* 73:701–42; We would like to thank the *Review* for permission to reprint.

1 *Unocal Corp.* v. *Mesa Petroleum Co.,* 493 A.2d 946, 953–54 (Del. 1985).
2 F. Easterbrook and D. Fischel, The Proper Role of a Target's Management in Responding to a Tender Offer, *Harvard Law Review* 94:1161 (1981) [hereinafter Proper Role]. For elaboration of the basic model see F. Easterbrook and D. Fischel, Auctions and Sunk Costs in Tender Offers, *Stanford Law Review* 35:1 (1982) [hereinafter Auctions].
3 See note 2, Proper Role, pp. 1176–7.

urged, managers could not be trusted to seek a proper level of monitoring even if it were attainable, as agency problems are apparently insurmountable when managers' jobs are on the line.[4] The Easterbrook–Fischel school therefore would ban managerial resistance to tender offers.

The opposition to managerial resistance is troubling. In the paradigm market, sellers (or their agents) are permitted to reject initial offers and bargain for higher ones. Sellers cannot bargain if they cannot reject an offer. The no-bargaining proposal for shares thus raises fundamental economic issues of considerable significance outside the corporate sphere. Resolution of these issues requires a more general understanding of the functions of property and of bargaining rights for assets traded in "thin" markets. Such an understanding is the objective of this article.

Section I shows that the market for corporate control is similar to other markets where bargaining – resistance – is the norm. In such markets, important benefits arise from allowing asset owners (including corporate shareholders) to bargain freely. Bargaining garners for sellers a greater share of the gains from exchange, and thus enhances owners' initial incentives to make value-maximizing investments in an asset.

The logical structure of Section I can be summarized point by point:

1. The ability to bargain is tantamount to the right to resist relinquishing an entitlement.
2. The expected strength of future bargaining rights affects the magnitude of the present investment one is prepared to make to enhance the value of an entitlement, with stronger bargaining rights implying greater willingness to invest.
3. Bargaining over an exchange of entitlements is symmetrical, so that strengthening the bargaining position of one party (here, bidders) simultaneously weakens the bargaining position of the other party (targets).
4. Hence, the proposed no-resistance rule might indeed augment investments in search by prospective bidders, but it would do so at a cost – it would simultaneously retard investments by prospective targets.

Ordinarily, one does not expect that owners of property rights will benefit if those rights are weakened. For a weakening of rights to benefit the owner, there must exist some market failure that cannot be overcome by voluntary contract. It is alleged that bargaining creates just such a failure in the market for corporate control. Targets' resistance to take-

4 Ibid., p. 1175.

over bids, it is claimed, imposes external costs on other firms because those other firms receive less monitoring from bidders.[5]

Section II points out that external effects are ubiquitous, but that only a subset of these effects merits legal intervention. Several additional theoretical and empirical criteria must first be satisfied, before intervention is warranted.[6] Yet, in the present debate about tender offer resistance, few of these criteria have been recognized or empirically investigated. The conditions necessary to justify intervention to eliminate an externality are stringent.

If the argument through Section II is accepted, then the wisdom of the Easterbrook and Fischel proposal is seen to hinge on several uninvestigated premises. Of particular interest would be a comparison between the two effects a no-resistance rule might have: increased bidder search, and decreased investment in targets. Because the gain from increased search need not exceed the loss from decreased target investment, the reserved judicial response that has greeted the no-resistance proposal is in fact appropriate.

Section III focuses on one of the conditions necessary to justify intervening against an externality, the requirement that the costs of private internalization exceed the costs of public intervention. We point out the following:

1. Mechanisms exist that permit an individual target to alter its own bargaining rules implicitly, thus achieving the level of monitoring desired.
2. Targets have an incentive to make such alterations as long as increased bidder investments add greater value than the value of target investments lost.
3. And, consequently, the cost to a firm of achieving the level of monitoring it desires (i.e., of avoiding any externality from other firms' resistance) seems modest.

When these private contract costs are contrasted with the costs of a mandatory no-resistance rule, therefore, such a rule appears inadvisable.

Section IV considers the agency cost objection to permitting resistance to tender offers. Initial entrepreneurs going public maximize their personal gains by maximizing the *net* present value of the firm, i.e., by considering both the costs and the benefits of various control techniques available to the public firm, including use of managerial agents. An agency "problem" would seem to exist in corporate control matters if

---

5 Ibid., pp. 1176–7.
6 See J. Buchanan and W. C. Stubblebine, Externality, *Economica* 29:371 (1962).

analysts focus solely on the cost side. But the use of agents, even in the context of corporate control, has its benefits. The proper response to agency costs is not to eradicate them; that can be done only by eliminating the use (and thus the benefits) of agents. The appropriate response is to structure agency contracts optimally, so as to maximize the benefits net of costs.

The chapter concludes, in Section V, by noting that new law may indeed be called for, though not that proposed by Easterbrook and Fischel. Instead, new law may be desirable to enhance the ability of private parties to internalize the effects of any relevant externalities in the market for corporate control. The distinction between this proposal and that of Easterbrook and Fischel is the distinction between expanded choice and compulsion.

I   Bargaining and property rights in assets

Bargaining over the price of assets is a familiar prelude to exchange. For example, in a real estate transaction, a seller could state a price as part of the contract with his selling agent that the seller would then be bound to accept. The seller, however, prefers to list a selling price higher than the one he would in fact insist upon, and then to haggle with potential buyers over the actual transaction price. Rules that allow negotiation have evolved for art, real estate, and other assets. These rules are protected by law; a prospective buyer may not automatically obtain such assets simply by bidding first or even highest. The owner may rightfully refuse to sell.

In other words, owners of assets typically are protected by property rules rather than liability rules.[7] Contractual rules that countenance

---

7 G. Calabresi and A. D. Melamed, Property Rules, Liability Rules, and Inalienability: One View of the Cathedral, *Harvard Law Review* 85:1089 (1972), p. 1092. "An entitlement is protected by a property rule to the extent that someone who wishes to remove the entitlement from the holder must buy it from him in a voluntary transaction in which the value of the entitlement is agreed upon by the seller."

Once bargaining is abandoned, however, the state must intrude into the valuation process. As Calabresi and Melamed note, "Whenever someone may destroy the initial entitlement if he is willing to pay an objectively determined values for it, an entitlement is protected by a liability rule. This value may be what is thought the original holder of the entitlement would have sold it for. But the holder's complaint that he would have demanded more will not avail him once the objectively determined value is set. Obviously, liability rules involve an additional stage of state intervention: not only are entitlements protected, but their transfer or destruction is allowed on the basis of a value determined by some organ of the state rather than by the parties themselves" (p. 1092).   [*Continued*]

bargaining are found in almost all markets involving nonfungible goods or services. This raises a point of more general economic significance. Where markets are "thin" (i.e., where the number of potential purchasers is small and there is no preexisting market price at which reasonable quantities of the asset can be purchased), parties to any exchange typically bargain as bilateral monopolists to establish the price. Bargaining is costly, yet it dominates other rules for exchange in thin markets. Why, then, is bargaining the rule in virtually every thin market?

A   *The role of bargaining in a theory of property rights*

Thick markets are characterized by frequent transactions of nearly homogeneous units. At any moment there is a "standard price quotation" for each of the traded items, which saves transaction costs. But items transacted in thin markets are not divisible or numerous enough to ensure that everyone values them equally at the margin. Because different persons value an item differently, they bargain whenever they attempt to trade.

It is possible to transact in thin markets without bargaining. If bargaining costs are high relative to the costs of other procedures for exchanging entitlements, an efficient legal system will dispense with property protection of entitlements, which endows traders with the bilateral vetoes necessary for bargaining to occur. Instead, transactions will be governed by liability protections, which enable one party to take an entitlement unilaterally. Compensation will be determined "objectively," or at least through a process not under the control of either party.[8] Ordinarily, liability remedies merely make whole the first party to lose his entitlement, meaning that all gains from trade go to the taker.[9]

Although shareholders may refuse the tender offer, and consequently seem to have property protection for their shares, by using a two-tiered bid the bidder can create a prisoner's dilemma among shareholders. This makes it desirable individually for shareholders to tender at the price unilaterally selected by the bidder, even though the shareholders would all be better off if none tendered and the bidder were forced to bargain with the shareholders' agent, usually the firm's management. See J. Macey and F. McChesney, A Theoretical Analysis of Corporate Greenmail, *Yale Law Journal* 95:13 (1985), pp. 19–27. So if defensive tactics are impermissible, the prisoner's dilemma enables the bidder to convert property protection into liability protection.

8 See note 7. Calabresi and Melamed, pp. 1106–07.
9 See, e.g., D. Haddock, F. McChesney, and M. Spiegel, "An Ordinary Economic Rationale for Extraordinary Legal Sanctions" forthcoming in *California Law Review* 78 (1990); D. Haddock and M. Spiegel, Property Rules, Liability Rules, and Inalienability: One View of the Edgeworth Box, *Proceedings of the European Association of*

By bargaining, each party tries to maximize his share of the gains
from trade, net of bargaining costs. Bargaining consumes resources, and
would be socially inefficient if it accomplished nothing but this short-
run division of gains from any given trade. But in two distinct ways,
bargaining is productive in the long run because it increases the magnitude of the gains to be partitioned. First, it assures that the traded
items are worth more in other hands (i.e., that gains from trade exist).
Liability rules cannot ensure the Pareto efficiency of exchanges because
subjective values are hard to measure and so may not be fully compensated.[10] Bargaining guarantees that no exchange occurs unless subjective
values are recognized. This is an important function of bargaining, but
it is not the focus here. Rather, this article focuses on the second role
of bargaining, that of enhancing the subjective and objective values of
the items to be exchanged.

At the moment of exchange, division of the gains is a zero-sum
activity, without allocative consequences. But the ability to capture a
greater portion of gains from trade tomorrow increases a party's incentive to augment the value of the asset today.[11] Creation (and destruction)
of an asset's value is a continuous process. The size of the gains to be

Law and Economics 1:47 (1984); W. Oi, The Economics of Product Safety, *Bell Journal of Economics* 4:3 (1973); S. Rose-Ackerman. I'd Rather Be Liable Than You: A Note on Property Rules and Liability Rules, *International Review of Law and Economics* 6:255 (1986); C. Veljanovski, The Employment and Safety Effects of Employers' Liability, *Scottish Journal of Political Economy* 29:256 (1982).

10 See, e.g., T. Muris, Cost of Completion or Diminution in Market Value: The Relevance of Subjective Value, *Journal of Legal Studies* 12:379 (1983); S. Rea, Nonpecuniary Loss and Breach of Contract, *Journal of Legal Studies* 11:35 (1982).

11 This is a central paradigm in several strains of economic literature, particularly those
analyzing alternative property rights. See, e.g., H. Demsetz, Toward a Theory of
Property Rights, *American Economic Review* (Papers and Proceedings) 57:347 (1967);
H. S. Gordon, The Economic Theory of a Common-Property Resource: The Fishery,
Journal of Political Economy 62:124 (1954). L. De Alessi, The Economics of Property
Rights: A Review of the Evidence, *Research in Law and Economics* 2:1 (1980) summarizes the link of concern here, that between ownership rewards and investment:
"To the extent that resource rights are held in common, individual choices regarding
the output to be produced, the production techniques to be used, the characteristics
(amount, type, and time profile) of the investment to be undertaken as well as the
time horizon and intensity of production will be affected. . . . Thus, since the individual
lacks exclusive rights to the output of any investment he might make on the commonly
owned resource, he has less incentive to invest this way."

For recent recognition of this paradigm in the corporate takeover context, see L.
Bebchuk, Comment: The Case for Facilitating Competing Tender Offers, *Harvard
Law Review* 95:1028 (1982), p. 1049 [hereinafter Competing Tender Offers]; Bebchuk,
The Case for Facilitating Competing Tender Offers: A Reply and Extension. *Stanford
Law Review* 35:23 (1982), pp. 42–3 [hereinafter Reply and Extension].

divided in the current period is determined by the myriad investment and other decisions made by asset owners before coming to the bargaining table. Restricting a party's ability to negotiate will decrease the returns from his value-increasing efforts, and will thus curtail such investments by him.

B   Value creation by target firms

Exchanges of blocks of corporate shares illustrate the role of bargaining in thin markets. When transacting relatively small numbers of a publicly traded corporation's shares, one deals in one of the thickest of markets. Hence, there is no bargaining, because by definition bargaining cannot alter relative prices in thick markets; there is no point to incurring bargaining costs if there are no benefits. Indeed, the buyer or seller rarely identifies his trading partner; every potential partner values the marginal share at the market price, so a partner's identity is irrelevant. But in the exchange of large blocks of shares, bargaining (with its concomitant costs) often occurs, suggesting that the block market is thinner, and that individual valuations differ at the margin. The market for controlling blocks is thinner still, and so costly bargaining is even more frequently observed. The market thins as a block of shares grows larger because a larger block confers greater ability to direct the corporation's behavior, a power most investors cannot properly exploit, and thus do not want.

Bargaining over blocks of shares allocates the gains from the transaction, and has consequences for the initial creation of valuable assets. A no-resistance rule would diminish incentives to create corporate wealth in two ways. First, it would decrease whatever investments would otherwise be made in anticipation of realizing the returns through future exchange. Second, inability to resist a takeover would diminish certain types of specific investments, the returns from which hostile acquirers could expropriate.

Wealth creation through takeovers. The theoretical takeover literature has focused almost exclusively on the value-increasing contributions of acquirers in ferreting out inept or dishonest management.[12] A no-resistance rule would be efficient, however, only if bidders created all the gains in takeovers, and targets none. If targets also make value-increasing investments, either at the time of a takeover or earlier, the

---

12 See, e.g., H. Manne, Mergers and the Market for Corporate Control, *Journal of Political Economy* 73:110 (1965).

desirability of mere liability protection depends on the elasticity of value creation by each side with respect to the rewards realized. The empirical literature is resolutely agnostic about the source of gains from takeovers.[13] Given that this source may vary substantially from one transaction to another,[14] compelling a no-resistance response seems unjustified.

Even adopting a short-run perspective of the takeover process, it is clear that bidders do not create all the gains. Firms do not always sit back and wait to be taken over. Some go looking for a bidder.[15] Indeed, a manager can enhance his own position by pointing out the undervalued nature of his firm to bidders, who will value his ability to discern such circumstances. When the firm is undervalued because assets should be reallocated out of the firm, insiders sometimes know this, and work toward an external remedy. By the same token, acquirers often do not actively search for targets, but merely hold themselves out as willing to entertain overtures from prospective targets.[16] Targets would have little incentive to inform potential bidders of their undervalued shares if the

13 See, e.g., M. Jensen, Agency Costs of Free Cash Flow, Corporate Finance, and Takeovers, *American Economic Review* (Papers and Proceedings) 76:323 (1986), p. 328. (There are "approximately a dozen theories to explain takeovers, all of which I believe are of some relevance.")

14 Jensen and Ruback note that "[v]arious sources of gains to takeovers have been advanced," but the studies showing gains from takeovers "cannot . . . distinguish between these alternative sources of gains." M. Jensen and R. Ruback, The Market for Corporate Control: The Scientific Evidence, *Journal of Financial Economics* 11:5 (1983), pp. 23–4. They remark that it "would be surprising to find that all the gains . . . are due to a single phenomenon such as elimination of inefficient target management." Idem p. 25.

15 When assets are unique, i.e., traded in thin markets, "sellers can also engage in search . . . in the literal fashion that buyers do." G. Stigler, The Economics of Information, *Journal of Political Economy* 69:213 (1961), p. 216, reprinted in G. Stigler, *The Organization of Industry* (Homewood, Ill., 1968), pp. 171, 175. For mention of this point in the takeover context, see note 11, Competing Tender Offers, p. 1049, and Reply and Extension, pp. 35–39. The search cost a party will undertake is a positive function of the expected reward. This is a fundamental aspect of the economics of information. See Stigler, p. 219, reprinted in G. Stigler, Economics of Information, p. 180; G. Stigler, *The Theory of Price* 3d ed. (New York, 1966). pp. 1–4. Bebchuk, Toward Undistorted Choice and Equal Treatment in Corporate Takeovers, *Harvard Law Review* 98: 1693 (1985), p. 1776 [hereinafter Undistorted Choice]; D. Mortensen, Property Rights and Efficiency in Mating, Racing, and Related Games, *American Economic Review* 72:968 (1982).

16 The following advertisement ran recently in the *Wall Street Journal*: "Acquisitions Wanted. Ocilla Industries Inc., a publicly traded OTC–National company with a significant cash position, is seeking acquisitions meeting the following criteria. . . . Brokers' inquiries welcome and brokers will be fully protected. Please call or write. . . . " *Wall Street Journal*, May 27, 1986, p. 62.

bidders received most of the resulting gain. Finally, some firms specialize in matchmaking, i.e., in facilitating corporate pairing between two other firms.[17] Matchmakers profit by taking a portion of the gains from the pairing. In short, while corporate acquisitions require investments in search, it is not just bidders who invest. There is no reason, then, to award all the gains from trade to bidders.

From a longer-run perspective, the importance of the target firm's own investments is even greater. The opportunity arises every day for a firm to make value-creating investments, the full returns from which may only be realized through a possible future takeover. Firms sometimes can create value by making initial investments that others are better able to develop, and so plan from the start to be acquired by another. For example, many computer software companies plan to be taken over if they successfully innovate even one important software package. This expectation enables them to concentrate on technical innovation and to ignore subsequent marketing, which is of no value until a technical advance has been completed. Much small-scale research in other fields follows a similar pattern.[18] The same process typifies both large-scale and personal real estate investments; property owners hesitate to make improvements unless they can "get their money out" when they sell.[19]

In other words, takeovers are not discrete events that begin at the moment the first bid materializes. All firms are "in play" from the day they are created, and the possibility of a later takeover only spurs greater innovation now. The more attractive the posttakeover asset configuration foreseen, the more effective the spur.

Forming a new company with the intention of being taken over is like planning to "go public" once the success of the company is manifest. Both techniques permit financing of untested projects by an entrepre-

---

17 See, e.g., Petre, Merger Fees That Bend the Mind, *Fortune,* January 20, 1986, pp. 18, 21 (investment bankers increasingly involved in acquisitions because they "devise clever stratagems and think up new kinds of transactions"); Sterngold, Wall Street's Army of Insiders, *N.Y. Times,* May 18, 1986, F1, F8. ("Merger teams originate many deals on their own today, rather than waiting for a client to ask for help, because they need a constant flow of transactions to keep the large staffs profitably employed"); Gupta, Intermediaries Play a Bigger Role in the Venture Business, *Wall Street Journal,* September 11, 1986, p. 1 (match-makers and advisers "wield increasing power").

18 One group puts together new Ph.D.s to create new research firms, then sells the firms to pharmaceutical companies. Boland, A Lot of Happy People, *Financial World,* May 13, 1986, p. 108.

19 For example, real estate ventures often issue prospectuses stating as their "investment objectives" the acquisition, holding, and ultimate disposal of various real estate properties.

neur adept at judging projects' potential, while freeing him from postinnovation management, a duty for which he may be poorly qualified. In other words, "inept" management may result from high opportunity costs, rather than from some moral failing or incompetence. That many fledgling companies anticipate the likelihood of going public is clear from contracts signed when the company is formed specifying who will pay the costs of the initial public offering.

Even entrepreneurs who do not intend their firms to become targets nevertheless foresee some probability that their firms will fail to achieve their principal goals. The potential for being acquired or for selling off assets provides insurance against such an event.[20] If the insurance payoff were reduced by a shift from property to liability protection, some risky ventures would never be initiated. Additionally, reduced rewards from secondary asset uses would shift the form of initial investments. Those ventures still undertaken after the takeover "insurance" payoffs were reduced would be investments in assets more highly specialized to their primary objective, and hence less suited to uses elsewhere.

Protecting existing quasi-rents of human capital. Aside from increasing targets' shares of the gains from trade, there is another way that bargaining (resistance) increases investments in potential targets. Bargaining makes takeovers less likely in cases where there are no gains, only transfers, at stake.

In their daily operations, firms face two types of risk, systematic and firm-specific. Coping with each type of risk requires different managerial skills. Adapting to systematic risk requires generalized skills readily marketable elsewhere. But, as Demsetz and Lehn have explained, firm-specific variations require investments in firm-specific human capital that are not readily transferable.[21] Individuals will make such investments only if the expected rewards exceed their best alternative by enough to provide a normal return.

Yet investments that are specific to assets owned by others place the

---

20 In general, the process of reclaiming failed ventures, managing them back to profitability, and then selling them off has become highly specialized. Practitioners are known as "turn-around venture capitalists," or "vulture capitalists." See Stevens, Lots of Business. *Financial World,* June 10, 1986, p. 32.
21 See H. Demsetz, Corporate Control, Insider Trading, and Rates of Return. *American Economic Review* (Papers and Proceedings) 76:313 (1986), p. 315; H. Demsetz, The Structure of Ownership and the Theory of the Firm, *Journal of Law and Economics* 26:375 (1983) [hereinafter Structure of Ownership]: H. Demsetz and K. Lehn, The Structure of Corporate Ownership: Causes and Consequences, *Journal of Political Economy* 93:1155 (1985).

investor at risk from those others' opportunistic behavior.[22] As long as the individual realizes at least as much as can be had in the best alternative, the invested human capital will remain, even if the returns are expropriated. The best alternative, of course, offers no premium for the firm-specific investment. Long-term guarantees may control the potential for opportunism by one party, but contracts that guarantee the other party's income invite shirking, i.e., opportunism by *that* party.[23]

22 See B. Klein, R. Crawford and A. Alchian, Vertical Integration, Appropriable Rents, and the Competitive Contracting Process, *Journal of Law and Economics* 21:297 (1978), p. 313.

23 If there is no danger that the trained employee will quit, initial investment in specific human capital will be borne entirely by the firm through wage rates in excess of realized marginal products during an initial training period. See G. Becker, *Human Capital* (New York 1964), pp. 18–29. After the investments have been completed, the firm reaps a return by paying wages equal to those available elsewhere, which are below the employee's (now enhanced) marginal product within the firm to which his human capital is specific.

   If the turnover rate is not zero, however, the situation is different: "If a firm had paid for the specific training of a worker who quit to take another job, its capital expenditure would be partly wasted, for no further return could be collected. Likewise, a worker fired after he had paid for specific training would be unable to collect any further return and would also suffer a capital loss. The willingness of workers or firms to pay for specific training should, therefore, closely depend on the likelihood of labor turnover (p. 21)."

   Becker notes that the likelihood of a quit is not fixed; because it depends on wages, a firm contemplating specific human capital investments in its employees might "offer employees some of the return from training. Matters would be improved in some respects but worsened in others, for the higher wage would make the supply of trainees greater than the demand, and rationing would be required (p. 22)."

   Moreover, the magnitude of investment would not be pursued to the proper margin: "The final step would be to shift some training costs as well as returns to employees, thereby bringing supply more in line with demand. When the final step is completed, firms no longer pay all training costs nor do they collect all the returns but they share both with employees. The shares of each depend on the relations between quit rates and wages, layoff rates and profits, and on other factors not discussed here (p. 22)."

   The firm-specific human capital embodied in a firm's top executives often is unique. At any given moment particular executives will be uniquely qualified to perform particular managerial tasks for the firm. The situation is akin to a bilateral monopoly, and an executive's well-timed strategic threat to withhold his services can leave the firm in an extremely poor bargaining posture. Consequently, in such instances the interests of shareholders will require that the executive's rewards approximate his marginal product, including the marginal product of his firm-specific human capital. In that way the executive himself will bear the full cost of a withdrawal of his services.

   But this analysis implies that there is no payoff to the firm for prior investment in firm-specific capital uniquely embodied in executives. If the initial investment is to be made, it must be made entirely by the executive; but, symmetrically, that leaves the

Consequently, those making firm-specific human capital investments sometimes defend against potential opportunism by taking control of the asset to which their investment is specific.[24] In the corporate context, those who specialize for the benefit of the firm often acquire a substantial block of shares in that firm. This implies a higher concentration of shareholding in firms benefiting from more firm-specific human capital, a prediction confirmed empirically.[25]

In effect, not all shares are equal. Controlling shareholders will divert greater rewards per share to themselves than to other shareholders. This is not thievery, but part of an implicit contract to induce investments in firm-specific human capital of general benefit to the firm and hence to all shareholders. The thick public market in shares will be populated only by "ordinary" shareholders, while controlling shareholders will sell their larger blocks more rarely and only for a higher price.

Yet each share typically has the same voting power. If establishing property rights were costless, those shareholders with more at stake would also have a more potent voice. Larger individual holdings in any firm imply the higher costs of diminished portfolio diversification[26] con-

executive at risk of expropriation of the returns to his investment, should the firm begin to bargain strategically.

24 This taking of control resembles vertical integration, which is one mechanism identified by B. Klein, R. Crawford and A. Alchian, note 22, p. 299, for controlling opportunism. Of course, ownership of shares is not the only device available to managers to mitigate the risk of expropriation. Pension rights, golden parachutes, severance pay, and the like, all raise the cost to the firm of carrying out an opportunistic threat. But to say there are alternatives does not mean that they are perfect substitutes for all firms in all situations. That, in turn, means that depriving managers of the ability to make and protect investments in blocks of shares must increase the overall cost of managerial services.

25 Demsetz and Lehn, note 21, pp. 1158–60. In Structure of Ownership, note 21, p. 388, Demsetz finds that managers and directors do indeed own substantial blocks of the employing firm's shares (usually 20% or more), except in the very largest corporations.

There is a link between controlling managerial malfeasance (upon which the takeover literature concentrates) and controlling passive shareholder opportunism. For both reasons, shares of firms that are relatively difficult to control are worth more to controlling shareholder–managers than to passive investors, and so one expects a high degree of integration of management and shareholding in those firms. See A. Alchian and H. Demsetz, Production, Information Costs, and Economic Organization, *American Economic Review* 62:777, (1972), pp. 785–6.

26 Acquiring control of one of the few largest corporations in the economy requires a nondiversified investment of impressive size, with daunting cost to the risk-averse. Although there are exceptions, Demsetz has shown that the stock interest of management in very large corporations tends to be low, averaging 2%–3% compared with

trolling shareholders still might own only a minority of the voting potential. Hence, "controlling" shareholders are usually only semi-controlling. But the free-rider situation created by widely dispersed share ownership normally affords (semi-) controlling shareholders sufficient protection from human capital expropriation by fellow shareholders.

This opens an avenue through which an outside bidder (for once, the term "raider" is appropriate) can profit. If defensive tactics are barred, a hostile bidder can overcome the free-rider problem among incumbent shareholders and expropriate the full value of controlling shareholders' firm-specific investments. The situation is similar to an eminent domain taking, where asset owners are paid only the "objective" or market value of what is taken. Owners who attach a higher subjective value to the asset taken will not be paid full value. Property-rule protection of the asset, forcing would-be takers to negotiate with owners, would guarantee that full compensation was paid. A liability rule permits the taker (the government in an eminent domain proceeding, the "raider" in a takeover) to acquire property for less than full value.[27]

Controlling shareholders can limit this risk by including provisions in the corporate charter or bylaws permitting resistance to hostile takeovers. In effect, they will minimize the overall cost of potential quasi-rent expropriation by mixing (costly) diversification-reducing but control-increasing tools with (also costly) takeover-resisting measures. This mix is beneficial to all shareholders because it induces appropriate investments in firm-specific capital in the first place.[28]

   smaller companies, where managers and directors typically hold 20%–30% of their corporations' voting shares. See Structure of Ownership, note 21, p. 388.
      If, in the face of their more tenuous minority voting control, managers of a giant corporation are to make value-increasing investments in firm-specific human capital, they must have greater latitude to resist hostile takeovers than managers holding controlling interests; otherwise, they cannot protect their quasi-rents from expropriation. When the relative cost of alternative cost of alternative tools differs between situations, the optimal mix of tools will differ also.
27 See R. Epstein, *Takings: Private Property and the Power of Eminent Domain* (Cambridge, Mass., 1985), pp. 216–18.
28 This notion of expropriation of managerial quasi-rents is similar to that analyzed by Knoeber, See, C. Knoeber, Golden Parachutes, Shark Repellants, and Hostile Tender Offers, *American Economic Review* 76:155 (1986), pp. 158–9. However, Knoeber focuses on potential expropriation of managerial compensation that has been deferred until better information on performance becomes available (p. 159). Deferral of compensation for past services creates a risk that payment will not be made in the event of a hostile takeover (pp. 159–60). At this point, our article focuses instead on firm-specific investments, the returns from which are to be realized in subsequent periods, and which are thus subject to similar opportunism in the event of a takeover.

The interests of controlling shareholders, who own large percentages of residual claims, are highly correlated with the interests of other shareholders and hence of the firm as a whole. To the extent that the correlation is not perfect, noncontrolling shareholders discount the price they pay for shares initially. To restrain that discount when seeking original or additional capital, controlling shareholders have an incentive to deny themselves any ability to resist takeovers not beneficial to the firm as a whole. Through the lower initial share price, the noncontrolling shareholders are compensated for any remaining costs of permitted resistance.

In addition to quasi-rents from human capital, returns to other valuable assets may be expropriable. Suppose that management has discovered changes in firm structure or activities that will enhance the value of the firm, but has not made the information public. An outside bidder who discovers that information could acquire shares from shareholders who are ignorant of the changes. To limit losses to an outside bidder, shareholders would want management to resist any takeover until the changes have been effectuated and the shares have risen in price.[29]

C   Search rates for targets

The issue of appropriate property rights in target firms' shares can be approached from another perspective. The search for undervalued targets, like the search for new ideas, is costly. When several different claimants to a profitable idea or asset emerge, some scheme for allocating the property right must also emerge. One possible scheme is first come, first served.

---

29 This hypothetical setting parallels an actual episode. Prior to the recent threat by Sir James Goldsmith to acquire control of Goodyear Tire & Rubber Company, Goodyear had hired two investment banking firms to study possible restructuring of Goodyear. Restructuring was recommended, but the information was to be kept private. Before Goodyear could act on the restructuring recommendations however, Goldsmith acquired a substantial minority stake in Goodyear. The stake was interpreted as preliminary to a takeover bid, after which Goldsmith would himself have restructured the company. There is no evidence that Goldsmith was privy to any inside information. See Winter and Stricharchuk, Goodyear, Responding to Takeover Bid, Seeks Buyer for Its Oil and Gas Unit, *Wall Street Journal,* November 4, 1986, p. 3. Goldsmith said that the company's restructuring plans were largely the same as his. Stewart and Revzin, Sir James Goldsmith, As Enigmatic as Ever, Bails Out of Goodyear, *Wall Street Journal,* November 21, 1986, p. 1. Partly because the prospects of Goldsmith's restructuring were becoming dimmer. Goldsmith eventually agreed to resell his shares at a premium to the firm, which then proceeded with its prior restructuring plans. Stricharchuk and Stewart, Goodyear Tire To Buy Interest from Sir James, *Wall Street Journal,* November 21, 1986, p. 3.

Various authors have shown, however, that establishing property rights by first possession ordinarily results in premature capture.[30] Moving resources to higher-valued uses as fast as possible is undesirable. Speed is costly. Rapid search consumes more resources per unit of discovery than does leisurely search.[31] Hence, attempting maximum speed in replacing poor management, or reallocating corporate resources for any other reason, is ill-advised. Finding better managers too soon makes them too expensive; found too soon, management is only "better" in an engineering, not an economic, sense.

The search for targets consumes resources which have valuable alternative uses. Resources will be diverted too soon if title to the entire increase in a corporation's value arising from reallocating control can be established only by racing to the firm before a competitor reaches it. Well-defined property rights control the race by forcing contenders to deal with an owner or agent capable of implementing an internally consistent plan of action.[32] Facing no resistance, first bidders would be more likely to be the only bidders, since no defense could be used to elicit competing bids.

II   Externalities from managerial resistance to tender offers

The preceding section illustrated various ways in which the ability to bargain is advantageous when assets, including blocks of corporate shares, are traded in thin markets. These advantages explain why bargaining is the norm in most thin markets, and why the law typically does not impose liability rules there that would prevent negotiation. Never-

---

30 Y. Barzel, Optimal Timing of Innovations, *Review of Economics and Statistics* 50:348 (1968); P. Dasgupta and J. Stiglitz, Uncertainty, Industrial Structure, and the Speed of R & D, *Bell Journal of Economics* 11:1 (1980), 25–6; Mortensen, note 15, pp. 969–70.

31 A. Alchian, Costs and Outputs, in *The Allocation of Economic Resources* (1959) pp. 23, 25. See Alchian, Reliability of Progress Curves in Airframe Production, *Econometrica* 31:679 (1963).

32 See R. Posner, *Economic Analysis of Law,* 3d ed. (Boston, 1986), pp. 33–9. E. Kitch, The Nature and Function of the Patent System, *Journal of Law and Economics* 20: 265 (1977), p. 276.

The "commons" effect can occur when common users of a given asset do not individually register marginal costs as the asset is depleted; thus, they overuse the asset to the point of exhaustion. The phenomenon draws its name from the overgrazing that typically took place on public commons. But see note 11, Gordon (if the rate of exploitation of an asset is decreased, as is appropriate in a commons, but no other aspect of the right to the asset is established, the cost of exploitation is increased until, at the margin, the entire value of the resource is dissipated).

theless, Easterbrook and Fischel have argued that the courts or legis-latures should prohibit managerial bargaining over takeovers by banning managerial resistance to takeover bids. The Easterbrook–Fischel model is well known, and needs little summary here. In effect, it argues, the market for corporate control is different from other markets for two reasons.

First, the expectation of a target firm's resistance acts as a disincentive to bidders, who therefore monitor all firms in the market less.[33] Reduced monitoring by bidders means that other firms pay for the target's resistance, creating an externality that allegedly requires a legal no-resistance rule for correction. This externality would arise even if target shareholders themselves, acting in their own interest, resisted takeover bids. But typically it is management that resists in the name of its shareholders. This, Easterbrook and Fischel claim, makes resistance undesirable for a second reason: Managers resist not only when resistance benefits their shareholders, but also when it wrongfully safeguards management jobs.[34] Thus, resistance not only creates externalities costly to other firms, but increases managerial agency costs to the target itself.

This section, and the next two, consider both objections to bargaining over corporate assets. Neither externalities nor excessive agency costs necessarily accompany takeover resistance. Furthermore, even if externalities and agency costs were substantial problems, they would not necessarily justify a legal ban on bargaining. The ability to bargain still has the value-enhancing advantages discussed in Section I. Even if these externality and agency cost problems exist, therefore, whether they justify a no-resistance rule is an empirical question; if the benefits of bargaining exceed the externality and agency costs, there is no good reason to ban resistance.

A   The externality problem

Easterbrook and Fischel argue that the application of a common-law business judgment rule to condone resistance would be wrong:[35] "[e]ven resistance that ultimately elicits a higher bid is socially wasteful."[36] There are two sources of alleged waste.

First the target firm's resistance consumes resources, while the gains

33 Proper Role, note 2, pp. 1176–7.
34 Ibid. p. 1175.
35 Ibid. p. 1195 (business judgment rule "should never serve to justify a decision to oppose a tender offer").
36 Ibid. p. 1175.

from resistance are asserted to be merely transfers from bidding firms, rather than the creation of new wealth. This is just a bargaining cost, however, neither more nor less troublesome in the takeover context than in any other thin market. Second, and more important, resistance by the target firm imposes an external cost on other firms, the managers of which are monitored less by potential takeover bidders:

[The] "externality" arises when a target's management resists a tender offer. The resulting increase in the prices paid for target firms will generally discourage prospective bidders for other targets; when the price of anything goes up, the quantity demanded falls. Changes in the incentives of bidders affect the utility of monitoring by outsiders, and that affects the size of [other firms' managerial] agency costs and in turn the pre-offer price of potential targets' stock.[37]

To end the perceived externality, Easterbrook and Fischel advocate legal intervention to prohibit a target firm's management from using any defensive tactics.[38]

The legal community has resisted the proposed no-resistance rule. Courts refuse to apply it[39] and commentators disagree with portions of the analysis.[40] For example, it has been noted that although resistance consumes real resources, resistance also avoids the transaction costs of subsequent transfers if the first bidder is not the highest-valuing user of the target firm's resources.[41] The debate has also focused on elasticities,

37 Ibid. pp. 1176–7.
38 Not all defensive tactics fit the Easterbrook–Fischel paradigm. Greenmail paid to prospective bidders, for example, has only trivial resource costs and can increase, not decrease, the amount of monitoring bidders do. note 7, Macey and McChesney, pp. 38–43.
39 See, e.g., *Unocal Corp.* v. *Mesa Petroleum Co.*, 493 A.2d 946 (Del. 1985). Citing Easterbrook and Fischel, the Delaware Supreme Court noted that "[i]t has been suggested that a board's response to a takeover threat should be a passive one.... [But] as the proponents of this rule of passivity readily concede, it has not been adopted either by courts or state legislatures." Idem, p. 955 n. 10; see also *Revlon, Inc.* v. *MacAndrews & Forbes Holdings, Inc.*, 506 A.2d 173, 180 (Del. 1986) (board of directors had the power to adopt a "poison pill" defense in response to a hostile takeover bid); *Moran* v. *Household Int'l, Inc.*, 500 A.2d 1346, 1357 (Del. 1985) (directors adopting poison pill defense in anticipation of a possible takeover attempt protected by business judgment rule).
40 See, e.g., note 11, Competing Tender Offers, pp. 1029–30; R. Gilson, Seeking Competitive Bids Versus Pure Passivity in Tender Offer Defense, *Stanford Law Review* 35:51 (1982), p. 66; D. Oesterle, Target Managers as Negotiating Agents for Target Shareholders in Tender Offers: A Reply to the Passivity Thesis, *Cornell Law Review* 71:53 (1985), pp. 55–6.
41 See note 11, Competing Tender Offers, pp. 1048–9. Easterbrook pp. 1048–49. Easterbrook and Fischel suspect the reverse, that auction costs exceed the costs of successive transfers. Auctions, note 2, 14. The issue is solely empirical, but neither side has presented any data to support its position.

i.e., on just how many bids are lost because firms can resist.[42] On the more fundamental externality point, however, there has been only acquiescence with the Easterbrook and Fischel model.[43]

B   Relevant versus irrelevant externalities

"Externality" is a slippery concept, one less often used to elucidate a supposed "problem" than to justify government intervention to "solve" it.[44] The efficiency issue is not whether any third-party impact takes place – that is inevitable – but whether the appropriate marginal conditions still hold. Many externalities are solely pecuniary; they change prices but do not raise efficiency concerns as long as prices still equal marginal cost.[45] A problem arises only when prices and costs diverge, creating a nonpecuniary (or "technological") externality.

There are really two distinct externalities connected with resisting

42 The elasticity debate has centered on the size of bidders' sunk costs, that is, on the extent to which costs can be recouped in the event bidders are thwarted by managerial resistance. The crux of the inquiry is, therefore, the overall effect of resistance on reducing bidders' search efforts. See, e.g., Reply and Extension, note 11, p. 30 (conceding that allowing managerial resistance reduces bidders' search, but arguing that the reduction "is unlikely to be substantial"). Again, no data are offered to support the claim that elasticities are low, so the empirical claim cannot be evaluated. But the Easterbrook and Fischel model does not depend on the size of the supposed externality; as long as there is any, it claims, too little monitoring and bidding will result. Auctions, note 2, p. 7.

43 See, e.g., G. Jarrell, The Wealth Effects of Litigation by Targets: Do Interests Diverge in a Merge? *Journal of Law and Economics* 28:151 (1985), pp. 151–4. Defensive tactics, Jarrell initially suggests, may seem to be "sensible gambles, rather than shameful self-dealing by managers" (p. 175). But Jarrell ultimately concludes that resistance is nevertheless welfare-reducing: "[T]his conclusion – that litigious defenses can be beneficial to target shareholders – does not imply that such actions enhance social welfare. Indeed, the opposite is more likely to be true, because litigious defenses redistribute some of the gains from corporate combinations from acquirers to the targets. This redistribution is analogous to a tax on acquirers."

But the redistribution is not analogous to a tax, because it does not simply disappear into an uninvolved treasury. It is received by the other party to the transaction, someone capable of reacting appropriately to the implied opportunity cost. See R. Coase. The Problem of Social Cost, *Journal of Law and Economics* 3:1 (1960), pp. 39–42.

44 Cf. E. Mishan, *Cost–Benefit Analysis* (New York, 1971) p. 107, n. 5. ("There are quite a number of economic phenomena . . . masquerading in the literature as external effects which cannot be admitted [as such].")

45 Ibid. pp. 103–5. Changes in prices "will lead to changes in the equilibrium output of goods and services, but each equilibrium will be equally efficient, or Pareto optimal." J. Due and A. Friedlaender, *Government Finance: Economics of the Public Sector.* 5th ed. (Homewood, Ill., 1973), pp. 80–81.

takeovers in the Easterbrook and Fischel model, although the model does not distinguish them. The first, fewer bids for targets, is merely pecuniary. This allegedly undesirable effect of resistance comes about because of the "resulting increase in the prices paid for target firms," meaning that "the quantity demanded falls."[46] Bidders are aware of the possibility – indeed, the virtual certainty – that their first bid will not be accepted, and at the margin adjust the amount of search and bidding they undertake to reflect the higher price of takeovers. Resources will be used differently, but no inefficiency arises. The pecuniary externality is real enough, but does not justify legal intervention on efficiency grounds.

The second externality arises because bidders adjust monitoring of potential target firms as takeover premiums rise. This externality admittedly is nonpecuniary, but that is not the end of the analysis. Five conditions still must be met before the legal system should intervene to correct even a nonpecuniary externality.[47] First, the actions of one party must affect other parties who have little or no influence over the decisions of the first party.[48] Second, the impact on the affected parties must alter their behavior.[49] Easterbrook and Fischel imply that these first two conditions for legal intervention are met, which is concededly plausible.

But these two necessary conditions are not sufficient to justify intervention that would *reduce* the level of an activity. An externality must also be an external cost, meaning that the affected parties would want the level of that cost-generating activity reduced.[50] In the corporate context, it is unclear whether third-party targets would want less takeover resistance, because it is unclear whether resistance results in a net cost to them. True, resistance decreases gains of bidders at the moment of takeover, which reduces bidder search for a given level of corporate investment. But as Section I noted, in the more dynamic market setting an ability to resist enhances target gains from a successful takeover and thus increases the amount of investment in place at any moment. This, in turn, makes a larger number of firms attractive targets. All else being equal, the increased population of potential targets *increases* bidder

46 Proper Role, note 2, at 1176–77; see note 37 and accompanying text.
47 If the actors in the legal system, such as the legislature, are themselves self-interested, these five conditions, while still necessary, will not be sufficient to assure the desirability of legal intervention.
48 Buchanan and Stubblebine, note 6, p. 372.
49 Ibid. pp. 373–74.
50 Ibid.

incentive to search by raising the likelihood that a bidder can locate a target of sufficient attraction.[51]

There is no apparent reason to believe that the first impact dominates the second, or vice versa. The issue is empirical. If the first impact, reduced bidder search, dominates, the externality is indeed an external cost, and shareholders in potential targets will want the resistance of other targets weakened. But if the second effect, increased incentive to search, dominates, the externality is a relevant external *benefit*, and shareholders will prefer that the ability of other targets to resist be *strengthened*. If the first and second impacts offset each other, the externality is irrelevant and need not be considered further.

Still a fourth condition necessary to justify legal "correction" of a relevant external cost requires that the cost of correction be less than the losses arising from the externality. By focusing solely on the benefits perceived from a no-resistance rule, Easterbrook and Fischel imply that the costs of correcting externalities due to resistance are negligible.[52] But as was noted in Section I, losses do arise from using a no-resistance rule, because initial investment incentives are altered. In effect, the technique suggested for controlling the perceived externality, nonresistance, has external effects of its own.

The fifth and final condition necessary to justify legal intervention to correct a Pareto-relevant externality is high private costs of internalization relative to the costs of public control.[53] Government solutions to problems cannot be optimal if private solutions are cheaper. This final necessary condition does not seem to be met in the case of tender offers, as is explained in the next section. If so, a no-resistance rule is inap-

---

51 An example underlines the point. A person is not required to accept the first marriage proposal received. One may spurn the first (or nth) suitor, even though that creates a risk of never getting a better offer. But the amount of search for spouses does not necessarily fall when such discretion is tolerated. True, the possibility of being refused is a disincentive to suitors' search, all other things equal. But the ability to refuse unattractive suitors makes marriage itself more desirable, and so gives a potential partner greater incentive to develop (i.e., invest in) attributes or skills that make that person more desirable to an acceptable suitor. When potential partners are more desirable, there will be more search, by more suitors.

52 According to Easterbrook and Fischel, both shareholders and bidders benefit from mandatory nonresistance. Auctions, note 2, pp. 7–9.

53 Demsetz makes the same point: "[P]roperty rights convey the right to benefit or harm oneself or others.... What converts a harmful or beneficial effect into an externality is that the cost of bringing the effect to bear on the decisions of one or more of the interacting persons is too high to make it worthwhile...." Demsetz, note 11, pp. 347–8.

propriate even if all the other necessary conditions for government intervention are met.

III   Private solutions to the "problem" of takeover resistance

If resistance generates Pareto-relevant, nonpecuniary externalities, they will be internalized when property rights are well defined and transaction (contracting) costs are low.[54] The common law has granted target firms unambiguous property rights to resist tender offers. That leaves the other issue: whether other potential targets can achieve contractually the level of bidder monitoring they prefer. If so, government intervention cannot be justified.

The monitoring of targets by bidders is not free; firms that get more of it will pay for the increase. A no-resistance promise is one way to pay for more monitoring. A firm selects the level of scrutiny by selecting the price of being acquired. Nonresistance means a lower expected price and so increases scrutiny. If a firm can credibly promise not to resist a takeover, it cannot be affected by other targets' resistance, and there cannot be any relevant externality.

Those who would ban defensive tactics because of alleged externalities implicitly assume that prospective targets cannot promise not to resist, that bidders cannot cheaply be informed of these promises, or that bidders will not believe the promises. But intrafirm contracts and third-party bonding through the formal rules of the organized stock exchanges allow firms to choose the level of resistance, and thus of monitoring, for which they are willing to pay.

A   Shareholder agreements

The obvious place for shareholders to invoke a ban on defensive tactics is within the firm itself. In theory, shareholders could use their firms' articles of incorporation to specify the types and amounts of defensive tactics their managers could use. But there are two potential problems with such intrafirm contracts: prebid agency problems created by unfaithful managers, and postbid opportunism against bidders by shareholders.

Prebid agency costs. When ownership is widely dispersed, no one shareholder will find it worthwhile to draft, and to obtain adoption of, cor-

54 See Coase, note 43, pp. 15–16.

porate charter changes. If changes are to be made, they must originate with management. Easterbrook and Fischel argue that since managers want to keep their jobs, they are unlikely to draft or support charter amendments or changes in bylaws that encourage tender offers.[55] But other contractual devices – phantom stock plans, stock option plans, and "golden parachute" contracts, for example – can align the interests of managers and shareholders in the event of a hostile tender offer.[56] Indeed, as Easterbrook and Fischel have recognized in another context, "[p]ublicly held corporations have developed a wide range of governance mechanisms that align managers' interests more closely with those of investors."[57]

Such internal arrangements are admittedly costly, but so is any method designed to induce monitoring. At the other extreme, shareholders might do no internal monitoring, relying instead on increased monitoring from outside bidders. But as noted above, more outside monitoring must be purchased by forgoing takeover premiums so as to promise greater gains to outside bidders. Contractual devices like golden parachutes merely substitute costly internal monitoring mechanisms for costly external monitoring by bidders. But there is no reason to think that internal monitoring is always more costly.

At the time of an initial public offering of securities there is no agency problem, because there is no separation of ownership and control. At this juncture shareholders would pay lower prices for the shares of firms that did not bar defensive tactics, if shareholders unambiguously would benefit from a no-resistance rule. Agency problems evolve subsequently due to the costliness of foreseeing all plausible eventualities.[58] But if nonresistance unambiguously maximizes the present expected value of a corporation, it should present no initial difficulties of foresight.

If it were indeed value-maximizing to do so, fledgling firms would install stringent rules prohibiting defensive tactics before hiring outside managers, and would install provisions making it hard to alter the anti-defensive rules. Ordinarily they do none of these things.

---

55 Proper Role, note 2, pp. 1175, 1181.
56 See Knoeber, note 28 159–61; Lambert and Larcker, Golden Parachutes, Executive Decision-Making, and Shareholder Wealth, *Journal of Accounting and Economics* 7:179 (1985), pp. 184–5, 200–1.
57 Easterbrook and Fischel, Close Corporations and Agency Costs, *Stanford Law Review* 38:271, (1986), pp. 277–8.
58 See S. Grossman and O. Hart, Takeover Bids, the Free-Rider Problem, and the Theory of the Corporation, *Bell Journal of Economics* 11:42 (1980), p. 48.

Postbid shareholder opportunism. An objection to the notion that initial charter provisions can limit the resistance that bidders will expect arises from the ability of shareholders to change their charter opportunistically when a takeover is anticipated. Postbid resistance is profitable. Any firm can adopt and announce a policy forbidding defensive tactics, but target shareholders can revoke the earlier policy and create an auction market after a bid is launched. Shareholders of all firms would be harmed if bidders could not distinguish firms that are likely to resist a bid from those that are not.[59] If bidders cannot distinguish, perhaps new law is called for, but only to ensure that firms honor their promises to refrain from resistance, not to bar all resistance.

But time is of the essence in struggles for corporate control. Shareholders can insert one provision in their charters to forbid all defensive tactics (or a specified subset) and another to prevent any changes in the charter until a specified period has passed. Such provisions would protect bidders from shareholder opportunism unless bidders were forced to reveal their intentions far in advance of their takeover move.[60]

Even without such delaying provisions, the structure of the corporate governance process prevents shareholders from making rapid changes in their articles of incorporation. Substantive changes require a shareholder vote,[61] which takes time, particularly if shareholders are widely dispersed. Furthermore, the mechanisms of soliciting proxies are controlled by federal rules[62] which again create delay.

These bonding mechanisms are not "perfect," that is, costless. But the cost of bonds must be compared to the costs of alternatives. It may be that a legal rule would provide enforcement of firms' no-resistance

59 Actually, few firms would keep their promises if bidders could not tell the difference. See Akerlof, The Market for "Lemons": Quality Uncertainty and the Market Mechanism, *Quarterly Journal of Economics* 84:488 (1970), pp. 495–6.

60 Perhaps the Williams Act, Pub. L. No. 90–439, 82 Stat. 454 (1968) (codified as amended at 15 U.S.C. secs. 78l–78n (1982 and Supp. III 1985)), has forced bidders to reveal their intentions so far in advance that preexisting corporate charters now offer insufficient restraints on resistance. But if that is so, the solution is not more law, but less – repeal or modification of the Williams Act.

61 See, e.g., Revised Model Business Corp. Act, secs. 10.01–03 (1985); Del. Code Ann. tit. 8, sec. 242 (b)(1)-(2) (1974).

62 The solicitation of proxies is controlled by the Securities Exchange Act, sec. 14, 15 U.S.C. secs. 78n (1982 and Supp. III 1985), and by Regulation 14A of the Securities and Exchange Commission, 17 C.F.R. sec. 240.14a (1986). SEC Rule 14a.6 requires that five copies of all proxy statements and accompanying forms be filed with the SEC ten days prior to the date such material is given to stockholders, 17 C.F.R. sec. 240. 14a.6(a) (1986), although the SEC may authorize a reduction in the ten-day period "upon a showing of good cause therefore."

promises more cheaply than would private bonding. If so, the appropriate legal response is to enforce voluntarily offered target promises rather than to ban all resistance.

B   Third-party bonds

When doubts exist about contractual reliability outside the corporate control market, third-party bonding to assure performance often resolves them.[63] Similarly, an explicit or implicit no-resistance bond could be posted with a third-party fiduciary, its value exceeding the expected gains from resisting once a bid materialized. The bond would be forfeited if the firm breached its promises. If credible mechanisms exist to bond shareholders to their promised responses to takeover bids, firms can choose their desired level of bidder monitoring by adjusting the contractual level of resistance.

State laws barring resistance by target firms comprise one possible sort of third-party bond. It is often suggested that state corporation statutes, reflecting interstate competition for charter revenues, furnish the most efficient rules of corporate governance.[64] If so, some states could enact no-resistance rules, and firms desiring to bond themselves to those rules could incorporate there.

If, for some reason, bonding through state law proved insufficient, the organized stock exchanges could serve as third-party guarantors of firms' promises of nonresistance. The exchanges have incentives to devise rules maximizing listed firms' values.[65] A firm will select as its forum for trading the exchange with the best rules for that firm's circumstances.

63 See C. Knoeber, An Alternative Mechanism to Assure Contractual Reliability, *Journal of Legal Studies* 12:333, (1983), pp. 335–43; B. Klein and K. Leffler, The Role of Market Forces in Assuring Contractual Performance, *Journal of Political Economy* 89:615, (1981), pp. 635–7.

64 See Winter, Government and the Corporation (1978) pp. 7–11. Fischel, The "Race to the Bottom" Revisited: Reflections on Recent Developments in Delaware's Corporation Law, *Northwestern University Law Review* 76:913, (1982), 919–20; R. Winter, State Law, Shareholder Protection, and the Theory of the Corporation. *Journal of Legal Studies* 6:251 (1977), pp. 289–92. But see D. Fischel, Efficient Capital Market Theory, the Market for Corporate Control, and the Regulation of Cash Tender Offers, *Texas Law Review* 57:1 (1978), 29 (competition among states may not be effective because a "corporation may be subject to the tender offer statutes of several states even if incorporated in a state with no such statute").

65 See Easterbrook, Managers' Discretion and Investors' Welfare: Theories and Evidence, *Delaware Journal of Corporate Law* 9:540 (1984), p. 556 [hereinafter Managers' Discretion] ("The willingness of people to trade depends . . . on their belief that they will get a fair deal. Thus it is in the interest of stock exchanges to establish rules for the protection of investors, and managers who seek to attract money will submit to these rules.").

Originally, simply listing on the New York Stock Exchange (NYSE) assured prospective bidders that the firm would not violate the exchange's rules. In the days before sophisticated computer technology, the NYSE was a natural monopoly. Firms that flouted exchange rules were delisted and lost access to this central marketplace, with a consequent fall in the firm's share prices.

Thus if firms could have gained by having enforceable no-resistance rules, the NYSE should have had them. Long before federal regulation of securities trading, the NYSE required independent audits and certain timely disclosures, and specified shareholder voting rights for listed firms.[66] But the NYSE has never had anything like a general no-resistance rule. Only two NYSE rules conceivably could be construed as discouraging defensive tactics, and these also serve purposes unrelated to takeovers. Listed firms must obtain shareholder approval before issuing new stock exceeding 18 percent of the value of the firm's outstanding stock,[67] and dual classes of voting stock are not allowed.[68] But the most common sorts of resistance – shark repellants, greenmail and the like – have never been limited by the NYSE, which seems inconsistent with the argument that the market's anticipation of resistance to a takeover decreases a firm's value.

The presence of rivals has diminished the value of the bond that NYSE listing once represented to prospective bidders.[69] Although the emergence of rival markets might explain why no exchange has adopted

---

66 G. Benston, Security for Investors, in *Instead of Regulation*, R. Poole ed. (1982), pp. 169, 170; R. Watts and J. Zimmerman, Agency Problems, Auditing, and the Theory of the Firm: Some Evidence, *Journal of Law and Economics* 26:613 (1983), p. 629.

67 Managers' Discretion, note 65 p. 556.

68 But see NYSE Formally Submits Proposal To Allow Unequal Voting Rights, *Securities (BNA) Regulations and Law Report* 18, no. 37:1337 (September 19, 1986). For text of proposed changes in NYSE rules, see p. 1389.

69 Neither the National Association of Securities Dealers (the industry self-regulatory organization that governs trading in the over-the-counter market) nor the American Stock Exchange forbids its listed firms from adopting dual-stock classes with unequal voting rights. Recently, several NYSE listed firms considered to be likely takeover targets violated exchange rules by adopting dual classes of stock with different voting rights (so-called "super shares") to avoid hostile takeovers. See J. Gordon, Ties That Bond: Dual Class Common and the Problem of Shareholder Choice. *California Law Review* 75 (October 1987) [see Chapter 3, this volume]. Rather than enforce its rule and lose listings to these competing markets, the NYSE has proposed changing its rules regarding voting rights for common stock. See note 68. At present, though, a firm can claim to be bonding itself not to engage in certain defensive tactics by listing on the NYSE, but then jump to another exchange or to the over-the-counter market when a bidder commits himself.

rules forbidding defensive tactics, it is significant that the NYSE never adopted rules forbidding resistance even when it had little fear of losing listings. But despite the modern competition among them, the exchanges still represent separate legal entities with standing to sue, a standing that is not contingent on the contracting party remaining listed on that exchange. Firms can sign legally enforceable bonding contracts with an exchange specifying a sum that the firm would forfeit if it resisted a hostile bid for control.[70] The bond would lessen the gains that a target might realize from defensive tactics. If shareholders valued such bonds, exchanges themselves would benefit from serving as guarantors or bonders, by providing a service of value to their listed firms and so being able to share in any of the resulting gains.

Because target firms can post bonds with exchanges, firms that desire more outside surveillance by potential bidders can purchase it, though two transactions (listing and bonding) may now be required where one sufficed earlier. External bonding admittedly is costly – as is any other device to obtain the level of monitoring the firm wants. The point is, first, that institutions with an incentive and an ability to bond targets' promises already exist. Moreover, the costs of writing effective and enforceable bonds appear to be slight, compared to the obviously costly alternative of banning valuable resistance. If Easterbrook and Fischel are correct that future target firms are systematically the victims of present target resistance, it is remarkable that none of the entities with an interest in the problem has done anything to solve it.

C   Firm variety and legal default rules

The amount of resistance the firm chooses determines the amount of external monitoring it receives in the market for corporate control. Firm owners combine this external monitoring with internal governance mechanisms, depending on the relative prices of external and internal devices, to achieve the optimal set of monitoring inputs overall. But different firms will demand varying amounts of monitoring, since they have managers with different attributes, industrial structures posing different problems, and different organizational practices. Likewise, to achieve a given level of monitoring, different firms will find it optimal to mix different amounts of the various monitoring inputs available.[71]

---

70 See Knoeber, note 63, pp. 335–36.
71 See Managers' Discretion, note 65, pp. 543–53; Jensen, note 13, p. 324. Shareholders have other mechanisms besides the market for corporate control to monitor managers, such as frequent trips to the capital markets, which subject firms to the scrutiny of

A principal disadvantage of a no-resistance rule is its inflexibility in the face of firms' demands for different types and degrees of monitoring.[72] A no-resistance rule forces at least some firms to buy more outside monitoring than they want. There is no such thing as *the* efficient amount of external monitoring inputs across firms, any more than there is a single optimum amount of labor or capital across all firms in all industries. Railroads have different capital–labor ratios than do drycleaning establishments. Similarly, different firms will prefer different combinations of external and internal monitoring inputs.

Casual empiricism verifies this phenomenon. Shareholders in many firms have agreed to restrict the payment of greenmail, or have refused to install poison pill provisions in their charters. Others have not.[73] Internally, many firms have stock option plans and golden parachute agreements. Others do not. In the face of such diversity in the use of monitoring inputs, the law's attempts to correct supposed imperfections must be cautious.

When, as in the takeover setting, there are dozens of internal and external monitoring choices available, and thus many thousands of possible input combinations, the likelihood that an appreciable number of firms would choose extremely large or extremely small amounts of many of those inputs is practically nil. Yet that is what a no-resistance rule would accomplish, by prohibiting firms from purchasing any combination of inputs that did not maximize outside monitoring. Such a rule would force an appreciable number of firms to purchase more external

investment banks and other institutional monitors. See F. Easterbrook, Two Agency-Cost Explanations of Dividends, *American Economic Review* (Papers and Proceedings) 74:650 (1984), pp. 652–6; Jensen, note 13, p. 324. Use of outside auditors, independent directors, and management consultants can also be an effective monitoring device. In addition, the market for managerial labor rewards and punishes managerial performance as appropriate. All else being equal, shareholders who utilize more of these other monitoring devices will demand less monitoring by takeover bidders, and will want their firms to engage in more defensive tactics in order to realize the full value of their monitoring activities.

72 "Politics is the art of compromise because political outcomes are very indivisible. The greater divisibility of market outcomes makes business the art of serving new wants without compromising old ones." H. Demsetz, *Economic, Legal, and Political Dimensions of Competition* (Amsterdam, 1982) p. 76. Perhaps this discussion seems to overstate a firm's ability to "fine tune" the allowable resistance prospectively. But a court does not have perfect foresight either. Judicial enforcement of a uniform and compulsory no-resistance rule would provide less flexibility than would interpretation of a voluntary no-resistance contract.

73 See B. Baysinger and H. Butler, Antitakeover Amendments, Managerial Entrenchment, and the Contractual Theory of the Corporation, *Virginia Law Review* 71:1257 (1985), pp. 1257–9.

monitoring (thus inducing less internal monitoring) than they would prefer. It is unlikely, that is, that many shareholders would wish to write the sort of contract that Easterbrook and Fischel's no-resistance rule would impose upon them.

As a standard-form contract for shareholders, the Easterbrook–Fischel proposal has a second defect. While a legal default rule merely forces all firms to accept the same missing term when they fail to provide for some contingency, the Easterbrook–Fischel proposal would override the explicit terms of charter provisions, employment agreements, and the like, when those contracts allowed managerial resistance to takeovers. Easterbrook and Fischel's rule is thus not a default option, around which firms can contract as they please. Rather, it mandates a set level of resistance – zero – regardless of the level shareholders have chosen. The ability of firms to contract around costly legal rules when lower-cost private alternatives are available must be a feature of any efficient standard-form contract.

Default options, like everything else, have their costs. In the takeover context, they may create uncertainty among bidders about what resistance rules a particular target has in force. But institutions like stock exchanges make it their business to minimize these costs. Moreover, firms that adopt no-resistance rules thereby increase the potential gains available to bidders in order to attract increased takeover attention. These firms then have every incentive to let bidders know what they have done, and bidders have every incentive to search for that information.

Of course, permitting firms to contract around legal rules means that courts must sometimes interpret and enforce contracts. But a rule requiring managerial passivity in the face of a takeover bid also requires costly interpretation and enforcement. As Easterbrook and Fischel concede, "Many legitimate business decisions could have the effect of making the corporation less attractive to the bidder and thus could be called resistance. . . . Distinguishing resistance from passivity will be simple in some cases and hard in others."[74]

Nor does it follow that corporate contracting should be ignored in the takeover context because some forms of resistance, such as poison pills or greenmail, were unknown at the time contracts were written. Legislatures are no more capable of predicting appropriate rules for things that do not exist than are the original entrepreneurs. Whatever statutory language a legislature might choose to proscribe takeover defenses is equally available to firms themselves if they want to use it.

74 Proper Rate, note 2. 1202.

IV   Agency costs

Whether or not important externalities attend takeover resistance, Easterbrook and Fischel believe resistance is undesirable because managers will resist to save their jobs, not to benefit their shareholders.[75] Indeed, to Easterbrook and Fischel the very existence of tender offers shows agency problems in target firms. Combinations between firms could occur through friendly mergers, which they claim dissipate fewer resources than hostile tender offers.[76] A bidder's resort to a tender offer, Easterbrook and Fischel argue, reveals target firm managers to have been protecting themselves by refusing to facilitate a beneficial merger.[77]

Mergers remain by far the most prevalent form of interfirm combination, while tender offers are comparatively rare.[78] This observation suggests that significant agency costs do not typify the takeover process, even by Easterbrook and Fischel's standards. It is also noteworthy that, for Easterbrook and Fischel, agency costs seem to be a significant problem only for tender offers. As Easterbrook has reported elsewhere, overwhelming empirical evidence from various aspects of corporate governance suggests that faithful managers are rewarded while the faithless are punished.[79] Shareholders apparently do monitor, and do devise corporate governance mechanisms that impose the costs of agency on agents themselves.[80] In advocating a no-resistance rule, Easterbrook and Fischel do not explain why tender offers are unique.

Especially curious is Easterbrook and Fischel's preference for mergers, rather than takeovers, to avoid agency costs. The potential for agency problems is no less in friendly mergers than in hostile tender offers. Managers of firms acquired in friendly mergers often receive substantial lump-sum payments from the acquiring firm or job guar-

75 Ibid., pp. 1174–75.
76 Ibid., p. 1169. To support this empirical claim. Easterbrook and Fischel cite a study of tender offer costs, but offer no data concerning the cost of mergers. (p. 1169 n. 22).
77 See Ibid., pp. 1169, 1174–5.
78 For a summary of the data, see note 28, Knoeber, p. 155 n.1. In 1982, the most recent year reported, tender offers constituted only 4% of all acquisition announcements.
79 Managers' Discretion, note 65 pp. 547–52.
80 Demsetz expresses similar skepticism about the importance, relevance, or even meaning of agency costs. See Structure of Ownership, note 21, cf. A. Alchian, Corporate Management and Property Rights, in H. Manne, ed. *Economic Policy and the Regulation of Corporate Securities* (1969), pp. 337, 344–7 (agency costs are higher because of dispersion of control among shareholders, but other advantages of this form of enterprise outweigh those costs).

antees for themselves prior to submitting the proposal to shareholders.[81] Moreover, managers typically do not accept the first bid from the prospective partner. They "resist" by bargaining for a better deal before submitting the offer for shareholder consideration. In negotiating merger terms, target firm managers seem to extract much, if not all, of the available gain from the combination, leaving the bidding firm with only a competitive rate of return.[82] Such hard bargaining presumably decreases the interest of other bidders in seeking merger targets, which again means less monitoring throughout the economy. If mergers are preferable to hostile tender offers, why is managerial resistance appropriate for the former but not the latter?[83]

Resistance (in the face of either merger offers or tender offers) can sometimes be used opportunistically by management.[84] But as Section

---

81 See, e.g., Hawkins, Tull Execs Guaranteed Pay for 3 Years in Buy-Out Plan, *Atlanta Constitution,* March 27, 1985, B3, col. 5.

82 See Jensen and Ruback, note 14, pp. 9–16.

83 Easterbrook and Fischel also overlook the fact that management's ability to enhance gains in merger negotiations depends on its ability to resist tender offers. A bidder encountering hard bargaining for a merger can go directly to shareholders by launching a tender offer. A target's tough line in merger negotiations is not credible if management can do nothing against a tender offer to force the bidder back to the merger bargaining table.

84 Partly because there are so many reasons behind corporate takeovers, see notes 13–14 and accompanying text, the empirical studies often cannot distinguish between desirable and undesirable takeover activities. See R. Roll, The Hubris Hypothesis of Corporate Takeovers, *Journal of Business* 59:197 (1986). Moreover, the empirical evidence on the effects of management resistance to takeover bids is itself complex and often contradictory. Empirical studies on greenmail, for example, are equivocal, but seem to indicate that target firms are better off when a raider buys into them and then is paid greenmail for his shares than they would be if greenmail were banned. See Macey and McChesney, note 7, pp. 43–8. Likewise, shareholders apparently benefit when management resists takeovers ex post by filing antitrust actions. Jarrell, note 43, p. 175. Study of ex ante antitakeover amendments has generated more inconclusive results. DeAngelo and E. Rice find that such amendments produce insignificant results on adopting firms' share prices. H. DeAngelo and E. Rice, Antitakeover Charter Amendments and Stockholder Wealth, *Journal of Financial Economics* 11:329 (1983), p. 355. Linn and McConnell find that such amendments have significant positive effects on adopters' share prices. S. Linn and J. McConnell, An Empirical Investigation of the Impact of "Antitakeover Amendments" on Common Stock Prices, *Journal of Financial Economics* 11:361 (1983), p. 397. A study by the SEC's Office of the Chief Economist, on the other hand, finds that antitakeover amendments have significant negative effects on share prices, although one type of amendment, fair-price provisions, has no effect at all. See Office of the Chief Economist, SEC, *Shark Repellents and Stock Prices: The Effects of Antitakeover Amendments Since 1980* (July 24, 1985), p. 43. This evidence is especially curious because the amendments studied were "[a]lmost always subject to approval by majority vote of shareholders" (p. 1). [*Continued*]

I pointed out, the ability to resist also can convey long-run benefits to shareholders. Whenever use of a tool such as resistance creates both costs and benefits for shareholders, they will want to optimize rather than eradicate its use.

V   Conclusion

Bargaining is the hallmark of exchanges in thin markets. Maximizing the value of assets often requires investments that owners cannot expect to be valued accurately by "objective" techniques, but only by negotiation. By definition, these investments involve more asset-specific risk, the management of which requires asset-specific investments in human capital. That capital can be expropriated unless bargaining is permitted.

It would be astounding if weakening well-defined property rights increased welfare. An externally imposed rule substituting liability for property protection can benefit neither bidders nor targets. It reduces the incentive to create value in potential targets. It causes too many bidders to search too much, too soon. There are good reasons why such a rule is not observed in other thin markets, even those in which sellers commonly use agents, and in which the good-faith efforts of the agent are costly to measure.

Unfettered discretion by asset owners over future bargaining strat-

In addition, a defensive tactic may hurt some but not all of the firms that adopt it. This is shown by another study by the Office of the Chief Economist, which looks at share price changes in firms adopting poison pills. Office of the Chief Economist, SEC, *The Effects of Poison Pills on the Wealth of Target Shareholders* (October 23, 1986). The study concludes that such devices have significant negative effects overall, p. 43. But it finds that, of firms adopting poison pills during control battles, the number that lost value when the pill defeated the takeover equaled the number that gained when the pill led to a later takeover at a higher price (p. 4). Such equivocal evidence hardly justifies a rule that supposedly would benefit firms that might not want a poison pill, but would prevent an equal number of firms from using a pill to benefit themselves.

Thus, the empirical case for banning resistance to takeovers is as unsettled as the theoretical argument. The empirical case, however, is largely irrelevant to our argument here. The typical event study examines the effect of a defensive tactic at the time it is imposed, normally as a response to a takeover bid. See, e.g., L. Dann and H. DeAngelo, Corporate Financial Policy and Corporate Control: A Study of Defensive Adjustments in Asset and Ownership Structure. (Managerial Economics Research Center, University of Rochester, Working Paper No. 86–11) (finding that managerial responses to attempted hostile takeovers by changes in asset or ownership structure have significant negative effects on firm share prices). Even if agency costs are significant at the time of an attempted takeover, the benefits of having a bargaining rule in effect will long since have been incorporated into share prices. An event study at the time of the takeover will miss these benefits.

egies cannot be shown to be inferior to a mandatory no-resistance rule. Target firms can contract for any monitoring for which they are prepared to bear the unavoidable resource costs. They may bond through both internal and external means any no-resistance promise they may make to potential bidders. The externality problem is a mirage. Imposing a single rule on firms with varying demands for outside monitoring would itself create inefficiencies where none now exist.

If the legal structure currently will not enforce voluntary commitments not to resist, the appropriate legal change is to enforce those promises, not to require nonresistance as a matter of law. Admittedly, judicial ability to interpret voluntary commitments is neither costless nor perfect. But to require costless perfection of a policy is to succumb to the Nirvana fallacy. The appropriate standard is not perfection but a real-world alternative. Against that standard it is difficult to imagine how voluntary commitments can be more costly to enforce than are compulsory ones.

As noted at several junctures above, resolution of all aspects of the controversy over resistance, particularly the externality issue, cannot be done at a purely theoretical level; some empirical judgments are required. Neither the proponents nor the opponents of managerial bargaining have provided quantitative evidence to support their position. But surely, given that low-cost private contractual solutions are available to solve any externality, and given that practically all other thin markets have evolved exchange rules allowing bargaining, the burden of persuasion must be on those who would ban bargaining. Likewise, firms differently situated inevitably want different bargaining rules, and are observed to impose different rules on themselves. Consequently, opponents of bargaining must shoulder the burden of showing why these private contractual solutions are undesirable, and why a single rule for all firms would be an improvement.

CHAPTER 5

A new approach to corporate
reorganizations

Lucian Arye Bebchuk

I   Introduction

The concern of this article is the way in which corporate reorganizations
divide the reorganization pie. The article puts forward a new method
for making the necessary division. This method can address some major
efficiency and fairness problems long thought to be inherent in corporate
reorganizations. Although the method is proposed as a basis for law
reform, it can also be used under the existing rules.

Reorganization is one of the two routes that a corporation in bankruptcy may take. When a corporation becomes insolvent and bankruptcy
proceedings are commenced, the corporation is either liquidated or
reorganized. In liquidation, which is governed by Chapter 7 of the Bankruptcy Code,[1] the assets of the corporation are sold, either piecemeal
or as a going concern. The proceeds from this sale are then divided
among those who have rights against the corporation, with the division
made according to the ranking of these rights.

Reorganization, which is governed by Chapter 11 of the Bankruptcy

A similar version of this paper appears in *Harvard Law Review* 101: 775 (1988). I
gratefully acknowledge the valuable comments of Bob Clark, Scott Edelman, Dan Fischel,
Ron Gilson, Henry Hansmann, Tom Jackson, Louis Kaplow, William Klein, Louis Kornhauser, Rainier Kraakman, Saul Levmore, Roberto Romano, Hal Scott, and Steve Shav-
ell. I also benefited from the helpful comments of participants in a conference at Harvard
Law School and in a workshop at the University of Pennsylvania Law School. Finally, I
would like to thank the National Science Foundation (grant SES–8708212) and the Harvard
Law School Program in Law and Economics for their financial support.

A mathematical derivation of all the elements of this article's analysis is included in
the discussion paper version of the article, which was issued as Discussion Paper No. 37,
January 1988, Program in Law and Economics, Harvard Law School.
1 11 U.S.C. secs. 701–86 (1982 and Supp. IV 1986).

Code,[2] is an alternative to liquidation. Reorganization is essentially a sale of a company to the existing "participants" – all those who hold claims against or interests in the company. This "sale" is of course a hypothetical one. The participants pay for the company with their existing claims and interests; in exchange, they receive "tickets" in the reorganized company – that is, claims against or interests in this new entity.

Why is the reorganization alternative necessary? The rationale commonly offered is that a reorganization may enable the participants to capture a greater value than they can obtain in a liquidation.[3] In particular, reorganization is thought to be especially valuable when (1) the company's assets are worth much more as a going concern than if sold piecemeal, and (2) there are few or even no outside buyers with both accurate information about the company and sufficient resources to acquire it. In such situations, liquidation might well leave the participants with less than the going-concern value of the company's assets; consequently, the participants will have more value to split if they retain the enterprise and divide it among themselves.

The development of U.S. bankruptcy law in this century suggests that public officials have long believed that reorganization is indeed desirable in an important set of cases. In 1938, Congress adopted Chapter X of the Chandler Act[4] to provide a detailed set of rules to govern reorganizations. Chapter 11 of the Bankruptcy Code replaced these rules in 1978.[5] Throughout this period, many corporations in financial distress, including major *Fortune* 500 corporations, have taken the reorganization route.[6]

This article takes as given the existence (and significant use) of the reorganization alternative to liquidation. Professors Baird and Jackson have recently challenged the conventional wisdom that it is desirable to have the corporate reorganization alternative; in their view, it might well be desirable to eliminate the reorganization alternative and resort

2 Ibid., secs. 1101–74.
3 See, e.g., Clark, The Interdisciplinary Study of Legal Evolution, *Yale Law Journal* 90: 1238–4 (1981), pp. 1252–4.
4 Pub. L. No. 75–696, 52 Stat. 840 (1938) (repealed 1978). Earlier, Congress had amended the Bankruptcy Act of 1898, 30 Stat. 544, by adopting section 77, 47 Stat. 1467, 1474–82 (1933), to govern railroad reorganizations, and section 77B, 48 Stat. 912, 912–22 (1934), to govern other reorganizations.
5 See The Bankruptcy Reform Act of 1978, 11 U.S.C. secs. 1101–74 (1982 and Supp. IV 1986).
6 See, e.g., LTV Corp. Files for Bankruptcy: Debt is $4 Billion, *N.Y. Times*, July 18, 1986, p. A1. At the time of filing, LTV was ranked as the 43rd largest industrial company in the U.S. (p. D4).

to liquidation in the case of each insolvent corporation.[7] This article does not enter that debate. Although the article seeks to improve the reorganization process, it does not advance, or indeed take any position on, the proposition that having reorganizations is desirable. Rather, it advances only the proposition that as long as reorganizations remain, the best method for dividing the reorganization pie is the one put forward below.

Section II of this article briefly describes the problems that have long afflicted the division process in corporate reorganizations. Because no objective figure is generally available for the value of the reorganized enterprise, the law has consigned the division of the reorganization pie to a process of bargaining and litigation among the various classes of participants. This process of bargaining and litigation frequently results in substantial deviations from participants' entitlements, commonly involves significant delays and litigation costs, and often produces an inefficient capital structure for the reorganized company.

Section III describes the proposed method of dividing the reorganization pie. The new method involves no bargaining or litigation, nor does it require that the value of the reorganized company be identified. Under the method, the participants in a reorganization would receive a set of rights with respect to the securities of the reorganized company. These rights are designed so that, whatever the reorganization value, the participants will never end up with less than the value to which they are entitled.

Section IV demonstrates the perfect consistency of the method's outcome with the entitlements of all participants. In particular, I show that the method will be effective even if the market is inaccurate in pricing the value of the rights distributed to the participants. Whether or not the market's pricing is accurate, no participant will have a justifiable basis for complaining about the method's outcome.

Section V discusses the implementation of the proposed method. Reorganization law, I suggest, should be reformed to facilitate and require use of the method in every corporate reorganization. Under such a regime, the division process will be effected swiftly, fairly, and efficiently. Moreover, the proposed method can be used even under the existing rules. Some participants will likely find it in their interest to use the method as a basis for reorganization plans filed for confirmation under the existing rules.

In describing the operation and effectiveness of the proposed method,

---

7 See T. Jackson, *The Logic and Limits of Bankruptcy* (1986), Chapter 9; D. Baird, The Uneasy Case for Corporate Reorganization, *Journal of Legal Studies* 15:127 (1986).

Sections III and IV use a simple example for convenience of exposition. Section VI shows how the proposed method can be adapted to deal with complex real-world features that are not present in that example.

II   The division problem in corporate reorganization

The division problem in corporate reorganization, on which this article focuses, may be stated briefly as follows: Given the set of all claims by participants, each claim defined by its size and relative priority, how should the reorganization pie (that is, the value of the reorganized company) be divided among the participants?

It is true that this issue of division, although central, is not the only element in corporate reorganizations. A reorganization inevitably must also include the preliminary process of determining the size and relative priority of the participants' claims. For example, it might be necessary to determine the amount the company owes to the holders of a certain bond issue or to certain business partners, as well as the relative priorities of these debts. Although this preliminary, inevitable process of determining the size and ranking of claims often involves significant delay and litigation costs, I will not discuss it. Rather, I will focus on the division problem, and to this end I will largely assume that the size and ranking of the participants' claims are already known.

As explained below, the existing reorganization process resolves the problem of division in a way that suffers from substantial imperfections. These imperfections are all rooted in a problem of valuation. It is generally impossible to place an objective and indisputable figure on the value that the reorganized company will have (the "reorganization value").[8] If such a figure were available, the distribution of tickets in the reorganized company would be easy to determine. Without such a figure, however, it is difficult to decide where, down the rank of creditors and preferred shareholders, it is necessary to stop issuing tickets in the newly reorganized entity.

This problem of valuation obviously does not exist in a liquidation, when actual sale to an outsider takes place. The liquidation results in an exchange of the company's assets for cash (or cash equivalents, such as marketable securities). Whether or not this cash represents the true value of the assets sold, there is no question as to the monetary value of the total pie available for distribution. The receiver running the liquidation thus can start by paying creditors that are most senior, until

8 See, e.g., Roe, Bankruptcy and Debt: A New Model for Corporate Reorganization, *Columbia Law Review* 83:527 (1983), pp. 547–8.

either no money is left or their claims are paid in full; the receiver then will pay money to creditors in the next tier, again until no money is left or their claims are paid in full; and the receiver will continue in this fashion until all the money runs out.

In contrast to liquidation, the sale of the company's assets in a reorganization is fictional. Consequently, no objective figure is available for the total monetary value to be distributed or, as a result, for the monetary value of the various tickets in the reorganized company. Although agreement over this reorganization value would be hard to achieve even among impartial observers, the clear conflict of interest among the participants makes it all the more difficult. Senior creditors have an incentive to advance a low valuation, because a low valuation would entitle them to a larger fraction of the tickets in the reorganized company.[9] For a similar reason, equity holders have an incentive to advance a high valuation.[10] It is of course possible to ask courts to estimate the reorganization value, and courts indeed sometimes must make such estimates. But no one suggests that we can rely on such judicial estimates to be generally accurate.[11]

The law has always dealt with this valuation problem by leaving the division of tickets in the reorganized company to a process of bargaining among the participants.[12] The law has sought only to provide a setup for this bargaining and to establish constraints within which the division must take place. Under existing rules, a plan of reorganization generally will obtain judicial confirmation if all the classes of participants approve it.[13] The legal rules governing this approval process prescribe how par-

---

9 Suppose, for example, that the senior creditors are owed $100 and that the reorganized company will have 100 common shares. Then, if the value of the reorganized company is determined to be $100, the senior creditors will be entitled to all of the reorganized company's shares. But if the value is determined to be $1,000, then the senior creditors will be entitled to only 10% of the company's shares.

10 For example, imagine that the company owes $100 to all of the creditors and that the reorganized company will have 100 common shares. Then, if the value of the reorganized company is determined to be $100, the equity holders will be entitled to nothing. But if the value is determined to be $1000, the equity holders will be entitled to 90% of the company's shares.

11 The difficulties involved in judicial estimates of a reorganized company's value are apparent to any reader of cases in which judges have to make such estimates. See, e.g., *In re* King Resources Co., 651 F.2d 1326, 1335–38 (10th Cir. 1980); *In re* Evans Products Co., 65 Bankr. 870, 875–6 (S.D. Fla. 1986).

12 For a description of the evolution of reorganization law in the last fifty years, see Coogan, Confirmation of a Plan under the Bankruptcy Code, Case Western Reserve Law Review 32:301 (1982), pp. 303–5, 309–26.

13 See. 11 U.S.C. sec. 1129(a) (1982 and Supp. IV 1986). For a discussion of the conditions for confirming a reorganization plan, see Trost, Business Reorganization Under Chapter 11 of the New Bankruptcy Code, *Business Law* 34:1309, pp. 1328–37.

ticipants may be grouped into classes, how their votes are to be solicited, and what majority counts as class approval.[14] The rules constrain the bargaining process by prescribing the limits within which the classes may bargain. In particular, the rules limit the concessions that a class may elect to make: The class may vote to make concessions but it may not, without unanimous agreement among the members of the class, concede to receive less than the class would get in a liquidation.[15] Similarly, the rules also limit the amount that a class can hope to extract in concessions from other classes: A plan will be confirmed in spite of the objection of a class if it can be shown that the value the class is receiving meets a certain standard.[16]

This process of bargaining and litigation is quite imperfect. First, and most importantly, the reorganization process often produces a division that substantially deviates from the participants' entitlements. Sometimes the deviation is unintentional, the result of inaccurate evaluation. Sometimes the deviation is deliberate: Participants might use their power to delay in order to extract a reorganization plan that gives them more than the value to which they are entitled. For example, equity holders, it is generally believed, often use their delaying power to extract a substantial value even in instances in which the creditors are entitled to all of the reorganization value.[17]

Second, the reorganization process often results in the choice of an inefficient capital structure for the reorganized company. The company's capital structure should be chosen solely to maximize the reorganized company's value. But under the existing system, the choice of the capital structure is often substantially affected by various strategic factors.[18]

Third, putting aside the severe shortcomings of the outcome of the division process, the process itself has substantial costs. The process usually involves significant litigation costs and frequently produces delay (beyond the time necessary to determine the size and ranking of the participants' claims). This delay might result from a genuine failure of

14 See 11 U.S.C. secs. 1122, 1125, 1126 (1982 and Supp. IV 1986); Coogan, note 12, pp. 328–36.
15 This limitation arises from the "best interest of the creditors" test established by 11 U.S.C. secs. 1129(a)(7) (1982). See Coogan, note 12, pp. 344–45.
16 A court will approve a plan over the objection of a class if the value given to the class satisfies the "absolute priority" standard. This possibility is established by the "cramdown" provision of 11 U.S.C. sec 1129(b) (1982). See Coogan, note 12, pp. 352–57.
17 See, e.g., Trost, Corporate Bankruptcy Reorganization: For the Benefit of Creditors or Stockholders? *UCLA Law Review* 24:540, (1973), p. 550.
18 For a discussion of the ways in which strategic factors shape the choice of the capital structure, see Roe, cited in note 8, pp. 536–46.

the participants to reach an agreement, but it also might be caused
deliberately by some participants whose interest would be served by a
postponement.[19] The resulting delay commonly involves significant
costs, some obvious and some subtle. For one thing, the company usually
cannot function efficiently during the reorganization period.[20]

Observers of the corporate reorganization process have long been
painfully aware of its substantial imperfections.[21] In 1978, Congress tried
to alleviate some of the widely perceived problems by making significant
changes in reorganization law. The 1978 changes, for example, sought
to provide more room for bargaining by giving classes the power to
make greater concessions to each other.[22] It is unclear, however, whether
the changes have made matters better or worse. Whether or not the
new rules are an improvement, there seems to be a consensus on one
thing – that although the division process can perhaps be improved, it
is bound to remain significantly imperfect, because of the impossibility
of accurate judicial valuation and the inevitable shortcomings of bargaining and litigation.[23]

Indeed, this perception concerning the inherent imperfection of the
division process in reorganizations has been the main basis for the view,

19 In particular, a delay often might be in the interest of equity holders. When the value
of the reorganized company is lower than the total value of creditors' claims, the equity
holders might have nothing to lose and something to gain from a delay.
20 Potential business partners, for example, might be reluctant to do business with the
company or might be willing to conduct business only on special terms. Furthermore,
management decisions during the reorganization period are afflicted with serious
conflict-of-interest problems. The company is usually run by the pre-reorganization
management, which represents the equity holders. The interests of the equity holders
in an insolvent corporation are likely to be served by courses of action that may not
be value maximizing. For example, it likely will be in the interest of the equity holders
for the company to take risks, even if taking such risks would not be value maximizing.
Taking a risky course of action will likely benefit the equity holders of an insolvent
corporation, because they might well have little to lose from a downward turn in the
company's fortunes and more to gain from an upward turn.
21 See e.g., D. Baird and T. Jackson, *Cases, Problems, and Materials of Bankruptcy*
(1985), Chapter 9; Blum, The Law and Language of Corporate Reorganization, *University of Chicago Law Review* 17:565 (1950), pp. 571–2; Brudney, The Investment-
Value Doctrine and Corporate Readjustments, *Harvard Law Review* 22:645 (1959);
Roe, note 8, pp. 536–49.
22 For a discussion and assessment of the 1978 changes, see Coogan, note 12, and Trost,
note 13.
23 Indeed, the perception that the division process is inherently imperfect is held even
by Professor Roe, who has put forward an important proposal for reforming the
process. See Roe, note 8. Although Roe's proposal would in my view be a substantial
improvement over the existing process, it would not perform as well as the method
proposed in this article. See pp. 165–6.

recently expressed by Professors Baird and Jackson, that it might be desirable to eliminate the reorganization alternative altogether and resort only to liquidation.[24] As explained below, however, this perception is wrong: The reorganization process can be greatly improved.

III   The proposed method

A   The example

To describe and assess the proposed method, it will be useful to consider it in the context of a concrete and simple example. Consider a publicly traded company that has three classes of participants. Class A includes 100 senior creditors, each owed \$1. Class B includes 100 junior creditors, each owed \$1. Class C includes 100 equity holders, each holding one unit of equity.[25]

The company is now in bankruptcy proceedings and is to be reorganized. The Reorganized Company, which I will call RC, is going to have a capital structure that for now I will assume to be given. For any chosen capital structure, it is of course possible to divide the securities of RC into 100 equal units. For example, if RC has 100 shares of common stock and 50 shares of preferred stock, then each of the 100 RC units will consist of 1 common share and 1/2 preferred share. The question for the reorganization process is how to divide the 100 units of RC among the three classes of participants.

B   Dividing the pie supposing its size is known

Let us denote the value of the reorganized company RC as V per unit. Thus, $100V$ is the total size of the pie to be distributed. As already noted, the division of the pie would be a straightforward matter if we could measure its size exactly (that is, if we could estimate V with precision). In such a case, we would simply proceed according to the ranking of the various classes involved.

Consider first the case in which the figure placed on V is no higher

---

24 See note 7, T. Jackson, Chapter 9; note 7, Baird, pp. 127–48.

25 As will be apparent, the method would also apply well to companies whose stock is not publicly traded, because the method's effectiveness does not hinge on the presence of market trading. Similarly, the other simplifying features of the example are not essential for the method's effectiveness. In particular, Section VI will show how the method might be adapted to situations in which the company has more than three classes of participants, secured creditors, and/or a class whose claims are concentrated in one hand.

than $1. In this case, the total pie is no greater than $100, which is the full value of class A's claims. Therefore, all the 100 units of RC should be given to the senior creditors (and divided among them pro rata).

Consider next the case in which the figure placed on V is greater than $1 but no greater than $2. In this case, the total pie is no greater than $200, which is the full value of the claims of the senior and junior creditors, and it thus should be divided only among the creditors. Because there is enough to pay the senior creditors in full, they should receive a value of $100, which can be accomplished by giving them 100/V units. When these units are divided among senior creditors pro rata, each senior creditor receives 1/V unit worth $1. The junior creditors should receive the remaining value of 100V − $100, which can be accomplished by giving them the remaining 100 − (100/V) units. Dividing these units among the junior creditors, each would end up with 1 − (1/V) unit.[26]

Finally, consider the case in which the figure placed on V is higher than $2. In this case, there is more than enough to pay both class A and class B in full. To be paid in full, the senior creditors as a class should receive 100/V units, with each senior creditor getting 1/V unit. The junior creditors, also paid in full, should also receive 100/V units total, or 1/V unit each. And the equity holders should receive the remaining value of 100V − $200. This would be accomplished by giving them − and dividing among them pro rata − the remaining 100 − (200/V) units (1 − (2/V) unit for each equity holder).[27]

The conclusions of the above analysis − showing how the reorganization pie should be divided if we could measure V precisely − are summarized in Table 5.1.[28]

---

26 For example, if V is $1.25, then class A should receive 80 shares (100/1.25), with each senior creditor receiving 0.8 share, and class B should receive 20 shares (100 − 100/ 1.25), with each junior creditor receiving 0.2 share.

27 For example, if V is $2.50, then the senior creditors should get 40 shares (0.40 share each), the junior creditors should get 40 shares (0.40 share each), and the equity holders should get 20 shares (0.20 share each).

28 Another way of expressing participants' entitlements as a function of V is by using the mathematical notation min(., .) and max(., .). (This notation has the following meaning: min(x, y) denotes the smaller of the values x and y; similarly, max(x, y) denotes the greater of the values x and y.) As we have seen, a senior creditor is entitled to receive the smaller of (1) $1, the full value of his claim, and (2) V, his pro rata share of the reorganization value. Thus, a senior creditor is entitled to min($1, V). A junior creditor is entitled to receive no less than the smaller of (1) $1, the full value of his claim, and (2) his pro rata share of the value left, if any, after the senior creditors are paid in full, which is max(0, V − $1). Therefore, the junior creditor is entitled to min($1, max(0, V − $1)).

Table 5.1. *Distribution of units supposing* V *is known*

Value of V	Distribution of units	
$V \le 1$	Senior creditors:	1 unit each (worth V)
	Junior creditors:	Nothing
	Equity holders:	Nothing
$1 < V \le 2$	Senior creditors:	$1/V$ unit each (worth \$1)
	Junior creditors:	$1 - (1/V)$ unit each (worth $V - \$1$)
	Equity holders:	Nothing
$V > 2$	Senior creditors:	$1/V$ unit each (worth \$1)
	Junior creditors:	$1/V$ unit each (worth \$1)
	Equity holders:	$1 - (2/V)$ unit each (worth $V - \$2$)

C   *Participants' entitlements as a function of reorganization value*

The question of division thus would pose no problem if we could measure V with precision. As already emphasized, however, the value of V – and thus also the monetary value to which each participant is entitled – cannot be determined with indisputable accuracy. But even though we cannot identify precisely the value to which each participant is entitled, we can precisely express this value as a function of V, the reorganized company's per unit value.

Consider first the senior creditors. As the analysis above has shown, a senior creditor is entitled to a value of V if $V \le \$1$ and a value of \$1 if $V > \$1$. Alternatively put, a senior creditor is entitled to a value of \$1 unless the reorganization value is less than \$100, in which case the senior creditor is entitled to his pro rata share of the reorganization value (that is, to one unit of RC).

Consider next the junior creditors. A junior creditor, we have seen, is entitled to nothing if $V \le \$1$, is entitled to $V - \$1$ if $\$1 < V \le \$2$, and is entitled to \$1 if $V > \$2$. Alternatively put, a junior creditor is entitled to a value of \$1 unless the reorganization value is less than \$200, in which case he is entitled to his pro rata share of the value that is left, if any, after the senior creditors are paid in full.

Finally, an equity holder is entitled to nothing if $V \le \$2$, and to $V - \$2$

Finally, an equity holder is entitled to no less than his pro rata share of the value left, if any, after the senior and junior creditors are paid in full. Thus, the equity holder is entitled to $\max(0, V - \$2)$. To summarize, the participants' entitlements are as follows: Senior creditors, $\min(\$1, V)$; junior creditors, $\min(\$1, \max(0, V - \$1))$; equity holders, $\max(0, V - \$2)$.

Table 5.2. *Participants' entitlements as a function of* V

	$V \leq \$1$	$\$1 < V \leq \$2$	$V > \$2$
Senior creditor	V	$\$1$	$\$1$
Junior creditor	0	$V - \$1$	$\$1$
Equity holder	0	0	$V - \$2$
Total	V	V	V

if $V > \$2$. Alternatively put, an equity holder is entitled to his pro rata share of the value that is left, if any, after the senior and junior creditors are paid in full.

Table 5.2 summarizes these conclusions concerning participants' entitlements as a function of the reorganization value.

D   The proposed approach

The idea underlying the proposed method is simple. Even though we do not know V and consequently do not know the value of participants' entitlements in terms of dollars or RC units, we do know precisely what participants are entitled to as a function of V (that is, for any value that V might take). With this knowledge, it is possible to design and to distribute to the participants a set of rights concerning RC's units such that, for any value that V might take, these rights would provide participants with values perfectly consistent with their entitlements.

Before describing the proposed approach, a preliminary remark on implementation is in order. As will be seen presently, each of the rights distributed to participants will have an "option" component.[29] In principle, the options should be for immediate exercise. However, because the participants might need a little bit of time to understand the terms of the options given to them, it might well be desirable to provide them with such time. The exercise date of the options, then, will be shortly after the distribution of the rights. For concreteness, I will assume below that the reorganized company will start its life and distribute the rights to participants on January 1, and that the exercise date for all the rights distributed will be four days later, on January 5.

29 As economists have recognized, it is often useful to break a security into its option components. Many securities can be described usefully as a set of certain options with respect to the assets of the issuing firm. See, e.g., R. Brearley and S. Myers, *Principles of Corporate Finance*. 2d ed. (1984), Chapters 20, 23.

Thus, on January 1, the reorganized company will start its life. But, under the proposed method, the units of RC will not be distributed at this point but rather will be retained by the company until January 5. Instead of receiving RC units, on January 1 the participants will get the following rights with respect to RC units:

Senior creditors. Each senior creditor will receive one type A right. A type-A right may be redeemed by the company on January 5 for $1. If the right is not redeemed, its holder on January 5 will be entitled to receive one unit of RC.[30]

To get some sense at this stage of the value to senior creditors of receiving type-A rights, consider a creditor that holds his type-A right until January 5. If the right is redeemed, then the creditor will be paid in full. If the right is not redeemed, then the creditor will receive a value of V. And indeed, the senior creditor is never entitled to receive more than either $1 or V (see Table 5.2).

Junior creditors. Each junior creditor will receive a type-B right. The company may redeem a type-B right on January 5 for $1. If the right is not redeemed, its holder will have the option on January 5 to purchase one unit of RC for $1. To exercise this option, the holder of the right must submit it to the company by January 5 accompanied by a payment of the $1 exercise price.[31]

Again, it might be worthwhile to describe briefly how receiving a type-B right will provide a junior creditor with the value to which he is entitled. If the creditor holds on to the type-B right and the right is redeemed, then the creditor will be paid in full. If the right is not redeemed, exercising it will provide the creditor with a value of $V - \$1$. And indeed, the creditor is never entitled to receive a value higher than both $1 and $V - \$1$ (see Table 5.2).

Equity holders. Each equity holder will receive one type-C right. A type-C right may not be redeemed by the company. The holder of a

30 In the terminology of options, a type-A right is equivalent to the following position: having one (call) option on one RC unit with an exercise price of $0, plus being short one (call) option on one RC unit with an exercise price of $1.

31 In the terminology of options, one type-B right is equivalent to the following position: having one (call) option on one RC unit with an exercise price of $1, plus being short one (call) option on one RC unit with an exercise price of $2. If the option on which the holder is short is not exercised, he will simply end up with an option to purchase one RC unit for $1. If the option on which the holder is short is exercised, he will end up with $1 (purchasing one RC unit for $1 and selling it for $2).

type-*C* right will have the option to purchase one *RC* unit on January 5 for $2. To exercise this option, the holder must submit the right to the company by January 5 accompanied by a payment of the $2 exercise price.[32]

Note that if an equity holder holds on to his right until January 5 and then chooses to exercise it, he will get a value $V - \$2$. And indeed, the equity holder is never entitled to a positive value exceeding $V - \$2$ (see Table 5.2).

These three types of rights will all be transferable. Thus, between January 1 and January 5, there will presumably be public trading in the rights. A participant that is given any one of the rights may thus either sell it on the market or retain it until the exercise date of January 5.

Table 5.3 summarizes the terms of the rights to be distributed to participants.

E   The exercise of rights

Adding up the obligations that *RC* will have toward the holders of type-*A,* type-*B,* and type-*C* rights shows that the net obligation of *RC* is to distribute 100 *RC* units on January 5, which is exactly what is available for distribution. Thus, *RC* should have no problem meeting all its obligations toward the holders of the three types of rights. Nonetheless, it is worth going through the mechanics of the process in detail.

Suppose first that all of the holders of type-*C* rights wish to exercise their options to buy *RC* units and that they submit a total of $200 to the company. *RC* then will provide them with all 100 units of *RC* (one unit for each right submitted), and it will use the $200 received from them to redeem all of the type-*A* and type-*B* rights.

Suppose now that no type-*C* rights are submitted for exercise, but that all holders of type-*B* rights wish to exercise their options to buy *RC* units at $1 and therefore submit a total of $100 to the company. In this case, *RC* will give all of the *RC* units to the holders of these type-*B* rights, and it will use the $100 received from them to redeem all of the type-*A* rights.

Next, suppose that no type-*B* or type-*C* rights are submitted for exercise. The mechanics of this case will be simpler still: The 100 units of *RC* will be distributed to the holders of type-*A* rights (one *RC* unit per right).

Finally, it remains to consider situations in which only a fraction of

32 In the terminology of options, one type-*C* right is equivalent to one (call) option on one *RC* unit with an exercise price of $2.

Table 5.3. *The distribution of rights*

Senior creditors

Each senior creditor receives one type-*A* right. A type-*A* right may be re-deemed by the company on January 5 for $1. If the right is not redeemed, on January 5 its holder will be entitled to receive one unit of *RC*.

Junior creditors

Each junior creditor receives one type-*B* right. A type-*B* right may be re-deemed by the company on January 5 for $1. If the right is not redeemed, on January 5 its holder will have the option to purchase one unit of *RC* for $1.

Equity holders

Each equity holder receives one type-*C* right. A type-*C* right may not be redeemed by the company. The holder of such a right on January 5 will have the option to purchase one unit of *RC* for $2.

---

the type-*B* or type-*C* rights are submitted for exercise. Such situations are unlikely to arise if there is public trading in the rights.[33] But in any event, given the design of the rights – in particular, the fact that the total net obligation of the company toward all right holders is to dis-tribute 100 units of *RC* – such situations will present no special problem for the execution process.

For example, suppose that only 50 type-*B* rights (and presumably no type-*C* rights)[34] are submitted for exercise. Then, those who submitted

---

33 To see why such situations are unlikely, imagine for example that as January 5 arrives, some holders of type-*B* rights (the "optimists") submit their rights for exercise while other holders of type-*B* rights (the "pessimists") do not submit their rights. The optimists' behavior indicates that they believe that *V* exceeds $1. The pessimists, as long as they do not intend to use their rights in any way, should be happy to sell them for any negligible positive price. Thus, as long as some shares are held by pessimists who are not going to use them, the market price of type-*B* rights must be negligible. But at such a market price, the optimists would buy the rights and submit them to the company for exercise. Alternatively put, if the optimists, but not the pessimists, view the rights as having some value and use, then, in the presence of market trading, the rights should all end up at the hands of the optimists, who would use them; no rights would remain idle in the hands of pessimists to whom the rights are of no use.

34 If some type-*B* rights are not submitted for exercise, then the market price of such rights must be negligible. In such a case, no holder of a type-*C* right will have a reason to submit it. If the holder did submit a type-*C* right, he would have to pay $2 to get one *RC* unit. Therefore, even if the holder does believe that *V* exceeds $2, he will still be better off not using his type-*C* right but instead purchasing a type-*B* right for the negligible market price, and then using this right to purchase an *RC* unit for only $1.

type-B rights will receive 50 units of RC (one unit per submitted right). The $50 submitted by them will be used for pro rata redemption of type-A rights. Consequently, each holder of a type-A right will end up with $0.50 and 0.50 units of RC.

More generally, RC will proceed in situations of partial submission of rights as follows. The money received from the exercise of type-C rights will be used half for pro rata redemption of type-A rights and half for pro rata redemption of type-B rights. The money received from the exercise of (unredeemed and submitted) type-B rights will be used for pro rata redemption of type-A rights. The 100 RC units will be given to those submitting type-C rights, those submitting type-B rights that are not going to be redeemed, and those holding type-A rights that are not going to be redeemed.[35]

IV   Consistency with participants' entitlements

This section demonstrates that the outcome of the proposed method of division will be perfectly consistent with the entitlements of the participants. As emphasized earlier, the problems of the division process arise from the difficulties involved in determining the monetary value of the reorganized company. The proposed method, however, makes no attempt to estimate this monetary value, nor does it require even a rough sense of the monetary value of the rights that the participants will receive. Although we may not know how much these rights are worth, we can be confident that whatever their worth is, they will provide the receiving participants with no less than the value to which they are entitled.

A   *The significance of not relying on accurate market pricing*

The rights given to the participants will be traded on the market in the brief period between the issue date and the exercise date. As the analysis

---

35 To consider a more complex example than the one above, suppose that only 50 type-C rights and all of the type-B rights are submitted for exercise. Those who submitted type-C rights will receive 50 RC units. The $100 received from them will be used for a pro rata redemption of 50 type-A and 50 type-B rights: Each holder of a type-A or a type-B right will have half of his right redeemed. The 50 remaining RC units will be divided among the holders of the 50 unredeemed, submitted type-B rights. The $50 received by the company from the exercise of these 50 type-B rights will be used to redeem the remaining 50 type-A rights. In sum, the units of RC will end up half in the hands of those submitting type-C rights and half in the hands of those holding type-B rights.

below will indicate, if the market does not underestimate the reorganized company's value, then the market price of any type of right will be no less than the value to which the participants receiving the right are entitled; consequently, the participants will be able to capture the value of their entitlement by immediately selling their rights on the market. Thus, the conclusion concerning the method's effectiveness follows immediately if one assumes that the market will not undervalue the distributed rights. As this section shows, however, such an assumption is not necessary to reach this conclusion: The method's effectiveness does not hinge on the market's not undervaluing the rights or even on the presence of market trading in the rights.

This feature of the method is very important. Many may believe that capital market prices are efficient not only in most cases but also in the particular case of companies in financial distress. But whatever one's views on the merits of this question, one must recognize that many public officials and commentators believe that the market often errs (and usually in the direction of undervaluation) in appraising the value of companies that emerge out of reorganization.[36] Indeed, the primary rationale for the existence of the reorganization alternative to liquidation is the concern that the market often undervalues such companies; if the market could be relied on to price such companies perfectly, there would be no reason to expect that a reorganization would ever provide the participants with a greater value than they would get from a going-concern sale effected through a Chapter 7 liquidation proceeding. Thus, any examination of the best reorganization method should take into account the concern that the market's estimate might be inaccurate. It is therefore a significant advantage of the proposed method that an inaccurate market pricing of the rights will not provide participants with a basis for objecting to the method's outcome.

This feature of the method is the main reason why it is superior to the method of division put forward by Professor Roe five years ago.[37] Roe was the first to seek, as I do in this article, a method of division that would not be based on the problematic process of bargaining among the various classes of participants. He proposed to estimate the value of the reorganized company by selling 10 percent of the reorganized company's securities on the market and then extrapolating the com-

---

36 See, e.g., *Citibank, N.A.* v. *Baer*, 651 F.2d 1341, 1347–48 (10th Cir. 1980); *In re* Interstate Stores, Inc., SEC Corporate Reorganization Release No. 322, 13 S.E.C. Docket 757, 786–87 (1977); Blum, note 21, pp. 566–67; Brudney, note 21, pp. 673–75.

37 See Roe, note 8.

166   **Lucian Arye Bebchuk**

pany's value from the sale price for these securities. Although Roe's method is, in my view, superior to the existing process of bargaining among classes, the method's reliance on market pricing makes it, as Roe himself recognized,[38] substantially imperfect. First, the method does not address the concerns of those who believe that the market might not perceive accurately the value of companies in reorganization. Second, even if the market's perceptions are accurate, selling a sample of the company's securities might produce an inaccurate figure, because some participants will have an incentive to manipulate the sale price. Third, Roe's method is inapplicable to companies whose securities are not publicly traded. Because the method that I propose does not hinge on the existence of accurate market pricing, it does not suffer from any of these problems.

Before proceeding to a detailed demonstration, it is worth stating briefly why accurate market pricing of the rights is not essential for the proposed method's effectiveness. Although participants may sell their rights on the market, they can always choose to retain them until the exercise date. If they do so, then, as is shown below, they will not end up with less than the value to which they are entitled. Consequently, even assuming that a given participant does not have, or attaches no value to, the opportunity to sell his rights on the market, the participant will have no basis for complaining about the method's outcome.

B   *The outcome in the example*

To demonstrate the method's effectiveness, I wish first to show that, in the example used in Section III, no participant has any basis for complaining about the method's outcome. Consider first the senior creditors. If they retain the type-*A* rights given to them, they will end up in one of two positions. First, their rights may be redeemed for $100 (if the holders of the type-*B* or type-*C* rights choose to exercise them). In this case, the senior creditors surely cannot complain about the outcome, as their claims will be paid in full. Alternatively, the senior creditors' rights may not be redeemed, in which case the creditors will end up holding all 100 units of *RC*. Again, they will have no basis for complaining, for they will be getting the whole reorganization pie: There is nothing more that could be given to them.

Now, the senior creditors surely might be unhappy about the way in which the market assesses the value of *RC* units and therefore also the value of type-*A* rights. Suppose that the senior creditors believe *V* to

38 Ibid. pp. 575–80.

be $0.90, and suppose that the market believes the value of V to be only $0.50. In this case, the senior creditors will not be able to sell their type-A rights for more than $0.50. Similarly, if and when they get the units of RC, they will be able to sell them for only $0.50. But the fact that others are unwilling to pay the senior creditors more than $0.50 for what in their view is worth $0.90 does not provide the senior creditors with a basis for complaining that the reorganization's outcome deprives them of the value to which they are entitled – for they will receive from the reorganization process all that there is to distribute. They can complain about the market ("Oh, the market is not what it is supposed to be") but not about the method's way of dividing RC units among the participants.

Consider now the junior creditors. If the junior creditors do not sell their type-B rights, they can end up in one of two positions. First, their rights may be redeemed by the company at $1 per right (if the type-C rights are submitted for exercise). In this case, the junior creditors will be paid in full and clearly have no reason to complain. Alternatively, the junior creditors may end up with options to purchase RC units at $1 per unit. The value of these options is by definition not lower than the value to which the creditors are entitled – for the junior creditors are entitled to no more than the value that is left, if any, after the senior creditors are paid in full. And having the option to receive all of the reorganization pie by paying the senior creditors' prior $100 claim makes the above value accessible to the junior creditors.

Again, the junior creditors might be unhappy about the way in which the market assesses the value of RC units and thus the value of their type-B rights. Suppose for example that the junior creditors believe that V is $1.90 and that the value to which they are entitled is thus $90 (the reorganization value of $190 minus the senior creditors' claims of $100). Suppose further that the market estimates V at $1.50 and thus prices the junior creditors' type-B rights at $0.50. The junior creditors will have no basis for complaining that the rights given to them have a $50 value, which is less than the $90 to which they are entitled. It would be inconsistent for them to assert both (1) that V is $1.90 and they are thus entitled to $0.90 each, and (2) that the value of their options is only $0.50 each. If V is $1.90, then the value of an option to buy an RC unit at $1 is $0.90; this value can be realized simply by exercising the option. The junior creditors thus should not sell their type-B rights to the unappreciative market; if they do sell, they will have only themselves to blame.

Finally, consider the equity holders. If they do not sell their type-C rights, they will on the exercise date have options to purchase RC units at \$2. These options will make accessible to them the very value to which they are entitled – which is all that is left, if anything, after the claims of the senior and junior creditors are paid in full.

Again, the equity holders may claim that the market undervalues the value of *RC* units and thus the value of their type-*C* rights. But then they should not sell their rights; rather they should retain and exercise them. Their perception (whether accurate or not) that such undervaluation takes place will provide them with no basis for complaining about the method's outcome – for reasons similar to those that have been discussed above with respect to the junior creditors.

C   *A more general defense*

Having examined in detail the method's outcome in our example, I now wish to state in general terms why any given participant will have no basis for complaining that the method's outcome is inconsistent with his entitlement. Suppose first that a given participant retains the right distributed to him until the exercise date. For him to assert that he has received less than the value to which he is entitled, he has to assert (1) that those above him in priority (or those who bought their rights) have received too much, or (2) that those below him in priority (or those who bought their rights) have received too much.

Those below the participant in priority (or those who bought their rights) will be able to capture any value only if they pay in full all the claims of those above them – including the participant's own claim. Thus, the participant will never have a basis for complaining that he is receiving too little because those below him are getting too much.

Similarly, the participant will be unable to complain that those above him in priority (or those who bought their rights) are getting too much – that is, that they are paid more than in full. By exercising the option given to him, the participant can ensure that, as far as his pro rata share of the company is concerned, those above him will not get more than the full value of their claims. The option automatically makes accessible to him his pro rata share of the value left after the preceding claims are paid in full – and he is entitled to no more.[39]

39 To illustrate the above reasoning, consider the position of a junior creditor in our example. For the creditor to have a justifiable complaint, he must assert either that the senior creditors are getting too much or that the equity holders are getting too much. The junior creditor cannot complain that the equity holders are getting too much, because they will get something only in the event that the junior creditor's type-*B* right is redeemed, in which case he will be paid in full. Similarly, the junior creditor's possession of a type-*B* right should prevent him from complaining that the senior

Thus, assuming that the participant's right is not transferable and that he must retain it until the exercise date, he will not end up with less than the value of his entitlement. And, clearly, he cannot be made worse off by the ability to sell his right, if he so wishes, in the period preceding the exercise date: If he believes that the market undervalues his right, he need not sell but rather can retain his right until the exercise date. Indeed, the ability to sell may improve the participant's situation: If he believes that the market accurately prices his right or overvalues it, he presumably will benefit from having the opportunity to sell.

D   Addressing the problem of differing estimates

An alternative way of explaining the proposed method's effectiveness is by showing how it addresses the valuation problem, which may be referred to as the problem of divergent estimates. Because no objective, indisputable figure is available for the reorganized company's value, participants may advance different estimates of this value. If the participants could all be expected to advance the same estimate, the question of division would be straightforward: Their common estimate could be used to divide the reorganized company's securities. The division question is difficult only because participants may well differ in the estimates they advance. Such differences may result from either strategic manipulation or genuine disagreement.

Strategic manipulation. Under the existing method of division, even if all participants actually share the same estimate of the reorganized company's value, they may well have strategic reasons for advancing different estimates. In the bargaining between any class and the classes preceding it, the preceding classes have an incentive to advance a low estimate whereas the junior class has the opposite interest.

Suppose, for instance, that the junior creditors and the senior creditors in our example have the same estimate of V, and consider what estimates they will find it in their interest to advance during bargaining and litigation under the existing method of division. The senior creditors will generally find it in their interest to advance an estimate below the participants' common estimate, for a low value of V would entitle them to a larger fraction of RC's securities. The junior creditors will generally

creditors are receiving too much – that is, more than $100, the full value of their claims. For, by exercising his right, the junior creditor can ensure that, as far as his pro rata share of the company is concerned, the senior creditors will not receive more than the full value of their claims.

find it in their interest to advance an estimate exceeding the participants' common estimate, for a high value of V would entitle them to a larger fraction of RC's securities.

Under the proposed method, however, no class will be able to benefit from strategic manipulation of estimates. The division of securities will in no way depend on what the participants or anyone else *claim* V is. The division depends only on what the participants *do* with their rights. And the participants' decisions whether to exercise their rights will necessarily reflect their true judgment concerning V. In particular, the junior creditors in our example will not be able to get any value simply by asserting that V exceeds $1; the only way for them to get any value is by exercising their rights (which of course they will do only if they estimate V to exceed $1). Similarly, the senior creditors will not be able to get a higher value by strategically advancing a low estimate of V; what they will end up with depends only on what the junior creditors elect to do with their rights.

Genuine disagreement. Strategic manipulation is not the only reason for the different estimates that parties may advance under the existing reorganization process. Parties also may differ in their estimates due to genuine disagreement. Such differences may exist not only among classes but also among the participants in any given class.

The proposed method addresses the possibility of different subjective estimates by enabling each participant to decide individually, based on his *own* estimate of the reorganized company's value, whether to exercise his rights. Consequently, each participant will get no less, and may indeed get more, than the value to which he believes he is entitled based on his *own* estimate of the reorganization value.

Consider, for instance, a junior creditor in our example. If the creditor believes that V is less than $1, then the value of his entitlement based on his estimate of V is zero (see Table 5.2). If the creditor keeps his right, which he will have to do if the right's market price is zero, he will not exercise it and indeed will end up with no value. But if others are more optimistic and believe that V exceeds $1, then the market price of type-B rights will be positive, and the creditor will be able to sell his right for this positive market price.

Next, suppose that the creditor believes that V is between $1 and $2, for instance $1.50, and that he thus believes that the value of his entitlement is $0.50 (see Table 5.2). By retaining and exercising his right, the junior creditor can capture a value that equals his own estimate of the value of his entitlement. If other parties are more optimistic and have higher estimates of V, however, the creditor will be able to capture a value that exceeds his own estimate of his entitlement. In such a case, the market price of his type-*B* right will exceed its \$0.50 value to him, and he will sell his right for this higher market price.

Finally, if the junior creditor believes that *V* exceeds \$2, then the value of his entitlement, based on his estimate of *V*, will be \$1 (a payment in full of his claim) (see Table 5.2). If others also believe that *V* exceeds \$2, then, because type-*C* rights will be exercised, type-*B* rights will be redeemed at \$1 (and will trade at \$1 beforehand). In such a case, the creditor will end up with a value that equals in his eyes the value of his entitlement. But if others are more pessimistic and believe that *V* is below \$2, then the participant's type-*B* right will not be redeemed, and by exercising it, he will end up with a value exceeding in his eyes the value of his entitlement.

E   Note on participants' information and financial resources

A question that some may raise is whether one can object to the proposed method by arguing that participants lack sufficient information or financial resources.

Information. Under the proposed method, as well as under the existing process of division, participants must make decisions on the basis of whatever information they have concerning the reorganized company's value. Therefore, it is necessary to examine whether, in comparison to the existing process, the proposed method might either increase the amount of information that participants need or decrease the amount of information that they possess.

The proposed method does not increase the participants' need for information. Under the existing process, each class of participants must make its bargaining and litigation decisions on the basis of whatever estimate of the reorganized company's value it happens to have. Assuming that participants will not have less information under the proposed method than under the existing process, they will be able to use the same estimate to make the necessary decisions about their rights.

Indeed, under the proposed method, participants will not even need to make a judgment, as they must under the existing process, concerning their best estimate of the reorganized company's value. They will only have to make the much more limited judgment whether the reorganized company's value exceeds the estimate that is implicit in the market price of their rights (that is, whether the value of their rights exceeds the rights' market price).

Finally, there is no reason to assume that participants will have less information under the proposed method than under the existing process. Indeed, the proposed method provides an important additional source of information – the market pricing of rights. To be sure, the proposed method may still reduce the amount of information that participants will have if it substantially decreases the extent to which participants take advantage of the available sources of information. Such a decrease may arguably take place because of collective action problems: Under the proposed method, participants will act individually rather than collectively, and they may have less incentive or ability to look for information. But the proposed method will not prevent participants from acquiring information as a class rather than individually when there are some advantages in doing so: In such cases, the committee representing the class will likely engage in information acquisition (say, by hiring an investment banker to do the job) and then disseminate its conclusions to individual class members.

Financial resources and willingness to invest. Another possible objection to the method arises from the fact that the method will require some participants to invest in the enterprise to capture the value to which they are entitled. Participants in an insolvent company, so the argument might go, may reasonably be reluctant to make such an investment or may lack the necessary financial resources.

It should initially be noted that most participants will not need to put in any money to capture the value of their entitlements. For one thing, many participants will have their rights redeemed by the company. Furthermore, even participants whose rights are not redeemed by the company will not have to put in any money if they believe that the market does not underestimate the reorganized company's value; in such a case, they can capture the value to which they believe they are entitled by selling their rights on the market. Thus, a given participant will need to invest money to capture the value of his entitlement only when the company does not redeem his rights and he believes that the market is underestimating the reorganized company's value.

Consider a junior creditor in our example who believes that V is $1.50 (in other words, that buying an RC unit at $1.50 will provide an "adequate" rate of return) – and who thus believes that he is entitled to $0.50. Suppose also that the market estimates V to be only $1.30 and thus prices the creditor's type-B right at $0.30. The creditor will be able to capture the value to which he believes he is entitled only if he invests the $1 necessary to exercise his right.

Let us first suppose that the amount at stake constitutes a small fraction of the creditor's wealth. In such a case, the creditor's need to put in $1 will not provide him with a basis for complaint, for if V is equal to $1.50 in his judgment, then from his perspective purchasing a unit worth V for $1 must be equivalent to his getting $0.50. To see this equivalency, observe that purchasing a unit for $1 is equivalent to receiving $0.50 plus being required to purchase an RC unit for $1.50. Given that the amount at stake is small relative to the creditor's wealth and that the creditor values the RC unit at $1.50, the creditor should be indifferent to the requirement that he purchase a unit for $1.50.

Thus, if the amounts that participants need to invest to exercise their rights are small relative to their wealth, which I suspect is the case for most participants in reorganizations of publicly traded corporations, then the need to invest will pose no problem. If participants' wealth is not sufficiently large relative to the amount at stake, however, problems may arise. Suppose, for instance, that the junior creditor in the example discussed above does not have the $1 necessary to exercise his right. In such a situation, the creditor may complain that his lack of funds forces him to sell his type-B right for a price below the value of his entitlements: Given the undervaluation of RC's units by the market, he will end up with only $0.30 rather than the $0.50 to which he believes he is entitled.

Even when such a liquidity problem does arise, it commonly can be eliminated or at least substantially alleviated by the participant's ability to borrow. In a well-functioning capital market, the junior creditor's borrowing power will be augmented by his ability to use as collateral the very RC unit that he will buy. In the example under consideration, if the market estimates the value of an RC unit at $1.30, then a junior creditor will be able to borrow the $1 necessary to exercise his option by pledging the purchased RC unit as a collateral.[40]

In sum, although the need to invest funds might pose some problems to the effectiveness of the proposed method, these problems appear to be quite limited. Most participants will not need to invest any amount in order to capture the value to which they believe they are entitled, because their rights will be either redeemed or valued sufficiently by the market. Furthermore, those who will need to invest will have no basis for complaining as long as the amount at stake is small relative to their wealth. Finally, as for those whose rights will be neither redeemed nor sufficiently valued by the market and whose wealth is not sufficiently

---

40 Lack of sufficient financial resources, then, may pose a problem only if the market's estimate of V is lower than not only the creditor's estimate but also the $1 that the creditor needs to exercise his right. For example, if the market estimates V at $0.80, then the junior creditor will not be able to borrow the full $1 necessary to exercise his right by pledging the unit as collateral.

large relative to the amount at stake, any problem resulting from the need to invest will be mitigated by their ability to borrow.

V   Implementation

A   *Under a new reorganization regime*

The proposed method of division is put forward as the basis for reform of reorganization law. The optimal reorganization regime, I suggest, is one that requires and facilitates the use of this method in every case of reorganization.

The proposed reorganization regime will include, as any reorganization regime must, a preliminary process of determining the size and ranking of participants' claims; this process may be straightforward at times, but it also may be complex and time-consuming at other times. Once the participants' claims are identified, however, the process of division will proceed smoothly and quickly.

Although the process of division will largely follow automatically from the method's principles, a reorganization plan will be necessary to fix some limited elements of the reorganized company's features. In particular, the plan would fix the reorganized company's capital structure.[41] Several possible parties can be charged with designing a reorganization plan for confirmation by the supervising court. Possible candidates include a trustee appointed by the court, incumbent management (which presumably represents the equity holders), or the committee representing a certain class of creditors. Note that assigning the role of designing the plan to representatives of a given class of participants will not create a conflict-of-interest problem. Given the way in which the proposed method operates, the choice of capital structure cannot be used to divert value from one class of participants to another. Therefore, in choosing the capital structure, the party charged with designing the reorganization plan will aim solely at maximizing the value of the reorganized company.

Because of the limited elements that the reorganization plan will cover, designing it and receiving the court's confirmation will presumably take relatively little time. Once the capital structure is specified, the division will proceed automatically and swiftly: Rights to the reorganized company's securities will be distributed to participants in accordance

41 As Section VI will explain, the plan may also include a few other elements, such as the treatment of secured claims and the reinstatement of some contracts with favorable terms.

with the method, the securities themselves will be distributed shortly afterward as the rights are exercised, and the company will be out of the reorganization process, hopefully on its way to a bright future.

This regime will best address the efficiency and fairness problems that have thus far afflicted the division process in corporate reorganizations. First, the outcome will always be in accordance with the entitlements of all the participants involved. Second, the choice of capital structure will be value maximizing. Third, the delay and litigation costs under the new regime will be the smallest possible under any reorganization regime (largely consisting of the unavoidable delay and costs involved in determining the size and ranking of claims).

B   Under existing law

The proposed method may be useful even under the existing reorganization rules. Some parties should find it in their interest to use the method as a basis for the reorganization plans that they file.

Under the existing rules, the equity holders usually have the exclusive right for a specified period of time to file (and seek confirmation of) a reorganization plan.[42] Subsequently, any participant may file a reorganization plan.[43] To obtain confirmation of a reorganization plan, its proponents must achieve either (1) acceptance of the plan by every class, or (2) if a class objects, a judicial overruling of this objection on the grounds that the plan provides the class with no less than its entitlement.[44] Achieving either (1) or (2) is often problematic or at least time-consuming: Securing class approval involves the complications of bargaining, and obtaining a judicial determination that the plan provides the class with the value of its entitlement involves the difficult problems of valuation.

Once the period in which the equity holders have exclusive right to propose plans has passed, it will be in the interest of the senior creditors to file a plan based on the proposed method. The proposed method will provide the senior creditors either with the full value of their claims or at least with all of the reorganized company's securities, which is all they can hope for. Furthermore, they will be able to secure confirmation of such a plan relatively quickly; given the way in which the method is designed, they should face no difficulty in demonstrating to the court

---

42 See 11 U.S.C. sec. 1121(b) (1982); Trost, note 13, pp. 1325–26.
43 See 11 U.S.C. sec. 1121(c) (1982 & Supp. IV 1986).
44 Ibid., sec. 1129(a)(7)(A), (b)(1); Trost, note 13, pp. 1328–44.

that their plan provides all other classes with no less than the value to which these classes are entitled.

Using the method will free the senior creditors from the threat of strategic behavior by participants junior to them. At present, juniors may seek more than the value to which they are entitled by threatening to oppose the plan and create protracted litigation. The proposed method will eliminate this threat by enabling the senior creditors to demonstrate easily that their plan provides all participants with a value consistent with their entitlements.

If parties do use the proposed method in their confirmation plans, some of the potential benefits of the method will be obtained even under existing rules. First, and most importantly, outcomes will come closer to those suggested by the participants' entitlements. Second, parties using the method as a basis for their reorganization plans will choose a capital structure solely on the basis of their judgment as to which structure would be value maximizing. Third, delays and litigation costs will decrease significantly.

VI   Extensions

The analysis in Sections III and IV used a concrete example for convenience of illustration. This section drops the simplifying assumptions used in constructing that example and considers four important complications that are present in reorganizations. I first show how the method can be adjusted easily to apply to situations in which there are more than three classes. I then discuss three issues that may arise and require treatment under any reorganization regime – contracts with favorable terms that are worth reinstating, secured claims, and concentration of claims in one hand. As I explain, the proposed method of division is consistent with any way that reorganization law might wish to treat these issues. Consequently, the potential presence of these problems does not undermine my earlier conclusion that the proposed method offers the best way of dividing the reorganization pie.

A   More than three classes

The example used above consisted of a company with three consecutively ranked classes, each with 100 units of membership. The method, however, can be applied easily in the general case of a company with any number of membership units. Describing the operation of the method in general terms, applicable to any such case, the rights distributed to participants will be as follows.

Each unit of membership in the most senior class will entitle its holder to receive a right that the company may redeem for the participant's pro rata fraction of the class's total claim. If this right is not redeemed, it will entitle its holder to receive (without any payment) his pro rata fraction of the reorganized company's securities.[45]

Each unit of membership in any intermediate class (any class below the most senior one and above the most junior one) will entitle its holder to a right that may be redeemed by the company for the participant's pro rata fraction of the class's total claim. If the right is not redeemed, it will entitle its holder to purchase his pro rata fraction of the company's securities for a price equal to his pro rata fraction of the total claim of the classes above his class.[46]

Finally, each unit of membership in the class of residual claimants (the most junior class) will entitle its holder to receive a right that may not be redeemed by the company. This right will entitle its holder to purchase his pro rata fraction of the company's securities for a price equal to his pro rata fraction of the total claim of all the classes above the residual claimants' class.[47]

B   Contracts with favorable terms

Prior to entering the reorganization stage, a company presumably has a whole set of outstanding contracts. To the extent that such contracts are breached or discontinued by the reorganization process or by preceding events, the other parties to the contracts are likely to have claims against the company. Some of the contracts, however, may be at terms that appear favorable to the company, given the information available at the reorganization stage. The breach or discontinuation of these contracts will not be in the interest of any participants except the parties

---

45 For example, if the total claim of the senior class is $300, then each member of the class will receive, for each $1 debt that he is owed, a right that may be redeemed by the company for $1 and, if not redeemed, will entitle its holder to receive 1/300 of the reorganized company's securities.

46 Consider, for example, a situation in which the total claim of a given intermediate class of creditors is $200 and the total claim of the classes above it is $540. In this case, any member of this intermediate class will receive, for each $1 debt that he is owned, a right that may be redeemed by the company for $1 and, if not redeemed, will entitle him to purchase 1/200 of the company's securities for a price equal to $2.70 (1/200 of the total preceding claims of $540).

47 For example, suppose that the total claim of the classes preceding the residual claimants' class is $1,800 and that the residual claimants' class includes 200 units. Then, each unit in this class will entitle the holder to a right to purchase 1/200 of the reorganized company's securities for $9 ($1800/200).

with whom the company has the contracts; the pie available to the other participants will be maximized by "reinstating" these contracts, that is, by having the reorganized company maintain them.

A typical case of a contract that is worth reinstating is one providing the company with a long-term loan at an interest rate that at the time of reorganization appears favorable to the company. Consider a company that took from a bank a $100,000 long-term loan with an interest rate of 5 percent and suppose that by the time of the reorganization interest rates have risen to 10 percent. In this case, the bank may wish to have the loan declared in default and consequently get a claim of $100,000 against the reorganizing company. But the pie available to the other participants may well be maximized by reinstating the loan contract, because, given the contract's 5 percent interest rate, the present value of the future installments on the loan will be much less than $100,000.

Any reorganization regime must determine whether and under what conditions reinstatement of contracts is allowed.[48] Existing reorganization law, for example, includes a detailed arrangement concerning the possibility of reinstating some contracts; participants whose contracts with the company are reinstated do not need to approve the reorganization plan because their claims are "unimpaired."[49]

Whichever approach we wish reorganization law to take to the issue of reinstating contracts, the operation of the proposed method of division will be consistent with that approach. Given the regime's rules concerning which contracts can be reinstated, the reorganization plan filed under the proposed method will specify those contracts that the plan's designers elected to reinstate (as well as the means of reinstating them). For the reasons noted earlier,[50] the designers of the plan presumably will choose to reinstate only those contracts whose reinstatement will maximize the pie available to the rest of the participants. The parties to the reinstated contracts will have claims that are not impaired and they therefore will not participate in the division of rights. The reorganized company, however, will be subject to the reinstated contracts, and the value of its securities will be affected by this fact. The division of rights among the participants whose claims are impaired will then proceed smoothly according to the proposed method.

48 For a discussion of some of the policy issues that are involved in this determination, see note 7, Jackson, pp. 35–44.
49 See 11 U.S.C. secs. 1124, 1126(f) (1982 and Supp. IV 1986).
50 See text accompanying note 41.

C   Secured claims

Thus far the analysis has assumed that the priority of a given claim over other claims necessarily applies to all assets of the debtor company. Some claims, however, are secured claims, which means that their priority over other claims is with respect only to a specific subset of the debtor's assets. Secured claims are often present in reorganizations.

In the presence of secured claims, any reorganization regime (and indeed any liquidation regime as well) must resolve two issues. First, the regime must choose both a method for deciding whether a claim secured by a given asset is *fully* secured (a method that may include estimating the asset's value) and, for claims that are not fully secured, a method for dividing these claims into fully secured and unsecured parts. Second, the regime must determine whether the holder of a secured claim has an *in rem* right to have the asset sold to pay his claim or only a right to be paid the appraised value of the asset. The existing reorganization regime includes an arrangement governing these issues,[51] and commentators have been debating the merits of this arrangement as well as possible reforms.[52]

Whichever arrangement we wish to apply to secured claims, the proposed method of division will be consistent with it. The arrangement will govern the identification of fully secured claims and their treatment under the reorganization plan.[53] The units of the reorganized company's securities that will then be available for distribution will be divided among the holders of unsecured claims and interests according to the proposed method of division.

D   Concentration of claims in one hand

The last complication to be discussed, which appears less frequently than those discussed above, is the possibility of a concentration of claims

---

51 See 11 U.S.C. secs. 506, 1111 (b) (1982 and Supp. IV 1986).
52 See D. Baird and T. Jackson, Corporate Reorganizations and the Treatment of Diverse Ownership Interests: A Comment on Adequate Protection of Secured Creditors in Bankruptcy, *University of Chicago Law Review* 51:97 (1984); Eisenberg, The Undersecured Creditor in Reorganizations and the Nature of Security, *Vanderbilt Law Review* 38:931 (1985).
53 If the arrangement requires or suggests making some immediate payments to the holders of the secured claims, then the reorganization plan may include provisions for selling assets or raising funds in some other way. For the reasons noted earlier, see p. 174, the designers of the plan presumably will seek to adopt that allowable method of treating secured claims that will maximize the pie available to the rest of the participants.

in one hand. Suppose, for instance, that 60 percent of the units in Class *A* in our simple example (the class of senior creditors) are held by a given bank. In such a case, if the type-*A* rights are not redeemed by the company, the bank will get 60 percent of the company's securities while the other members of the class will get 40 percent of these securities. The rights given to the bank will be worth more per right than those given to the other senior creditors, because shares in a controlling block are worth more than minority shares. Consequently, the value given to the senior class will be divided disproportionately, with the bank getting more than the value of its entitlement and the other members of the class getting less than the value of their entitlements.

Such a problem can arise, however, in any reorganization regime that divides the reorganized company's securities among the participants.[54] As long as the division proceeds under the assumption that any two shares of the reorganized company are worth the same amount, a concentration of claims may lead to a given participant's receiving a controlling block; as a result, this participant will end up with more than the value of his entitlement, whereas others will receive less than the value of theirs. Because this problem may arise and require a solution under any reorganization regime, its potential presence does not weaken my earlier conclusion that the proposed method is the best way of dividing the reorganization pie.

Although the problem of concentrated claims is unlikely to arise frequently and is in no way unique to the proposed method, I do wish to note what appears to be the best means of addressing it.[55] If the exercise of rights provides someone with a controlling block of the reorganized company's equity, then the holder of this controlling block should be required to dispose of his controlling position – by selling enough shares to go below a specified control threshold – within a specified period of time. Under such a rule, those who exercise rights will be able to count on receiving shares that, at least after a specified period of time, will not be minority shares.

VII   Conclusion

This article has put forward a new method of division for corporate reorganizations. This method can eliminate certain efficiency and fairness problems that have been long viewed as inherent to the reorgan-

---

54 Thus, for example, Roe, in discussing his proposed reorganization regime, recognized the existence of this problem. See Roe, note 8, pp. 575–76.

55 The endorsed approach is that suggested by Roe, note 8, pp. 575–76.

ization process. Under the method, once the size and relative priority of the participants' claims are determined, the division of the reorganization pie will be resolved quickly and efficiently – and in perfect consistency with the entitlements of all the participants. The method is put forward as a basis for law reform: The optimal reorganization regime is one that requires and facilitates the application of the proposed method in every reorganization case. Furthermore, the method can be used even under the existing legal rules, as a basis for reorganization plans that participants may want to file. It is hoped that the method will indeed prove useful to public officials overseeing corporate reorganizations and to participants in such reorganizations.

CHAPTER 6

The corporate contract

Frank H. Easterbrook and Daniel R. Fischel

For a long time public and academic discussion of corporations has started from the premise that managers have "control" and use this to exploit investors, customers, or both. The usual prescription is some form of public control. This may take the form of regulation of the firm's output and prices. It may take the form of regulation of the securities markets. It may take the form of intervention through corporate law, which establishes minimum voting rules and restricts how managers can treat the firm and the investors.

The argument is simple. In most substantial corporations – firms with investment instruments freely traded, which we call public corporations – each investor has a small stake compared with the size of the venture. The investor is therefore "powerless." The managers, on the other hand, know how the business is running and can conceal from investors information about the firm and their own activities. As a result the managers can divert income to themselves, stealing and mismanaging at the same time. Diversion and sloth may be subtle, but it exists. Even when it does not, the potential for misconduct remains. Only some form of regulation can protect investors. And the limit on regulation is to be found not in principles of free contracting – for the corporate charter is at best a contract of adhesion by which the managers call all the shots – but in a concern that regulation not go "too far." Thus in the debate about whether public corporations should be permitted to issue non-voting stock, most people assume that nonvoting stock is bad because it insulates the managers further from investors' control, and the only question is whether an outright ban (as opposed to severe regulation) would restrict "too much" the ability of firms to raise capital.

Yet although the language of regulation is everywhere, corporate law has developed along a different path. The corporate code in almost

A version of this chapter appears in *Columbia Law Review* 89:1416–48 (1989) and in our forthcoming book, *The Economic Structure of Corporate Law*.

every state is an "enabling statute." An enabling statute allows managers and investors to write their own tickets, to establish systems of governance without substantive scrutiny from a regulator and without effective restraint on the permissible methods of corporate governance. The handiwork of managers is final in all but exceptional or trivial instances. Courts apply the "business judgment doctrine," a hands-off approach that they would never apply to the decisions of administrative agencies and other entities the officials of which do not stand to profit from their decisions – and therefore, one might think, are not subject to the pressures that cause managers' goals to diverge from those of investors.

Why does corporate law allow managers to set the terms under which they will govern corporate assets? Why do courts grant more discretion to self-interested managers than to disinterested regulators? Why do investors entrust such stupendous sums to managers whose acts are essentially unconstrained by legal rules? Our work seeks to offer answers to these questions, explanations for the economic structure of corporate law. The corporation is a complex set of explicit and implicit contracts, and corporate law enables the participants to select the optimal arrangement for the many different sets of risks and opportunities that are available in a large economy. No one set of terms will be best for all; hence the "enabling" structure of corporate law. And although managers are self-interested, this interest can be aligned with that of investors through automatic devices, devices that are useless when those in control are "disinterested." Hence the apparent contradiction that self-interested managers are more free than disinterested regulators. Of course "automatic" controls come at a cost, and much of corporate law is designed to reduce the costs of aligning the interests of managers and investors. Before we explore the nature of the legal rules, however, we develop the framework within which all of our analysis proceeds: The corporate structure is a set of contracts through which managers and certain other participants exercise a great deal of discretion that is "reviewed" by interactions with other self-interested actors. This interaction often occurs in markets, and we shall sometimes call the pressures these interactions produce "market forces." No one should assume from this shorthand, however, that we personify "markets." All economic activity is an interaction among real people, and the interactions that shape the corporate form are among the most interesting.

I   The dynamic shaping of the corporate form

The view you take of corporations and corporate law is apt to depend on your assumption about how investors, employees, and other players come to be associated in a common venture. You are likely to be driven to a regulatory view of corporations if you assume that corporations are born with a complement of managers, employees, and investors. Suppose the world is static. Everyone awakes one morning to find himself a manager or an investor. The veil of ignorance is suddenly parted. The manager exalts: "Aha! No one can stop me!" The investors gasp: "Woe is me, I'm powerless. Only the government can save me now!" This is a natural view if you draw a line at a moment in time without asking how the world came to be as it is.

Yet managers and investors do not wake up in this way. They assume their roles with knowledge of the consequences. Investors part with their money willingly, putting dollars in equities instead of bonds or banks or land or gold because they believe the returns of equities more attractive. Managers obtain their positions after much trouble and toil, competing against others who wanted them. All interested people participate in the process. The process affects the terms on which the corporations operate. Firms are born small and grow. They must attract customers and investors by promising *and delivering* what those people value. Corporations that do not do so will not survive. When people observe that firms are very large in relation to single investors, they observe the product of success in satisfying investors and customers.

How is it that managers came to control such resources?[1] It is not exactly secret that scattered shareholders can't control managers directly. If the investors know that the managers have lots of discretion, why did they give their money to these managers in the first place? If managers promise to return but a pittance, the investors will not put up very much money. The investors simply pay less for the paper the firms issue. There is therefore a limit on managers' efforts to enrich themselves at investors' expense. Managers may do their best to take advantage of their investors, but they find that the dynamics of the market drive them

1 The discussion that follows owes much to M. Jensen and W. Meckling, Theory of the Firm: Managerial Behavior, Agency Costs and Ownership Structure, *Journal of Financial Economics* 3:305 (1976). They and we write in a tradition that began with R. H. Coase, The Nature of the Firm, *Economica* 4 (n.s.):386 (1937). Other important contributions include A. A. Alchian and H. Demsetz, Production, Information Costs, and Economic Organization, *American Economic Review* 62:777 (1972); E. Fama and M. Jensen, Separation of Ownership and Control, *Journal of Law and Economics* 26:301 (1983), and Agency Problems and Residual Claims, idem p. 327; H. Manne, Some Theoretical Aspects of Share Voting, *Columbia Law Review* 64:1427 (1964); H. Manne, Mergers and the Market for Corporate Control, *Journal of Political Economics* 73:110 (1965); and R. Winter, State Law, Shareholder Protection, and the Theory of the Corporation, *Journal of Legal Studies* 6:251 (1977). See also J. Pratt and R. Zeckhauser, eds., *Principals and Agents: The Structure of Business* (Boston, 1985) and N. Wolfson, *The Modern Corporation: Free Markets vs. Regulation* (New York, 1984).

to act as if they had investors' interests at heart. It is almost as if there were an invisible hand.

The corporation and its securities are products to as great an extent as the sewing machines or other things the firm makes. Just as the founders of a firm have incentives to make the kinds of sewing machines people want to buy, they have incentives to create the kind of firm, governance structure, and securities people value. The founders of the firm will find it profitable to establish the governance structure that is most beneficial to investors, net of the costs of maintaining the structure. People who seek resources to control will have to deliver more returns to investors. Those who promise the highest returns – and make the promises binding and hence believable – will obtain the largest investments.

The first question facing entrepreneurs is what promises to make, and the second is how to induce investors to believe the promises. Empty promises are worthless promises. Answering to the first question depends on finding ways to reduce the effects of divergent interests; answering the second depends on finding legal and automatic enforcement devices. The more automatic the enforcement, the more investors will believe the promises.

What promises will the entrepreneurs make in order to induce investors to hand over more money? No set of promises is right for all firms at all times. No one thinks that the governance structure used for a small business will work well for Exxon or Hydro Quebec. The "best" structure cannot be derived from theory; it must be developed by experience. We should be skeptical of claims that any one structure – or even a class of structures – is best. But we can see the sorts of promises that are likely to emerge in the competition for investments.

Some promises may entail submitting to scrutiny in advance of action. Outside directors watch inside ones; inside directors watch other managers; the managers hire detectives to watch the employees. At other times, though, prior monitoring may be too costly in relation to its benefits, and the most desirable methods of control will rest on deterrence, on letting people act as they wish but penalizing certain conduct. Fiduciary obligations and derivative litigation are forms of subsequent settling-up that are among these kinds of devices. Still other methods operate automatically. Managers enjoy hefty salaries and perquisites of office; the threat of losing these can induce managers to act in investors' interest.

Managers in the United States must select the place of incorporation. The fifty states offer different menus of devices (from voting by shareholders to fiduciary rules to derivative litigation) for the protection of investors. The managers who pick the state of incorporation that is most desirable from the perspective of investors will attract the most money. The states that select the best combination of rules will attract the most corporate investment (and therefore increase their tax collections). So states compete to offer – and managers compete to use – beneficial sets of legal rules. These include not only rules about governance structures but also fiduciary rules and prohibitions of fraud.

Managers select when to go public. Less experienced entrepreneurs start with venture capital, which comes with extensive strings. The venture capitalists control the operation of the firm with some care. Only after the managerial team and structure has matured will the firm issue public securities.

Entrepreneurs make promises in the articles of incorporation and the securities they issue when they go public. The debt investors receive exceptionally detailed promises in indentures. These promises concern the riskiness of the firm's operations, the extent to which earnings may be paid out, and the domain of managerial discretion. These promises benefit equity investors as well as debt investors. The equity investors usually receive votes rather than explicit promises. Votes make it possible for the investors to replace the managers. (Those who believe that managers have unchecked control should ask themselves why the organizers of a firm issue equity claims that enable the investors to replace the managers.) The managers also promise, explicitly or otherwise, to abide by the standards of "fair dealing" embedded in the fiduciary rules of corporate law. Sometimes they make additional promises as well.

To sum up: Self-interested entrepreneurs and managers, just like other investors, are driven to find the devices most likely to maximize net profits. If they do not, they pay in lower prices for corporate paper. Any one firm may deviate from the optimal measures. Over tens of years and thousands of firms, though, tendencies emerge. The firms and managers that make the choices investors prefer will prosper relative to others. Because the choices do not impose costs on strangers to the contracts, what is optimal for the firms and investors is optimal for society. We can learn a great deal just by observing which devices are widely used and which are not.

It is important to distinguish between isolated transactions and governance structures. There are high costs of operating capital and managerial markets, just as there are high costs of other methods of dealing with the divergence of interest. It is inevitable that a substantial amount of undesirable slack or self-dealing will occur. The question is whether its costs can be cut by mechanisms that are not themselves more costly. We accept some costly conduct because the costs of the remedy are even greater. We also use deterrence (say, the threat of punishment for fraud) rather than other forms of legal control when deterrence is the least-cost method of handling a problem. Deterrence is a particularly inexpensive method of controlling agency costs. The expensive legal system is not cranked up unless there is evidence of wrongdoing; if the anticipated penalty (the sanction multiplied by the probability of its application) is selected well, there will not be much wrongdoing, and the costs of the system are correspondingly small. A regulatory system (one entailing scrutiny and approval in advance in each case) ensures that the costs of control will be high; they will be incurred even if the risk is small.

Markets that let particular episodes of wrongdoing slide by, or legal systems that use deterrence rather than structural change to handle the costs of management, are likely very effective in making judgments about optimal governance structures. Governance structures are open and notorious, unlike the conduct they seek to control. Costs of information in knowing about a firm's governance are low. Firms and teams of managers can compete with each other over time to design governance structures and to build in penalties for malfeasance. There is no substantial impediment to the operation of the competitive process at the level of structure. The pressures that operate in the long run are exactly the forces that shape structure.[2] Contractual promises and fiduciary rules arise as a result of these considerations.

Elsewhere we plan to discuss evidence that helps us to determine whether this picture is a plausible one or just wishful thinking. Before dipping into the evidence, however, it is useful to step back and ask whether corporation-as-contract is a satisfying way of looking at things even in theory. No one portrays the relation between trustee and beneficiary as one of arm's-length contracting, and legal rules impose many restrictions that the trustee cannot avoid. Why think about corporations differently?

II   Markets, firms, and corporations

"Markets" are economic interactions among people dealing as strangers and seeking personal advantage. The extended conflict among selfish people produces prices that allocate resources to their most val-

---

2 Our treatment has much in common with R. Nelson and S. Winter, *An Evolutionary Theory of Economic Change* (Cambridge, 1982), even though it is an application of neoclassical analysis that Nelson and Winter challenge. Survivorship stories have been used in economics for a long time. The more sophisticated and rapid the process of natural selection, the better these analyses work. Firms are a paradigm for evolutionary pressure in economic organization.

uable uses. This is an old story, and Adam Smith's *The Wealth of Nations* (1776) remains the best exposition. A series of short-term dealings in a market may be more useful for trading than for producing goods, however. The firm – an aggregation of people banded together for a longer period – permits greater use of specialization. People can organize as teams with the functions of each member identified, so that each member's specialization makes the team as a whole more productive than it would otherwise be.

Teams could be assembled every day, the way casual labor is hired. Some production is organized in this way. The construction and longshore industries assemble separate teams for each project. More often, however, the value of a long-term relation among team members predominates, and, to the extent it does, recognizable firms grow. Yet as the size of the firm grows, there must be more and more transactions among members. A manufacturer of cars that makes its own paint must decide how much paint to use and of what quality. Does it make sense to add extra paint, or to make the paint job a little less durable? This depends on the value of the paint the firm uses – and on whether someone else could provide the paint for less. The integrated firm has difficulty assessing the value of the paint it makes for itself, however. It must take expensive steps to give the paint a value (called a "transfer price"), which at best duplicates information that markets produce and at worst may be quite inaccurate, leading the firm to make inefficient decisions. Managers may specify transfer prices that, if inaccurate, will lead firms to produce paint they should have bought, or to use too much or too little paint in their products. Transacting for paint in markets has risks (will the seller deliver on time? will the quality be good?) that are costly to deal with. Letters of credit, the courts, organized exchanges and credit bureaus, and other institutions are among the costs of markets. Transacting for paint inside the firm is costly too. The firm grows until the costs of organizing production internally exceed the costs of organizing things through market transactions.

One cost of cooperative production inside the firm is the divergence of interest among the participants. It is sometimes useful to think of the atoms dealing in markets as individual people who reap the gains and bear the expenses of their own decisions. The organization of production in teams is not so simple. The firm may hire labor by the hour ("hourly employees") or the year ("salaried employees"); this arrangement hires a segment of time but not a specified effort. It may be very difficult to induce the employee to devote his best effort to the firm's fortunes. Why should he? His pay is the same no matter his performance. Although it may be possible to penalize sluggards by reducing their wages or firing them (a process sometimes called "ex post settling up"), it is costly to monitor effort (and who monitors the monitors' efforts?). On top of that, often it is very difficult to determine the quality of the work performed. A team of designers may put together an excellent airplane (the Lockheed L–1011 comes to mind) that fails in the market either for reasons beyond their control or because it was "too good" and so too costly. A system of monitoring that asked only whether the employees' work was profitable for the firm would lead to very inaccurate rewards when there are risks beyond the control of the employees or knowledge beyond the reach of the monitors.[3] Unless someone knows the quality of each person's work in relation to the demand, settling up must be imperfect; and given that accounts may be settled well after the work has been performed, the time value of money sometimes will make a balancing of accounts impossible.

Another way around the difficulty of monitoring the work of the firm's employees is to give each the right to claim the profits from the firm's success. Then he will work hard and monitor the work of his colleagues, lest their subpar performance reduce his rewards. But the allocation of the venture's profits to the employees – and by employees we mean managers too – is just another cost. It reduces the return to those who contribute the venture's capital. And it, too, is imperfect. Much production is performed in teams. Teams of employees sweep the floor, teams of engineers design new products, teams of managers decide whether and where to build new plants. So long as no monitor can determine what each member's marginal contribution to the team's output is, each member will be less than a perfectly faithful representative of the interests of the team as a whole. Unless one person receives all the rewards of success and penalties of failure, his incentives are not properly aligned with those of the venture as a whole.[4] "Let George do it" is a predictable response, when any given employee gets some of the benefits of George's hard work and does not get all the benefits of his own hard work.

Sometimes this division of interests will lead the employee to divert the firm's assets to himself. Theft is the dramatic way to do this; diversion

---

3 There is an extensive economic literature on the design of optimal systems of rewards for work under conditions of risk and incomplete (or asymmetric) knowledge. We need not explore this flourishing field, because the proposition that monitoring is costly, imprecise, or both holds under any system of rewards yet designed.

4 See S. Grossman and O. Hart, The Costs and Benefits of Ownership: A Theory of Vertical and Lateral Integration, *Journal of Political Economics* 94:691 (1986), for a discussion of the difficulties that follow when it is not possible to assign the whole profit stream to one person.

of "corporate opportunities" may be another, and in general the discretion managers possess gives them an opportunity to favor themselves in dealing with the other actors. Sometimes this division of interests will lead to less diligent work. The employee may engage in goldbricking, and the upper manager may "slack off" by working seventy hours per week rather than the seventy-five he would work if he received more of the reward from his effort. Sometimes the division of interests influences by dulling the willingness to take risks. The quiet life may be a perquisite of employment. All of these are costs. Monitoring by outsiders to reduce these costs also is costly.

Employees may reduce the amount of monitoring that is necessary by giving "bonds" – not physical certificates but automatic devices that impose penalties for a shortfall in performance. When managers hold the stock of their firm, they are "bonding" their performance (in part) by exposing their wealth to erosion if their performance, and hence the firm's profits, is substandard. Every firm uses a different mix of bonding devices, monitoring devices, and residual costs of the divergence of interest. The trick is to hold the total costs of these things as low as possible. It is foolish to spend $2 in monitoring to reduce by $1 the perquisites of employees. We refer to the combination of monitoring, bonding, and residual costs as "agency costs."

So far we have been describing the firm as an extramarket, team method of production with certain benefits and costs. Corporations are a subset of firms. The corporation is a financing device and is not otherwise distinctive. A corporation is characterized by a statement of capital contributions as formal claims against the firm's income that are distinct from participation in the firm's productive activities. The corporation issues stock in exchange for an investment; stock need not be held by the firm's employees. Investors bear the risk of failure (sometimes we call them risk bearers) and receive the marginal rewards of success. Equity investors are paid last, after debt investors, employees, and other investors with (relatively) fixed claims. These equity investors have the residual claim in the sense that they get only what is left over – but they get all of what is left over.

The separation of risk bearing from employment is a form of the division of labor. Those who have wealth can employ it productively even if they are not good managers; those who can manage but lack wealth can hire capital in the market; and the existence of claims that can be traded separately from employment allow investors to diversify their investment interests. Diversification makes investment as a whole less risky, in ways to which we return, and therefore makes investment both more attractive and more efficient. Investors bear most of the risk of business failure, in exchange for which they are promised most of the rewards of success. The penalty for this arrangement is that separation of management and risk bearing at least potentially increases agency costs by driving a broader wedge between employees' interests and those of the venture as a whole. Employees will receive less of the return; investors, on the other hand, will be less effective monitors to the extent holdings are widely scattered, for then no one investor has a good reason to monitor. (In other words, investors face their own agency costs that dissuade them from monitoring, which is why investors in public firms often are ignorant and passive.) The corporation will flourish when the gains from the division of labor exceed the augmentation of the agency costs.

Sometimes it is said that the distinctive features of the corporation are limited liability, legal identity, and perpetual existence, but these are misleading descriptions.[5] "Limited liability" means only that those who contribute equity capital to a firm risk no more than their initial investments – it is an attribute of the investment rather than of the corporation. This attribute of investors' risk is related to the benefits of widely held, liquid investment instruments. It often is altered by contract when these benefits are small. Legal identity and perpetual existence mean only that the corporation lasts until dissolved and has a name in which it may transact and be sued. It is convenient to think of the firm as an "it." Many other firms, such as business trusts, are treated in the same way. It would be silly to attach a list of every one of Exxon's investors to an order for office furniture just to ensure that all investors share their percentage of the cost.

The "personhood" of a corporation is a matter of convenience rather than reality, however; we also treat the executor of an estate as "a" legal entity without submerging the fact that the executor is a stand-in for other people. It is meaningful to speak of the Legislative Branch of the U.S. Government, or Congress, or of Members of Congress, depending on context, but it would be misleading to think of Congress – an entity with a name – only as an entity, or to believe that its status as an entity is the most significant thing about the institution. "Congress" is a collective noun for a certain group of independent political actors and their employees, and it acts as an entity only when certain forms have been followed (such as majority approval in each house). So too with corporations. There are disparate independent actors, from pro-

---

5 See R. Hessen, *In Defense of the Corporation* (Stanford, 1979); P. Blumberg, Limited Liability and Corporate Groups, *Journal of Corporate Law* 11:573 (1986), pp. 577–604 (tracing the history of limited liability).

duction employees to managers to equity investors to debt investors to holders of warranty and tort claims against the firm. The arrangements among these persons usually depend on contracts and on positive law, not on corporate law or the status of the corporation as an entity. More often than not a reference to the corporation as an entity will hide the essence of the transaction. So we often speak, following Jensen and Meckling, of the corporation as a "nexus of contracts" or a set of implicit and explicit contracts. This reference, too, is just a shorthand for the complex arrangements of many sorts that those who associate voluntarily in the corporation will work out among themselves. The form of reference is a way to remind you that the corporation is a voluntary adventure, and that we must always examine the terms on which real people have agreed to participate.

The agreements that have arisen are wonderfully diverse, matching the diversity of economic activity that is carried on within corporations. Managers sometimes hold a great deal of the firm's stock and are rewarded for success through appreciation of their investment prices, as other employees may be paid on a piecework basis; sometimes compensation is via salary and bonuses. Corporations sometimes are organized as hierarchies, with the higher parts of the pyramid issuing commands; sometimes they are organized as dictatorships; sometimes they are organized as divisional profit centers with loose or missing hierarchy. The choice of organization and compensation devices will depend on the size of the firm, the identity of the managers, and the industry (or spectrum of industries) in which the corporation participates. Organization and compensation in an investment bank are vastly different from organization and compensation in an industrial conglomerate.

The organization of finance and control is equally variable. Small, close corporations may have only banks as outside investors, and these banks hold "debt" claims that carry residual rights to control the firm; highly leveraged public firms may concentrate equity investments in managers while issuing tradable debt claims to the public; the public investors in these firms have no effective control, because debt conventionally does not carry voting rights. Public utilities and national banks may have more traded equity but still no effective shareholders' control, given both regulatory structures and the nature of the risks in the business. Many growing firms have almost no debt investment, and the equity investment pays no dividends; these firms are under the dictatorial control of the entrepreneur. (Some firms go public under rules that stifle any attempt at control; Ford issued nonvoting stock, leaving the firm in family hands for a long time.) Mature firms may be more bureaucratic, with boards of directors "independent" of managers and answerable to equity investors. Some managerial teams attempt to insulate themselves from investors' control in order to carry out programs that they view as more important than profits. Both the *New York Times* and the *Wall Street Journal* have established structures that give the managers substantial freedom to produce news at the (potential) expense of profit.

The way in which corporations run the business, control agency costs, raise money, and reward investors will change from business to business and from time to time within a firm. The structure suited to a dynamic, growing firm such as Xerox in 1965 is quite unsuited to Exxon in 1965 (or to Xerox in 1988). The participants in the venture need to be able to establish the arrangement most conducive to prosperity, and outsiders are unlikely to be able to prescribe a mold for corporations as a whole or even a firm through time. The history of corporations has been that firms failing to adapt their governance structures are ground under by competition.[6] The history of corporate law has been that states attempting to force all firms into a single mold are ground under as well. Corporations flee to find more open-ended statutes that permit adaptations. This is the reason for the drive toward enabling laws that control process but not structure.

To say that a complex relation among many voluntary participants is adaptive is to say that it is contractual. Thus our reference to the corporation as a set of contracts. Voluntary arrangements *are* contracts. Some may be negotiated over a bargaining table. Some may be a set of terms that are dictated (by managers or investors) and accepted or not; only the price is negotiated. Some may be fixed and must be accepted at the going price (as when people buy investment instruments traded in the market). Some may be implied by courts or legislatures trying to supply the terms that would have been negotiated had people addressed the problem explicitly. Even terms that are invariant – such as the requirement that the board of directors act only by a majority of a quorum – are contractual to the extent that they produce offsetting voluntary arrangements. The result of all of these voluntary arrangements will be contractual.

Just as there is no right amount of paint in a car, there is no right relation among managers, investors, and other corporate participants. The relation must be worked out one firm at a time. A change in

6 O. Williamson, *The Economic Institutions of Capitalism* (Cambridge 1987); cf. A. Chandler, *The Visible Hand* (Cambridge, 1977).

technology – whether the technology of applying paint or the technology of assembling blocs of shares to change control of a firm – will be reflected in changes in the operation or governance of corporations. To understand corporate law you must understand how the balance of advantage among devices for controlling agency costs differs across firms and shifts from time to time. The role of corporate law at any instant is to establish rights among participants in the venture. Who governs? For whose benefit? But without answering difficult questions about the effectiveness of different devices for controlling agency costs, we cannot tell the appropriate allocation of rights. We will have trouble establishing background rules (i.e., principles that apply in the absence of a different term incorporated in a particular corporate contract). We certainly cannot answer questions whether and when it is appropriate to override contractual choices actually made or to fetter the ability of participants to change the terms established when the firm was created.

We use economic arguments about agency costs to attempt to answer questions about background terms, mandatory terms, and changes in terms. The analogy to contract focuses attention on the voluntary and adaptive nature of any corporation. We treat corporate law as a standard-form contract, supplying terms most venturers would have chosen but yielding to explicit terms in all but a few instances. Our normative thesis is that corporate law should contain the terms people would have negotiated, were the costs of negotiating at arm's length for every contingency sufficiently low. The positive thesis is that corporate law almost always conforms to this model. It is enabling rather than directive. The standby terms grant great discretion to managers and facilitate actual contracts. They leave correction to the interplay of self-interested actors rather than to regulators. But many standby terms – for example, the presumption that equity shares have one vote apiece, that these votes can be used to oust the managers and govern the firm, and that debt investors have no voice in governance – have both important effects and solid economic rationales.

III   Real and unreal contracts

The rhetoric of contract is a staple of political and philosophical debate. Contract is a term for voluntary and unanimous agreement among affected parties. It is therefore a powerful image. It shows up in argument about "social contracts" that justify political society. The founding of the United States was accompanied by much contractarian reasoning. Philosophers who resort to the "original position" to establish a definition of justice are using a contractarian argument. Yet arguments about social contracts are problematic. They are constructs rather than real contracts. And even if our forebears had entered into an actual contract, why would these rules bind later generations? Such doubts are also part of our political heritage; Jefferson accordingly suggested that the Constitution expire and be renewed whenever half of the living had been born since the last renegotiation. Perhaps the corporate contract, like the social contract, is no more than a rhetorical device. After all, investors do not sit down and higgle among themselves about the terms. As a rule investors buy stock in the market and know little more than its price. The terms were established by entrepreneurs, investment banks, and managers. Changes in the rules are accomplished by voting rather than unanimous consent. So why not view the corporation as a republican government rather than as a set of contracts?

The corporate venture has many real contracts. The terms present in the articles of incorporation at the time the firm is established or issues stock are real agreements. So with the rules in force when the firm raises new money – whether by issuing debt, the terms of which often are negotiated at great length over a table, or by issuing equity, the terms of which affect the price of the issue. Employees often negotiate in detail with the firm and with each other. Many changes in the rules are approved by large investors after negotiation with management. And of course the rules that govern how rules change are also real contracts. The articles of incorporation typically allow changes to be made by bylaw or majority vote; they could as easily prevent changes, or call for supermajority vote; or allow change freely but require nonconsenting investors to be bought out. That the articles allow uncompensated changes through voting is a real contractual choice. And many remaining terms of the corporate arrangement are contractual in the sense that they are presets of fallback terms specified by law and not varied by the corporation. These terms become part of the set of contracts just as provisions of the Uniform Commercial Code become part of commercial contracts when not addressed explicitly.

These contracts usually are negotiated by representatives. Indenture trustees negotiate on behalf of bondholders, unions on behalf of employees, investment banks on behalf of equity investors. Sometimes terms are not negotiated directly but are simply promulgated, in the way auto rental companies promulgate the terms of their rental contracts. The entrepreneurs or managers may adopt a set of rules and say "take them or leave them." This is contracting nonetheless. We enforce the terms in auto rental contracts, as we enforce the terms of a trust even though the beneficiaries had no say in their framing. The terms in rental contracts, warranties, and the like are rental contracts because their value (or detriment) is reflected in price.

The corporation's choice of governance mechanisms does not create third party effects. Let us suppose that entrepreneurs simply pick terms out of a hat and foist them on investors. They cannot force investors to pay more than the resulting investment instruments are worth; there are too many other places to put one's money. Unless entrepreneurs can fool the investors, a choice of terms that reduces investors' expected returns will produce a corresponding reduction in price. So the people designing the terms under which the corporation will be run have the right incentives. Suppose they must decide whether to allow managers to take corporate opportunities or instead require them to be used by the firm (or sold to third parties unaffiliated with the firm). The ability to appropriate opportunities poses obvious risks of diversion to managers; it may also allow efficient use of opportunities and be a source of compensation for managers, which benefits investors. The net effects, for good or ill, will influence the price investors pay for stock. If the managers make the "wrong" decision – that is, choose a rule or term inferior as investors see things – they must pay for their mistake. To obtain an (inefficient) right to divert opportunities they must pay in advance. The same process applies to terms adopted later; undesirable terms reduce the price the stock fetches in the market, so that investors who buy thereafter will get no less than they pay for. In general, all the terms in corporate governance are contractual in the sense that they are fully priced in transactions among the interested parties. They are thereafter tested for desirable properties; the firms that pick the wrong terms will fail in competition with other firms competing for capital. It is unimportant that they may not be "negotiated"; the pricing and testing mechanisms are all that matters, so long as there are no effects on third parties. This should come as no shock to anyone familiar with the Coase Theorem.[7]

Are terms priced? The provisions in articles of incorporation and bylaws often are picky and obscure. Many are not listed in the prospectus of the firm's stock. Buyers of the original issue and in the aftermarket alike may know nothing of the terms in use, let alone whether a staggered board of directors or the existence of cumulative voting will make them better off. They do not consult the *Journal of Financial Economics* before buying. Yet it is unimportant whether knowledge about the nature or effect of the terms is widespread, at least for public corporations.

---

7 R. H. Coase, The Problem of Social Cost, *Journal of Law and Economics* 3:1 (1960).

The mechanism by which stocks are valued ensures that the price reflects the terms of governance and operation, just as it reflects the identity of the managers and the products the firm produces.

The price of stocks traded in public markets is established by professional investors, not by amateurs.[8] These professionals – market makers, arbitrage departments of investment banks, managers of mutual funds and pension trusts, and others – handle huge sums that they are willing to use to purchase undervalued stocks. They study the firm's profits and prospects and bid or sell accordingly. People who do this poorly will find the funds at their disposal dwindling; people who do it well will command additional sums. At any given instant, the professional traders are those who have generally been successful at assessing the worth of stock. If the price of a stock at any time is not right in relation to the price it will have in the future, then professionals can make a lot of money. If the terms of corporate provisions and the details of corporate structure have any effect on investors' welfare, this will be reflected in the profits of the firm and hence the eventual price of the stock. Professionals trade among themselves in a way that brings the present value closer to the future value; if it is known that the stock will be worth $20 in a year, then people will bid that price (less the time value of money) now; no one has a good reason to hold off in this process, because if he does someone else will take the profit. The more astute the professional investors, and the more quickly they can move funds into and out of particular holdings, the faster the process of adjustment will occur. The process eventually makes it difficult even for professional traders to make money, unless they are the first to obtain or act on a piece of information affecting future value. A great deal of data, including evidence that most professional investors are unable to "beat the market," supports the position that prices quickly and accurately reflect public information about firms. Amateur investors then trade at the same price the professionals obtain. These amateurs do not need to know anything about corporate governance and other provisions; the whole value of

8 The process we describe below is reasonably well understood, and it has been so completely discussed elsewhere that we offer only a sketch. See J. Lorie and M. Hamilton, *The Stock Market: Theories and Evidence* (1973), Chapter 4; R. Brealey, *An Introduction to Risk and Return from Common Stocks* 2d ed. (1983), Chapter 2; R. Gilson and R. Kraakman, The Mechanisms of Market Efficiency, *Virginia Law Review* 70:549 (1984). See also J. Cragg and B. Malkiel, *Expectations and the Structure of Share Prices* (1982). The process of adjustment to information that we describe happens exceptionally fast, usually within the day the professional investor learns the information. D. Pearce and V. Roley, Stock Prices and Economic News, *Journal of Business* 59:49 (1985).

these mysterious things is wrapped up in the price established by the professionals. The price reflects the effects, good or bad, of corporate law and contracts, just as it reflects the effects of good and bad products. This is yet another example of the way in which markets transmit the value of information through price, which is more "informed" than any single participant in the market.[9]

To say that the price of a stock reflects the value of the firm's governance and related rules is not necessarily to say that the price does so perfectly. There may be surprises in store, for a firm or for all firms, that make estimates about the effects of governance provisions inaccurate. But these problems of information and assessment also affect any other way of evaluating the effects of governance devices. That is, if professional investors with their fortunes on the line are unable to anticipate the true effects of nonvoting stock or some other wrinkle in a concrete case, how are members of state legislatures or other alternative rule givers to do better? To put this differently, it does not matter if markets are not perfectly efficient, unless some other social institution does *better* at evaluating the likely effects of corporate governance devices. The prices will be more informative *than the next best alternative*, which is all anyone can demand of any device.

This means that we need not enter the debate about whether stocks are priced perfectly.[10] Prices do not reflect very well information that is not available to the public. They reflect the value of stock to public investors with scattered holdings rather than to insiders or others with the ability to control the firm's destiny. For any given firm, there will be an irreducible amount of error in the pricing – after all, information that increases the accuracy of prices is costly, and the "perfect price" may cost more to achieve than it is worth. The more accurate the price becomes, the less private gain is available to pros who study the stock to find bargains; they therefore do not find it profitable to pursue perfection. None of this matters for our purposes, unless some better device is available. No one argues that regulators are better at valuing terms of corporate governance than are markets.

9 See T. Sowell, *Knowledge and Decisions* (1982); S. Grossman and J. Stiglitz, Information and Competitive Price Systems, *American Economic Review* 66:246 (1976); and R. Verrecchia, Consensus Beliefs, Information Acquisition, and Market Information Efficiency, *American Economic Review* 70:874 (1980). See generally the symposium, The Behavioral Foundations of Economic Theory, *Journal of Business* 59:S181–S505 (1986).

10 See J. Gordon and L. Kornhauser, Efficient Markets, Costly Information, and Securities Research, *New York University Law Review* 60:761 (1985), for a summary of data on the efficiency of market prices.

One might say that the effects of obscure terms in articles of incorporation will be too small to affect price, but prices turn out to be sensitive to changes in governance. Elsewhere we discuss many studies showing how changes in the articles and other structural features have measurable, and predictable, effects on price. It turns out to be hard to find any interesting item that does *not* have an influence on price! And even those who believe that markets are less efficient than generally supposed concede that changes in prices reflect the marginal value, to investors outside the managerial group, of publicly disclosed information about the firm. Governance structures are known to anyone seeking the information, so the pricing mechanism will embody their effects for good or ill.

Let us now suppose, however, that not all terms induce accurate changes in the price of stock. Unless prices are systematically *wrong* about the effects of features of governance, as opposed to being noisy and uninformative, managers still have appropriate incentives. The long run will arrive sooner or later, and terms that are not beneficial for investors will stand revealed; the firm will lose out in competition for investors' money. We therefore treat even hard-to-value terms as contractual. To disregard the terms that appear in corporate documents or to attempt to require corporations to employ governance devices that they have attempted to avoid would just induce the firms to make offsetting adjustments. For example, if corporate law should forbid managers to divert corporate opportunities to themselves, they might respond by drawing higher salaries or working less hard to open up new business opportunities. Similarly, a mandatory term that increased the length of a warranty supplied with a refrigerator would lead to an increase in the price. If the longer warranty was worth the price, the seller would have offered the term in the first place, charged the higher price, and made more money. One cannot tinker with one term in a contract in any confidence that the change will make any party better off after other terms have been adjusted.[11] Because so many terms are open to explicit contracting, it is almost always possible to make an end run around any effort to defeat a particular term.

If it is possible to demonstrate that the terms chosen by firms are both (a) unpriced, and (b) systematically perverse from investors' stan-

---

11 This is the Coase Theorem again. See also R. Epstein, The Social Consequences of Common Law Rules, *Harvard Law Review* 95:1717 (1982) and A. Schwartz, Justice and the Law of Contracts: A Case for the Traditional Approach, *Harvard Journal of Law and Public Policy* 9:107 (1986). On warranties see G. Priest, A Theory of the Consumer Product Warranty, *Yale Law Journal* 90:1297 (1981).

dards, then it might be possible to justify the prescription of a mandatory term by law. This makes sense, however, only when one is sure that the selected term will increase the joint wealth of the participants – that is, that it is the term that the parties would have selected with full information and costless contracting. But this, too, is a contractual way of looking at the corporation. This formula is the one courts use to fill the gaps in explicit contracts that inevitably arise because it is impossible to cover every contingency. Any system of law that recognizes explicit contracts must deal with gaps and ambiguities. The gap-filling rule will call on courts to duplicate the terms the parties would have selected, in their joint interest, if they had contracted explicitly. It promotes clear thought to understand that the silence or ambiguity in corporate documents itself is a problem of contract, one the parties could solve if they wished and if the costs of negotiating were worthwhile in light of the stakes. High information costs – the ones that impede accurate reflection of governance features in the price of stock – are the same things that impede more complete transacting.

This is not to say that corporate documents are ideal. Perhaps there are third party effects. Perhaps there are obstacles to reaching the appropriate agreements. Perhaps optimal terms, once reached, will be altered in ways that enable managers to escape the consequences of their acts; terms changed by voting may fit in this category. The next section discusses the limits of contracts, both actual and implied.

IV   Trumping the corporate contract

Many parts of the law contain contract-defeating doctrines. Some of these may be applicable to corporate contracts. We look at the principal ones.

A   Protecting contracting parties

Think of the principal reasons why private agreements may not be honored.[12] Contracts signed under threat of force displace voluntary arrangements and are unjust as well; force is therefore illegal. Some contractual choices are thought unreliable. Fraud will vitiate an agreement. Infants and others who do not know their own interests cannot contract. An expansion and combination of the fraud and deficient knowledge of self-interest lines would emphasize that sometimes peo-

---

12 See C. Sunstein, Legal Interference with Private Preferences, *University of Chicago Law Review* 53:1129 (1986).

ple's perceptual apparatus does not work well. They underestimate the chance that certain risks (floods, earthquakes, failures of the products they buy) will come to pass, so they may not choose rationally when confronted with choices about such risks; at other times they may think the probability greater than it is (nuclear calamity). When a person is confronted with a problem or risk for the first (or only) time in his life, the chance of error is greatest. Choices that are made repeatedly and tested against experience are more likely to be accurate – both because each person learns from experience, and because the mass of persons contains many astute searchers, who identify "bargains" and so influence the terms on which all may trade.

Some contracts are not honored because they have adverse effects on third parties. Contracts to pollute affect people who are not parties to the deal. Cartels (contracts among business rivals to raise prices) affect customers. So we have laws to control pollution and monopolies, and much regulation (such as rate regulation of electrical utilities) is based on a belief that a dearth of competition has produced monopoly prices. Legal rules that protect people in need of rescue (passengers on a sinking ship) from excessive prices charged by saviors serve a similar function. Sometimes the argument for intervention by the state is reinforced by a claim that the person paying the price should be a beneficiary of an income transfer; for example, rent control and minimum wages sometimes are justified by reference to the relative wealth of landlord and tenant (or employer and employee).

None of these justifications for intervention applies to intracorporate affairs. Investors are not candidates for transfers of wealth; this is not a branch of poverty law. Investors and other participants agree on the stakes: money. They therefore would agree unanimously to whatever rule maximizes the total value of the firm. Questions of distribution among investors are unimportant because that just causes the price they pay for their stakes to change. There is no fraud; the rules of corporate governance are open for all to see. (There may be fraud in the operation of the firm, but concealed violations of any rules are wrongful; recall that our concern is with the selection of rules of governance.)

It might seem that the argument based on perceptual biases justifies intervention. Few investors know much about corporate governance; few are repeat players; therefore most are likely to misunderstand the risks they take. Yet as we have explained, in corporate transactions risks are priced through the stock market, and these prices respond to the knowledge of professional investors. These prices protect ignorant investors automatically. The "game" of corporate governance is most assuredly a repeat play game in which people learn from experience. Each corporation has an extended life, so the effects of governance devices may be observed, and when scores of corporations use similar devices, it is possible to find out how they fare compared with each other. Investors as a whole (and therefore prices) will be informed and informative, even though most investors are baffled by the rules embedded in corporate contracts.

Participation in corporations is uniquely amenable to contracting because even the ignorant have an army of helpers. The stock market is one automatic helper. Employees work at terms negotiated by unions (and nonunion employees can observe the terms offered at other firms, which supply much information). Managers and corporations employ professional search firms (headhunters) to convey information and match person to job. Holders of bonds are protected by trustees, which negotiate terms and monitor compliance. Many people invest in corporations through their bank accounts; syndicates of banks (after conducting thorough reviews) pool the money of depositors for investment in corporations. Much pension money is under professional management; the funds hire expertise for the benefit of investors who need not even know what stocks they indirectly hold. Individual investors can hire professional advice directly (through brokerage houses) or indirectly (by investing in mutual funds). They can hedge their bets by buying diversified portfolios of investments, getting the return of the market as a whole (or some subset) rather than an individual firm.

In sum, knowledge about corporate transactions does not depend on the wisdom of individual investors. What is not understood through professional advice is priced, so that the investor gets what he pays for (in the absence of fraud). If we honor one-shot contracts for once-in-a-lifetime transactions, such as the construction of a house, the case for treating as binding contracts the terms under which corporations operate is ironclad. No contract used in our society is more likely to satisfy the conditions for enforcing voluntary agreements.

B   The inefficient term

Third party effects and collective decisions. The argument that contracts are optimal applies only if the contracting parties bear the full costs of their decisions and reap all the gains. It applies only if contracts are enforced after they have been reached. The argument also depends on the availability of the full set of possible contracts. If some types of agreements are foreclosed, the ones actually reached may not be optimal. Some of these problems crop up in corporate law and require careful attention to the limits of contracting.

One type of third party effect is created by the peculiar nature of information and the difficulty of arranging reciprocal disclosure of information among firms. A detailed set of mandatory rules is imposed on corporations by the securities laws. One possible reason for such mandatory rules is that firms would disclose too little information unless compelled. Managers seek to disclose all the information that is privately optimal to investors, because that will induce investors to part with more money for their shares. But some disclosures may be beneficial to other firms, too, and unless legal rules set up a requirement of reciprocal disclosure neither firm may find it optimal to disclose information that is valuable to investors. Some kinds of disclosure may be complex, and legal rules can establish a common language that will facilitate transmission of information.

To see another way in which one firm's acts may affect another's, consider tender offers, bids for the outstanding stock of a firm. A tender offer is a way of gathering up the equity interests to make some fundamental change in the firm that the existing managers oppose; it is an appeal over managers' heads to the equity investors. Usually a tender offer is made at a substantial premium over market price. Investors contracting at the time the firm goes public may wish to make tender offers easy to arrange. Bids are delightfully profitable events; more, putative bidders serve as possible monitors, holding down the agency costs of management whether or not a given firm is the object of a bid. So before a firm knows whether there will be a bid (that is, ex ante), all involved may find it useful to invite scrutiny and bids. But once potential bidders have become interested, or there is a bid on the table, it may be in the interest of the target's managers and investors alike to change plans and conduct an auction. This will raise the price they realize. It may also discourage monitoring, but after the monitoring has occurred and the bidding has begun, the investors in the target no longer care about this benefit. The contract that is optimal ex ante may not be optimal ex post. The investors in the target may quickly change their own contracts, creating an auction. But if such change is possible, then it is not possible to enforce the contract that (by hypothesis) was optimal at the beginning.

Note that this presents a partial view of the available contracts. It assumes that only contracts among participants in targets are possible. Suppose, however, investors in targets could also make contracts with putative bidders. Perhaps they could sell options to purchase their shares at certain prices or under defined conditions. If it were possible to contract in advance with bidders, they could restrain themselves from adopting new strategies only when it looks like a bid is in prospect. Such options turn out to be both impractical (because they imply contracts with a world of potential bidders, at prohibitive transaction costs) and illegal (because the Williams Act forbids bidders to line up shares in advance of making a public announcement, and it also forbids the preferential purchases that such options imply). The impracticality and illegality of an important contractual device may mean that the contracts actually adopted are not optimal. This may – just may – mean that legal rules can improve on the corporate contracts.

The difficulty of enforcing contracts and observing them also may create opportunities for beneficial intervention. The enforcement problem is simple to see. Suppose a contract to hold an auction for a target is optimal, both ex ante and ex post, for investors in the putative target. They adopt such a contract explicitly. They also explicitly forbid the managers' "defending": that is, they want the firm sold at the highest possible price, not kept "independent." But can they get what they want? Any auctioneering strategy creates some risk of the bid falling through. If today's bids are not high enough, an auctioneer may take a painting off the market for a short time, until a higher-valuing bidder appears. The duration of an auction is flexible, and the highest bidder may not appeal for a while. Yet any device that allows the managers to defeat all of the first few bids – such as a rule that no bid may be made without the managers' approval, a rule that poison pill stock approximates – also can be used to defeat any bid. How could anyone tell which strategy was being followed? Would the managers themselves know? They might set an unrealistic reservation price, subjectively believing that they were peddling the firm while objectively making the sale impossible. The difficulty of assuring compliance with the terms of the corporate contract may make particular kinds of contracts less useful.

As for observing contracts, consider this: A strategy of easy-to-acquire may be optimal ex ante, and a strategy of auctioneering may be optimal ex post, yet if an auctioneering strategy becomes known, bids may not materialize; therefore the best strategy for a given firm may be to *look* easily acquired at all times, but to follow an auctioneering strategy at all times. The strategy privately optimal for the target, in other words, is to fool the bidders. This does not violate any rule of contracting; the strategy is beneficial to parties to the contract. Putative bidders have no entitlement to learn the target's true strategy, any more than owners of land have an entitlement to be told what use the buyer will make of the land. Holding information in confidence often is both privately and socially optimal; firms prospecting for ore would do less searching if they had to reveal to the world what they had found before acquiring the mineral-bearing lands. Yet if some putative targets adopt this hidden strategy, other firms with different strategies will be injured. Some firms may have adopted *genuine* easy-to-acquire policies. Putative bidders will have a hard time telling which firms will resist and which will not, and therefore they may reduce their monitoring and bidding activities even with respect to firms that would not conduct auctions. The uncertainty concerning the contractual strategy selected will interfere with the process of governance of other firms.

This introduces still another sort of problem: There may be a divergence between private and social optimality. We have assumed so far that investors and other corporate players design rules that are best for their firm. And so they do. Yet there is another perspective from which investors do not care about the performance of a given firm. They can invest in any or every firm. In the long run, therefore, they care about the performance of the economy, not a given firm in it. Some firms may do better, some worse, but an investor who does not know beforehand which firm will be which wants only to maximize the average performance. It is possible to show that investors who look only to the welfare of targets will set up rules with too much defense, from the perspective of society.[13] Investors who think themselves likely to hold interests in either bidders or targets are not interested in rules that try to engross a greater portion of gains for targets; they want instead to facilitate the process with the least possible cost devoted to attempting to allocate the gains among firms.

An example shows why. Suppose the FCC is going to award a license to operate a TV station, and ten firms are in the running. An investor in one of these firms will want it to spend money on lawyers, market surveys, etc., until the marginal dollar on trying to capture the license brings in one dollar's worth of anticipated profits from having the license (discounted by the probability of not receiving the award). If the license is worth $1 million, each firm might spend $50,000, for a total of $500,000 among firms. An investor with stakes in all ten firms would want nothing of the sort, however. He would want all ten firms to do nothing, compelling the FCC to award the license by lot. That way the winner would get the highest possible net value of the license,

13 S. Grossman and O. Hart, Takeover Bids, the Free-Rider Problem, and the Theory of the Corporation, *Bell Journal of Economics* 11:42 (1980); Grossman and Hart, The Allocational Role of Takeover Bids in Situations of Asymmetric Information, *Journal of Finance* 36:253 (1981); and A. Schwartz, Search Theory and the Tender Offer Auction, *Journal of Law Economics and Organization* 2:49 (1986).

$1 million, and the investors would bear no costs at all and therefore receive the whole profit. The privately beneficial rule (spend until the marginal return is zero) is neither the socially beneficial rule nor the rule that is best for an investor holding stock in all firms. When situations of this sort occur, there are gains to be had in overriding the corporate contracts. (The investor could achieve the gains without the state's aid by buying all ten firms, but that would come at a cost in diversification. And sometimes the problem of fighting over a fixed pie comes about precisely *because* an investor tries to gather up all of the interests. Suppose a TV magnate had started making tender offers for the stock of the firms that were trying to acquire the license. Then we could have had a series of costly auctions as each firm tried to capture all of the gains to be had from bringing all under a common umbrella to save the costs of bidding!)

The idea underlying much of this section is that the investor wants to maximize the value of his holdings, not the value of a given stock. The value of holdings is highest if the value of each stock is highest. Whenever there is a question about the *apportionment* of gain, the investor prefers whatever rule maximizes the net gain to be had – which means increasing the probability of a gain-producing transaction and reducing the costs of realizing each gain. The rules for dealing with gain-creating opportunities will be established before any particular opportunity is in sight, and so each investor will prefer the set of rules that maximizes the total value (wealth) enjoyed by the investors, without regard to how the return is shared among corporations. It is possible to show this with formal logic.[14] It follows that corporate rules that facilitate costly fighting over who gets the gains from some profitable transaction

---

14 H. DeAngelo, Competition and Unanimity, *American Economic Review* 71:18 (1981); L. Makowski, Competition and Unanimity Revisited, *American Economic Review* 73:329 (1983); and Makowski and A. Pepall, Easy Proofs of Unanimity and Optimality Without Spanning: A Pedagogical Note, *Journal of Finance* 40:1245 (1985). The most important assumption leading to unanimous support for wealth maximization is a competitive capital market. Roughly speaking, this means that any one firm's production and financing decisions have negligible effects on both the price of any given investment (that is, any given bundle of risk and return from one firm or many), and on the menu of risk–return combinations that investors can obtain by holding portfolios of instruments issued by different firms. When there is competition, investors agree that the corporation should have the objective of maximizing wealth because greater wealth gives them the ability to consume or purchase portfolios with greater cash returns – in either event, they exercise greater command over resources. Given the depth and richness of the world's capital markets, it is fair to conclude that the conditions for investors' unanimity are satisfied in practice.

are not likely to survive in practice and that in filling gaps in existing contracts it is safe to disregard questions of allocation.

So in thinking about tender offers, an investor does not know whether his firm will be a bidder or a target, and we therefore should not expect him to worry much about creating rules that will transfer money to targets (if there is a bid), for that is likely to cost him if his firm turns out to be a bidder. Almost all investors are repeat players; if they do not get cut in on gains today, they will tomorrow, and they seek to reduce the process costs along the way. There is one potential objection to this way of looking at optimal corporate contracts: risk aversion. We have assumed so far that an investor is indifferent between a 10 percent chance of receiving $1,000 and a certainty of receiving $100. Most investors are risk-averse, which implies that dividing gains may have a role in optimal contracts after all. Perhaps investors seek ways to cut down on risk even if that also cuts down on anticipated return. If so, it has substantial implications for how to supply missing terms in corporate contracts – maybe even for when to override real contracts.

We shall nonetheless largely ignore risk aversion with respect to public corporations. Our rationale is simple: diversification. Investors who dislike risk can get rid of risk easily. They may hold low-risk instruments (high grade bonds and Treasury obligations). If they hold equity instruments, they may do so through mutual funds or by selecting some other broad basket. A diversified portfolio will not get rid of risk that goes with the market as a whole. It will, however, essentially eliminate the risk that goes with conflicts among firms and scraps over the allocation of gains and losses. A person who holds a diversified portfolio has an investment in the economy as a whole and therefore wants whatever social or private governance rules maximize the value of all firms put together. He is not interested in maximizing one firm's value if that comes out of the hide of some other corporation. Diversification is cheap in the current economy. It costs less to buy and hold a diversified fund than to trade a small number of stocks.

This appears to overlook the fact that many people are not diversified. Some are undiversified by design. Corporate managers have much of their wealth tied up in the firms they manage, and this lack of diversification reduces the agency costs of management. These managers, as investors, will be risk-averse and interested in the allocation of gains and losses. This is not a reason to treat corporate law as if it ought to care about these allocations, however; the risk aversion of managers is a regrettable cost of the corporate form, not a reason to select a rule other than the wealth-maximizing one. As for other undiversified investors, the stock pickers who hold five to ten stocks and trade actively: These people are simply telling us that they are not risk-averse. Recall that the only reason to care about diversification is because some people may be risk-averse and therefore might not want whatever approach maximized social wealth. If the people who do not like risk can look after themselves, then there is no remaining reason not to select whatever rule maximizes value. And for what it is worth, the vast majority of investments are held by people with diversified portfolios. The principal investors in most firms are institutions of one sort or another: mutual funds, trust departments of banks, pension funds, and other instrumentalities for diversifying holdings. It is a bad idea to reduce the wealth of the prudent many for the dubious benefit of gamblers.

Mistakes. Some people take particular provisions of corporate organization as proof that the provisions could not have been selected by any contractual process. Suppose the articles of Acme Widget Corp. provide that in deciding whether managers may take a corporate opportunity for their own benefit, interested directors are entitled to vote. Suppose the articles thrust on investors the burden of showing that a self-dealing transaction was unfair to the firm, whether or not the manager disclosed the transaction and obtained approval beforehand. Would not such provisions be so one-sided, so fraught with danger to investors, that their very existence shows managerial domination and overreaching? Would not that justify the imposition by law of terms more favorable to investors?

Two kinds of argument might be at work here. One is that some third-party effect of the sort mentioned in the preceding section has caused the interests of a given corporation to diverge from the social optimum. The other is that the particular term in the corporate charter is a blunder, as its investors see things. Divergence between private and social interest is rare and does not appear to be at work in these examples. That leaves mistake. But whose mistake? The investors', for not seeing through the ruse and reducing the price paid for the securities? Or the critics', for believing that the terms disserve investors' interests? Unless the person challenging the portion of the corporate contract can make a convincing argument that the consequences of the term could not have been appreciated by investors and priced efficiently, there is no reason for intervening to correct a mistake. Any complexity that might prevent professional investors from recognizing the true effects of a given term probably has no less a baleful effect on the critics' ability to do so. So the presumptive hypothesis is that the mistake has been made by the critic, not by the firm and the investors.

Whenever the costs and benefits of a practice are knowable, they will be reflected in the prices at which the corporation's stock trades. The critic who says that some important term of corporate governance has escaped this mechanism is saying either that the costs and benefits are not knowable or that he alone knows the costs and benefits. Now of course he can reveal these; if people believe him, the market will respond without the need for governmental intervention. The more likely hypothesis, however, is that the people who are backing their beliefs with cash are correct; they have every reason to avoid mistakes, while critics (be they academics or regulators) are rewarded for novel rather than accurate beliefs. Market professionals who estimate these things wrongly suffer directly; academics and regulators who estimate wrongly do not pay a similar penalty. You should trust those who wager with their own money to do the calculations correctly. They may be wrong, but they are less likely to be wrong than are academics and regulators, who are wagering with other peoples' money.

Corporate governance devices that have survived in many firms for extended periods are particularly unlikely candidates for challenge as mistakes. We have emphasized that the durability of a practice both enables people to gauge its effects and allows competition among firms to weed out the practices that do not assist investors. There is no similar process of weeding out among academic ideas or regulations. Quite the contrary, mandatory terms prescribed by law halt the process of natural selection and evaluation. Unless there is a strong reason to believe that regulation has a comparative advantage over competition in markets in evaluating the effects of corporate contracts – a showing that depends on the sort of features discussed in the preceding section and the one that comes next – there is no basis for displacing actual arrangements as "mistakes," "exploitation," and the like.

C   The latecomer term

Much of the discussion so far has proceeded as if all parts of the corporate contract were established at the beginning. "The beginning" for any participant is when he enters the venture – when he becomes an employee, invests, and so on. This is the critical time for most purposes because the time of entry is when the costs and benefits of governance arrangements are priced. If a term is good (or bad) at the beginning, adjustments in the prices even everything up. But of course many things change after the beginning. The firm may reincorporate in Nevada. It may adopt staggered terms for members of the board of directors or a "fair price amendment." It may abolish the executive committee of the board or get rid of all the independent directors (or create a board with a majority of independent directors). What are we to make of these changes?

Changes of this sort have some things in common: They are proposed by the existing managers (unless approved by the board of directors, no change in an ongoing firm's rules will be adopted), the proposals are accepted by voting among the equity investors, and the winning side in the vote does not compensate the losing side. If the changes are adverse to existing participants in the venture, there will be price adjustments – but these adjustments do not compensate the participants. If an amendment reduces the expected profitability of the firm by an amount worth $1 per share, the price will fall, and existing investors will experience a capital loss of $1 per share. They can sell, but they can't avoid the loss. The buyers will get shares worth what they pay; the investors at the time of the change are out of luck. The mechanism by which entrepreneurs and managers bear the cost of unfavorable terms does not work – not in any direct way, anyway – for latecomer terms. It will work eventually. Latecomer terms that injure investors will reduce the firm's ability to raise money and compete in product markets. But these eventual reactions are not remedies; they explain why firms that choose inferior governance devices do not survive, and they show why widespread, enduring practices are likely to be beneficial, but they do nothing for participants in the ventures that are about to be ground under by the heel of history.

The process of voting controls adverse terms to a degree but not perfectly. Investors are rationally uninterested in votes, not only because no investor's vote will change the outcome of the election but also because the information necessary to cast an informed vote is not readily available. Shareholders' approval of changes is likely to be unreliable as an indicator of their interests, because scattered shareholders in public firms do not have the time, information, or incentives to review all proposed changes. Votes are not sold, at least not without the shares. The difference between governance provisions established at the beginning and provisions added later suggests some caution in treating the two categories alike. Some of the hardest questions in corporate law concern arrangements that are adopted or changed after the firm is under way and the capital has been raised. Thus doctrines of corporate law refusing to allow shareholders to ratify waste (except unanimously) are well-founded. Yet the rules for amending the rules are themselves part of the original articles, and it is (or should be) possible to draft limitations

on amendment. These most commonly take the form of provisions des-
ignating some amendments as transactions from which investors may
dissent and demand appraisal. Moreover, amendments to governance
structures may spark proxy contests in which investors' attention is focused, and they also may call forth takeover bids. So voting, or at least
the opportunity for review set in place by the voting mechanism, is a
partial substitute for the pricing mechanism that applies at the beginning.

One candidate for a rule of law that could overcome a problem in
the contracting process is a rule that differentiates between terms according to the time of their adoption. It could provide that terms in
place at the beginning (at the time the firm is founded, goes public, or
issues significant amounts of stock) are always to be honored unless
there are demonstrable effects of the sort discussed in Section IV B,
while terms adopted later that appear to increase the agency costs of
management are valid only if adopted by supermajority vote at successive annual meetings or if dissenting investors are bought out. (The dual-
meeting rule would allow an intervening proxy or takeover contest to
prevent the change from going into effect.) Yet if such a constraint on
amendments is beneficial to investors, why are supermajority and dual-
meeting requirements so rare in corporate documents? Investors can
and do appreciate the risk that latecomer terms will be damaging, yet
perhaps rules that slow down the adoption of changes would be more
damaging still on balance. It is not our purpose here to draft rules of
law. It is important, however, to keep the latecomer term in mind as a
potential problem in a contractual approach to corporate law.

D   Why is there corporate law?

One natural question after all this business of corporation-as-contract
is: Why law? Why not just abolish corporate law and let people negotiate
whatever contracts they please? The short but not entirely satisfactory
answer is that corporate law is a set of terms available off the rack so
that participants in corporate ventures can save the cost of contracting.
There are lots of terms, such as rules for voting, establishing quorums,
and so on, that almost everyone will want to adopt. Corporate codes
and existing judicial decisions supply these terms "for free" to every
corporation, enabling the ventures to concentrate on matters that are
specific to their undertaking. Even when they work through all the issues
they expect to arise, they are apt to miss something. All sorts of com-
plexities will arise later. Corporate law – and in particular the fiduciary
principle enforced by courts – fills in the blanks and oversights with the
terms that people would have bargained for had they anticipated the

problems and have been able to transact costlessly in advance. On this view corporate law supplements but never displaces actual bargains – save in situations of third-party effects or latecomer terms.

And there is a ready source of guidance for corporate codes and judicial decisions to draw on in filling in blanks (or establishing background terms): the deals people actually strike when they bargain over the subject. These actual bargains offer models for other firms too. It is possible that firms that have come to actual bargains on a subject are different from firms that remain silent; the very difference is the reason for the bargain. Possible, but unlikely; differences in transaction costs or perspicacity are more plausible, unless there is some identifiable difference that calls for different rules of governance. Larger firms will find it worthwhile to make specific things others leave open, because the gains from resolution increase with the size of the firm. As amateur investors benefit from the work of professionals, so smaller firms and courts can benefit from the work of the professional negotiators who solve problems for larger firms.

The story is not complete, however, because it still does not answer the question "Why law?" Why don't law firms or corporate service bureaus or investment banks compile sets of terms on which corporations may be constructed? They can peddle these terms and recover the cost of working through all the problems. Yet it is costly for the parties (or any private supplier of rules) to ponder unusual situations and dicker for the adoption of terms of any sort. Parties or their surrogates must identify problems and then transact in sufficient detail to solve them. This may all be wasted effort if the problem does not occur. Because change is the one constant of corporate life, waste is a certainty. Often the type of problem that the firm encounters does not occur to anyone until after the venture is under way. Court systems have a comparative advantage in supplying answers to questions that do not occur in time to be resolved ex ante. Common law systems need not answer questions unless they occur. This is an economizing device; it avoids working through problems that do not arise. The accumulation of cases dealing with unusual problems then supplies a level of detail that is costly to duplicate through private bargaining. To put it differently, "contractual" terms for many kinds of problems turn out to be public goods!

Even if law firms, investment banks, or other private suppliers of solutions could specify optimal solutions, they could not readily supply answers for all marginal cases. No one firm could capture all of the gains from working out all problems in advance, because other firms could copy the answers without paying the creator. If the value of new solutions is hard to appropriate, and if the gain from private bargaining is small, people will leave things to be worked out later. As we have emphasized repeatedly, what should be worked out and supplied by corporate law is the rule that, if uniformly applied, will maximize the value of corporate endeavor as a whole. The law completes open-ended contracts. There is no reason why it should be used to impose a term that defeats actual bargains or reduces the venturers' joint wealth.

V   Maximands

An approach that emphasizes the contractual nature of a corporation removes from the field of interesting questions one that has plagued many writers: What is the goal of the corporation? Is it profit (and for whom)? Social welfare more broadly defined? Is there anything wrong with corporate charity? Should corporations try to maximize profit over the long run or the short run? Our response to such questions is, Who cares? If the *New York Times* is formed to publish a newspaper first and make a profit second, no one should be allowed to object. Those who came in at the beginning actually consented, and those who came in later bought stock the price of which reflected the corporation's tempered commitment to a profit objective. If a corporation is started with a promise to pay half of the profits to the employees rather than the equity investors, that too is simply a term of the contract. It will be an experiment. We might not expect the experiment to succeed, but such expectations by strangers to the bargain are no objection. Similarly, if a bank is formed with a declared purpose to prefer loans to minority-owned businesses, or to Third World nations, that is a matter for the venturers to settle among themselves. So too if a corporation, on building a plant, undertakes never to leave the community. Corporate ventures may select their preferred "constituencies."

The one thing on which a contractual framework focuses attention is surprises. If the venture at its formation is designed in the ordinary fashion – employees and debt investors holding rights to fixed payoffs and equity investors holding a residual claim to profits, which the other participants promise to maximize – that is a binding promise. If the firm suddenly acquires a newspaper and declares that it is no longer interested in profit, the equity investors have a legitimate complaint. It is a complaint for breach of contract, not for derogation from some ethereal ideal of corporate governance.

The role of corporate law here, as elsewhere, is to adopt a background term that prevails unless varied by contract. And the background term should be the one that is either picked by contract expressly when people get around to it or is the operational assumption of successful firms. For most firms the expectation is that the residual risk bearers have contracted for a promise to maximize long-run profits of the firm, which in turn maximizes the value of their stock. Other participants contract for fixed payouts – monthly interest, salaries, pensions, severance payments, and the like. This allocation of rights among the holders of fixed and variable claims serves an economic function. Risk bearers get a residual claim to profit; those who do not bear risk on the margin get fixed terms of trade.

One thing that cannot survive is systematic efforts to fool participants. If investments are attracted on the promise of efforts to maximize profits, then that plan must be executed; otherwise new money cannot be raised and the firm will fail. If investors should come to doubt the worth of promises made to them, investment in the economy as a whole would fall. Similarly, if a firm building a new plant undertakes to operate it only so long as it is profitable and then to lay off the employees and move away, an effort to change the terms later on (if the feared condition materializes) to lock the plant in place or compel severance payments would be a breach of the agreement. Fear of such opportunistic conduct ex post would reduce the willingness of investors to put up new plants and hire new workers.

Notice that a contractual approach does not draw a sharp line between employees and contributors of capital. Employees may be investors in the sense that portions of their human capital are firm-specific – that is, are adapted to the corporation's business and are worth less in some other job. Holding firm-specific human capital is a way of investing in the firm. The question is not whether employees and other "constituencies" of the firm have entitlements or expectations – they do – but what those entitlements are. If employees negotiate for or accept a system of severance payments to protect their firm-specific human capital, they cannot turn around later and demand an additional device (such as a contract for a term of years) when business goes bad. Each investor must live with the structure of risks built into the firm. Equity claimants lose out to debt claimants when times are bad and are not thereby entitled to some additional compensation. It is all a matter of enforcing the contracts. And for any employee or investor other than the residual claimant, that means the explicit, negotiated contract.

The choice of maximand is still important if political society wishes to change corporate behavior. Given wealth as a maximand, society may change corporate conduct by imposing monetary penalties. These reduce the venturers' wealth, so managers will attempt to avoid them. So, for example, a pollution tax would induce the firm to emit less. It would behave as if it had the interests of others at heart. Society thus takes advantage of the wealth-maximizing incentives built into the firm in order to alter its behavior at least cost. Nothing in our approach asks whether political society should attempt to make firms behave as if they have the welfare of nonparticipants in mind. We do not address optimal ways to deal with pollution, bribery, plant closings, and other decisions that have effects on people who may not participate in the corporate contract. Society must choose whether to conscript the firm's strength (its tendency to maximize wealth) by changing the prices it confronts, or by changing its structure so that it is less apt to maximize wealth. The latter choice will yield less of both good ends than the former.

CHAPTER 7

The state competition debate in corporate law

Roberta Romano

A perennial issue in corporate law reform is the desirability of a federal system. For notwithstanding the invasive growth of regulation by the national government, principally through the federal securities laws, corporate law is still the domain of the states. While no two corporation codes are identical, there is substantial uniformity across the states. Provisions typically spread in a discernible S-shaped pattern, as one state amends its code in response to another state's innovation.[1] The revision process is often analogized in the academic literature to market competition, in which states compete to provide firms with a product, corporate charters, in order to obtain franchise tax revenues.[2] This characterization is the centerpiece of the federalism debate in corporate law – whether competition, and hence a federal system, benefits shareholders. The hero – or culprit – in the debate is Delaware, the most successful state in the market for corporate charters.

I would like to thank Rick Antle, Lucian Bebchuk, Bob Clark, Henry Hansmann, Lewis Kornhauser, Saul Levmore, Isaac Meilijson, George Priest, Jeff Strnad, Elliott Weiss, and Oliver Williamson for helpful comments and suggestions. This chapter is an abridged version of an article published in the *Cardozo Law Review* 8:709 (1987).
1 See R. Romano, Law as a Product: Some Pieces of the Incorporation Puzzle, *Journal of Law, Economics, and Organization* 1:225 (1985), pp. 233–5. The enactment of general incorporation statutes in the 19th and early 20th centuries follows a pattern similar to what we observe today. See W. Shughart and R. Tollison, Corporate Chartering: An Exploration in the Economics of Legal Change, *Economic Inquiry* 23:585 (1985). A recent graphic example of statutory invention and imitation is Maryland's second generation takeover statute which requires a supermajority vote in certain business combinations. Md. Corps. and Ass'ns Code Ann. secs. 3–601 to –603 (1985 and Supp. 1986). This statute was enacted in 1983 and in less than two years had been adopted by nine other states.
2 See, e.g., R. Winter, State Law, Shareholder Protection, and the Theory of the Corporation, *Journal of Legal Studies* 6:251 (1977), p. 255.

216

Delaware's preeminence and its impact on who benefits from competition is the subject of this chapter, which is essentially a survey of recent learning on state competition. After a sketch of the conventional moves in the state competition debate, I summarize a transaction cost explanation for Delaware's success. Next, I briefly examine a controversial subset of state laws – antitakeover statutes – whose problematic place in corporation codes muddies the debate. Thereafter, I review the findings of empirical studies that have sought to arbitrate the state competition debate by employing financial econometric techniques. I conclude by discussing the implications of this new learning on state competition for public policy.

I   The state competition literature

A   The classic positions revisited

The foundation of the federalism debate in corporate law is that revenues derived from franchise taxes provide a powerful incentive for state legislatures to implement corporation codes that will maintain the number of domiciled corporations, if not lure new firms to incorporate in their state. All participants in the debate believe that the income produced by the chartering business spurs states to enact laws that firms desire.[3] This behavioral assumption is plausible: There is a positive linear relation between the percentage of total revenues that states obtain from franchise taxes and states' responsiveness to firms in their corporate codes.[4] The more dependent a state is on income from franchise tax revenues, the more responsive is its corporation code. The potential revenue from this tax source can be substantial for a small state. Delaware's franchise tax revenue averaged 15.8 percent of its total revenue from 1960 to 1980, and while it is impossible to generate a precise figure, this income considerably outdistances the cost of operating its chartering business.[5]

Given the shared assertion that revenues compel states to be responsive to firms' demands for legislation, the crux of the dispute is, therefore, whether this responsiveness is for the better. Because of the separation of ownership and control in the management of many large public corporations, when a firm's managers propose a reincorporation

3 E.g., ibid. (supporting state codes); W. Cary, Federalism and Corporate Law: Reflections upon Delaware, *Yale Law Journal* 83:663 (1974) (supporting national regulation).
4 Romano, note 1, pp. 239–40.
5 Ibid. pp. 240–2.

or urge the enactment of a statute, no less the adoption of a charter provision, we are concerned about whether they are maximizing the value of the firm. This is the classic agency problem, which goes to the heart of corporation law in a pluralist democracy: How do principals (the shareholders) ensure that their agents (the managers) behave faithfully?[6]

Advocates of a national corporation law have termed state competition a race for the bottom because they believe that managers' discretion is unfettered, enabling them to promote laws that are detrimental to shareholders' welfare.[7] They base this conclusion on a characterization of the statutes and case law of Delaware – which is the most frequent location for a reincorporation – as excessively permissive, by which they mean tilted toward management. Proponents of the current federal system, however, question this phrasing of the issue, typically viewing the agency problem as trivial. They maintain that the many markets in which firms operate – the product, capital, and labor markets – constrain managers to further the shareholders' interests. Accordingly, in their view, conflict between investors and managers over the content of state laws is largely illusory, and the laws that are promulgated can best be explained as mechanisms for maximizing equity share prices.

The initial articulation of the market argument in the state competition debate was by Ralph Winter.[8] Responding to William Cary, who launched the first salvo in the modern debate,[9] Winter contended that if management chose a state whose laws were adverse to the shareholders' interests, the value of the firm's stock would decline relative to stock in a comparable firm incorporated in a state with value-maximizing laws, as investors would require a higher return on capital to finance the business operating under the inferior legal regime. This impact in the capital market would affect managers by threatening their jobs. Either the lower stock price would attract a takeover artist who could turn a profit by acquiring the firm and relocating it in a state with superior laws, or the firm would go bankrupt by being undercut in its product market by rivals whose cost of capital would be lower because they were incorporated in value-maximizing states. In either scenario, in order to maintain their positions, managers are compelled, by

6 See R. Romano, Metapolitics and Corporate Law Reform, *Stanford Law Review* 36:923 (1984), pp. 928–9, 955–6, 1013–14.
7 E.g., Cary, note 3, p. 666.
8 Winter, note 2.
9 Cary, note 3.

natural selection, to seek the state whose laws are most favorable to shareholders.

Winter's critique is devastating to Cary's analysis because Cary completely overlooked the interaction of markets on managers' incentives. Yet Cary's position cannot be entirely dismissed: More sophisticated proponents of national chartering can move to another line of attack by maintaining that there is a true difference in opinion that turns upon Cary's and Winter's assessments of the disciplining effect of markets on managers. Winter can assume away the agency problem because of his view that the capital market is efficient such that information concerning the impact of different legal regimes is publicly available and fully assimilated into stock prices. In contrast, support for national chartering presupposes a market that is, at best, only weakly efficient, such that it does not digest information concerning legal rules. In addition, even if stock prices accurately reflect the value of different legal regimes, if product markets are not competitive or the costs of takeovers are substantial, then a manager's livelihood may not be jeopardized by the choice of a nonvalue-maximizing incorporation state. When the debate is phrased in this way, the disagreement is over an empirical question concerning market efficiency, for which, in principle, there is a clean answer.

To be sure, Cary sees a failure not only in financial and product markets, but also in local politics. His recommendation of national standards for corporations implies that the political process at the national level differs fundamentally from that of the states. Cary considers the flaw in Delaware's code to be a function of that state's desire for revenue and the close personal connections between Delaware legislators, judges, and corporate law firms.[10] The national government certainly would not be as sensitive to franchise tax dollars as would a small state, and practically speaking, there would be no competing sovereigns to attract dissatisfied corporations.

But even if we grant Cary's premise that the states' responsiveness is the source of the problem, the elimination of intergovernmental competition is not necessarily the cure. The hitch in Cary's position is that he leaves unexplained why national legislators in pursuit of reelection would be less susceptible to the political influence of managers for "pet" statutes than state legislators. For why should diffuse and unorganized shareholders be appreciably better able to communicate their views

10 Ibid. pp. 690–2.

to Congress when they cannot do so to state legislatures?[11] There are countless pieces of legislation produced by pork barrel politics in Congress – the tax code is perhaps the most notable example – and there is no convincing reason to believe that firms' managers would be any less skilled at protecting their interests when it comes to a federal corporation code.[12]

B   An extension of the debate: product differentiation stories

Both Cary's and Winter's explanations of state competition predict a trend toward uniformity across state corporation codes. In addition, they imply a process of constant disequilibrium in which the system swings back and forth between corner solutions: As soon as one state innovates with a new provision, all managers should, theoretically, reincorporate in that state in order to increase firm value (or to entrench themselves in their positions). Then a second state, to avoid losing revenue, should respond by introducing a further innovation, causing all of the firms to migrate to it, and so forth. However, the market for corporate charters is more stable than this. Most firms that relocate do so only once, some never change their incorporation state, and Delaware continues to attract the vast majority of all reincorporations.[13] Accordingly, although Cary's and Winter's depiction of the competitive process is intuitively appealing, it has the undesirable property of being a disequilibrium rather than an equilibrium story. If we assume optimizing

---

11 If the claim is that communication costs are lower when there is only one legislature, the obvious response is that even with state competition, only one state matters, Delaware, where a large number of firms reside. Putting it this way makes clear that competition is the linchpin of the argument. Cary must argue that another state would come to the managers' rescue if shareholder lobbyists succeeded in Delaware, thereby making such expenditures futile, whereas no such alternatives would exist in a national scheme. The transaction cost explanation of state competition discussed in notes 26–40 and accompanying text suggests that there is friction in the chartering market, involving transaction-specific assets that tie together particular states and firms, and that prevents overnight shifts in a state's market share while simultaneously protecting firms' interests in a responsive corporation code.

12 See R. Romano, The Future of Hostile Takeovers: Legislation and Public Opinion, *University of Cincinnati Law Review* 57:457 (1988).

13 Romano, note 1, p. 244 (82% of reincorporations of publicly traded firms in the period 1960–1980 were in Delaware). In my sample of firms, those with multiple reincorporations consisted primarily of a group of Michigan manufacturing companies that went to Delaware in the 1960s and 1970s upon Delaware's revision of its corporation code, and then moved back to Michigan in the 1980s after a change in that state's taxation. Michigan had also revised its code to duplicate Delaware's in the interim (p. 258).

behavior, as Winter and Cary assume of managers, a disequilibrium story is unsatisfactory because it implies that deals could still be made between firms and states, and consequently, that the actors have not optimized.

Recognizing this snag in the classic exposition of the corporate charter market, some scholars sought to refine Winter's explanation of the value-maximizing properties of state competition. Richard Posner and Kenneth Scott, in a short note in their corporate law reader, hypothesized that states differentiate their products by tailoring their codes to attract different types of firms.[14] In particular, they suggested that Delaware specializes in providing charters for large publicly traded firms. While this is an interesting insight, there are serious difficulties with it. First, competition is not necessary for product differentiation because it can be achieved within one state's code. Many states, including Delaware, offer different rules for smaller, closely held corporations through the enactment of close corporation statutes.[15] Second, only slightly more than one-half of the largest firms are incorporated in Delaware. Thus, to be useful, Posner and Scott's conjecture must be refined, as size alone is not a distinguishing characteristic. However, comparison tests across numerous attributes of large public firms incorporated in Delaware and in other states fail to show any statistically significant differences.[16] Consequently, Posner and Scott's speculation is, at best, incomplete.

While a specialization story avoids a disequilibrium result, it does not provide the normative edge for asserting that state laws are value-maximizing: The welfare implications of product differentiation models are indeterminate, as their equilibrium need not be optimal.[17] A product differentiation story that fits the formal economic models of the Posner and Scott intuition accordingly does not have to be attached to the position that state laws are in the interest of shareholders. In fact, Barry

14 R. Posner and K. Scott, *Economics of Corporation Law and Securities Regulation* (Boston, 1980), p. 111. A fuller exploration of such a view of corporate charters derived from an economic theory of federalism – Charles Tiebout's theory of local public goods in which citizens move to the locality whose tax and spending program matches their preferences – was provided by Frank Easterbrook. Easterbrook, Antitrust and the Economics of Federalism, *Journal of Law and Economics* 26:23 (1983).
15 E.g., Del. Code Ann. tit. 8, sec. 342 (1984).
16 Romano, note 1, pp. 262–65. The only statistically significant differences were that the Delaware firms have been in existence for fewer years than non-Delaware firms and that they average more acquisitions over their shorter lives. This difference can be explained by the transaction explanation of reincorporation; see notes 26–40 and accompanying text.
17 See M. Spence, Product Selection, Fixed Costs, and Monopolistic Competition, *Review of Economic Studies* 43:217 (1976), pp. 231–3.

Baysinger and Henry Butler have combined a product differentiation explanation with pieces of both sides of the state competition debate.[18] They begin by agreeing with Cary that some state codes, such as Delaware's, are lax and favor managers, while others are strict and favor shareholders. The analysis then takes an interesting turn. Baysinger and Butler's thesis is that firms will locate in the state whose laws match their shareholders' needs: In particular, firms with diffuse ownership will select lax states because these shareholders can sell their shares if management's performance is poor, while firms with a controlling shareholder or concentrated ownership will choose strict states whose codes facilitate shareholder activism because exit is costly for large shareholders.

Baysinger and Butler sought support for this self-selection thesis by examining the ownership concentration of firms in states with strict and lax laws. They compared the mean holdings of various types of shareholders across firms that had remained in and firms that had reincorporated away from four states that were classified as strict. Rather than derive the classification from the content of state corporation codes, upon which the point of the exercise is premised, they defined a strict state to be a state from which headquartered firms migrate. They found that the shareholder groups' holdings were significantly smaller in firms that had left the strict states.

Unfortunately, their definition of strictness is unsatisfactory; a migration index of strictness is a noisy signal because some states have larger firm populations than others, which generates some movement independent of the relative differences in legal regimes. Although Baysinger and Butler alleviate this problem by using percentages rather than absolute numbers of firms per state, the adjusted criterion is still an inaccurate proxy for what they want to measure. One of the four states they identified as strict by the migration criterion, New York, is in fact a relatively permissive state, and a number of states with high corporate retention rates that are permissive under Baysinger and Butler's definition, such as South Dakota, are strict states if we examine the actual content of their codes.[19] This objection is not trivial. Because the sample for testing their thesis consisted of an equal number of firms from each

---

18 B. Baysinger and H. Butler, The Role of Corporate Law in the Theory of the Firm, *Journal of Law and Economics* 28:179 (1985).

19 I have developed a measure of states' corporate law responsiveness that is a function of both the substance and timing of enactment of corporation code provisions in order to better examine the state competition hypothesis. See Romano, note 1, pp. 233–42. The responsiveness measure identifies strict and lax legal regimes more precisely than migration because it is derived directly from the content of corporation codes.

of the four states they classified as strict, the misclassification of one state renders one-quarter of the observations questionable, and we cannot be sure what effect this has on their results.[20]

More important, Baysinger and Butler's thesis is problematic because it calls for behavior that is not observed. If legal regime and shareholder concentration are paired, as they maintain, then when a firm is taken over and ownership becomes more concentrated, it should move to a strict state. Yet this rarely occurs. In the cases where we see a change of incorporation state at the same time or shortly after a merger, the destination state is typically Delaware, the most "lax" state.[21]

In addition, reincorporation patterns raise a further question concerning their results. Because corporations reincorporate in order to undertake specific types of transactions for which legal rules matter,[22] if there is a systematic relation between transaction-type and ownership concentration, this would create an omitted variable problem, weakening the power of Baysinger and Butler's test. For the type of legal regime, strict or permissive, might actually be related to the transaction motivating the reincorporation and not to the ownership pattern. For example, when firms go public they frequently reincorporate in Delaware.[23] While this fact superficially appears to further Baysinger and Butler's thesis because the firm moves to a lax state as ownership becomes less concentrated, it in fact underscores a difficulty in testing their explanation – the transaction of interest, reincorporation when going public, coincides with a change in ownership pattern, and thus confounds the test.

Moreover, it is misleading to characterize firms that have gone public as having diffuse ownership, because even though their ownership has become less concentrated when they go public, the original owners retain, at minimum, working control. This phenomenon is therefore an additional problem for their thesis: Since there are still large controlling shareholders, the firm should not have moved to a permissive state. In

---

20 An additional difficulty is that we do not know whether the variable for director and officer holdings excludes family members who are also managers. Presumably, the tests controlled for such individuals. If not, then the finding of no difference in management holdings would be misleading. Moreover, the conclusion that strict laws are important for firms with higher family holdings would be illusory because if family members are also managers, then the basis for maintaining that the legal regime matters is weakened because there is less separation of ownership and control in such firms.
21 I found this to be so in the data collected for Romano, note 1.
22 Ibid. pp. 250–1. See also notes 26–28 and accompanying text (discussing transaction costs of reincorporation).
23 Romano, note 1, pp. 255–6.

no case does the original owners' holding drop to a sufficiently small number of shares such that the difficulty of selling the stock that Baysinger and Butler posit would disappear.[24] Indeed, most of the statistically significant ownership differences in their sample, given conventional wisdom, would not significantly affect shareholders' control of their firm.[25] Furthermore, the mean holding in the migrating firms of all types of shareholders for which the difference across firms was statistically significant is still a very substantial block of stock. Accordingly, these investors do not have the ability to sell shares easily in either case, casting further doubt on Baysinger and Butler's explanation of state competition.

Given these factors, the more plausible explanation for the ownership pattern in conjunction with migration is not that large shareholders necessarily prefer stricter laws, but rather that the initial legal regime may be irrelevant to such shareholders. The corporation code does not have the monitoring role that Baysinger and Butler ascribe to it because for firms with controlling shareholders that move upon going public, as well as for the average firm in their sample, it is not very helpful to talk about the separation of ownership and control. In short, some other feature must be driving corporations to Delaware. While Baysinger and Butler offer an elegant twist – corporate self-selection – to the state competition debate, the data do not satisfactorily accord with their identification and explanation of the basis for self-selection.

C   *A transaction cost explanation of the market for corporate charters*

The feature in Cary's and Winter's analysis that implies system instability is the assumption that there are no transaction costs of moving. If there are costs to reincorporating, then it is less likely that a corner solution

---

24 It might make sense for Baysinger and Butler note 18, to emphasize absolute levels of ownership rather than the relative measure of a difference in means test. This would eliminate the problem discussed in the text by excluding most firms that go public. But it would also weaken the link between their thesis and state competition. In their story, it is the preferences of migrating firms that drives the selection of corporation codes. Because going-public firms comprise the largest group of reincorporating firms (pp. 250, 253) to be complete, any theory of state competition must explain those decisions.

25 For example, the corporate ownership of "leavers" averages 11.28%, compared to 15.69% for "stayers." Baysinger and Butler, note 18, p. 187. Yet in both situations, the lower percentage is well within what is generally thought to be enough for working control in a public corporation, and constitutes insider status for the purpose of the federal securities laws.

will develop. The importance of transaction costs enters into the product differentiation explanations that emphasize variety in corporation codes. It is explicit in Posner and Scott's size hypothesis – they suggest that only large firms can afford to relocate in Delaware. And while it may not be crucial to Baysinger and Butler's thesis, they do maintain that information costs prevent firms from choosing the most liberal state and then tailoring their charters to meet shareholder preferences.

My explanation of the corporate charter market relies on transaction costs. This transaction cost explanation of state competition has two prongs: One concerns the reasons why firms move, and the other concerns the persistence of Delaware's extraordinary market share. The cost of migration[26] must produce a commensurate benefit for a move to be undertaken, a benefit that relates to a reduction in the cost of operating the firm under the new regime. In addition, unlike the product differentiation stories, my thesis predicts substantial uniformity in state laws, in keeping with the classic positions of Cary and Winter, as well as the more salient characteristic of corporation codes. Under this explanation, variety in corporation codes is primarily a function of diffusion – the differential in time by which innovations are enacted by legislatures across the states – rather than of different preferences across firms.[27]

Why do firms reincorporate? I expected that reincorporations would accompany changes in business operation and organization that would be cheaper in a different legal regime. The cost reduction could involve direct costs (for instance, where the legal rules governing specific transactions differ across the states, thereby imposing different costs on those transactions) or it could involve indirect costs (for example, different regimes affect the likelihood and cost of litigation over transactions differently). My data on reincorporations support this contention: Firms reincorporate when they are preparing to initiate a discrete set of transactions, the most frequent being a public offering, a merger and acquisition program, or defensive maneuvering against takeovers.[28] A number

---

26 See Romano, note 1, pp. 246–9 (reincorporation costs range from a few thousand to millions of dollars).

27 In my analysis, because most states are behaving defensively in the charter market and differences in legal regimes are of interest to firms undertaking certain types of transactions, firm self-selection could still be a factor in statutory variety in the following circumstance: If no or very few firms in a state will ever undertake specific transactions for which another state has innovated, then the former state does not have to amend its code to retain the firms in its jurisdiction.

28 Romano, note 1, 242–3. These three categories comprised 72% of the reincorporations where an associated transaction type could be identified. Romano, note 1, p. 250. My

of legal rules that vary across the states, including the conditions for shareholder voting and appraisal rights, affect the cost of engaging in such activity. For instance, corporation codes may limit merger voting and appraisal rights of the acquiring firm's shareholders, which reduces acquisition costs. They may also regulate takeovers or make charter amendment flexible, reducing the cost of resisting a bid. Finally, different organizational rules, including the requirements for shareholder meetings, written consent, and board communication, both ease the transition to, and reduce the cost of operating, a newly publicly traded firm.

In addition, a common characteristic of the transactions motivating reincorporations is an increase in the likelihood that a firm will be embroiled in litigation. Acquisitions and efforts to thwart them frequently produce protracted lawsuits over the fairness of the offer or the appropriateness of management's actions. Going public sets the stage for potential fiduciary breaches by bringing into the firm a new class of stockholders whose interests may differ from those of manager-shareholders. In all of these situations, a legal regime that reduces expected litigation costs is desirable. A well-developed case law and expertise in corporate law are mechanisms by which a state can lower those costs. Such a regime enables counsel to provide management quickly with opinion letters concerning the transactions they wish to pursue, which facilitates business planning to circumvent problems that could spark litigation.

Reincorporating firms' interest in finding legal regimes that reduce their cost of doing business is further supported by survey responses: Firms that reincorporate to undertake the transactions mentioned earlier perceive a significant difference in the laws of the origin and destination states and emphasize that the difference is an important factor in their decision to move more frequently than do other firms.[29] Moreover, firms that reincorporate to pursue the identified transactions choose more

---

data consisted of survey responses and public information on the reincorporations of several hundred industrial corporations that were publicly traded in 1982 and had changed their incorporation state during the 20-year period, 1962–1981.

29 Ibid., pp. 258–60. The other firms moved primarily to realize tax savings. Firms that move to a more responsive state also more frequently report a difference in origin and destination state legal regimes and that the difference is an important factor in their decision to move. The chi-square statistic for both crosstabulations was statistically significant, although the statistic for the table of transaction-type by questionnaire response is not reliable because more than 20% of the cells had very low expected frequencies.

frequently to relocate in the most responsive state, Delaware.[30] If there is a self-selection story to be told about state competition for corporate charters, it is more likely to be one that matches responsive states with firms engaging in particular types of transactions, which may or may not be correlated with shareholder concentration, rather than with firms of specified ownership structures per se.

While the transaction cost explanation of reincorporation tells us why firms change their incorporation state, it is inconclusive concerning who benefits from the move. If firms reincorporate to reduce transaction costs, then migration is value-maximizing for shareholders by definition, because cost minimization is an inherent aspect of equity share price maximization. However, if reincorporation merely reduces potential litigation costs, the direction of the effect becomes muddied. These lawsuits involve shareholder claims, and the beneficiaries of the cost reduction may therefore include managers, who are the defendants in the suit and whose interest in this context may conflict with that of the shareholders. Moreover, even when the cost reduction consists of making a specific transaction cheaper to undertake, the move is value-maximizing only if the transaction itself benefits shareholders.[31]

Why is Delaware the destination state of choice? The transaction cost explanation of the corporate charter market provides a different perspective on state competition. Delaware's persistent large market share is maintained by a first-mover advantage created by the reciprocal relation that develops between the chartering state and firms due to their substantial investment in assets that are specific to the chartering transaction. The concept of a transaction-specific asset, developed by Oliver Williamson, arises in an intertemporal context and refers to an asset that cannot be redeployed in an alternative use at a price anywhere comparable to its value in the original contract should that contract be disrupted.[32] Contracts involving such assets transform the parties' exchange relationship from a competitive market transaction into a bilateral monopoly. A simple example of a transaction-specific asset is the specialized racks that are used to transport finished automobiles to market. Such racks are customized for specific car models and cannot be

---

30 Ibid. pp. 255–6.
31 Some would argue that particular transactions, such as takeover defensive tactics, do not benefit shareholders. For some discussion of this issue, see notes 53–57 and accompanying text.
32 For a complete exposition of the theory, see O. Williamson, *The Economic Institutions of Capitalism* (New York 1985), pp. 163–206.

used to transport models of different manufacturers. As a consequence, they are valuable only in certain transactions, and both transporter and car manufacturer are vulnerable and have holdup power. At the outset, there are a number of transporters and automobile manufacturers with which to negotiate, but once parties enter into an agreement, the manufacturer needs that particular hauler to get its cars to market and the hauler needs that manufacturer to earn a return on the racks.

The key feature for analysis is that the nonredeployable character of the asset makes the parties to a contract vulnerable and necessitates additional institutional arrangements – which Williamson terms "governance structures" – that reduce the possibility of exploitation and safeguard investments in the transaction-specific asset. One such mechanism is the bilateral use of hostages – the contracting party may place him or herself in an analogously vulnerable position to the asset owner by giving up something of value, by posting a bond so to speak. This action credibly guarantees his or her performance and thereby maintains the other party's incentive to invest in the transaction-specific asset.[33] In cases of asset specificity, the exchange of hostages may be a prerequisite for the transaction itself to occur.

How does this analysis apply to the corporate charter market?[34] Because the transactions between a firm and its incorporation state extend over a long period of time and reincorporation is not costless, relocation makes a firm vulnerable to exploitation by the state. In particular, the state may charge a premium for incorporation and then alter its code or simply not implement the latest innovations, to the firm's detriment, knowing that the firm cannot quickly migrate again without incurring additional expenses. Hence, due to this non-simultaneity in performance, a state with a favorable corporation code must guarantee its code's continued responsiveness to be successful in the corporate charter market.

Of all the states, Delaware is best positioned to commit itself credibly

33 Ibid. The typical solution to the automobile racks example discussed in the text involves informal contracting in conjunction with ownership of the racks by the carrier, rather than a bilateral exchange of hostages; the typical solution for the shipment of automobile parts, which also require specialized racks, is ownership by the shipper. T. Palay, Avoiding Regulatory Constraints: Contracting Safeguards and the Role of Informal Agreements, *Journal of Law, Economics, and Organization* 1:155 (1985). Good examples of pure hostages are far too complex to be useful for the text's pedagogic point of an illustration of a transaction-specific asset. For specific examples, see O. Williamson, note 32, pp. 180–9, 197–203.
34 The discussion in the text sets out the thesis put forth in Romano, note 1, pp. 235–6, 240–2, 257–60, 273–9.

to responsiveness. First, its very success in the incorporation business serves, ironically, to constrain its behavior: The high proportion of total revenue it derives from franchise taxes guarantees continued responsiveness because it has so much to lose. For unlike states less dependent on franchise revenues, Delaware has no readily available alternative source to which it can turn in order to maintain expenditures. It cannot afford to lose firms to other states by failing to keep its code up-to-date. In this way, Delaware offers itself as a hostage by its reliance on franchise taxes to finance its expenditures.

Second, an additional institutional mechanism warranting responsiveness is Delaware's constitutional provision mandating that all changes in the corporation code be adopted by a two-thirds vote of both houses of the state legislature.[35] This makes it difficult to renege on provisions already in the code and, correspondingly, on the overall policy of being responsive to firms. While the provision would appear to make future changes equally difficult, if firms are risk-averse when it comes to corporation codes, they might favor a maximin strategy in which the constitutional provision would be desirable, since it helps to ensure that the legal regime will never be worse than it is at the time of incorporation. This provision thus complements Delaware's high proportionate franchise tax, for while the constitution is backward-looking, limiting radical revamping of the code, the incentives provided by the franchise tax revenue are forward-looking, as the state reacts to the high proportion of franchise tax revenues in the past by maintaining its responsiveness to incremental change in the future.

Third, Delaware has invested in assets that have no use outside of the chartering business. These assets, which can best be characterized as legal capital, consist of a store of legal precedents forming a comprehensive body of case law, judicial expertise in corporate law, and administrative expertise in the rapid processing of corporate filings. These features are not as easily duplicated by other states as the provisions of a corporation code because of the start-up costs in developing expertise and the dynamic precedent-based nature of adjudication by courts.[36]

---

35 Del. Const. art. IX, sec. 1. Only one other state, Iowa, has such a constitutional provision. Iowa Const. art. 8, sec. 12.

36 While a state could explicitly legislate the principle of statutory construction that when it enacted a Delaware law it intended to include all of the existing judicial interpretations, see, e.g., *Wilmington City Ry.* v. *People's Ry.*, 47 A. 245, 251 (Del. Ch. 1900), this would not protect firms concerning future adjudicative issues. The state would have to bind its courts to follow future Delaware precedents, and hope that no case of first impression decided by its own courts would conflict with a subsequent Delaware

The combination of these factors – the high proportion of franchise tax revenue, the constitutional supermajority requirement, and the investments in legal capital – create an intangible asset with hostagelike qualities, a reputation for responsiveness,[37] that firms weigh in their incorporation decision. The large number of firms already incorporated in Delaware further solidifies its commanding position in the market by giving it a first-mover advantage. There is safety in numbers – the more firms there are, the higher the level of franchise tax paid and the more the state relies on its incorporation business for revenue, which provides the incentive to behave responsively. In addition, the large number of firms makes it more likely that any particular issue will be litigated and decided in Delaware, providing a sound basis for corporate planning. This attracts even more firms for the more responsive a state and the more settled its law, the cheaper it is for a firm to operate under that legal regime. The first-mover advantage is self-sustaining because the more firms there are paying a franchise tax, the greater the return Delaware earns on its reputation for responsiveness, and the stronger its incentive not to engage in an end-game strategy of exploiting firms that would damage, if not destroy, its investment in a reputation.

This brings us to the demand side of the market, which also aids Delaware in maintaining an edge. There is a third party affected by the incorporation system, legal counsel, and the features of Delaware's legal regime that are attractive to firms – a well-developed case law with a pool of handy precedents and a means for rapidly obtaining a legal opinion on any issue – are also advantageous to corporate lawyers. For these features of Delaware law lower the cost of furnishing advice to clients. This is especially important for outside counsel, who service firms that are headquartered in different states and who are instrumental in choosing the incorporation state.[38] They realize cost savings by having

decision. Such a system would involve overwhelming problems of constitutional delegation and parties' rights of appeal, in addition to problems concerning the coherency of local decisional law and the granting of retroactive relief should the hypothesized conflict arise.

37 The connection between reputations and hostages is straightforward: In the corporate charter market where both firms and states have potentially infinite lives, the party with the reputation, Delaware, has an incentive to maintain it because the costs of building up its reputation will not be recouped if it behaves irresponsibly in the short run. For then domestic firms will relocate, new firms will not migrate to it, and tax revenues in later periods will be lost. In other words, a cooperative equilibrium can emerge from a "tit-for-tat" strategy. See generally R. Axelrod, *The Evolution of Cooperation* (New York, 1984) (reciprocity strategies are self-reinforcing and powerful tools to create cooperation).

38 Romano, note 1, pp. 274–6. Jonathan Macey and Geoffrey Miller suggest that the

clients operate under one legal regime. In addition to encouraging the choice of Delaware as the incorporation site for clients, specialization also provides an incentive for advising firms to remain in Delaware, because moving will diminish the attorney's human capital. Counsel's desire to recoup the investment in mastery of the institutional detail of Delaware law ties firms reciprocally to Delaware, just as Delaware is tied to firms.

Human capital is important in another way. Delaware's stake in the chartering business exceeds the revenues it receives from the franchise tax. A number of its citizens specialize in providing services to nonresident Delaware corporations. Accordingly, it is in the interest of those individuals that Delaware be responsive to corporations so that the demand for their services does not decline.[39] Delaware's supermajority constitutional provision therefore serves an important function aside from credibly precommitting it to be responsive to firms: It protects the value of these individuals' personal investments by making it more difficult for a political realignment in the state to alter the long-standing course of corporate responsiveness.

failure to find investment bankers as the source of the decision may be because "the questionnaire...used did not list investment banks as potential parties to suggest reincorporation" (see J. Macey and G. Miller, Toward an Interest-Group Theory of Delaware Corporate Law, *Texas Law Review* 65:469 [1987], p. 487 n. 69.) The questionnaire included investment bankers as an explicit choice; the respondents did not choose that answer.

39 Romano, note 1, pp. 276–7. A number of years ago, Joe Bishop made the point concerning the importance of lawyers in Delaware's lack of a security-for-expenses requirement for shareholder derivative suits. He wrote: "It might...occur to a cynical mind that this curious anomaly of the Delaware law may not be wholly unconnected with the fact that the prosecution or defense of a derivative suit in a Delaware court requires the retention of Delaware counsel." Bishop, New Cure for an Old Aliment: Insurance Against Directors' and Officers' Liability, *Business Lawyer* 22:92 (1966), pp. 94–5. Macey and Miller, note 38, also stress the importance of lawyers in Delaware. They appear to suggest that the input of lawyers in Delaware's legislative process has negative implications for a theory of state competition. Such a conclusion would be wrong – the role of lawyers is peripheral to the debate, particularly from the transaction cost view of state competition that they appear to be advancing. If Delaware passed corporate laws that systematically favor lawyers to the detriment of firms on a large scale, it would lose its chartering business to another state whose lawyers were not as avaricious. Delaware maintains its position by mutual cooperation with, and not by exploitation of, firms. This is not to say that lawyers do not profit in Delaware. While lawyers are actively and intimately involved in Delaware's profitable chartering business, their participation provides no clear-cut insight concerning whether it benefits managers at the shareholders' expense. The important question, which Macey and Miller do not answer, is how any rents are divided among Delaware, the bar, and the participants in firms.

This transaction-specific human capital, which creates a "mutual reliance relation"[40] between firms and Delaware, joins the parties in long-term cooperation because of their reciprocal vulnerability, and cements Delaware's market position, as it makes it difficult for a rival state to compete successfully. Another state cannot simply offer corporations the same code at a lower price and attract the marginal firm, because a switch would increase operating and legal costs, and more importantly, the state cannot provide a credible commitment of superior service. In particular, a rival state cannot place itself in the same vulnerable position as Delaware because it starts from a low franchise tax ratio and has not yet invested in legal capital.[41] In order for a state to begin to compete, a significant number of firms would have to agree to move to it in concert. But there is no incentive for corporations to move to another state so long as Delaware continues to cooperate, and there are powerful incentives for Delaware to continue to do so.

II   Takeover statutes: anomaly or exemplar?

More than most provisions in corporation codes that are the technical terrain upon which the state competition debate is fought, state takeover statutes are a source of substantial controversy. The statutes were enacted in two waves. The first generation statutes, which spread rapidly across states in the 1970s, directly regulated tender offers by establishing waiting periods and administrative hearing requirements for bids for target firms that often had dubious jurisdictional contacts with the legislating state. After the Supreme Court held in 1982, in *Edgar v. MITE Corp.*,[42] that Illinois' statute burdened interstate commerce, new statutes with more plausible jurisdictional bases were devised.

The new statutes had three major forms: (1) control share acquisition statutes that require acquisitions of stock that constitute control, or the voting rights of such shares, to be approved by a majority vote of disinterested shareholders,[43] (2) fair price statutes that require either a supermajority shareholder vote, disinterested board approval, or pay-

---

40 The term is from O. Williamson, Credible Commitments: Using Hostages to Support Exchange, *American Economic Review* 73:519 (1983), p. 528.
41 Nevada, one of two states to experience a net immigration of corporations in the period 1960–1980, Romano, note 1, p. 246, has sought to compete for corporate charters. It has been styled the "Delaware of the West," yet it has failed in its quest for a commanding share of the market.
42 457 U.S. 624 (1982).
43 E.g., Ohio Rev. Code Ann, sec. 1701.831 (Anderson 1985).

ment of a fair price for the second step of a two-tier acquisition,[44] and (3) redemption rights statutes that give all shareholders cash redemption rights against any acquirer of at least 30 percent of the firm's stock.[45] The fair price provision was the most popular of the three, having been enacted by fourteen of the twenty-one states to adopt second generation statutes by 1986.[46]

In 1987, the Supreme Court upheld Indiana's control share acquisition statute in *CTS Corp* v. *Dynamics Corp. of America*.[47] Thereafter the pace and scope of the state legislation changed: Fourteen new statutes were adopted within six months of the decision, and these statutes increased the constraints on bidders even further by banning business combinations (which are very broadly defined) between bidder and target for several years.[48] All four types of takeover statutes can raise the price of an acquisition, although unlike the first generation statutes, they codify tactics that firms could undertake by self-help through charter provisions and permit firms to opt out of the legislation's coverage. Their potential to discourage unfriendly acquisitions is, of course, what gives them bite, and, correspondingly, what makes them controversial.

Takeover statutes are of particular interest because they generate a puzzle for the state competition literature. Some commentators who contend that state competition produces laws that benefit shareholders have also maintained that mechanisms which facilitate management's efforts to thwart hostile bids, such as the actions codified by takeover statutes, are not in the shareholders' interest and should be banned.[49]

44 E.g., Md. Corps. & Ass'ns Code Ann. sec. 3–602 (1985). New York recently passed a more restrictive fair price statute that bans a second-step combination for five years after the first step, with limited exceptions. N.Y. Bus. Corp. Law sec. 912 (McKinney 1986). Its version appears to have replaced Maryland's as the model for states adopting fair price provisions. See, e.g., 1986 N.J. Sess. Laws Serv. ch. 74 (West).
45 E.g., 15 Pa. Cons. Stat. Ann. sec. 1910 (Purdon Supp. 1986).
46 R. Romano, The Political Economy of Takeover Statutes, *Virginia Law Review* 73:111 (1987), pp. 117–18. Only three states adopted a redemption rights provision and six chose control share acquisition statutes, of which two also enacted a fair price provision. For a discussion of why the fair price statute was the most popular, see pp. 117–20, 168–70.
47 481 U.S. 69 (1987).
48 Variants of the New York statute (see note 44) and the Indiana statute upheld in *CTS* are the most popular provisions.
49 E.g., Easterbrook, note 14, p. 35 (state competition benefits shareholders); D. Fischel, The "Race to the Bottom" Revisited: Reflections on Recent Developments in Delaware's Corporation Law, *Northwestern University Law Review* 76:913 (1982), pp. 943–4 (same); F. Easterbrook and D. Fischel, The Proper Role of a Target's Management in Responding to a Tender Offer, *Harvard Law Review* 94:1161 (1981), pp. 1165–82 (defensive tactics harm shareholders).

The difficulty for this position is that many firms choose their incorporation state to facilitate defensive maneuvering against takeovers. To be consistent, it would seem that the commentators must argue either that state competition is managerialist, or that defensive tactics are beneficial to shareholders.[50]

A   *The politics of a takeover statute*

I set out to explore this apparent inconsistency in the literature concerning the effects on shareholder welfare of state competition and takeover defensive tactics by examining the politics behind the adoption of a second generation takeover statute.[51] My initial hypothesis, which was sparked by newspaper accounts, was that corporation code provisions might be differentiated as value-maximizing or managerialist, by who lobbied for their passage. In particular, if takeover laws were supported by a coalition of labor, local community leaders, and managers, it would support a managerialist explanation. Namely, managers would be better positioned to have enacted a law adverse to shareholders' interests when they could appeal for support to a broadbased constituency that had no particular interest in the everyday technicalities of corporation codes. I expected to find that takeover laws would be aberrational in their politics and, hence, sharply distinguishable from other provisions in corporation codes.

The hunch was wrong. In Connecticut, the passage of a fair price statute was of moment only to the business community. A major corporation in the state promoted the bill with the aid of a trade group similar to a state chamber of commerce.[52] The only other group interested in the legislation was the executive committee of the corporate law section of the state bar association. The bar group opposed the

---

50 Ralph Winter distinguished state takeover laws from state competition over corporation codes because of takeover laws' extraterritorial effects – the first generation statutes applied to more than domestically incorporated firms. Winter, note 2, p. 268. He maintained that this enabled the states to restrain competition for charters, pp. 287–9. The second generation statutes, however, have a narrower jurisdiction and thereby lack the external effects with which he was concerned, for they apply only to domestically incorporated firms. Therefore, they cannot be so readily differentiated from other corporation laws.

51 The discussion that follows is from Romano, note 46, pp. 122–41.

52 There was no opposition within the business community to the firm's proposal: The number of firms affected by the statute was small – a substantial number of the publicly traded firms had similar provisions in their charters and there are few acquiring companies in Connecticut. Moreover, the statute would matter to those acquirers only if they wanted to acquire other Connecticut firms.

statute, largely on procedural grounds; they had not been consulted and thought that such a statute should be scrutinized more carefully before enactment.[53]

Apart from the statute's quirky procedural status and consequent bar opposition, the experiences of other states are very similar to that of Connecticut: The only groups who are active in the enactment of second generation takeover statutes are business organizations and the bar. The statutes proceed through state legislatures at an extraordinarily rapid pace, with virtually unanimous bipartisan support, at the behest of the local business community and, most frequently, one concerned firm. This data supports what I term a putting-out-fires explanation of the enactment of takeover legislation, in which legislators simply react to a constituent's immediate concrete demands. To mitigate the problem of sampling error from relying on a case study, I also performed several statistical analyses to see which explanation – the coalition or the putting-out-fires explanation – best predicts which states adopt second generation statutes. Regressions including predictor variables that represented both theses, as well as economic variables indicating a state's prosperity, were estimated. But the results were inconclusive; the estimations offered some support for both explanations.[54] I prefer the putting-out-fires explanation to the coalition hypothesis because it is supported by both anecdotal accounts and statistical data.

B   When should we question takeover statutes?

While the micro examination of the political process identified the parties involved in the legislation, it did not provide much evidence for resolving the issue motivating the study: Whom do takeover statutes benefit? I therefore returned to first principles by trying to determine when shareholders would voluntarily adopt as a charter

53 Unlike the enactment of most other Connecticut corporate law provisions, the corporate bar was not consulted about the fair price statute and learned of it only after it was about to be approved by the state senate. The limited opportunity for involvement by the corporate bar in the legislation was connected to the peculiar procedural posture of the bill – having missed or waited until after the session's filing deadline, the fair price statute's sponsors had it attached as an amendment to an inconsequential bill providing for changes in corporate names. This procedure made it possible to bypass the requirement of a public hearing on the fair price statute. Romano, note 46, pp. 122–8.

54 The estimated equations were significant, explaining approximately 40% of the variation across the states of statute adoption, and having a statute was positively related to union membership and negatively related to the presence of domestic hostile bidder firms. Ibid. pp. 142–5.

provision the requirements that the second generation statutes codify, for if we had a plausible explanation of which firms voluntarily adopt shark repellent amendments, we would be better able to assess how legislation incorporating such provisions impacts on firms, and whether managers promoting the statutes were acting in their shareholders' interest.

To study the incentive effects of the different provisions that the statutes codify, I examined the shareholder's decision problem in the takeover context – whether or not to tender – using a decision tree analysis that incorporates the findings of empirical research on takeovers.[55] The analysis indicates under what conditions the provisions encourage shareholders not to tender their shares in the hope of receiving a higher price later. I then add to the analysis two important institutional details which aid in explaining why not all firms adopt shark repellent amendments: the typical multistage techniques bidders employ to obtain control, and the systematic differences across investors in information costs. The confluence of these factors creates a disproportionate sharing of takeover premiums in multistage offers across shareholders, with better-informed investors typically receiving the greater share. In the takeover situation, therefore, in contrast with the norm for corporate law, shareholders' interests may differ markedly. Consequently, views on the welfare-enhancing properties of shark repellent provisions may not be uniform across the common-stock class. In particular, because provisions such as a fair price requirement enable small investors to realize information cost savings by equalizing bid prices, small shareholders should tend to favor the adoption of such provisions while large institutional and individual investors, whose costs in obtain-

---

55 Ibid. The discussion that follows summarizes the conclusions on pp. 145–87. The analysis suggested why fair price provisions are more popular in charters than are control share acquisition or redemption rights rules. The latter two consist of separate features that are combined in a fair price provision, supermajority approval, and equal premium payments, respectively. These proposals thus offer acquiring firms fewer options for the structuring of an acquisitive transaction than does a fair price provision. As a result, a fair price provision introduces fewer barriers to an acquisition. In addition, target shareholders' decisions to tender or not vary under the three takeover rules, such that only under a fair price regime is there a decision strategy in which the investor sometimes tenders and sometimes does not. These two factors suggest that shareholders approving shark repellent amendments could be rationally trading off a decrease in the probability of receiving an initial bid against an increase in the certainty of receiving an equal share of the bid premium. For the most frequently chosen tactic, a fair price provision, has the smallest impact on the likelihood of initial bids while at the same time, by providing an incentive to not tender in some cases, retains the possibility of receiving a higher premium.

ing information are lower and enable them to benefit from a disproportionate premium structure, should not. A firm's voluntary adoption of an antitakeover provision should correspondingly be dependent upon its ownership concentration.[56]

The corollary of an ownership-composition explanation of shark repellent amendments is that the impact of a statute will differ across firms, and, accordingly, can become quite problematic. For example, it could be a means for managers to circumvent shareholders where a favorable charter amendment vote would be doubtful. Given that management can place a proposal on the agenda with less difficulty than can a shareholder, this troubling possibility could be mitigated by opt-in rather than opt-out regimes.[57] But opting in also has disadvantages: Because a vote is still required, it negates much of the transaction cost savings of a statute for those corporations whose shareholders would approve a charter provision.

I sought to test whether ownership concentration would be an accurate predictor of firms with shark repellent amendments by comparing concentration measures for firms with and without fair price provisions. None of the differences were statistically significant. I also divided the firms in the sample by incorporation state, based on whether or not they had a second generation statute, and compared the concentration levels for those with and without fair price provi-

---

56 Barry Baysinger and Henry Butler maintain that support for shark repellent provisions comes from shareholders who have special relations with firm management such that their shares would be worth less under new management and are worth more to them than the premium paid by an outsider. B. Baysinger and H. Butler, Antitakeover Amendments, Managerial Entrenchment, and the Contractual Theory of the Corporation, *Virginia Law Review* 71:1257 (1985). They further contend that this stock relation, which they view as a transaction-specific asset, is independent of the size of the holding (pp. 1284–8). They do not connect their thesis concerning firms' choice of incorporation state (see text accompanying notes 18–25) and firms' adoption of shark repellent amendments, although the two choices are related because firms often choose their incorporation state to facilitate adopting such measures, as well as to be protected by a takeover statute. Even if we assume that the concept of transaction-specific stock is sensible (and I have serious doubts about this that cannot be pursued in this article without going off on an unrelated tangent), an analysis of the effects of the most popular shark repellent amendments indicates the problem with the thesis: These provisions do not unambiguously favor shareholders with special relations to managers, unless they are the managers themselves. See Romano, note 46, pp. 170–87. Moreover, if certain shareholders have special relations with management that were beneficial to all shareholders of the firm, then we need an explanation for why those relations would not be continued by new management.

57 Only a few states have opt-in rather than opt-out provisions. E.g., Ga. Code Ann. sec. 14–2–235(a) (Supp. 1986); Minn. Stat. Ann. sec. 302A.167 (West Supp. 1987).

sions within the subgroups separately. The concentration ratios differed significantly across the states, with the concentration ratios being lower in states with second generation statutes.[58] This appears to support a transaction-cost-reducing view of the statutes – states that have enacted the legislation have more firms with diffuse ownership, which are the firms, under my conjecture, whose shareholders would approve such provisions. But in an equal-sized sample, the difference was not significant. In addition, there is anecdotal evidence in support of the opposite proposition: The firm that promoted the Connecticut legislation has a relatively high concentration ratio which, in keeping with the ownership composition thesis, suggests that its management might have had difficulty obtaining shareholder approval.[59] These two pieces of information are not, however, necessarily inconsistent: Takeover statutes may be promoted by managers who fear a negative shareholder vote, while the rest of the local business community does not object to the proposal because their shareholders would voluntarily adopt a provision.

The impact of takeover statutes remains, then, a troubling, open question, as some firms can use a statute to undermine the shareholder sovereignty on which corporation law is premised. In this sense, the Connecticut experience suggests that state chartering may not always be an unmitigated good. Yet it also implies a positive assessment of Delaware's role in the corporate charter market. Delaware has consistently been slow to enact a takeover statute, and the ones it has adopted have not been as hostile to bids as those in other states: There was no hearing requirement in its first generation statute, and firms could opt out of its coverage. Its second generation statute, enacted after much debate and a far more open process than that of other states, has a shorter prohibition period and more ways to exempt bids from its coverage than other states' post-*CTS* statutes banning business combina-

---

58 Romano, note 46, p. 179. As a conceptual matter, concentration measures have no strict implication for the enactment of statutes because firms with diffuse ownership, which could presumably adopt such provisions on their own, might want a law to reduce drafting costs, yet, managers of firms with concentrated ownership might also want a law because they cannot employ voluntary solutions. If enactment of takeover statutes evinces a permissive state, then this data supports Baysinger and Butler's pairing of more diffusely owned firms and lax jurisdictions; see text accompanying notes 18–25. But when I used a random sample with an equal number of firms in each subset to provide a more powerful test of the difference of means, as Baysinger and Butler used for their analysis, the difference in shareholder concentration across the states was not significant.

59 The sponsoring firm was also doing poorly at the time, and shortly after the statute's passage there was a change in top management.

tions. This is not coincidental: Delaware is better able to resist political pressure for takeover laws because of the large number of incorporated firms, which includes both acquirers and targets.[60] Delaware legislators have to be responsive to a corporate constituency whose interests are varied and conflicting. In addition, other interested parties who oppose restricting takeovers, such as financial intermediaries, would find it more worthwhile to lobby in Delaware than in other states because its statute would have a greater impact on acquisitions, as it would apply to so many firms. Consequently, it is unlikely that any one firm could have the political clout in Delaware that individual firms display in other states like Connecticut, in having second generation statutes enacted.[61] As a result, we can expect a different political equilibrium in Delaware than in other states when it comes to takeover defenses, in which target firms rely primarily on self-help and shareholder approval rather than on a mandated statutory solution.

III   Event studies as arbiters of the debate

The debate over the efficacy of state corporation codes essentially boils down to an empirically testable hypothesis: whether managers or shareholders benefit from the market for corporate charters. If we could identify the beneficiaries, then fashioning a political consensus regarding the optimal level of government regulation would be straightforward.[62] The best available means of generating information bearing on this issue is to examine the impact of reincorporations on stock prices, for a change in equity value conveys investors' assessment of the event's[63] expected

60 The second generation statutes create an externality, though of a different sort described by Winter's analysis of first generation statutes; see note 50. States like Connecticut may be benefiting local target firms at the expense of nonresident acquiring firms.

61 There is very little research, although there is need for some, on the modern political history of Delaware. Some have contended that the DuPont family and their corporation run the state (see J. Phelan and R. Pozen, *The Company State* (New York, 1973) pp. 113–32), but that claim is disputed, and viewed with skepticism by local historians (see, e.g., C. Hoffecker, *Corporate Capital: Wilmington in the Twentieth Century* (Philadelphia, 1983), pp. 260–1).

62 Of course, the issue may be resolvable only in theory: Limitations of data and statistical techniques may render an answer impossible. Moreover, an analyst's priors will affect the weight he or she attributes to empirical findings, which may result in an exceedingly slow updating of beliefs that hinders the development of a consensus on policy.

63 An "event" can be technically defined as a change in the information set about firms from which price expectations are formed. An event's effect can be isolated from the effects of other factors that influence the market by standard econometric techniques. The regressions typically employ a version of the capital asset pricing model of security

effect on shareholder wealth. A stock price increase upon a firm's reincorporation would mean that investors expect the change in incorporation state to increase the firm's future cash flows, and from this it
could be concluded that shareholders benefit from a move. Similarly, a
decline in stock price would indicate the anticipation that shareholder
welfare will be diminished by the move and confirm the managerialist
position.

Several event studies have been performed that bear on the state
competition debate. Researchers have addressed the issue directly by
investigating the impact of reincorporating, and indirectly by looking at
the effect of state court decisions and state takeover laws. The results
are summarized in Table 7.1. None of the studies support the managerialist position, for none found a negative effect on stock price.
Rather, to the extent they can be used to buttress any position, it is the
value-maximizing view associated with Ralph Winter.

A   Event studies on state competition

Peter Dodd and Richard Leftwich, in the first empirical study concerning
state competition, found statistically significant positive abnormal returns to the stock of reincorporating firms over the two-year period
preceding the reincorporation.[64] The returns around the event date were

valuation. That model asserts that there is a positive linear relation between an asset's
risk and return, and in particular that the risk premium varies in direct proportion to
the stock's sensitivity to market movements, which is referred to as the stock's beta.
Betas estimated from stock prices in a period prior to the event are used to predict
stock prices at the time of the event. The regression residuals, which are the difference
between the predicted prices and observed prices, measure abnormal returns that can
be attributed to the event. Event studies are therefore tests of semistrong-form market
efficiency – the hypothesis that all publicly available information is reflected in stock
prices and changes in the information set are instantaneously reflected in price adjustments. To ensure that only the effect of the event of interest is being measured,
a portfolio of firms that have experienced the event is created and the average residual
of the group is studied. In addition, when there is uncertainty over the precise date
of the event – that is, the day on which the information that is conveyed by the event
became publicly available in the market – the average residuals are cumulated over
an interval in event time and the relevant datum is the cumulative abnormal return.
When event dates are well-specified, the methodology is very accurate. See S. Brown
and J. Warner, Using Daily Stock Returns: The Case of Event Studies, *Journal of
Financial Economics* 14:3 (1985) [hereinafter Brown and Warner II]; S. Brown and
J. Warner, Measuring Security Price Performance, *Journal of Financial Economics*
8:205 (1980).
64 P. Dodd and R. Leftwich, The Market for Corporate Charters: "Unhealthy Competition" versus Federal Regulation, *Journal of Business* 53:259, (1980), pp. 274–5.

Table 7.1. *Research findings on state competition*

Study	Type	Results
1. Dodd and Leftwich (1980)[a]	Event study of reincorporation	Positive cumulative average residuals, 2 years before event
2. Jarrell and Bradley (1980)[b]	First-generation takeover statutes (event = acquisition)	Premium higher, more shares acquired, in states with statutes
3. Romano (1985)[c]	Event study of reincorporation, firms grouped by motive for move	Positive cumulative average residuals, 1–10 days around event, for merger and aggregate portfolios
4. Guerin-Calvert, McGuckin and Warren-Boulton (1987)[d]	First-generation takeover statutes (event = acquisition; other techniques also employed)	Premium higher, more multiple bids, in states with statutes
5. Romano (1987)[e]	Event study of second-generation takeover statutes	No effect
6. Weiss and White (1987)[f]	Event study of Delaware court decisions	No effect

[a]See note 64.   [b]See note 76.   [c]See note 1.
[d]See note 76.   [e]See note 46.   [f]See note 67.

not, however, significant. While this finding undermines Cary's position, it is difficult to assert that it bolsters Winter's view, because the period of abnormal returns is so far before the announcement of the move that it is possible the abnormal returns are due to some other factor affecting the firms.

I sought to refine the Dodd and Leftwich study by partitioning the portfolio of reincorporating firms according to the reasons for which the reincorporation was undertaken, and by using daily rather than monthly stock price data.[65] I found that firms which reincorporated in order to embark on merger-and-acquisition programs, as well as the aggregate portfolio of reincorporating firms, experienced statistically significant

65 Romano, note 1, pp. 265–73. Tests relying on daily data are more accurate than those using monthly data, as daily data allow for more precise identification of events, assuming the event date is accurately specified. Brown and Warner II, note 63, p. 12.

positive abnormal returns on and around the event date. The signs of the cumulative average residuals for the other groups were also positive, although they were not significant.[66] This finding creates further difficulty for the Cary thesis, and provides more clear-cut support for Winter's value-maximizing interpretation of state competition. Elliot Weiss and Lawrence White challenge my conclusion and assert that the abnormal returns are not due to reincorporating because they begin to accrue prior to the event date.[67] Weiss and White are mistaken. Although, as I stated in that article, the positive revaluation of the firm's stock may be generated by the activity associated with the reincorporation rather than the reincorporation itself, the rise in price that occurred in the months preceding the event date is almost surely caused by leakage concerning the plan to reincorporate and engage in the associated activities rather than any other unrelated events, because all firms that were the subject of any report in the *Wall Street Journal* in the two months preceding and one month following their event dates were excluded from the sample.

Weiss and White examined another theme in the literature to get at the crux of the state competition debate: Who is helped out by Delaware court decisions?[68] They investigated the effect of seven Delaware opinions that they characterized as reversals or departures from existing corporate law rules. They hypothesized that if the decisions benefited shareholders, firms would experience abnormal positive returns, and if not, there would be negative returns. They found no statistically significant abnormal returns earned by Delaware firms, and the signs of the residuals were not consistent with any particular thesis.[69]

---

66 I had expected to find a negative effect on the stock of firms that had reincorporated for antitakeover purposes, but none could be detected. This provided further evidence of the inconsistency in some commentators' positions on state competition and takeover defensive tactics (see text accompanying note 49) and spurred me to investigate the politics behind state takeover laws as a possible explanation.
67 E. Weiss and L. White, Of Econometrics and Indeterminacy: A Study of Investors' Reactions to "Changes" in Corporate Law, *California Law Review* 75: 551 (1987).
68 Ibid.
69 Because Delaware firms make up a large segment of the market, and thus may invalidate the abnormal returns methodology, they also examined the effects of the decisions on a portfolio of non-Delaware firms. Again, the results were largely statistically insignificant, and the signs of the residuals were not always the opposite of the signs of the residuals of the Delaware firms, as they had hypothesized (pp. 582–83). I do not believe, however, that this technique deals adequately with the problem. To the extent that state competition tends to produce uniformity in corporation codes,

As a further test of the state competition debate, Weiss and White sought to explain the relative size of the cumulative average residuals for one of the decisions – *Singer* v. *Magnavox Co.*[70] – by examining the firms' likelihood of being taken over. They put forth two alternative scenarios: If the decision was detrimental to shareholders because it discouraged takeovers, companies that are more likely to be targets would have larger negative residuals, and if the decision was favorable to investors because it decreased the likelihood of an exploitative cash-out, companies that are more likely to be taken over would have larger positive residuals. This is their more interesting test because most of the judicial opinions are of concern only to a subset of firms – potential targets – and hence, in a randomly constructed portfolio of Delaware firms, only some of the firms would fit this category. Any effect of the event on those firms could be overwhelmed by the insignificant effect of the event on the aggregated portfolio. The regression failed, however, to explain much of the variation in the residuals: Only one of the characteristics of targets that they identified – firm growth – was significant.

Weiss and White conclude from the failure to find abnormal returns and the lack of explanatory power of their regression of the residuals on target characteristics, that investors do not believe that changes in corporate law affect stock value and that, correspondingly, investors are not concerned about differences in statutory regimes. As a result, they maintain that there is no state competition to speak of. Their study makes an important contribution to our understanding of the impact of certain court decisions, but the implications they derive for the state competition thesis from their data are questionable. In the first place, a plausible alternative interpretation of the data is that investors anticipate Delaware court decisions better than do researchers.[71] Indeed, they provide no persuasive evidence that the corporate bar was taken

then, corporate law rules embodied in court decisions will be contributing to systematic risk and not unsystematic risk, and therefore will not be picked up as an abnormal return for either set of firms. Weiss and White recognize this possibility as an interpretation of their finding of no statistical significance but then reject it as unrealistic without any convincing reason (p. 591).

70 380 A.2d 969 (Del. 1977). The decision affected the rights of dissenters in cash-out mergers. Because we do not have very good theories for predicting which firms will become targets, an interesting ad hoc test would be to examine the residuals of firms that subsequently were acquired.

71 If we adopt a strong rational expectation view of the market, then we would also not predict any reaction to court decisions because, as investors expect all decisions to have only welfare enhancing (or diminishing) effects, all of the value of those decisions would be impounded in the stock price at the time of incorporation or reincorporation in Delaware.

by complete surprise by the decisions. A complementary explanation is that it is likely that shareholders anticipate that the state legislature will reverse any undesirable decision. For example, Delaware recently revised its code to allow firms to limit outside directors' liability.[72] This move is presumably a reaction to the Delaware Supreme Court's decision in *Smith* v. *Van Gorkom*,[73] which held outside directors liable for accepting too hastily an acquisitive offer. In addition, given the complexity of corporate acquisitions, many of the decisions in the study could have offsetting positive and negative effects on shareholder welfare, which could result in insignificant residuals. Weiss and White's uncertainty as to the impact of *Singer* and the fact that a firm that is the acquirer in one transaction may be the target in another, are instances of the complexity of the effects that need to be sorted out.

Although some participants in the state competition debate have emphasized the role of the Delaware judiciary in furthering the state's market position while disputing who has benefited from state law doctrine,[74] there is another important role for courts, with sharply different implications. One factor that transaction cost economics emphasizes is that reducing uncertainty reduces the cost of doing business. Hence, certainty concerning the structuring of a transaction is valuable. One of the benefits stressed by firms reincorporating in Delaware was its pool of precedents, and the corresponding ability to receive opinion letters on contemplated transactions quickly. In this regard, the substantive content of the rule is less important than having a rule. A rule defines the rights of the parties, enabling them to bargain around it if they so wish, and provides guidance as to how a transaction should be structured if liability is to be avoided. This feature permeates corporate law: Corporation codes are enabling statutes that set presumptions to govern specific issues and allow firms to tailor their internal organization around the rule. Indeed, the costs of particular rules could be offset by the benefits of having a rule around which future transactions can be planned. Thus,

---

72 Act of June 18, 1986, ch. 289, 65 Del. Laws secs. 1,2 (codified at Del. Code Ann. tit. 8, sec 102(b)(7)(1987)).

73 488 A.2d 858 (Del. 1985). For a critique of the decision, see D. Fischel, The Business Judgment Rule and the *Trans Union Case, Business Lawyer* 40:1437 (1985).

74 Compare Cary, note 3, p. 670 (Delaware courts create a "favorable climate" for management to further its own interests at the expense of shareholders' interests) and Fischel, note 73 (criticizing certain Delaware decisions for decreasing firm value) with Fischel, note 49, p. 943 (shareholders benefit by recent Delaware decisions) and Winter, note 2, pp. 260–61 (decisions which seem to favor management are not necessarily unfair to shareholders).

from the transaction cost perspective, it is not surprising that the market did not react to the decisions in any systematic way, and the statistical insignificance would not indicate that being subject to Delaware's legal regime is detrimental to shareholders.

In addition, Weiss and White's findings must be interpreted with caution. Besides the obvious fact that, given the standard understanding of statistical techniques, a failure to find significance does not provide evidence supporting the alternative hypothesis (such as the Cary position that Weiss and White prefer to the Winter position), their conclusion is built upon a description of the evolution of corporate law rules produced by court decisions over time that is inconsistent with the methodology they applied. Courts are depicted as engaging in a balancing process that continually adjusts and reconciles the interests of shareholders and managers, in which no one decision can be evaluated separately. Such a story is most in keeping with an explanation that Weiss and White reject, that the event study methodology is inappropriate for determining the effect of court decisions, rather than the position that there is no such thing as state competition. If judicial decision making is the perpetual adjustment process they describe, it does not consist of discrete events.[75] Event studies do not – and cannot – evaluate the effects of evolutionary processes. The methodology presupposes information of a lump-sum nature that is introduced in the market instantaneously with a single event, and its accuracy is a function of the correct specification of an event date. Thus, given their characterization of the judicial process, their study can provide no information on the crucial issue of who benefits from state competition, nor can they draw any conclusion concerning the process of, or investors' attitudes toward, state competition.

B   Studies on the effect of takeover statutes

Research on first generation takeover statutes has produced uniform findings, although only one of the two empirical studies on this topic sought to relate the findings to the state competition debate. Gregg Jarrell and Michael Bradley, and Margaret Guerin-Calvert, Robert McGuckin, and Frederick Warren-Boulton (the Economic Analysis Group), using both cumulative average residual techniques to estimate bid premiums and actual bid prices, found that the premiums received by target firms in states with takeover statutes were significantly higher

---

75 This is also true if legislatures systematically overturn judicial opinions.

than those received by firms in states without regulation.[76] There is variation in the studies' findings on whether state regulation reduces the number of acquisitions. The Economic Analysis Group found no clear evidence that the proportion of successful takeovers declined as a result of regulation. In contrast, Jarrell and Bradley found that the relative frequency of successful cash tender offers for firms in states with statutes declined after the legislation was enacted. Of course, none of these results resolve the state competition debate. At best, they point to a possible trade-off of premium size against initiation of bids, which makes it difficult to decipher whether shareholders are losers or gainers under these laws.

The Economic Analysis Group did, however, relate their research directly to the incorporation debate. Jarrell and Bradley appear to have restricted their identification of regulated firms to those whose incorporation state had a takeover statute, thereby possibly misclassifying some targets whose bids were, in fact, subject to regulation. The Economic Analysis Group included and distinguished targets by their susceptibility to both place of business and charter regulation. They found that when they partitioned their sample of regulated targets by type of jurisdiction, the dummy variable for jurisdictional type was significant. They had hypothesized that this would be so, because they believed that regulation based on a firm's physical location more clearly constitutes a negative externality than regulation by incorporation state, since moving assets is more costly than moving a charter. They concluded that place-of-business regulation might be the most important component of

---

76 G. Jarrell and M. Bradley, The Economic Effects of Federal and State Regulations of Cash Tender Offers, *Journal of Law and Economics* 23:371 (1980); M. Guerin-Calvert, R. McGuckin and F. Warren-Boulton, State and Federal Regulation in the Market for Corporate Control, *Antitrust Bulletin* 32: 661 (1987) (hereafter Economic Analysis Group). Jarrell and Bradley also found that acquirers of firms in states with statutes purchased a higher percentage of shares, and the Economic Analysis Group found that targets in states with statutes were more frequently the subject of multiple bids. In this regard, it would be useful to remove the multiple-bid firms from the sample to see how much of the difference in premiums across states is due to actual auctions rather than the effect of statutes alone. However, it may be difficult to disentangle the effects of statutes and auctions, because bidders, knowing that the statutes make auctions more probable, may raise their initial bids to make competition less likely. A study of second generation statutes, published after this chapter was completed, found evidence of a decrease in the number of successful bids and a smaller increase in the total number of bids in states with statutes compared to states without them. See Second Generation Takeover Statutes and Shareholder Wealth: An Empirical Study, *Yale Law Journal* 97:1193 (1988).

the significant effects of state regulation on bid premiums in the estimations in which no jurisdictional variable was included.

Second generation statutes are only of the incorporation state jurisdictional variety, and thus, examination of their effect might shed more light on the Economic Analysis Group's work. I studied the effect on stock prices of each type of second generation statute, rather than their impact on bid premiums.[77] Because most second generation statutes are passed quickly, with little debate and virtual unanimity, they are better suited than most laws for an event study in which pinpointing the event date is crucial to the power of the statistical tests. The statutes I examined were those adopted by Connecticut (fair price provision); Missouri (control share acquisition statute); and Pennsylvania (redemption rights provision). All of these states enacted the legislation within a month or so after their bills' introduction, and are thus good candidates for an event study.[78]

No effects were discernible in any of the regressions: The average residuals were not significant on or near the event date, and the cumulative average residuals were not significant in any of several intervals around the event date, revealed no nice pattern, and were of small negative magnitude.[79] Of course, since not all firms are potential takeover targets, not all firms should be expected to experience abnormal returns upon the enactment of these statutes. This seriously weakens

77 Romano, note 46, pp. 181–86.
78 I chose Connecticut for the study of a fair price statute, even though its small population of publicly traded firms reduces the power of the test, because, in addition to my ability to date precisely its enactment, my knowledge of the legislative history could provide a useful interpretative gloss on any results. Pennsylvania has the benefit of having a large pool of firms as well as a short time from introduction to enactment, and Missouri had the shortest time from introduction to passage of the states with control share acquisition statutes for which accurate dates were available, although like Connecticut, it has too small a number of firms to provide a powerful test.
79 The cumulative average residuals of Missouri firms that did not have fair price charter provisions at the time the statute was enacted show an upward trend after the bill passed the state senate (t-statistic 1.2), in contrast to the residuals of the firms that already had such provisions. In addition, in all the regressions, some average residuals were significant approximately one week after the event dates, but trying to draw conclusions from such data would be equivalent to reading tea leaves. Since this chapter was completed, several studies have found negative stock price effects of second generation statutes. See M. Ryngaert and J. Netter, Shareholder Wealth Effects of the Ohio Antitakeover Law, *Journal of Law, Economics, and Organization* 4:373 (1988); L. Schumann, State Regulation of Takeovers and Shareholder Wealth: The case of New York's 1985 Takeover Statutes, *Rand Journal of Economics* 19:557 (1988).

the power of the tests, because the aggregate portfolio could be burying the impact of the legislation on the unidentifiable subset of future target firms (although presumably the market also cannot predict in advance which firms are future targets). An ad hoc examination to see if this was a factor, by looking at the residuals of firms that subsequently turned out to be targets, did not help. One Connecticut firm, Scovill, Inc., was involved in a takeover fight shortly after the Connecticut statute's enactment.[80] However, Scovill's abnormal performance was not greater than that of other Connecticut firms. In addition, the returns of the proponent of the Connecticut legislation were insignificantly negative.

In sum, the financial research on takeover statutes does not provide much information on the state competition debate. It cements the intuition that these statutes, like most defensive tactics, will increase the premiums target shareholders receive, possibly at the cost of a reduction in the aggregate number of bids. Such a trade-off does not indicate whether shareholders, managers, both, or neither, are better off. To be sure, the event studies on reincorporation, which go directly to that question, offer far greater support to the Winter position than to the Cary position – there is no evidence of negative returns to migrating firms (or to firms operating under Delaware law) and some evidence of positive returns. But studies of specific statutes' impact are even more inconclusive and are subject to substantial methodological difficulties, given the limitations on obtaining precise event dates for legislation. What we can say with some degree of confidence is that reincorporation produces abnormal positive returns for some firms (those engaging in certain transactions), and for the rest it is a zero net present value transaction.[81]

IV   Policy implications of the new learning on state competition (or where do we go from here?)

The new learning on state competition provides us with a good understanding of the economics, and some inkling of the political dynamics, of the corporate charter market. What conclusions can we draw for public policy?

  1.   A middle ground between Cary's and Winter's positions on the efficacy of state competition seems to me to be most appropri-

80 While Scovill's management was not involved in the drafting or passage of the legislation, it hoped it would be protected by the law. In the end, the statute did not affect the bid because it was an any-or-all offer.
81 Romano, note 1, pp. 272–73.

ate. Such a view recognizes that shareholders benefit from state competition, while granting that, on occasion, competition may well produce laws that shareholders in some firms would not choose to adopt voluntarily. To review the data informing this conclusion:

(a) Event studies indicate that state competition does not harm shareholders. None of the studies found any negative effect on investor wealth from state regulation, whether they investigated changes made by the states in statutes or doctrine, or changes made by firms in their choice of incorporation state, and more importantly, they found a positive effect of reincorporation on stock prices.

(b) There is a plausible logical scenario, supported by anecdotal evidence, that suggests that managers promote second generation takeover statutes because they cannot obtain shareholder approval for the tactics these laws codify, although statistical tests related to this thesis were inconclusive.

(c) There is good reason to believe that the political equilibrium in Delaware differs from that of other states when it comes to a potentially managerialist provision like a second generation takeover statute, because its diverse corporate constituency and the corporate bar's input into the legislative process check any one firm's ability to have a pet bill passed.

(d) Simple stochastic models of the dynamics of a corporate charter market indicate that the processes that capture some key features of state competition spend a significant amount of time in the more optimal states (value-maximizing laws passed), but some time will be spent in suboptimal states (non-value-maximizing laws), unless we adopt quite strong constraints on legislative behavior, such as perfect foresight, which require that value-maximizing laws always be adopted and never repealed.[82]

Staking out a position somewhere between Cary's and Winter's views – and I locate my position as closer to the Winter than the Cary endpoint of the interval – is not that appealing because it both conveys the appearance of hedging one's bets and requires detailed empirical analysis of individual code provisions before any conclusion can be reached. But it is, in my opinion, the most reasonable position to advocate, given current

82 See R. Romano, The State Competition Debate in Corporate Law, *Cardozo Law Review* 8:709 (1987), pp. 740–52.

knowledge. It recognizes the agency problem that Winter's position downplays, while concurring in his assessment of the important advantages derived from having a federal system. A corollary of the position is that we should invest less energy in discussing whether national chartering is needed,[83] and more in examining state regulation at a micro level, to determine how we can improve the federal system.

2. One method to protect shareholders without having to identify precisely which rules maximize shareholder wealth and which do not, is to require that corporation code amendments entailing a major change in relations between shareholders and managers, where we can intuit conflicting interests, such as second generation takeover statutes, contain opt-in rather than opt-out provisions.[84] For an opt-in regime can minimize the possibility that management will lobby successfully for legislation that shareholders might not support, since shareholders must explicitly approve the law's application to their firm. An opt-in policy is an extension of the basic feature of corporation codes – that they are enabling. The benefit of this approach is that it is a strategy by which shareholders, rather than managers, lobbyists, or legislators, have the ultimate say on corporate governance by voting.[85] In addition, by increasing the cost of

---

83 Even apart from the lack of empirical support, the analytical case for national chartering, in my opinion, has not been made. Most of the benefits of federalism have been emphasized in the debate, such as the incremental experimentation and innovation in corporate law rules created by having numerous decision makers. One benefit often overlooked in the corporate law literature, that I find important, is the supportive relation between a federal structure and individual liberty. Vital state governments can check a powerful national government (for an interesting effort to revitalize this view of Federalism, see A. Amar, Of Sovereignty and Federalism. *Yale Law Journal* 96:1425 [1987]), just as private organizations protect individuals from encroachment by the state by counterbalancing the state's power; see J. Coleman, *The Asymmetric Society* (Syracuse, 1982), pp. 51–5. If corporations were subject to comprehensive national regulation, they would be less effective performers of such a checking function.

84 Cf. M. Eisenberg. *The Structure of the Corporation: A Legal Analysis* (Boston 1976), (shareholders should vote on fundamental changes). A similarly spirited proposal is to require shareholder approval of defensive tactics, such as poison pills; see SEC Advisory Committee on Tender Offers, Report of Recommendations, reprinted in Fed. Sec. L. Rep. (CCH), Special Report No. 1028, pp. 37–40 (July 15, 1983) (recommending annual shareholder advisory votes on golden parachutes, standstill agreements, and supermajority and disenfranchisement charter provisions).

85 Delaware's latest revision to its code is a good example of such a policy: It does not eliminate director liability, but rather, it permits a firm to limit its directors' liability

corporate decision making by requiring a shareholder vote, it tends to add to the stability of the status quo of no shark repellent amendment.[86] This is a desirable feature if shark repellent amendments are harmful to shareholders. The disadvantage is, for firms whose shareholders want the statute's protection, the cost is greater in an opt-in than opt-out regime where no such vote is required.

(a) The conventional objection to relying on such a device is that voting is a sham because shareholders lack either the information to vote intelligently or the inclination to expend time and resources to obtain the information. I do not find the claim of massive shareholder ignorance and misinformation compelling. But even if the objection is granted, it can be resolved directly, by ensuring the provision of the pertinent information to investors.[87] Government intervention is not always necessary to ameliorate a market failure. In this context, institutional investors, who are typically informed voters, have recently begun to create national organizations for pooling information and research on corporate policies.[88] These voluntary networks could, in due course, produce substantially more informed voting.

by charter amendment. S.B. 533, enacted June 18, 1986, to be codified at Del. Code Ann. tit. 8, sec. 102(b)(7). The political process of this bill provides an interesting comparison with that of other state statutes. In contrast to the adoption of Connecticut's takeover statute, in which the corporate bar organization was excluded from the drafting process, Delaware's director liability statute was approved by the corporate law section of the state bar association prior to its enactment. This practice of bar approval is the rule, and not the exception, in Delaware. See A. Moore, State Competition: Panel Response, *Cardozo Law Review* 8:779 (1987), pp. 780–1.

86 Cf. H. Bruff, Legislative Formality, Administrative Rationality, *Texas Law Review* 63:207 (1984), pp. 218–22 (describing how government structure mitigates faction and increases stability of legislation).

87 There is no convincing basis for asserting that shareholders will be so overwhelmed by the information that an indirect solution of prohibition should be adopted. Cf. D. Grether, A. Schwartz and L. Wilde, The Irrelevance of Information Overload: An Analysis of Search and Disclosure, *Southern California Law Review* 59:277 (1986) (questioning the contention of an information-overload problem in commercial law). If the fear is the free-rider problem that afflicts all voting processes, supermajority conditions could be attached to the amendment process, although I am skeptical that such a solution would be optimal.

88 For example, in 1985, a group of public and private pension fund trustees formed the Council of Institutional Investors to "protect their rights as shareholders" by collecting data and providing information and consulting services for members. Pension Fund Trustees Form Council, *Washington Post*, January 25, 1985, D1; Institutional Investors Join Forces for Clout, ibid. May 12, 1985, F1. See also Appearances Likely to Prove

(b) One potential problem for even informed shareholder voting is that management controls the proxy apparatus. This is a problem because if there are many points in the set of majority-preferred outcomes, then management can place on the agenda the particular proposal that it prefers from the winning set.[89] But if shareholder preferences are homogeneous – which is a plausible assumption in most contexts in corporate law for all shareholders have the same goal of equity share price maximization – then the majority-preferred set will consist of a single point and management's control of the agenda cannot determine the outcome.

3. If institutional investors' interests differ sharply from those of individual investors, who are uninformed and/or who do not vote, then reliance on voting rights to protect all shareholders will be unsuccessful. This possibility might conjure up the specter of management agenda manipulation, but if the differences are such that shareholder preferences can be represented as single-peaked, arrayed along a single line – which is reasonable given the value-maximizing goal – then, again, there will be no voting cycle and the shareholders determine the outcome regardless of management's position. The concern is therefore not that the outcome will be chosen by management but that the interest of the majority is in direct conflict with that of the minority. In other contexts where shareholders' interests may differ because of institutional characteristics, such as the different positions of high- and low-tax-bracket investors on distribution policies, there is evidence of a clientele effect, in which investors segregate themselves by firm according to similar interests, and thereby avoid the potential conflict so that majority rule poses no difficulty.[90] But this solution may not be available to diffuse the conflict with which we are concerned: For example, takeover policies affect so many firms that clienteles may be unable to form because it may be difficult to exclude investments in targets, assuming they can be identified, and achieve optimal portfolio diversification. The policy punch of

Deceiving When It Comes to T. Boone Pickens, *Wall Street Journal*, August 22, 1986, 6, col. 1 (corporate raider to establish group to lobby for shareholder rights). In addition, the Investors' Responsibility Research Center compiles annual reports on institutional investors' voting on corporate governance questions.

89 See K. Shepsle, Institutional Equilibrium and Equilibrium Institutions (draft May 1984).

90 See W. Lewellen, K. Stanley, R. Lease and G. Schlarbaum, Some Direct Evidence on the Dividend Clientele Phenomenon, *Journal of Finance* 83:1385 (1978).

these considerations is not clear-cut. We may have to rethink the use of majority rule to alter rights in corporate law, for it presupposes shareholder unanimity on ends. But there are at least three factors mitigating such a concern. First, majority rules that permit disproportionate premiums may not be objectionable; the non–pro rata sharing may be a return on the shareholder's investment in information. Such rewards to information-seeking may be necessary for market efficiency.[91] Second, there have been and may continue to be fundamental changes in the form of ownership of public corporations, such that uninformed investors with small holdings may come to hold shares only indirectly via mutual funds,[92] which would moot the potential conflict. Third, if prices or some other datum signal to uninformed shareholders the view of the informed, then the voting outcome may be identical to the voting outcome under complete information.[93]

4. When we consider the issue of informed voting by shareholders in light of the politics of Connecticut's second generation takeover statute, a further recommendation is in order: Bills substantively revising corporation codes should be scrutinized and debated in a public hearing. This policy will raise the cost of legislating, but it will also provide a check on the passage of hastily drafted statutes that can have unintended, adverse consequences. A legislature should be more than a clearing house for pork barrel. With a public hearing, a legislature could improve the quality of decision making, by drawing on the insights of experts testifying concerning the probable consequences of particular policies, in reaching a judgment on a bill.[94] It would, at least, promote a more active role for the corporate bar in

---

91 See generally R. Gilson and R. Kraakman, The Mechanisms of Market Efficiency, *Virginia Law Review* 70:549(1984) (discussing market efficiency). The rewards may also be shared by the uninformed – some of the information of sophisticated investors will be conveyed in the stock price as they trade, and some uninformed shareholders will tender in two-step offers and receive the same disproportionate share as the informed.

92 See R. Clark, The Four Stages of Capitalism: Reflections on Investment Management Treatises, *Harvard Law Review* 94:561, 564–5 (1981).

93 See R. McKelvey and P. Ordeshook, Information, Electoral Equilibria and the Democratic Ideal, *Journal of Politics* 48:909 (1986) (complete information equilibrium attained despite incomplete information as uninformed voters update from very general and cheap information sources such as opinion polls).

94 See W. Muir, *Legislature* (Chicago 1982) (state legislature is a school in which legislators are educated by lobbyists and other informed individuals).

the legislative process. The bar's participation offers the benefit that its members represent clients with diverse interests, and a package that meets their approval would be more likely attuned to the problems of unintended consequences, if not more balanced in its effects, than a draft submitted by one anxious corporation.[95] In addition, hearings create a record of a proposal's strengths and weaknesses that shareholders can use in assessing whether to agree to conform their charters to the revised codes.

5. A middle ground on state competition has specific implications for the direction of research. In particular, we need to undertake more comparative studies of the political process across states and statutes, and compile information on shareholder attitudes and voting patterns on different corporate policies or management actions. To the extent that the events of importance involve evolutionary processes, we may need to seek out new and refine existing techniques on how to determine the impact of specific policies on investor wealth. Without such information, discussion will devolve into ill-informed a priori assertions about the probable effects of particular rules, and we will correspondingly be unable to raise the quality of public decision making.

---

95 The introduction of attorneys obviously creates the potential for additional agency problems concerning their advocacy of the clients' interests in the legislative process. In addition to the constraints placed on attorneys from the forces of state competition (see note 39), a competitive market for legal services should constrain attorneys from favoring their own interests at a cost to shareholders.

CHAPTER 8

The positive role of tax law in corporate and capital markets

Saul Levmore

I   Intrusions of tax law into corporate law

Taxes normally and correctly are considered to be unfortunate and annoying intruders in the elegant world of capital markets and in the already complicated world of corporate law. There are no fewer than eleven different types of intrusions which may be recognized easily. First, because tax law focuses on "recognition" events rather than periodic appraisals of wealth and does not excuse or defer tax on gains from the sale of stock and other capital assets completely, exchanges are discouraged.[1] Similar to brokers' commissions, taxes add to transaction costs and, therefore, discourage transactions.[2] Second, by taxing dividends more harshly than income realized from the sale of stock, and by taxing such dividends less harshly when they are of the intercorporate

A similar version of this chapter appears in *Journal of Corporation Law* 12:483 (1987). Alan Auerbach, Henry Hansmann, Roberta Romano, Paul Stephan, and participants at a Harvard Law School Conference on the Economics of Corporate and Capital Markets provided helpful suggestions.

1 The intrusion is not limited to capital assets. For example, inventories might be accumulated and disposed of differently in the face of taxes which are triggered by various transactions. I have, however, slanted the generalizations in the text toward matters most relevant to contests for corporate control and other topics of current interest.

2 To the extent that transactions are entered into voluntarily and are the means by which assets move to their highest valued uses, taxes can be said to cause a reduction in welfare. The question often is how to raise revenue for projects that may improve welfare in a manner that is least harmful. See generally M. Feldstein, Personal Taxation and Portfolio Composition: An Econometric Analysis, *Econometrica* 44:631 (1976); M. Feldstein, J. Slemrod, and S. Yitzhaki, The Effects of Taxation on the Selling of Corporate Stock and the Realization of Capital Gains, *Quarterly Journal of Economics* 94:777 (1980); B. Sprinkel and B. K. West, Effects of Capital Gains Taxes on Investment Decisions, *Journal of Business* 35:122 (1962).

variety, tax law may affect the dividend policy of a firm.[3] To the extent
that a firm's dividend policy is affected, its overall reinvestment policy
probably will be affected.[4] Third, the compensation packages offered
to managers and other agents of the firm likely will be influenced by tax
laws. Recipients may prefer deferred compensation, certain fringe benefits, and particular types of profit-sharing plans. These preferences may
make it worthwhile for employers to structure compensation differently
than they would have if taxes did not depend on the form of compensation. Stated in terms of the literature on agency costs, a certain compensation package offered to agents may minimize the monitoring costs
of the shareholders and creditors of a firm, but tax law may encourage
the use of a different package that causes higher agency costs even
though such a package may include stock options which on their own
may decrease agency costs.[5] Fourth, although in the absence of taxes
there may be an optimal means of financing the firm, tax laws will make
some capital structures appear more attractive than others. For example,
tax laws that allow deductions for interest expenses but not dividend
payments encourage debt financing.[6] Fifth, the treatment of financial
intermediaries, such as banks and stock and mutual insurance companies, is sufficiently uneven to suggest that the existing mix of these

3 Tax law, thus, causes corporate and individual shareholders to have different attitudes
toward the distribution of dividends. Note that the elimination of the preference for
capital gains in the Tax Reform Act of 1986 does not make shareholders indifferent
between dividends and stock sales. When selling stock, shareholders are given immediate credit for the cost or basis of their stock.

4 For example, if the firm can earn 10% on its next available project, and shareholders
can earn 11% on their own, reinvestment rather than distribution, nevertheless, may
occur because of the tax cost of the distribution. Shareholders may be able to invest at
11% with funds they will borrow on the strength of their shareholdings, which, in turn,
are affected positively by the firm's retention of earnings. In general, tax laws probably
encourage larger businesses. See A. Feld, *Tax Policy and Corporate Concentration*
(1982), pp. 55–100 (treatment of retained earnings and reorganizations encourages big
businesses).

5 For the seminal presentation of the agency cost insight *without* taxes, see M. Jensen
and W. Meckling, Theory of the Firm: Managerial Behavior, Agency Costs, and Ownership Structure, *Journal of Financial Economics* 3:305 (1976).

6 The question is debated frequently. Compare M. Miller, Debt and Taxes, *Journal of
Finance* 32:261 (1977), and F. Modigliani and M. Miller, The Cost of Capital, Corporation Finance and the Theory of Investment, *American Economic Review* 48:261
(1958) with S. Myers, The Capital Structure Puzzle, *Journal of Finance* 39:575 (1984);
see also S. Ross, Debt and Taxes and Uncertainty, *Journal of Finance* 40:637 (1985).
For a discussion of the possibility that the reactions are bifurcated, see A. Auerbach
and M. King, Taxation, Portfolio Choice, and Debt–Equity Ratios: A General Equilibrium Model, *Quarterly Journal of Economics* 98:587 (1983).

intermediaries is influenced more strongly by tax considerations than by organizational qualities.[7] Sixth, because inputs such as labor and property often are taxed separately and differently, the mix of inputs that is utilized in a given enterprise is different from that which is most efficient in terms of real productivity.[8] Seventh, inputs aside, the very size of an enterprise probably will be influenced by taxes. The tax system encourages the retention of earnings, and therefore growth,[9] and it allows multidivision enterprises to offset the gains and losses of different divisions while smaller single-division firms are unable to transfer the full tax value of their losses to profitable enterprises.[10] Eighth, similarly, the treatment of business losses and the progressive character of tax rates may discourage risky investments even when the expected values of such investments exceed those of investments with less variance in possible outcomes.[11] Ninth, tax laws may encourage a mix of ownership forms different from that which would prevail as a result of agency cost and other real or non-tax considerations. Examples of such rules are those that encourage or discourage leasing, and those that deny certain treatments when there are more than some specified number of shareholders.[12] Indeed, an ownership change as important as a leveraged buyout

7 See M. Graetz, ed., *Life Insurance Company Taxation: The Mutual Versus Stock Differential* (1986); R. Clark, The Federal Income Taxation of Financial Intermediaries, *Yale Law Journal* 84:1603 (1975).

8 Of course, there is a significant amount of literature on the assessment and collection of property taxes. Unfortunately, less work has been done on unemployment-related taxes. See M. Kelly, Taxes, Depreciation, and Capital Waste, *National Tax Journal* 24:31. (1971).

9 See M. Campisano and R. Romano, Recouping Losses: The Case for Full Loss Offsets, *Northwestern University Law Review* 76:709 (1981). Note also that because losses suffered by one enterprise sometimes can be applied against gains of another or gains at a different time, a conglomerate normally can offset gains against losses in this manner as a matter of course (pp. 721–2). The treatment of losses, thus, is "intrusive" and encourages large firms, even though such enterprises *may* be suboptimal from the standpoint of agency costs or other "real" concerns.

10 See J. Lintner, Distribution of Incomes of Corporations Among Dividends, Retained Earnings, and Taxes, *American Economic Review* 46:97 (Supp. 1956); see also M. J. Brennan, Taxes, Market Valuation and Corporate Financial Policy, *National Tax Journal* 25:417 (1970).

11 See generally M. Campisano and R. Romano, note 9, pp. 722–30; J. Fellingham and M. Wolfson, Taxes and Risk Sharing, *Accounting Review* 60:10 (1985).

12 For a discussion of leasing, see R. Brealy and S. Myers, *Principles of Corporate Finance,* 2d ed. (1984), pp. 547–61. For a discussion of the choice among the partnership, corporate, and "S" Corporation entity forms, see S. Thompson, The Federal Income Tax Impact of the Operating Function on the Choice of Business Form: Partnership, Subchapter C Corporation, or Subchapter S Corporation, *Black Law Journal* 4:11

may be motivated largely by tax considerations. The significant premiums enjoyed by those who sell their interests to insiders in these buyouts may reflect little more than their proportionate shares of the tax savings.[13] Tenth, and most simply, capital may be deployed in various geographic locations in spite of inferior resources, labor, or transportation, because relatively low taxes are associated with these locations. Last, tax laws intrude upon the allocation of resources among industries. The various exclusions, depreciation schedules, and accounting rules which are the soft underbelly of the tax system yield different marginal and average tax rates – and, therefore, different incentives to invest – in different types of enterprises.[14] To the extent that such differentials reflect accidental political arrangements rather than sensible social policies regarding externalities and public goods, resources surely are misallocated. Unfortunately, the tax system itself makes it difficult to assess these differentials, because it imposes taxes not only on the firm, but also on the receipts of shareholders and bondholders. Inasmuch as these payments to investors *themselves* may play roles in the efficient allocation of resources, a comparison of all the taxes associated with various enterprises and industries is necessary before concluding that apparent differentials inefficiently bias investment.

The length and relentless quality of this list suggests that intrusions under the tax laws are tolerated, at least partially. This tolerance is the product of a political and an economic reality. As a political matter, those who draft and enforce tax laws are most concerned with the ability and ingenuity of taxpayers to avoid taxes. From this perspective, the efficiency cost of a tax actually may be welcome because the cost usually forms a constraint on tax avoidance. For example, because there are organizational or efficiency reasons to offer employees certain compensation packages, employers will not use those packages that minimize taxes. Similarly, because there are real efficiencies gained by conducting business in given forms, sizes, and locations, taxpayers often will fail to take advantage of all avoidance strategies, including transformations of

(1974); D. Wolfe and R. DeJong, The S Corporation as an Alternative Form of Business Organization After ERTA, TEFRA, and the Subchapter S Revision Act of 1982, *De Paul Law Review* 32:811 (1983).

13 Prior to the Tax Reform Act of 1986, the basis of a firm's assets could be "stepped up" – an occurrence that was advantageous for depreciation purposes – at the cost of one capital gains tax assessment. The general point was not lost on legislators. See H. R. Rep. No. 426, 99th Cong. 1st Sess. 281–82 (1985) (tax benefits induce liquidations and asset transfers).

14 See C. Hulten and J. Robertson, The Taxation of High Technology Industries, *National Tax Journal* 37:327 (1984).

form and relocations, because there are real costs to such strategies. A less ambitious way to state this point is as follows: Lawmakers are wary of taxpayers avoiding all forms of taxation and, therefore, when a tax appears to distort economic behavior on the margin, these lawmakers might focus less on the inefficiencies generated by the particular tax than on the inframargin where taxpayers are locked in sufficiently and unable to escape the tax.

The economic explanation of why so many intrusions of tax law in the functioning of capital and other markets are tolerated begins with the observation that every major tax in our collective arsenal is intrusive. For example, property taxes distort the use of inputs, and income taxes reduce the incentive to earn more income. Given the government's need to raise substantial amounts of money, every method of raising revenues may be intrusive in some market, and these intrusions progressively become more serious as additional revenue is sought through increases in any one method of taxation. Therefore, intrusions of the kind discussed above may be tolerated because alternatives are thought to entail other or more serious inefficiencies.

This last explanation becomes less abstract if a familiar contemporary example is reviewed. A tax on the sale or exchange of capital assets, or any assets for that matter, is intrusive in the sense that taxpayers may retain such assets longer than they would have if the exchanges would not trigger taxation. Therefore, efficiency might be enhanced if this tax were repealed, or if appreciation were taxed periodically, regardless of whether an exchange had taken place. Assuming away the latter possibility for either political or administrative reasons, and assuming an unrelenting demand for the revenues currently raised from the taxation of capital gains, eliminating the taxation of gain on the sale of stock or real estate would require an increase in the tax rates applicable to other less favored income. In turn, these higher rates would discourage work, as opposed to leisure, and encourage efforts to avoid taxes or to engage in tax-favored, but unproductive activities. This familiar illustration, and the more general arguments or explanations of why so many intrusions by the tax laws are tolerated, emphasizes the premise of this essay: Our tax system contains numerous moderate intrusions *but* to expect that the system could be otherwise is unrealistic.

In spite of the preceding sketches and arguments regarding the seemingly endless set of intrusions by tax law into corporate and capital markets, the goal of this essay is to arrive at an opposite conclusion that does not depend upon an agreement about the magnitudes of various intrusions. Rather, the aim is to show that there are ways in which tax law complements or supports, rather than intrudes upon, the efficient functioning of corporate and capital markets. These illustrations are meant to be revealing and interesting on their own, while also suggesting that there are important interactions between tax law, agency cost, and other efficiency considerations. Although one may be able to study some industries and markets without considering the effect of the tax laws, to separate an understanding of the market for corporate control, for example, from an understanding of the taxes levied upon assets and transactions in that market, is not possible.

In exploring the "positive interactions" of tax law and corporate law, this author does not mean to imply that the various intrusions are somehow less important than the positive interactions. For some time these intrusions have been the focus of the tax policy literature, and for good reason. On the other hand, some of the interactions between tax law and corporate law are quite subtle, and exploration of these interactions requires considerable familiarity with, and sensitivity to, the world of corporate law, rather than the world of public finance, which is the normal background for academics who write about tax policy.

Stated somewhat differently, although the central argument of this essay, that there are subtle, positive roles played by taxes which should be considered seriously, the essay has other broader aims. Tax law, especially corporate tax law, too often is seen as something to be ignored or left to the specialists who examine legislative histories and drive trucks through seemingly small loopholes. This essay seeks to tempt those who think about the corporate and capital markets to study and think about tax law because these subjects regularly overlap. There are two specific areas of interaction explored in this essay. First, the ways in which tax law influences the mix of debt and equity used in financing the corporate firm. Second, the way in which certain kinds of stock acquisitions are treated and influenced by tax legislation. The detail and complexity of these examples suggest that tax law, at least in part, must become the province of those who think carefully about corporate law.

II   The positive influence of tax law on the capital structure of firms

As noted above, taxes may interfere with the central message of the Modigliani-Miller irrelevance proposition.[15] This intrusion certainly will result if a significant number of tax-exempt or low-taxed investors such as pension funds, businesses that lend money to pension funds, and charitable foundations, can invest in corporate debt. Inasmuch as in-

15 See generally F. Modigliani and M. Miller, note 6.

terest payments on such debt are deductible to the issuing corporation, while dividend payments are not, high debt–equity ratios may result from such intrusions.[16] The existence of these abnormal investors or creditors is an important part of the story, because without their presence the deductibility of interest payments by firms with high debt–equity ratios would be no more advantageous than is the deductibility of interest payments by individuals who, in accordance with the classic story of homemade leverage, borrow money in order to buy stock in firms with low debt–equity ratios. However, when there are many tax-exempt investors, and when it is easier, for institutional and legal reasons, for those investors to lend to firms rather than to many dispensed individuals, there will be a significant amount of debt at the firm level rather than at the individual level, because firms obviously will find it less expensive to borrow, from eager, tax-exempt lenders, than will individuals.

If everything else about capital structure were irrelevant, none of this activity would be troubling. Firms simply would have high debt–equity ratios but as a normative matter no combination of debt and equity would be better or worse than another. An argument against excessive debt, for instance, must incorporate an assumption or rely upon a set of facts that is contrary to the assumptions of the irrelevance proposition. Thus, one could assert that bankruptcy generates great private and social costs while also arguing that large amounts of debt are undesirable because the probability of bankruptcy and unanticipated displacement increases. In turn, one could argue that debt can and should be discouraged, either by requiring tax-exempt institutions to pay tax on the receipt of interest income, or by denying interest deductions to issuers, to the extent that creditors do not pay tax on their receipts of interest payments.[17] I prefer, however, to construct this argument around agency costs instead of bankruptcy costs, because the expected value of the latter may be small.[18] Arguably there is an optimal capital structure for each firm because some combinations of secured debt, unsecured debt, and equity – and even preferred stock and convertible securities – generate lower agency costs than other combinations. There is little point

---

16 See P. Canellos, The Over-Leveraged Acquisition, *Tax Lawyer* 39:91, (1985), pp. 100–01.
17 Issuers could be required to withhold taxes unless payees demonstrated or affirmed that they pay taxes.
18 Of course, not everyone agrees that the expected value of bankruptcy is low. Compare J. Gordon and B. Malkiel, Corporation Finance, in *How Taxes Affect Economic Behavior* (1981) and Brealy and Myers, note 12, pp. 390–401, with R. Haugen and L. Senbet, The Insignificance of Bankruptcy Costs to the Theory of Optimal Capital Structure, *Journal of Finance* 33:383 (1978).

262 Saul Levmore

in reviewing the literature regarding these matters; suffice it to say that for a given firm, some capital structures may reduce monitoring and bondings costs better than others – perhaps by encouraging some creditors to monitor the firm and by giving a firm's managers a great incentive to maximize profits without encouraging so much risk-taking that the cost of borrowed capital becomes excessively great[19] and that tax laws may intrude inefficiently on financing decisions, as discussed earlier.[20] Again, the solution may be to require the issuer to withhold taxes unless the recipient pays tax on interest payments.

With this "negative" effect which taxes exert upon financial policy in mind, consider now the following set of tax laws that may have a "positive" effect. Section 351 of the Internal Revenue Code[21] allows parties who pool capital and form a corporation to receive stock and securities, including bonds (that are not very short in term), in return for the property that they contribute, without recognizing gain on the transaction. If, for instance, A, B, and C contribute cash, appreciated real estate, and appreciated stock of some other company (X) to a corporation in return for its stock and bonds, neither the corporation nor A, B, and C will recognize any gain; all tax is deferred. C, for example, will take the basis that he had in his appreciated shares of the X Corporation as the basis for the stock and securities that he receives. Note, however, that section 351 does not apply to a situation in which an *ongoing* firm distributes bonds to its shareholders. To the extent that these bonds are received in a non–pro rata fashion, the difference between the value of the bonds and the basis of the assets exchanged will be taxed as gain from an exchange. If the bonds are distributed in a pro rata fashion, they will be treated under section 301 as dividends.[22] The tax treatment of such bonds often is explained as differing from that of stock dividends, which can be received from an ongoing corporation in pro rata fashion without triggering a tax, because a given corporation's bonds are more liquid than its stock. Thus, bonds, like cash, are taxed upon receipt. This explanation merely highlights the remarkable difference between the treatment of different bond distributions. Section 351 governs if the bonds are distributed at the time of formation[23] while section 301 provides the rule when bonds are distrib-

19 See generally M. Jensen and W. Meckling, note 5; S. Levmore, Monitors and Free-riders in Commercial and Corporate Settings, Yale Law Journal 92:49 (1982).
20 See text accompanying note 6.
21 I.R.C. sec. 351 (1982).
22 Ibid., secs. 301, 351. The uninitiated reader might consult B. Bittker and J. Eustice, Fundamentals of Federal Income Taxation of Corporations and Shareholders (1980).
23 Shareholders who contribute property in midstream to an ongoing corporation also

uted by an ongoing firm. The difference is extreme: Bonds are favored at formation, but are as disfavored as cash afterward.[24]

In Modigliani-Miller terms ("irrelevance" or "invariance") these rules seem senseless.[25] Given that shareholders can borrow on their own, purchase stock in the firm, and thus create whatever risk-and-return combination they desire, the tax laws' penalization of leveraging by the ongoing firm is odd and intrusive. Individuals do *not* recognize gain when they borrow on their own, indeed they do not even recognize gain when they borrow on the strength of assets that have appreciated in their hands without being taxed.[26] Stated differently, assuming that an individual's role in controlling a firm is not at issue, or is not affected significantly by the firm's capital structure, when the individual contemplates joining a group that is forming a new corporation he is not likely to care about the capital structure of the new corporation. If the corporation's organizers choose a high debt–equity ratio which appears to be too risky for the investor's portfolio and taxes, the investor can buy fewer shares and become a creditor. If the opposite is true, the investor can borrow and buy more shares. Assuming either that the individual and corporate tax rates are roughly equal, and that both the investor and the firm can use their interest deductions to the fullest extent[27] or that the market price of the debt reflects any tax advantages

may be able to receive nonrecognition treatment under sec. 351. However, satisfying the control requirement of sec. 351 may be more difficult. Inasmuch as this possibility at first may seem to contradict the argument developed in the next few pages, note that any ability to alter cheaply the capital structure, of debt–equity balance, of the firm is constrained by the value of the property transferred.

24 Note that if recognition *is* desired by the taxpayer, the corporation can be started without bonds, and it can borrow against the new collateral after incorporation. Sec. 351, thus, is quite friendly because it is, for the most part, elective.

25 A reader unfamiliar with the elegance and reach of the invariance notion should see R. Brealey and S. Myers, note 12, pp. 377–83; W. Klein and J. Coffee, *Business Organization and Finance.* 2d ed. (1980).

26 See M. Chirelstein, *Federal Income Taxation.* 4th ed. (1985), pp. 234–45 (showing how rules seem to include initial borrowing in basis and exclude subsequent borrowing from basis, but how a taxpayer can include both if he so desires). Note that if one views all this as a problem, because taxpayers can use appreciated assets as a means of borrowing for immediate consumption purposes and yet defer recognition, it will not do to tax borrowing only when specific assets are used as collateral. Such a rule would discourage secured transactions that may have an important economic purpose in the form of reducing agency costs. This solution would, instead, require that all borrowing be taxed and, therefore, a different set of problems would be created.

27 That is, that all the parties have sufficient outside income to make interest deductions useful. One also might add an assumption that any rules discounting "passive income" should be unconstraining, even though such rules might strengthen the argument that

and handicaps,[28] the initial capital structure is irrelevant to each investor. At the corporate level, section 351 simply mirrors the treatment of borrowing at the homemade or individual level. Just as an investor can use appreciated property as collateral and borrow money without recognizing any gain, so too he can contribute such assets to a corporation and let the corporation issue debt without any gain recognition.

By way of comparison, a shareowner of an ongoing firm also can manipulate his risk-and-return at any time by lending or borrowing on his own. However, in this situation the shareowner is *not* indifferent to the firm's maneuvers. If the ongoing firm distributes bonds, the shareholder will have income to report because section 301, and not 351, governs the transaction; if the firm is passive and the shareholder borrows in order to buy more shares – and, thus, fashions the risk-and-return package that would have been formed by the firm's issuing bonds – there is no tax liability.

At first, this difference may seem to be indicative of yet another intrusion of tax law into the smooth functioning of corporate and capital markets. However, a more pragmatic perspective yields just the opposite conclusion. The practical message of the irrelevance proposition for corporate managers, after all, is that time and energy are best spent on real rather than financial variables; managers should try to lower real production costs and increase outputs because effort spent on determining and achieving the "optimal capital structure" is wasted. Arguably, the distinction between sections 301 and 351 *reinforces* this message because by taxing the distribution of bonds the tax law discourages managers from fiddling with the capital structure of an ongoing corporation. Thus, the law can be described as adopting a Modigliani-Miller perspective and encouraging managers to focus on real, rather than financial, variables.

The positive effect of tax law in this setting can be stated even more strongly. One can view the Code as recognizing that excessive debt (compared to agency cost considerations alone) will be encouraged by the combined presence of tax-exempt investors and the interest expense deduction. The task, in support of efficient corporate and capital markets (in agency cost, or real terms), is to discourage debt, and the rules governing midstream distributions of debt, whether in redemption, reorganization, or dividend distribution, accomplish just that by refusing

follows. It is also helpful to ignore any problems arising from an Internal Revenue Service recharacterization of debt as equity.

28 See Miller, note 6, p. 267.

nonrecognition treatment.[29] The tax laws governing exchanges involving debt, thus, can be deemed to discourage both excessive debt financing and irrelevant or even destructive "financial fiddling" by managers with the capital structure of the ongoing corporation.

The obvious objection to this proposition is as follows: Financial fiddling and excessive debt also should be discouraged at the time that a corporation is formed and bonds should be regarded as the equivalent of cash even at the time of incorporation. There are three lines of response to this objection. First, debt is an important factor in pooling arrangements because someone who contributes more capital than his co-venturers may conveniently be given debt. This debt financing serves two important objectives: it gives maximum incentive in the form of equity shares to other parties and it eliminates the financier's fear that his coventurers will act to dissolve the firm and capture his contribution.[30] Debt, is therefore more important at the time of a firm's formation than at a later time. Second, the irrelevance proposition suggests that there may be an optimal capital structure that exists at the time of a firm's formation. Some firms may wish to appeal to low-tax-bracket investors by instituting a financing structure with a high debt–equity ratio. Others may raise capital most inexpensively by appealing to high-tax-bracket investors who prefer retained earnings (deferred gains) to current distributions.[31] Indeed, many investors would prefer a firm to announce or display its capital structure initially and *not change* this structure. Investors would be able to choose investments according to their individual tax and portfolio circumstances, and engage in homemade leverage or unleverage if they wish to adjust the risk-and-return qualities of their investments. However, investors must continue to readjust investments if the firms that they have invested in alter their capital struc-

---

29 The debt–equity ratio *can* be altered at no tax cost by contribution of unappreciated property in return for bonds or by corporate-level borrowing from banks or other lenders. The argument in the text points out that these devices are difficult to block without other instrusions. The point is not that all debt-equity manipulations are discouraged, but rather that tax law strikes at those that can be discouraged easily.

30 The financier will not want his coventurers to be prepaid for their services in any way that allows them to take advantage of this compensation before contributing all the effort that is expected of them. The point is illustrated and developed in D. Herwitz, Allocation of Stock Between Services and Capital in the Organization of a Close Corporation, *Harvard Law Review* 75:1098 (1962).

31 See A. Auerbach, *The Taxation of Corporate Income* (1983), pp. 87–90 (argument that wealth maximization is not accomplished by maximizing the firm's market value); M. King, Taxation and the Cost of Capital, *Review of Economic Studies* 41:21, (1974), pp. 25–9; R. Brealey and S. Myers, note 12, p. 385.

tures. Again, the taxation of debt which is distributed to shareholders discourages such alterations, at least in the sense that the resulting tax disadvantage is so obvious that an explanation of the distribution of debt, as a strategy that is in every investor's best interest, will be difficult.[32] Finally, one should combine this last point with an agency cost analysis. Fiddling with the capital structure of an ongoing firm may reduce agency costs, but such fiddling may upset expectations about risk-and-return and tax considerations more than it improves agency arrangements, despite the fact that these arrangements optimally would change over time.

In short, the relatively harsh treatment surrounding the receipt of debt from ongoing corporations can be explained as partially offsetting the tendency to finance with excessive debt and as discouraging financial fiddling in the face of both the irrelevance proposition and settled investor expectations. In contrast, the relatively friendly treatment surrounding the receipt of debt by those involved in the formation of corporations can be viewed as a treatment that is in harmony both with the notion that some amount of debt is optimal for agency cost reasons and with the need for debt in pooling arrangements among coventurers who will supply different proportions of capital and labor.

The treatment of preferred stock supports the idea that there is a positive link between the law and Modigliani-Miller's irrelevance proposition. Section 351 protects the issue of preferred stock just as it protects bonds. Sections 305 and 306,[33] however, provide rules for the distribution of preferred stock by an ongoing corporation that are more generous than the rules available for the distribution of bonds. Similar to pure stock dividends, preferred stock can be received, even in pro rata fashion, without the recognition of gain. Taxes are assessed only when such stock is sold. The rules in this area are a bit complicated because these taxes attempt to compensate for the earlier tax-free receipt of what now has the appearance of a dividend, but this complexity need not concern us.[34] For purposes of this analysis, one must note only that

---

32 If one believes in signaling explanations of the mystery of dividend distribution, then it may be tempting to argue that midstream debt distributions come at a high tax cost, but may be worthwhile as signals of the successful firm. These signals seem too expensive for this function. Moreover, one does not observe as many successful firms distributing debt to shareholders as firms distributing cash dividends. The market thus appears to have developed one signal and not the other. This development may have resulted because debt distribution throws shareholders' homemade portfolios out of balance.

33 I.R.C. secs. 305, 306 (1982).

34 Ibid., sec. 306; B. Bittker and J. Eustice, note 22, para. 10.04, pp. 10–5 to –7. The

preferred stock is treated more kindly than debt. Tax law makes each form of financing attractive at formation, but has less patience for bonds than for preferred stock that is distributed by the ongoing corporation.[35] The usual explanation for these treatments as a positive matter is adequate; Congress is said to have recognized that preferred stock can be a useful tool for providing intergenerational succession in business ownership while bonds, although equally useful in this regard, are too liquid to permit their tax-free or tax-deferred distribution.[36]

The treatment of preferred stock is doubly explicable if one also thinks in terms of the irrelevance proposition. Homemade leverage is possible because an investor can borrow and take a stronger equity position in a firm, but "homemade preferred stock" is not manufactured so easily. If an investor wishes that a firm have more preferred stock in its capital structure – assuming that preferred stock plays some role in the construction of an optimal portfolio[37] – there is little that he can do, because normally he cannot find a third party who will advance funds to him under conditions that resemble those surrounding the issue of preferred stock.[38] In short, because homemade preferred stock is created much less easily than homemade debt, tax law can be viewed as making it easier for a firm to distribute preferred stock, rather than debt, to its shareholders.

centerpiece of the system provides that if the shareholder sells the stock and thus reveals that the stock is not to be held as part of a long-range scheme to promote intergenerational succession, an ordinary income tax is collected to the extent that earnings and profits were sufficient for such a tax at the time the preferred stock dividend initially was distributed.

35 Tax is collected only if the preferred stock is sold or redeemed, whereas bonds are taxed immediately. The tax law could adopt a "wait and see" policy with respect to what will happen with the bonds. Such an approach would be similar to the treatment of preferred stock, but the code does not contain such an approach. See S. Levmore, Identifying Section 306 Stock: The Sleeping Beauty of Revenue Ruling 66–332, *Virginia Tax Review* 2:59, 60–2 (1982)

36 Ibid. p. 60.

37 This role may be explicable in terms of agency cost theory. See Levmore, note 19, pp. 74–5. Of course, there may be a simple tax explanation for preferred stock in the hands of corporate investors (see R. Brealey and S. Myers, note 12, pp. 288–9), but reliance on this explanation causes the argument presented in the text to become circular.

38 The investor would need to contract for a nonrecourse loan bearing an "interest" rate that was tied to the performance of a particular firm. There is no need to continue on and imagine a homemade counterpart to a provision that grants preferred shareholders the right to elect directors in the event that dividend payments are missed, because finding someone to extend such a loan would be difficult and expensive in terms of transaction costs.

Perhaps the most forceful objection to the claim that the tax laws concerning the receipt of bonds and preferred stock by common stockholders work in tandem with, rather than intrude upon, efficient capital markets, is that a firm always can fiddle with its capital structure by issuing more common stock for value or by redeeming stock. Moreover, because there is not a tax disadvantage either in distributing bonds, to existing shareholders or other investors, for fair value or in paying off debt, the firm has a number of options that enable it to engage in financial fiddling. Only some of these methods – those that involve the distribution of debt by an ongoing corporation to its shareholders for less than full value – are discouraged by the tax laws. One must, however, consider the constraints under which tax jurisprudence operates. The goal of the tax system is to tax income. Any approach that did not give credit for the value given up by an investor in return for bonds or other debt would be inconceivable.[39] To be sure, a tax could be imposed at the firm level and the occurrence of debt financing could be made a taxable event based on the theory that such tax is a proxy for the tax on the unrecognized gain in appreciated assets. Nevertheless, the question remains: Which borrowers should be taxed? If all borrowers are taxed, including firms at the time of their formation, tax law *will* intrude upon attempts to minimize agency costs through careful arrangement of capital structures. Debt financing will be discouraged, notwithstanding the absence of any reason to believe that it is efficient to discourage debt and encourage equity. Additionally, if only corporate borrowers are taxed, pooling of capital will be discouraged inefficiently. Finally, if borrowing is taxed, but section 351 continues to favor corporate borrowing at the time of formation, firms may dissolve inefficiently or sell their assets to firms that are in the formation stage. Such a system would cause more pressure to be exerted in an area where the corporate tax system has the most difficulty, namely the treatment of liquidation-reincorporations.

Even more difficult to imagine is the tax law's interfering with the issue and distribution of equity shares which form the denominator of the debt–equity ratio. The inefficiencies of various alternatives are obvious enough and, as a legal matter, one only need note that even the nontaxation of pure stock dividends has a history that borders on con-

---

39 Taxing someone who invests $300 and sells out for $600 differently than someone who begins with $100 and emerges with $400 would be terribly odd and inefficient. Of course, the best method of giving credit for investment is less obvious. See M. Chirelstein, note 26, pp. 25–8.

stitutional invincibility.[40] In sum, while only radical changes in tax law would leave firms and investors entirely free to arrange capital structures in ways that minimize agency costs, one can argue that *within* its own historically and economically determined confines, tax law supports, rather than intrudes upon, the practical lessons of modern financial theory with regard to capital structure.

III   The positive role of tax law in stock and asset acquisition

Consider the tax treatment of an acquisition of a target, T's stock by an acquiring corporation, A. Assuming that A pays cash, or that it uses its own stock to effect this acquisition, but intentionally fails to meet the requirements for a tax-free reorganization,[41] there are means by which A can receive credit for its purchase price toward the tax cost of "stepping up" the basis of T's assets for depreciation purposes. If A had purchased T's assets rather than equity instruments, this step-up would have been automatic. Thus, any means provided by tax law for asset step-ups in stock acquisitions should be considered as an attempt to be neutral or nonintrusive. If A's ability to step-up asset basis is limited to one method of acquisition, tax law will have intruded on this important business decision.[42] When A purchases less than 80 percent of T's stock, or when A is an individual, the step-up of T's assets is easy – although under the Tax Reform Act of 1986 it may be unattractively expensive to effectuate such a step-up. A simply liquidates T. This liquidation is an occasion for recognition and normally generates a tax at the shareholder level under section 331 as well as a step-up in the assets' bases under section 334. However, the recognition is painless because A, having just purchased T's stock from shareholders of T who will have paid tax on any previously unrecognized appreciation when selling these shares, will have no gain to report on the shares of T that are exchanged in liquidation. Under new

40 Cf. B. Bittker and J. Eustice, note 22, para 7.60, pp. 7–41 to –44.
41 Some acquirers, in effect, will be able to choose whether to "reorganize" with the target and inherit most of the target's tax attributes including asset basis on which depreciation deductions are figured, or to purchase the target's assets or stock and allow the target to step up (or force it to step down) its asset basis for depreciation purposes. Other advantages and disadvantages, such as the recapture of prior deductions, also may be at stake in this choice. Roughly speaking, the latter (step-up through purchase) route requires a tax on previous appreciation, while the reorganization route can allow the continuing nonrecognition of gain.
42 If asset acquisitions are more attractive than stock acquisitions, incumbent managers will have greater power to prevent takeovers or demand side-payments for their role in enabling such takeovers.

section 336 of the Tax Reform Act of 1986, the liquidation also will trigger a corporate level tax so that the step-up requires the payment of a second tax, or "asset tax," in addition to the "stock tax" paid by these who sold shares to A. Because of the absence of a preference for capital gains – under the initial rules of the 1986 Act – an acquisition and liquidation of the sort just described would require unusual tax circumstance or expectations or a strong nontax motivation.

As every student of corporate tax knows, special Code provisions are needed only when an acquiring corporation owns 80 percent or more of T's stock. The liquidation of T in such situations is a tax-free reorganization, with no step-up in asset basis.[43] Section 338 works in this setting to preserve neutrality between stock and asset acquisitions. The analysis could stop here, sketch section 338, and repeat the main point about the positive role of tax law: The idea that section 338, like its predecessors was designed to ensure that acquirers and sellers would not be limited to one form of acquisition strongly supports the point that tax law works hard to avoid intrusions. Indeed, this small area of tax law in which corporate acquirers of stock are entitled to step-up the bases of assets, and are not, therefore, discouraged from stock – as opposed to asset – acquisitions is an excellent example of the positive role stressed in this essay.

However, the role played by section 338 is deeper, richer, and more striking than what first meets the eye. The rather intricate mechanics of section 338 contain less obvious evidence about the positive interaction between tax and corporate law. These mechanics, summarized presently, are understood most easily if one bears in mind that the Code's treatment of business sales, at least through 1986, generally has been to collect one full tax on all unrecognized appreciation or gain and to give in return a full step-up in the basis of assets to the level of present fair market value. In the case of these stock acquisitions, one should be mindful of the contributions toward this tax collected from the past and present shareholders of T. Although the Tax Reform Act of 1986 now collects *two* taxes in most acquisitions, as the price of a step-up, section 338 continues to play a substantial part of the role that it played in the one-tax scheme.

In the pages that follow, an argument about the positive role of tax law in terms of the rules in place *prior* to the Tax Reform Act of 1986 will be presented. A related and equally intricate argument about the

---

43 I.R.C. secs. 332, 334(b) (1982). See also Tax Reform Act of 1986 sec. 337. I.R.C. sec. 337 (1986).

post-1986 rules is developed in the notes.[44] The reasons for dwelling on these rules are several. First, the argument is a bit more elegant under the older rules, and the purpose of this essay is to explore the nature of the interaction between tax law and corporate law, rather than to sketch the latest rules on corporate acquisitions. The occasional notes should assist the purist who wishes to reformulate every aspect of the argument in terms of the 1986 act. Second, because the Tax Reform Act of 1986 essentially imposes two taxes, rather than one, on complete corporate acquisitions, the details of the argument are made more complex by the act. As will be apparent below, the matter is complicated sufficiently with one tax in tow. Finally, and not unimportantly, the old rules are by no means obsolete. A substantial number of transactions initiated before August 1986 are grandfathered and treated under the old rules.[45] Moreover, the old rules apply until 1989 for target corporations that have 50 percent of their stock held by ten or fewer individuals, including trusts and estates, and whose value is less than $5 million. Corporations worth more than $5 million but less than $10 million are entitled to some of the old (one-tax rather than two-tax) treatment on their liquidation.[46] In short, not only will the argument be easier to follow in one-tax terms, but also the one-tax *General Utilities*[47] world will continue to exist for some time, even if no future legislative changes return us more completely to its rules.

A   Section 338

Section 338 operates[48] in the following manner. First, if corporation *A* buys 100 percent of *T's* stock, *A* can elect to step up the basis of *T's* assets, as if the assets were sold, without paying any tax.[49] Note that all those who sold stock to *A* will pay taxes on their gain. Second, if *A*

44 See note 56.
45 Tax Reform Act of 1986 sec. 633(c).
46 Ibid. sec. 633(d).
47 *General Utils. & Operating Co.* v. *Helvering*, 296 U.S. 200 (1935).
48 I.R.C. sec. 338 (1982). Section 631(b)(2) of The Tax Reform Act of 1986 repealed sec. 338(c) and, therefore, the mechanism described in the text as contained in sec. 338. The use of the present tense in the text's description of sec. 338 must be understood as applying to small or grandfathered corporations. See note 56 for a more complicated argument, applying the rules in sec. 338 after the repeal of subsection (c).
49 Under sec. 631 of the Tax Reform Act of 1986, which repeals the General Utilities rule that had forgiven corporate level recognition of gain upon liquidation, there will be a corporate level tax under sec. 338(a)(1). The discussion in note 56 includes this tax.

buys between 80 percent and 100 percent of *T's* stock, there is a full 100 percent step-up as if all the assets were sold in a taxable transactions but *T*, now controlled by *A*, must pay tax on the hypothetical sale of these assets according to how many old *T* shareholders have *not* sold – and therefore not paid tax on appreciation in – stock to *A*. Thus, if *A* buys 85 percent of *T's* stock and elects under section 338, there is a complete step-up of *T's* assets, but *T* must pay 15 percent of the tax that would be due if all of *T's* asset were sold in a taxable transaction. If *A* buys 95 percent of *T's* stock, there is an "asset tax" on 5 percent of the asset appreciation, and so forth. Finally, for those who do not follow corporate tax law but would like to know that the system is comprehensive, if *A* buys more than 80 percent of *T's* stock and has purchased some *T* stock at some time in the past, it still can choose a complete step-up in *T's* assets, but must pay tax on appreciation in its own old holdings of *T* stock. The basis in these holdings also is stepped up.[50]

I will argue that these rules are sensitive to the decision-making processes that surround tender offers, but it is useful first to sketch the alternative means by which section 338 could have allowed a step-up in basis in order to maintain neutrality between asset and stock acquisitions in return for one tax. Instead of giving a 10 percent step-up in return for less than a 100 percent stock purchase, and collecting the balance of the tax in the form of an "asset tax" from the corporation, the Code, instead, could have chosen to give a step-up only to the extent that a tax has been collected from the shareholders who sell to *A*. When *A* purchases 85 percent of *T* stock, for example, an 85 percent step-up would follow. Recall that section 338 gave a 100 percent step-up in these circumstances and collected a 15 percent asset tax from *T*. The alternative is to collect no such "asset tax," but simply to give an 85 percent step-up. We might label this "Alternative 1." Note that the rules of Alternative 1 might permit the acquirer to freeze out the remaining shareholders and, in return for the taxes they pay on selling these shares, enjoy a full step-up in *T*'s assets.

The approaches found in section 338 and described by Alternative 1 both suffer from what can be called a "correspondence fallacy" that lurks throughout much of corporate tax. Unrecognized gain is unlikely to be distributed evenly across the outstanding stock of a firm. The amount of unrecognized gain represented, for example, in 10 percent of the outstanding stock of a company is not likely to equal the amount

50 I.R.C. sec. 338(b) (1982). This feature of sec. 338 survives the 1986 Act. See note 56 for some discussion of the 80% requirement of sec. 338.

of unrecognized gain in 10 percent of that firm's assets. When *all* the stock appreciation is taxed, the government can be sure that it has received the equivalent of a tax on all asset appreciation because the market value of the stock presumably represents, at least, the value of all the assets held by the corporation. However, when less than all the stock has been traded and taxed there is no way of knowing in the abstract what part of the overall unrecognized gain contained in all the stock or all the assets is in this subject of the stock. Indeed, because old shares with significant untaxed appreciation are the least likely to be traded on a given day, a scheme that steps up assets according to the percentage of stock that is traded recently will provide opportunities for step-ups too cheaply when compared to the treatment of a 100 percent stock sale and step-up. Moreover, taxpayers surely will take advantage of the correspondence fallacy and adversely select against the fisc by electing under section 338, or Alternative 1, readily whenever the unsold stock contains a disproportionately high share of unrecognized gain. Inefficient acquisitions also might be generated by such rules because tax advantages in the form of depreciation deductions from higher bases would be available from otherwise inefficient, unprofitable transfers of control when unrecognized gain is contained disproportionately in relatively few unsold shares.

To see this correspondence fallacy, assume that a firm, T, begins with ten shares owned by A Corporation, and $10 invested in a machine, but that over time both become worth $1,000 because of inventions or marketing by employees of the firm. T now sells ninety shares to new investors, who contribute $100 in assets for each share. Each share will represent a 1/100 claim on an enterprise now worth $10,000. If, after a year with no further appreciation, the ninety new shareholders all sell their stock to A, they will have no gain to report. A can now make a section 338 election. Under the rules of section 338, T will need to pay, on behalf of the nonselling shareholders, 10 percent of the tax that it would have paid in a complete and taxable asset sale (10% of $990). The machine's basis is stepped up completely to $1,000 even though only 10 percent of its appreciation has been taxed. This is the correspondence problem inherent in section 338.

Under Alternative 1's rules, the correspondence problem is at least as great as under pre-1986 section 338. The machine would be stepped up by 90 percent of the full differential between the adjusted basis, $10, and the fair market value, $1,000, or from $10 to $901 with no tax cost at all. Superficially, the correspondence fallacy is the same under this method as it is under section 338. Both approaches might be said to give the first $891 of step-up at no tax cost, but under section 338 the corporation must continue and take another $99 step-up at the cost of a corporate-level tax on $99 of gain. Sometimes this extra step-up will be welcomed by the taxpayer, perhaps because some depreciation schedules are friendly to investment. However, sometimes the tax, and step-up, will be unwanted because it involves an immediate tax liability with consequent depreciation deductions available only in later years. Finally, sometimes the extra step-up will be a matter of indifference because the advantages of increased deductions and the disadvantages of a present tax liability will be offsetting. My own sense is that the two methods often will be roughly equal from the perspectives of the taxpayer and the government, but that in a significant subset of acquisitions the loss to the government arising out of the correspondence fallacy is likely to be less under the method actually employed in section 338 than under Alternative 1. Stated differently, taxpayers in the aggregate would prefer Alternative 1, earning a step-up to the extent that stock changes hands. The section 338 rules, in contrast, force additional gain recognition. There is reason to think that taxpayers generally prefer to have maximum control over the timing of recognition and the section 338 technique removes from taxpayers some of their control over the timing of recognition. In short, the two methods may generate equal correspondence fallacies, in which case the choice of the technique actually used in section 338 simply can be regarded as a matter of indifference. On the other hand, one might estimate that the correspondence fallacy in Alternative 1 (that is, step-up according to purchase, and no more) is greater than that in section 338, in which case the statute can be understood as reflecting a decision to minimize the correspondence problem.

The correspondence problem might have been avoided altogether, while collecting a full tax and giving a complete step-up in a manner alluded to in the 1982 changes to the Code and suggested by a case that was regarded widely as too harsh to nonselling minority shareholders.[51] This approach, which might be labeled "Alternative 2," would permit a full step-up of *T's* assets even when *A* has bought less than 100 percent of *T's* stock, and would collect a tax from the nonselling shareholders of *T* rather than from *T* itself. By imagining and forcing these nonselling shareholders to sell their *T* stock to themselves and to recognize gain, the correspondence fallacy is avoided because there is 100 percent recognition.

With Alternatives 1 and 2 and the notion of the correspondence fallacy now set out we are positioned to consider the interaction between

---

51 *Kass* v. *Commissioner*, 60 T.C. 218 (1973), aff'd without opinion, 491 F.2d 749 (3d Cir. 1974).

the mechanics of section 338 and the dynamics of the market for corporate control. The nonselling shareholders – as opposed to offerees in general – surely will be pleased to learn that the drafters of section 338 did not opt for Alternative 2. Alternative 2 would be unattractive to such shareholders because, in contrast to the normal tax law rules that allow the individual to decide on the timing of such recognition, it would force gain recognition. In some settings, these nonselling shareholders may have dissented from, or turned down, an acquirer's offer for their stock precisely because the tax consequences of a sale made the offer less attractive than it was to most other shareholders. Here, the ability to control the timing of recognition is relatively clear.

A difficult question is whether economic efficiency would be promoted by Alternative 2's insensitivity to the nonselling shareholders' personal tax consequences. Arguably, the market for corporate control works best when owners freely decide whether to accept an offer, await other offers, or hope that current management over time will cause shares to be worth even more than what a bidder offers presently. Inasmuch as tax law, by collecting revenue when there are recognition events, *already* intrudes on this decision, this distorting, inefficient intrusion possibly could be neutralized by a rule that withdraws from the shareholder the ability to trigger or prevent such a recognition event. Stated differently, nonselling shareholders may have good tax reasons to turn down offers for their shares, but society's interest could be served best by encouraging a decision on each offer that is unaffected by tax considerations. Therefore, Alternative 2 may be good for the market despite the fact that it is costly to some individuals.

A problem with this argument is that it tries to stop short of repeating the familiar notion that the tax system would be less intrusive if changes in wealth or consumption were assessed daily or yearly rather than calculated only when certain recognition events occur. Shareholders may reject offers from acquirers, who signal with their generous offers that they could put the firm's assets to more productive use, simply to postpone their personal tax liability; a smaller amount of money taxed later, unfortunately, is more attractive than more money taxed now. But, what are the alternatives to the present regime? Alternative 2 may generate perverse behavior because targets, acting through their managers, may resist acquisitions more vigorously in order to avoid tax liabilities. Some shareholders may be able to pay or influence the firm to behave in this way, whereas without Alternative 2 they will have less reason to care about the responses of their fellow shareholders. More generally, Alternative 2 does not necessarily cause offerees to ignore taxes and to focus on "real" things, because if enough shareholders decline the offer, no qualifying acquisition will take place and section 338, like Alternative 2, cannot be triggered. Nor can this distortion in the responses of offerees be avoided by decreeing that all offers of acquisition trigger a stock tax, so that target shareholders do not include tax considerations in the calculus of their responses; it is simply too difficult to distinguish true offers from strategic offers. Any further step in this direction is nothing more than a call for daily recognition of gain and is so far removed from the norms of the present tax system that it is best left unconsidered in this essay.

Alternatives 1 and 2 are thus relatively unattractive. Alternative 1, which would allow a step-up only to the extent that taxes have been collected from selling shareholders, is undesirable because the correspondence problem probably is greater under its terms than under those of section 338. Alternative 2, which would give a full step-up but would assess taxes against all nonselling shareholders similar to those collected from sellers, also is unattractive, not only because as a matter of legal tradition, it suggests the unthinkable[52] and forces shareholders to recognize gains or losses in a way that seems unfair in the context of a system that normally allows taxpayers to control the timing of recognition events, but also because it might cause targets to resist outside offers even more than they do under existing tax rules.[53]

B   *The positive role of section 338*

With all this in mind, the design of the second prong of section 338 itself can be reexamined. We have seen how section 338 compromises on the correspondence problem,[54] but there has been no discussion of section 338's effect on offerees' inclinations to accept or reject offers for their shares. At first glance, the design of section 338 seems flawed because when the corporate-level tax on appreciated assets is paid "on behalf of" the less than 20 percent nonselling shareholders, no step-up or other credit is given to these shareholders, so that there is potential for overtaxation in comparison with the complete stock or asset sale norm. For example, if T's assets have risen in value from \$100 to \$200, if T has 100 shares outstanding each with a basis of \$1 and fair market value of \$2, and if 80 of the 100 shares of T stock were sold to A who elects under 338, T will pay tax on 20 percent of the \$100 asset appreciation.

---

52 See text accompanying note 39.
53 That is, the rules contained in (now repealed) sec. 338(c), giving a full step-up, but requiring an asset tax from T "on behalf of" the nonselling shareholders.
54 See text preceding note 50.

If the nonselling shareholders sell their stock to A or some other purchaser shortly after the original sale to A, they will pay tax on their gain. Thus, the government could collect tax on $80 from the first group of selling shareholders, $20 from T after the 338 election, and $20 from the second group of originally nonselling shareholders. This results in a total tax of $120 when only $100 would have been taxed in a normal stock or asset sale. Section 338, contrary to its obvious purpose, thus intrudes upon the choice between an asset and stock acquisition, because the tax assessments associated with the latter can be more expensive.[55]

Having examined the alternatives to the second prong of section 338, it becomes apparent that the failure of section 338 as just described may simply be the least of all evils. Allowing those minority shareholders who eventually sell their stock to avoid taxation, or, equivalently, giving the nonselling shareholders a step-up in the basis of their stock in T when a partial asset tax is paid "on their behalf" by T would be unacceptable. Such treatment would encourage offerees to reject an offer – even when it is one they think beneficial – in the hope that the offer would succeed at the 80 percent level and then be followed by a section 338 election. This set of events not only would allow those who turn down the offer to benefit by paying less than their proportional share of the tax cost of a full step-up in the corporation's assets, but also would give them a tax-free sale of their stock. Any hope of neutral, efficiency-enhancing responses to offers, or responses not influenced primarily by tax considerations, therefore, depends on treating nonsellers no better than sellers. In addition, because the alternatives to section 338 also are flawed, one can argue that the imperfection of section 338's step-up technique, including the potential for overtaxation, is, in fact, the least of all evils.[56]

---

55 The tax liability also *could* be lower because of a combination of the correspondence problem and deferral. However, taxpayers can be expected to select adversely against the fisc. Note that even this imperfection sometimes will be avoidable after an 80% acquisition, because the acquirer and the nonselling shareholders may be able to strike a deal to liquidate within a year, in which case the nonsellers will upon liquidation pay a tax and, appropriately, sec. 338(c)(1) will forgive the asset-based tax that otherwise would be collected from the target in return for the full step-up.

56 The Tax Reform Act of 1986 deleted sec. 338(a)(1)'s reference to old (repealed) sec. 337 and sec. 338(c), which had contained the rule requiring A to pay an asset tax on behalf of nonselling shareholders. Under the new rules, if A purchases 100% of T stock and elects under 338, T's assets are stepped up in return for a complete asset tax on the appreciation of these in T's hands. Although the Code generally frowns on "self-triggered" recognition, see, e.g., sec. 1239, it is reasonable for the Code to allow this self-triggered step-up, because the fair value of the assets is determined accurately by referring to the price just paid by A for all of T's stock. [*Continued*]

I suppose that it might have been slightly more elegant for the statute to provide a 100 percent step-up, collect an asset tax from the target "on behalf of" the nonsellers, *and* give the nonsellers a "corresponding," rather than a full, step-up in their stock basis linked to

The more serious design problem is the treatment of a purchase by A of, let us say, only 80% of the T stock. It is useful to think of the following five possibilities and the attendant advantages and disadvantages of each.

1. The Code could deny any step-up in T's assets, despite the collection of a full asset tax, on the grounds that it can be reckless to extrapolate from the price paid for 80% of the stock to the fair value of 100% of the assets of a firm. A might even find it worthwhile to overpay for the 80% stock in order to generate a high basis. For example, if T is worth $85,000. A might pay $80,000 for 80% of T's stock and claim that a straight line extrapolation indicates that $100,000 is the apparent value of 100% of T's stock and, therefore, of all T's assets. On the other hand, the denial of any step-up following an 80% stock purchase would deter acquirers from stock acquisitions and, therefore, endow targets' managers with great power to extract payments and promises in return for the engineering of asset sales.

2. The Code could pick some dividing line, such as 80%, and allow 80% stock purchasers to extrapolate and step up 100% of T's assets in return for a full (anti-*General Utilities*) asset tax and the 80% "stock tax" paid by the selling shareholders. Stated differently, while allowing a full step-up in the case of a 20% stock purchase (in return for a full asset tax and a 20% stock tax) would overly encourage stock purchases by acquirers who sought advantage from both the extrapolation technique and from the correspondence fallacy, in the case of an 80% purchase it is arguable that the extrapolation and correspondence problems are relatively small and are more than offset by the advantages of enabling some (less than 100%) stock acquisitions as an alternative to asset acquisitions. Withholding step-ups from all but 100% purchasers would give great holdout power either to target managers or to minority target shareholders.

3. The Code could collect two full taxes by levying an asset tax on T, once again, and requiring all nonselling T shareholders to pay tax and step up their stock bases as if they sold their shares. This is a harsh rule although it *would* promote neutrality between stock and asset acquisitions.

4. The Code could collect a full asset tax and then grant a step-up to the degree that stock is sold and taxed. An 80% stock purchase would thus enable T to step up its assets 80% of the way from their old adjusted basis to their present fair market value – determined, once again, by extrapolation from the 80% purchase.

5. Finally, if method 3 seems too harsh, either because of the tradition of awaiting voluntary recognition events or because when A buys T's assets only one tax need be paid in order to enjoy an asset basis step-up (the stock tax is due only when money is received by shareholders), methods 2, 3, and 4 can be compromised. The Code could extrapolate from the 80% purchase to give a full step-up as in 2, so long as a full asset tax is paid, but withhold this step-up to the extent that A itself owns the nonselling stock (as in 4) – unless A

the asset tax paid by the target. Some overtaxation would be prevented by this "Alternative 3," and yet no incentive to dissent would be created.

Imagine, for example, that every one of the ten shares of a target has a basis of $10 and a fair market value of $100, that its assets have appreciated from $100 to $1,000, and that only one share is not sold to the acquirer who elects under 338 with Alternative 3 incorporated. Alternative 3 provides a full asset basis step-up, extracts a tax on $90 ($100 minus $10) from the nine shareholders ($810 total), collects a corporate-level tax on 10 percent of the $900 asset appreciation, and, unlike actual section 338, gives the nonselling shareholder a basis in his stock of $19. This step-up of $9 is equal to the 10 percent proportion of the $90 asset appreciation taxes to the corporation because of the nonseller. This corresponding, or partial, stock basis step-up probably is insufficient to encourage more dissent or nonselling than is already influenced by section 338, because in dissent, under the rules actually contained in section 338, one might indirectly pay a greater part of the asset tax paid on behalf of nonsellers.[57]

Had Alternative 3 been chosen by the tax law, one could not overstate the positive interaction of corporate law and tax law in the context of acquisitions. Inasmuch as section 338 contains rules very similar to Alternative 3 and is much less complicated administratively,[58] I feel comfortable arguing that section 338 is an impressive example of the positive role of tax law. Not only does section 338 aim to give acquirers the

pays tax on the unrecognized gain in these shares (as in 3). Remarkably this most complicated alternative is precisely the current pattern of sec. 338 (a) and (b). For example, if A bought 10% of T stock some years ago for $10 and now it buys 80% more for $160, and elects under sec. 338, it is given a step-up to $190. T is entitled to a basis of 200 in its assets only if A recognizes gain on the extrapolated increase in value of its old T stock (20 minus basis of 10).

I suspect that some of this is the patchwork remains of the recent round of tax reform, and that in the future sec. 338 will evolve to look more like method 2 and less like method 5. Nevertheless, the positive role of tax law is quite striking. Both methods 2 and 5 – that is, current sec. 338 – reflect a compromise between sensitivity to the extrapolation and correspondence problems, on the one hand, and, on the other, an appreciation of the need to leave open both the asset and stock acquisition routes in the market for corporate control.

57 I.R.C. sec. 338 (c) (1) (1982).

58 Frequently the Code utilizes what conceptually is a second-best solution because the optimal solution is available only at a higher administrative or articulation cost.

flexibility of choosing between asset and stock acquisitions, but also the mechanics of stepping up asset bases in stock acquisitions reflect remarkable sensitivity to the dynamics of stock sales. The Code appears elegant and efficient rather than intrusive.

IV   Conclusion

One could not claim that taxes do not intrude upon or distort decisions that take place in corporate and capital markets.[59] I have tried to suggest in this essay that alongside these intrusions there also is positive interplay. There is reason to think that the positive interactions described in this essay are not accidental in the evolutionary sense, either because the drafters of the relevant Code sections knew just what they were doing or, more likely, because they could perceive some weaknesses in the available alternatives. On the other hand, the more one can explain those areas of tax law that interact positively with various policy goals, the more mysterious or troubling are those areas in which taxes appear to be violent intruders. But whatever the explanation of the positive role of tax law, the study of positive interactions between tax and other law will assist reformers who, when trying to minimize the intrusions of tax law, need to understand that tax and other law are sometimes complementary.

---

59 Even if current stock prices reflect all pertinent factors, the fact remains that at the margin the tax system's preference for recognition, rather than periodic appraisals, affects the decision to hold or sell an asset.

CHAPTER 9

Ownership of the firm

Henry Hansmann

I.   Introduction

Most large-scale enterprise in the United States is organized in the form
of the conventional business corporation, in which the firm is collectively
owned by investors of capital. Other ownership patterns are prominent
in a number of important industries, however. Many firms, for example,
are owned by their customers. These include not just consumer retail
cooperatives, which are relatively rare, but also business-owned wholesale and supply cooperatives, which are quite common, as well as public
utility cooperatives, mutual insurance companies, mutual banking institutions, and cooperative and condominium housing. Further, many
firms are owned by persons who supply the firm with some factor of
production other than capital. Worker-owned firms, which predominate
in professional services such as law and accounting, are conspicuous
examples, as are the agricultural processing and marketing cooperatives
that dominate the markets for many farm products. Finally, a number
of important service industries are heavily populated by nonprofit firms,
which have no owners at all. In this essay I explore the economic factors
responsible for these different patterns of ownership.

In recent years a number of scholars have explored various aspects

This chapter appears, in more complete form, in *Journal of Law, Economics, and Organization* 4:267 (1988). The subjects it deals with are explored much more extensively
in a forthcoming book, tentatively titled *The Ownership of Enterprise*.

Helpful comments on previous drafts were offered by Bruce Ackerman, Bengt Holmstrom, Reinier Kraakman, Michael Levine, Saul Levmore, Roberta Romano, Alan
Schwartz, Jeff Strnad, and Oliver Williamson, by participants in the Conference on the
Economics of Corporate and Capital Markets Law at Harvard Law School and the Conference on the Economics of Institutional Choice and Design in Vienna, and by participants
in workshops at New York University, the University of Toronto, and Yale.

of enterprise ownership. In particular, Williamson[1] and Klein, Crawford, and Alchian[2] have dealt insightfully with the influence of transaction-specific investments on the assignment of ownership, and I shall draw heavily here on the concepts they have developed. Similarly, a number of writers have looked at questions of ownership in particular contexts. A particularly common focus has been worker ownership versus investor ownership, which has been examined thoughtfully by, among others, Jensen and Meckling.[3] This essay extends the work of these and other authors[4] by viewing ownership in a more general framework. In the process I seek to provide better perspective on existing theories, develop some significant considerations that have previously been neglected, and offer a more comprehensive and convincing explanation for the prominence of noninvestor-owned firms in many important industries.

The primary focus here is on firms, such as the publicly held business corporation, in which ownership is shared among a numerous group of persons. One reason for this emphasis is that such firms are the dominant actors in the contemporary economy. But another reason is that widely shared ownership gives rise to problems that call for special attention. In particular, one of the central themes of this essay is that large costs can be engendered by conflicting interests when the ownership class is heterogeneous, and that these costs are a primary determinant of the relative efficiency of alternative assignments of ownership. Such costs have previously received little attention in the literature on the organization of the firm.[5]

Although this inquiry is largely an exercise in positive social science, it also has an important policy dimension. There is considerable enthusiasm today for forms of ownership other than the conventional capitalist firm. This is particularly true of worker ownership, which is being pro-

---

1 The most recent and comprehensive treatment appears in Oliver Williamson, *The Economic Institutions of Capitalism* (1986).

2 Benjamin Klein, Robert Crawford, and Armen Alchian, Vertical Integration, Appropriable Rents, and the Competitive Contracting Process, *Journal of Law and Economics* 21:297 (1978).

3 Michael Jensen and William Meckling, Rights and Production Functions: An Application to Labor-Managed Firms and Codetermination, *Journal of Business* 52:469 (1979). See also the authors cited in Section V below.

4 E.g., Eugene Fama and Michael Jensen, Agency Problems and Residual Claims, *Journal of Law and Economics* 26:327 (1983).

5 For example, Williamson's work focuses most closely on situations involving single owners, as in his analysis of the considerations bearing on the efficiency of vertical integration between two firms. He has himself noted the need for further investigation of the relative efficiency of collective ownership of the firm by labor and other parties; see note 1, Williamson, pp. 265–8 ("The Producer Cooperative Dilemma").

moted by large tax preferences, by the recently chartered National Co-operative Bank, and by special corporation statutes for employee-owned firms that have been enacted in several states and are on the legislative agenda in others.[6] It is important that we have some understanding of the efficiency of these alternative forms of ownership.

Furthermore, by considering patterns of ownership in general, we can achieve a better appreciation of the strengths and weaknesses of the type of investor ownership that is the norm in our economy. For example, we can obtain important insight into the familiar problem of the separation of ownership and control in large firms, and into the significance of the market for corporate control as a means of dealing with this problem.

A general framework is set out in Section II. That framework is then illustrated and elaborated in subsequent sections by application to the ownership patterns that appear in a number of different industries. Section III deals with investor-owned firms. Section IV examines customer-owned retail, wholesale and supply firms – an important and interesting class of firms that has largely been neglected in the economics and legal literature. Section V deals with worker-owned firms and seeks to offer a more convincing explanation for their pattern of development than has previously been given. Finally, Section VI briefly considers mutual and nonprofit firms.

II   A theoretical framework

A   The structure of ownership

A firm's "owners," as the term is conventionally used and as it will be used here, are those persons who share two formal rights: the right to control the firm and the right to appropriate the firm's residual earnings.[7] The reference here to "formal" rights is important. Often the persons who have the formal right to control the firm – which typically takes the form of the right to elect the firm's board of directors – in fact exercise little effective authority by this means over the firm's management. It is sometimes said that the owners of such firms do not "control" them – hence the familiar references to the "separation of ownership

---

6 E.g., Massachusetts Employee Cooperative Corporations Act, Mass. Gen. Laws Ann. ch. 157A (West 1987). Connecticut, New York, Vermont, and Washington have adopted similar statutes.

7 The term "residual earnings" is used here to encompass all net returns to the firm, including net current earnings and the net increase in capital value of any assets or other rights that the firm itself owns.

and control." Nevertheless, I shall be concerned here principally with explaining the way in which the *formal* (legal) rights to control and residual earnings are assigned. Indeed, an important implication of the analysis and examples offered below is that it is often efficient to assign the formal right of control to persons who are not in a position to exercise that right very effectively.

In theory, the rights to control and to residual earnings could be held by different persons. In practice, however, they are generally joined, since those with control would otherwise have little incentive to use their control to maximize the residual earnings. To be sure, if all aspects of control could be contracted for ex ante, then this problem would not arise. But control can usefully be thought of as authority over precisely those aspects of firm policy that, because of high transaction costs or bounded rationality, cannot be specified ex ante in a contract, but rather must be left to the discretion of those to whom the authority is granted.[8]

Nevertheless, not all firms have owners in the sense defined here. In particular, nonprofit firms are characterized by the fact that the persons who have formal control of the firm are barred from receiving its residual earnings.[9] The same considerations, however, that determine the class of persons to whom ownership is efficiently assigned also determine when it is efficient for a firm to have no owners at all.

In the discussion that follows it will be helpful to have a term to comprise all persons who transact with a firm, either as purchasers of the firm's products or as suppliers to the firm of some factor of production, including capital. Such persons – whether they are individuals or other firms – will be referred to here collectively as the firm's "patrons."

Most firms are owned by persons who are also patrons. This is conspicuously true of producer and consumer cooperatives. It is also true of the standard business corporation, which is owned by persons who lend capital to the firm. In fact, the conventional investor-owned firm is in a sense nothing more than a special type of producer cooperative – a lenders' cooperative, or capital cooperative. Because we so commonly associate ownership in general with invested capital, and because the comparison of investor-owned firms with other types of cooperatives will be at the core of the analysis that follows, it may be useful to elaborate on this point.

8 See Sanford Grossman and Oliver Hart, The Costs and Benefits of Ownership: A Theory of Vertical and Horizontal Integration, *Journal of Political Economy* 94:691 (1986).
9 See Henry Hansmann, The Role of Nonprofit Enterprise, *Yale Law Journal* 89:835 (1980).

Consider, first, the structure of a typical producer cooperative. A representative example is a dairy farmers' cheese cooperative, in which a cheese factory is owned by the farmers who provide the raw milk for the cheese. The firm pays the members a predetermined price for their milk on the occasion of each sale. (In keeping with conventional usage, the term "member" will be used here to refer to the patron-owners of cooperatives.) This price is usually set low enough so that the cooperative is almost certain to make a profit from its operations. Then, at the end of the year, any profits that have been earned from the manufacture and sale of the cheese are distributed pro rata among the members according to the amount of milk they have sold to the cooperative during the year. Voting rights are held only by those who sell milk to the firm, either on the basis of one member–one vote or with votes apportioned according to the volume of milk each member sells to the firm. Some or all of the members may have capital invested in the firm. In principle, however, this is unnecessary; the firm could borrow all of the capital it needs. In any case, even where members invest in the firm, those investments typically take the form of preferred stock that carries no voting rights and is limited to a stated maximum rate of dividends. Upon liquidation of the firm, the net asset value – which may derive from retained earnings or from increases in the value of rights held by the firm – is divided pro rata among the members, usually according to some measure of the relative value of their cumulative patronage.

In short, ownership rights are held exclusively by virtue of the fact, and to the extent, that one sells milk to the firm. On the other hand, not all farmers who sell milk to the firm need be owners; the firm may purchase some portion of its milk from nonmembers, who are simply paid a fixed price and do not participate in net earnings or control. (Consumer cooperatives are set up similarly, with net earnings and votes apportioned according to the amounts that a member purchases from the firm.)

A business corporation is also organized in this fashion, except that it is owned not by persons who supply the firm with some commodity, such as milk, but rather by some or all of the persons who lend capital to the firm. To see the analogy clearly, it helps to characterize the transactions in a business corporation in somewhat stylized terms: The members each lend the firm a given sum. For this they are paid a fixed interest rate, set low enough so that the firm has a reasonable likelihood of running at a profit. Then at the end of the year, any profits earned by the corporation (after all contractual expenses, including wages and the cost of materials as well as the fixed interest rate on the capital borrowed from the members, have been paid) are distributed pro rata among the lender–members according to the amount they have lent. The firm may also have lenders who are not members. These lenders, commonly banks or bondholders, simply receive a fixed market interest rate and have no share in profits or participation in control.

As it is, in a business corporation the interest rate that is paid to lender–members (i.e., shareholders) is generally set at zero for the sake of convenience. Moreover, the loans from members are not arranged annually or for other fixed periods, but rather are perpetual; the principal can generally be withdrawn only upon dissolution of the firm. In the typical cooperative, by contrast, members generally remain free to vary their volume of transactions with the firm over time, and even to terminate their patronage altogether. This distinction is not, however, fundamental. Investor-owned firms can be, and sometimes are, structured so that the amount of capital invested by each member can be redeemed at specified intervals or even (as in the typical partnership) at will. Conversely, cooperatives can be, and often are, structured so that members have a long-term commitment to remain patrons. Electricity generation and transmission cooperatives, for example, commonly have requirements contracts from their members (which are local electricity distribution cooperatives) that run for thirty-five years.

Indeed, we can view business corporation statutes as simply specialized versions of the more general cooperative corporation statutes. In principle, there is no need to have separate business corporation statutes at all; business corporations could just as well be organized under a well-drafted general cooperative corporation statute. Presumably we have separate statutes for business corporations simply because it is convenient to have a form that is specialized for the most common form of cooperative – the lenders' cooperative – and to signal more clearly to interested parties just what type of cooperative they are dealing with.[10]

In short, ownership need not be, and frequently is not, associated with investment of capital. Rather, lending capital is simply one of many types of transactions to which ownership of a firm can be tied. A general theory of corporate ownership, therefore, must explain both why ownership is generally tied to transactions and what factors govern the particular class of transactions – whether lending capital, supplying other factors of production, or purchasing the firm's products – to which ownership is tied in any particular case.

---

10 Nevertheless, the term "cooperative" will be used below, as is conventional, to refer to patron-owned firms other than investor-owned firms, and without regard to whether the firm is organized under a cooperative corporation statute or (as is common for many cooperatives) under a business corporation statute or as a partnership.

B   An overview of the theory

In principle, a firm could be owned by someone who is not a patron. Such a firm's capital needs would be met entirely by borrowing; its other factors of production would likewise be purchased on the market, and its products would be sold on the market. The owner(s) would simply have the right to control the firm and to appropriate its (positive or negative) residual earnings.[11] Such firms are rare, however. Ownership commonly is assigned to persons who have some other transactional relationship with the firm. The reason for this, evidently, is that the ownership relationship can be used to mitigate some of the costs that would otherwise attend these transactional relationships if they were managed through simple market contracting.

More particularly, market contracting can be especially costly in the presence of those conditions loosely called "market failure," such as limited competition or asymmetric information. In such circumstances, the total costs of transacting can sometimes be reduced by merging the purchasing and the selling party in an ownership relationship, hence eliminating the conflict of interest between buyer and seller that underlies or aggravates many of the avoidable costs of market contracting.

Ownership can itself involve substantial costs, however, and, as we shall discuss below, these costs can be quite different for different classes of patrons. Efficiency will be best served if ownership is assigned so that total transaction costs for all patrons are minimized. This means minimizing the sum of both the costs of market contracting[12] for those patrons who are not owners, and the costs of ownership for the class of patrons who are assigned ownership. Thus, if there are N different classes of patrons who transact with a given firm, ownership will be assigned most efficiently to that class j that minimizes

---

11 To be sure, the exercise of control, even if it amounts only to the choice of a manager, may require some effort. The owner might therefore be considered a contributor of labor to the firm, and the residual earnings might be considered a return for that labor. Viewed this way, such a firm is simply a reductive form of worker-owned firm.

12 The discussion here is framed in terms of two polar ways of structuring transactional relationships: market contracting and ownership. In fact, as Williamson has emphasized, a variety of different types of "governance structures" are available for transactions. In particular, what here is loosely termed "market contracting" can take various forms, ranging from simple spot market contracting, in which competition is essentially the only safeguard for the parties, to highly interdependent forms of "obligational contracting." See note 2, Williamson, Chapter 3. In general, the term "market contracting" will be used here to comprise all forms of contracting other than ownership.

$$CO_j + \sum_{\substack{i=1 \\ i \neq j}}^{N} CC_i,$$

where CO_i and CC_i are, respectively, the cost of ownership and the cost of market contracting for class i. To the extent that efficient ownership forms are selected by market forces, or simply by rational choice among alternatives by the interested parties, the result will be the differential survival of those forms in which ownership is assigned to economize on transaction costs in this fashion.

To give this theory more substance, I shall survey the most significant types of costs that attend market contracting and ownership, respectively. Because most of these categories of costs are familiar, this survey will be brief, emphasizing only those considerations that have not been well analyzed before and that have special bearing on problems of collective ownership.

C   The cost of market contracting

Although a variety of factors can make market transactions costly, there are three characteristic types of problems that arise commonly and can often be mitigated by assigning ownership to the patrons involved.

Market power. An obvious reason for assigning ownership to a given class of patrons is that the firm, owing to the relative absence of effective competition, has a degree of market power vis-à-vis those patrons. If, in such a situation, the patrons own the firm, they can avoid not only the efficiency losses that result from setting prices above marginal cost, but also the larger private costs that such prices would impose on the patrons.

Ex post market power ("lock-in"). As Williamson has noted, problems of price or quality exploitation can arise *after* a person begins patronizing a firm even when the firm has a substantial number of competitors at the time of initial contracting.[13] These problems appear where the patron must make substantial transaction-specific investments[14] upon entering into the transactional relationship and where complexity requires that some elements of the transaction be left unspecified initially and dealt with according to experience. Once such a transactional relationship has

13 See note 1, Williamson, Chapter 2.
14 That is, investments whose value cannot be fully recouped if the transactional relationship with the firm is broken.

been entered into, the patron becomes locked in to a degree, losing the option of costless exit in case the firm seeks to renegotiate the terms of the transaction in its favor as events unfold. Ownership of the firm by the patron reduces the incentives for opportunistic behavior of this sort. This consideration is now widely recognized as an important incentive for vertical integration between individual firms.[15] It can also help explain why ownership is extended to whole classes of patrons.

Asymmetric information. Finally, contracting can also be costly when a firm has significantly better information than its patrons concerning the quality of performance that the firm offers or renders. Ownership by the patrons reduces the incentive for the firm to exploit such an information advantage.

Who owns whom? In the preceding discussion, I have been speaking of mitigating the costs of market contracting by having the patrons own the firm. Sometimes those costs could also be avoided by having the firm own its patrons. Where there is only one patron involved, and where that patron is itself a firm, there is frequently no distinction between these two forms of vertical integration. But, as Grossman and Hart have emphasized, the costs and benefits of ownership are sometimes asymmetric between the parties to a transaction; if the parties are to be integrated, one party may be the less costly owner. This is often the case in the situations of principal interest here, where multiple patrons are involved and where the patrons are sometimes individuals: Ownership of the patrons by the firm may be costly or infeasible where the reverse is not true. This is obviously the case when the patrons are individuals – customers or workers, for example – rather than firms; legal prohibitions on personal servitude as well as a variety of practical contracting problems then bar the firm from establishing effective ownership (and especially control) of its patrons. But ownership of the patrons by the firm may also be impractical even where the patrons are themselves firms. Consider, for example, the common case of wholesale cooperatives owned by the retail stores to which they sell. Ownership of the stores by the wholesaler may lead to loss of the strong incentives for efficient operation that exist when the stores are owned by their local managers, while the reverse is not true.[16]

---

15 See note 1, Williamson, Chapters 4 and 5; note 2 Klein, Crawford, and Alchian.
16 The essence of the problem is – as Grossman and Hart, note 8, describe – that even when two parties have been vertically integrated some decisions must be left to the discretion of the original parties themselves. A local retail store manager's actions,

D   *Costs of ownership*

As already emphasized, the ownership relationship itself can involve substantial costs. The most significant of these costs can be grouped conveniently under three headings.

Monitoring. If a given class of patrons is to exercise effective control over the management of a firm, they must incur the cost of (1) becoming informed about the operations of the firm, (2) communicating among themselves for the purpose of exchanging information and making decisions, and (3) bringing their decisions to bear on the firm's management.[17] These costs, which Jensen and Meckling have labeled "monitoring" costs,[18] can vary widely among different classes of patrons. They are most likely to be small, relative to the value of the patrons' transactions with the firm, where, for example, the patrons involved are relatively few in number, reside in geographic propinquity to each other and the firm, and transact regularly and repeatedly with the firm over

for example, cannot be entirely controlled by the wholesaler even if the wholesaler owns the store; the manager necessarily retains some discretion over her own effort. Costs may be better internalized, therefore, if the manager is given (shared) ownership of the wholesaler, so that the residual returns from her personal actions, and control over those actions, are both left largely in her own hands.

17 It will be taken for granted here that a firm of any substantial size and complexity needs a hierarchical form of organization for decision making, which means that the firm must have a single locus of executive power with substantial discretion and authority. This means that, where ownership of the firm is shared among a large class of patrons, highly participatory forms of decision making will not be efficient. Rather, in such situations, control will generally be exercised by the firm's owners indirectly through election of the firm's directors; direct participation in decision making will be confined to approval of major structural changes, such as merger and dissolution.

   Williamson, note 1, Chapter 9, presents a convincing analysis of the advantages of hierarchical decision making in the context of a discussion of worker management. He there argues for the superiority, in efficiency terms, of the capitalist firm with a strong central management over a highly participatory ("communal") form of worker ownership. By itself, however, Williamson's analysis simply shows the virtues of centralized management; it does not tell us which class of patrons – workers, or lenders of capital (or yet some other group of patrons) – can most effectively exercise the right to elect that management. See Louis Putterman, On Some Recent Explanations of Why Capital Hires Labor, *Economic Inquiry* 22:171 (1984); Raymond Russell, Employee Ownership and Employee Governance, *Journal of Economic Behavior and Organization* 6:217 (1985); and Oliver Williamson, Employee Ownership and Internal Governance: A Perspective, *Journal of Economic Behavior and Organization* 6:243 (1985).

18 Michael Jensen and William Meckling, Theory of the Firm: Managerial Behavior, Agency Costs and Ownership Structure, *Journal of Financial Economics* 3:305 (1976).

a prolonged period of time[19] for amounts that are a significant fraction of their budget.

To the extent that the owners of the firm fail to exercise effective control over its managers, the managers are free to engage in self-dealing transactions and exhibit slack performance. As the literature on agency costs has emphasized, the costs from such managerial opportunism are sometimes smaller than the costs of effective monitoring, and thus it may be efficient for the owners to bear these costs rather than to seek to impose discipline on the firm's managers.[20]

An equally important but less familiar point is that for a given class of patrons the costs of managerial opportunism may be worth bearing as an alternative to having no ownership at all. That is, just because a given class of patrons cannot monitor effectively, and thus cannot exercise much control beyond that which they would have simply by virtue of market transactions with the firm, it does not follow that there is no substantial gain to those patrons from having ownership of the firm. Or, put differently, it may be efficient to assign ownership to a given class of patrons even where, for those patrons, voice adds little to exit in the way of control.[21] By virtue of having ownership, the patrons in question are assured that there is no *other* group of owners to whom management is responsive. It is one thing to deal with managers who are nominally your agents but serve you poorly; it is another to transact with managers who are actively serving owners with an interest clearly adverse to yours. Although managers may be able to appropriate, in the form of cash or perquisites, some of the potential gains from exploiting patrons, their ability to do this is limited. The self-dealing transactions necessary for managers to divert to themselves a significant fraction of the potential residual in a large firm will usually be difficult to conceal, and can generally be explicitly proscribed by contract or by law, thus exposing the managers to a variety of moral, contractual, tort, and criminal sanctions.[22] This is in contrast to the situation of owners, who can easily and

19 The importance of the frequency of transacting in making "unified governance" – essentially ownership – an efficient form for transactional relationships has been emphasized by Williamson, note 1, Chapter 3.
20 See note 18, Jensen and Meckling.
21 Cf. Albert Hirschman, *Exit, Voice and Loyalty* (1970).
22 There is, however, one very costly managerial perquisite that may not be easy to proscribe or detect – namely, excessive retention of earnings. Retentions can benefit managers by creating a financial buffer against adversity and by increasing the size of the firm and thus the scope of the empire that they manage. To the extent that the returns from these retentions are below their opportunity cost, or simply cannot be recovered by the current owners of the firm, whatever their rate of return to the firm, the owners stand to lose. The excessive financial reserves accumulated by mutual

lawfully distribute to themselves directly any net earnings that accrue to the firm from exploiting patrons. Owners thus have a much stronger incentive to engage in such exploitation than do managers who are simply pursuing their own self-interest.

To be sure, while legal, contractual, and moral constraints may effectively prevent most managers from taking grossly excessive compensation from the firm, they will not necessarily insure that managers work hard and make effective decisions. Thus, if the firm's owner–patrons are poor monitors, managers might nevertheless exploit them severely and then simply waste the resulting earnings through organizational slack – in effect extracting the potential gains in the form of an easy life. But, while theory and empiricism on this issue both remain in flux, there is reason to believe that the incentive and opportunity for managers to engage in substantial waste in this fashion may be distinctly limited. For example, the desire of managers to keep and enhance their jobs, or to get another job in the future,[23] probably serves as an important check on such behavior.[24] Consequently, the fact that the firm's nominal owners are unable to exercise effective control may result in only a modest amount of organizational slack.[25] Indeed, large groups of firms that have prospered over long periods of time in competitive environments without any effective exercise of control by owners whatever – and even without any owners.[26]

In summary, if all else is equal, then the patrons who are the lowest-cost monitors are the most efficient owners. But all else is often not

insurance companies seem to be a conspicuous case in point. See John Hetherington, Fact v. Fiction: Who Owns Mutual Insurance Companies, *Wisconsin Law Review* 1969:1068 (1969). This is arguably a problem in investor-owned firms as well. See Michael Jensen, Agency Costs of Free Cash Flow, Corporate Finance, and Takeovers, *American Economic Review* 76:323 (1986).

23 Incentive pay schemes, such as stock options, can also help align managers' interests with those of owners. But if the owners are not in direct control, they are presumably in a poor position to design the compensation mechanism.

24 For a thoughtful survey of the general issue see Bengt Holmstrom and Jean Tirole, The Theory of the Firm, in Richard Schmalensee and Robert Willig, eds., *Handbook of Industrial Organization* (forthcoming).

25 This is an important point that is often neglected in the literature on corporate control, with its emphasis on the incentives for efficient management that accompany receipt of residual earnings. See, e.g., note 18, Jensen and Meckling; also Michael Jensen and Eugene Fama, Separation of Ownership and Control, *Journal of Law and Economics* 26:301 (1983) (emphasizing that a board with outside directors may exercise a significant check on managerial discretion even in nonprofit firms in which the directors are not in the service of owners).

26 See, in particular, the discussion of mutual life insurance companies and nonprofits below.

equal; sometimes a class of patrons who face high costs of monitoring also face unusually high costs of market contracting (owing, for example, to severe problems of asymmetric information). Those patrons may then be efficient owners, in spite of their high monitoring costs. The costs of market contracting that are avoided by giving such patrons formal ownership rights may well outweigh any accompanying increase in the costs of managerial opportunism. This was apparently the case with depositor-owned life insurance companies in the middle of the nineteenth century, and it is arguably true of most large investor-owned corporations today.

In the discussion that follows, the term "monitoring costs" will be used to denote the sum of (1) the costs actually incurred by the owners in monitoring management and (2) the costs of managerial opportunism that result from the failure to monitor perfectly. This is essentially equivalent to Jensen and Meckling's "agency costs"; the term "monitoring costs" is used here simply to focus attention on the factor that determines the upper bound of these costs, namely the costs that the firm's nominal owners would incur if they were to oversee management effectively.[27]

Collective decision making. When ownership of a firm is shared among a class of patrons, a method for collective decision making must be devised. Most commonly a voting mechanism of some sort is employed, with votes weighted by volume of patronage, although some cooperatives adhere to a one member–one vote scheme.

As methods for aggregating the preferences of a group of patrons, such collective choice mechanisms often involve substantial costs in comparison to market contracting. Little attention has been devoted to these costs in the literature on corporate control and the economics of organizational form.[28] Nevertheless, they appear to be crucial in determining the efficiency of alternative assignments of ownership. These costs might, to be sure, simply be included as part of the monitoring costs discussed above. They appear to be of such special importance in

27 See note 18; Jensen and Meckling include a third element, "bonding expenditures by the agent," in their definition of agency costs. These bonding costs are not distinguished here from the other costs undertaken to control the managers.

28 A significant exception are Jensen and Meckling, note 3, who refer to this issue as "the control problem." They do not analyze the issue in detail, observing simply that "no one today has a viable theory of . . . political processes" (pp. 488–9), and suggesting that the problem of reconciling diverging interests may be an important obstacle to worker-managed firms. They also make the important observation, which will be reaffirmed below, that one of the most important sources of the efficiency of investor-owned firms may be the limited opportunity they afford for advantaging one group of owners at the expense of another (p. 494).

determining the patterns of ownership actually observed, however, that they call for separate treatment.

Although a variety of factors influence the magnitude of these costs, a fundamental consideration is the extent to which the patron-owners have divergent interests concerning the conduct of the firm's affairs. Where the patrons involved all have essentially identical interests – for example, where they all transact with the firm under similar circumstances for similar quantities of a single homogeneous commodity, as in the case of the farmers' cheese cooperative described above – the costs associated with collective decision making are naturally small. Absent such circumstances, however, these costs may be large relative to those of market transactions. The costs can come in several different forms.

To begin with, even if no patron acts strategically, such processes may yield decisions that are collectively inefficient in the sense that they do not maximize aggregate patron surplus. Thus, if the preferences of the median voter are not those of the mean, a majority voting mechanism may yield decisions that are not only inefficient but inferior, from a welfare standpoint, to those that would be reached if the patrons simply contracted as individuals with a profit-maximizing firm.[29] A more serious version of this problem can arise if one group of patrons self-consciously seeks to use the collective choice mechanism to exploit another group – for example, by raising prices or cutting quality for services consumed primarily by the disfavored group. If becoming an owner requires making a transaction-specific investment that is at risk (such as a contribution of capital that is not easily recouped when the patron withdraws from membership in the firm), then the disfavored group could be much worse off as owners than if they dealt with the firm simply through market contracting.[30]

Further, the process of collective decision making itself can have high transaction costs in the face of heterogeneous interests. Because there is a strong incentive for individuals to form coalitions to shift benefits in their direction, efforts to form and break such coalitions may consume substantial effort.

The essential distinction between ownership and market contracting here is that, when patrons deal with the firm simply through market

---

29 Kenneth Shepsle and Barry Weingast, Political Solutions to Market Problems, *Journal of Political Economy* 78:471 (1984).

30 For example, consider purchasing a top-floor apartment in a four-floor cooperative apartment building. Can one count on the occupants of the first three floors to support maintenance of the elevator or the roof?

contracting, they have no leverage over firm policy beyond the threat of withdrawing their individual patronage. With a collective decision-making mechanism, by contrast, subgroups of patrons with particular interests can often achieve disproportionate influence. Moreover, this problem is likely to be accentuated if, as is often the case, some patrons are better situated to participate effectively in collective decision making than others – for example, because of geographic accessibility to the firm, low opportunity cost of time, or special expertise.

On the other hand, even where patrons diverge considerably in interest, the costs associated with collective decision making may be low if there is some simple and salient criterion for balancing their interests. For example, where it is easy to account separately for the net benefits bestowed on the firm by each individual patron, dividing up net returns according to such an accounting is likely to be both natural and uncontroversial even if the nature and the volume of the transactions with individual patrons differ substantially. The empirical literature indicates strongly, however, that, in the absence of such a clear focal point for decisions, agreement may take a long time to reach and often in fact is never reached.[31]

There are, to be sure, also some potential *advantages* to collective decision making over market transactions. As Hirschman has pointed out, there are many circumstances in which voice can be more effective than exit as a method of communicating patron preferences to the management of a firm.[32] The evidence suggests strongly, however, that collective decision making is more costly than markets in this respect in cases of even modest heterogeneity of interest among the class of patrons in question. For example, there are very few large firms in which ownership is shared among more than one class of patrons, such as customers and suppliers, or investors and workers. The conspicuous exceptions –

---

31 One striking example is the extreme difficulty in organizing multiple owners of drilling rights in a common oil pool to act collectively, even when the potential efficiency gains are very large and the number of owners is relatively small. See Gary Libecap and Steven Wiggins, Contractual Responses to the Common Pool, *American Economic Review* 74:87 (1984).

   Elizabeth Hoffman and Matthew Spitzer, Experimental Tests of the Coase Theorem with Large Bargaining Groups, *Journal of Legal Studies* 15:149 (1986), report results in which even groups with as many as nineteen persons experienced little difficulty in agreeing collectively to contract on efficient terms with an opposing individual or group. In these experiments, however, all of the individuals within a given group faced essentially identical payoffs; consequently, the results do not provide much insight into situations in which interests differ significantly among the individuals involved.

32 See note 21, Hirschman.

such as German codetermination – have generally been imposed by law, and they apparently do not involve much true sharing of control.[33]

Risk bearing. The preceding discussion has focused on the costs associated with the first element of ownership: the exercise of control. But costs are also associated with the second element of ownership: the receipt of compensation in the form of residual earnings. Most conspicuous among these is the cost of bearing the risk of the enterprise and is typically reflected in residual earnings. One class of a firm's patrons may be in a much better position than others to bear such risk, for example, through diversification. Assigning ownership to those patrons can then bring important economies.

This is a familiar explanation for the prevalence of investor-owned firms. It is not true, however, that lenders of capital are the only low-cost risk bearers. For example, consumers can also be in a good position to bear the risks of enterprise, particularly where the goods or services involved make up a small fraction of the consumers' budget or where the consumers are themselves firms that can pass the risk on to customers of their own who in turn are good risk bearers.

Another important consideration here, and one that has been little remarked upon, is that market contracting with a given class of patrons itself sometimes *creates* a substantial degree of risk that can be avoided by assigning ownership to those patrons. This is particularly likely to be the case where the patrons must enter into a long-term relationship with the firm, so that the terms of the contract between them become a gamble on future contingencies.

E.   Applying the calculus

Any assignment of ownership involves important trade-offs between the costs of market contracting and the costs of ownership. The efficient assignment of ownership, to repeat, is that which minimizes the sum of such costs among all the patrons of the firm.

---

33 The German Codetermination Act of 1976 in essence gives shareholder representatives on the board of directors a casting vote in cases of impasse between labor and shareholder representatives. For a brief description, see Jan Svejnar, West German Codetermination, in Frank H. Stephen, ed., *The Performance of Labour-Managed Firms* (1982), p. 214. It seems plausible that the most important efficiency advantage of codetermination lies simply in giving worker representatives access to inside information, and thus reducing the possibilities for strategic or opportunistic behavior by management toward workers. See Masahiko Aoki, *The Cooperative Game Theory of the Firm* (1984), p. 167.

In the discussion that follows I explore the particular costs of ownership and of market contracting that affect various classes of patrons in different industries, and I seek to explain the patterns of ownership in terms of those costs. Although the six categories of costs set out above do not comprehend all the transactional efficiency considerations relevant to ownership, they usefully organize those that appear most important. Sometimes, to be sure, public subsidies or legal constraints also influence organizational form, and these will be acknowledged where they seem important.[34] Other considerations – such as the "horizon problem"[35] – that have been emphasized by other authors but do not seem fundamental in determining which forms of ownership survive, will be discussed in the context of particular industries that illustrate the issues involved.

The simple analytic framework outlined here, of course, does not provide a precise calculus for determining the efficient assignment of ownership in any given industry. Rather, its principal object is simply to help in asking the right questions. More particularly, by viewing the prevailing ownership pattern in different industries with this framework in mind, we can gain a much stronger appreciation for the relative magnitudes of the various costs associated with both market contracting and ownership.

III   Investor-owned firms

Although many of the efficiencies of investor-owned firms are familiar, it is useful to review them in terms of the framework developed above.

A   Costs of market contracting

Because capital markets today are highly competitive, market power is rarely an incentive for lenders of capital to become owners of a firm to which they lend. Rather, problems of asymmetric information and lock-in provide the strongest incentive for assigning ownership to investors.

---

34 For efforts to determine empirically the relative efficiency of cooperative and investor-owned firms in industries in which cooperatives benefit from subsidies, see Henry Hansmann, The Law and Economics of Cooperative and Condominium Housing (Working Paper No. 57, Center for Studies in Law, Economics, and Public Policy, Yale Law School [1987]), and Philip Porter and Gerald Scully, Economic Efficiency in Cooperatives, *Journal of Law and Economics* 30:489 (1987). (The latter authors, however, seem to impute to cooperatives in general some characteristics that may be induced by the tax laws.)

35 See note 66.

In theory a firm could borrow 100 percent of the capital it needs, with the owners of the firm – whether they be another class of the firm's patrons, or third parties who do not otherwise transact with the firm – investing no capital themselves. And if, in practice, the owners could be constrained by the terms of the loan contract to devote the borrowed funds only to the most efficient projects, and to take for themselves only a specified rate of compensation until the loan had been repaid, this approach would be workable. But it is extremely difficult to write and enforce such a contract. And, without such contractual terms, the owners have an incentive to behave opportunistically, distributing to themselves dividends (or perquisites) that are unjustified by the firm's earnings or (what is harder to police) investing the proceeds of the loan in high-risk projects whose gains will go disproportionately to the owners and whose losses will fall disproportionately on the lenders.[36]

If the loan proceeds are invested in assets that are not organization-specific, these problems can be largely avoided by giving the lenders a lien on the assets. Yet, as other scholars have emphasized, where the loan proceeds are in some part invested in organization-specific assets – and this will be the usual case – this solution is unavailable.[37]

These problems of asymmetric information are substantially magnified by lock-in. If lenders could withdraw their investments from the firm at will, there would be a substantial check on the possibilities for managerial opportunism. But firms typically must undertake long-term investments, and these require long-term financing. Short-term borrowing not only involves the transaction costs of continuous refinancing but, more importantly, threatens inefficient runs on the firm's assets by its creditors.

As a consequence, the costs of managerial opportunism can often be significantly reduced only by having the lenders themselves, or some subset of them, own the firm.

B   Costs of ownership

Diversification of risk is of course a conspicuous advantage of investor ownership. Another great strength of investor-owned firms is the fact

---

36 This problem has been well recognized in the context of determining debt–equity ratios for investor-owned firms. See Jensen and Meckling, note 18.

37 See note 2; Klein, Crawford, and Alchian, p. 321, seem to be the first to note clearly that problems of opportunistic expropriation of firm-specific assets are an important reason "why the owners of the firm (the residual claimants) are generally also the major capitalists of the firm."

that the owners generally share a single well-defined objective: to maximize the net present value of the firm's earnings per dollar invested.
To be sure, differences in tax status or risk preference may lead investors
to differ about the most appropriate financial policy for the firm. But
even these differences can be eliminated to some extent if investors sort
themselves among firms.[38]

The great liability of investor-owned firms, on the other hand, is that
investors frequently are in a poor position to engage in meaningful
supervision of the firm's management – particularly where, in order to
obtain access to a large pool of capital and to diversify risk, the firm's
capital is drawn from a numerous group of relatively small investors. It
is commonly argued that the market for corporate control – more precisely, the threat of takeover by a concentrated group of large investors
who are in a position to act effectively – is an effective surrogate for
the direct exercise of oversight and control by the firm's current owners
in keeping corporate management in line. But, whether or not this view
has some validity as a description of current reality,[39] the existence of
the market for corporate control seems both inadequate and unnecessary
to explain the great success of large business corporations with broadly
dispersed share ownership. The market for corporate control has been
highly active only for the past decade or two. Prior to that, hostile
takeovers were rare, possibly because the managerial, financial, and
legal innovations necessary to effect them were not well developed.[40]
Yet widely held business corporations have been commonplace for the
past century.

We might, therefore, draw another conclusion from the success of
such corporations: Direct exercise of oversight and control by owners
is not of decisive importance for the efficient conduct of enterprise; it
is often worth trading off in favor of the other cost factors outlined
above.[41] Under this view, much of the protection that the investors in
a widely held investor-owned firm have from opportunistic behavior on
the part of the firm derives simply from the absence of a class of owners

---

38 Cf. Harry DeAngelo, Competition and Unanimity, *American Economic Review* 71:18
(1981).
39 See Michael Jensen and Richard Ruback, The Market for Corporate Control: The
Scientific Evidence, *Journal of Financial Economics* 11:5 (1983).
40 See, e.g., note 1 Williamson, p. 321.
41 This is arguably supported by the findings of Harold Demsetz and Kenneth Lehn, The
Structure of Corporate Ownership: Causes and Consequences, *Journal of Political
Economy* 93:1155 (1985), who report no empirical correlation between ownership
concentration and profitability of investor-owned firms.

with interests contrary to theirs.[42] But, as suggested earlier, this may be important protection, and worth the costs of some managerial slack.

IV   Customer-owned retail, wholesale, and supply firms

A   Retailers of consumer goods

In the popular mind, customer-owned firms are commonly exemplified by retail stores organized as consumer cooperatives. Yet consumer cooperatives have an almost negligible share of the market for nearly all ordinary retail items, amounting to only 0.25 percent of the overall consumer goods market.[43]

The small market share held by retail cooperatives is understandable in terms of the cost considerations outlined above. The costs of customer ownership for many consumer goods and services are high: The customers of any given retail firm are commonly so numerous, transitory, and dispersed that organizing them effectively would be excessively difficult. And for those goods for which the costs of customer ownership might be manageable – for example, items such as food and clothing that comprise a significant share of consumer budgets – the costs of market contracting are typically low: Retail markets for such items are sufficiently competitive to keep prices close to cost, and the goods and services themselves are sufficiently simple or standardized, or are purchased so repetitively, that asymmetric information about quality is not a serious problem.

The single retail market in which consumer cooperatives have established significant market share is the market for books, where cooperatives account for nearly 10 percent of all sales.[44] This large market share reflects the prevalence of cooperative book stores on university campuses, where a significant fraction of the nation's books are sold. The principal incentive for adopting the cooperative form here is apparently market power in the textbook market; there is usually room for only one important seller of textbooks on a campus, evidently be-

---

42 In investor-owned firms the problem of managerial opportunism may also be mitigated by the fact that, when it comes to investment policy, there is good reason to believe that – contrary to the behavior to be expected of owners who are not investors – the managers will be too conservative rather than too speculative, since their own human capital is on the line if the firm goes bankrupt. See, e.g., Yakov Amihud and Baruch Lev, Risk Reduction as a Managerial Motive for Conglomerate Mergers, *Bell Journal of Economics* 12:605 (1981).

43 Richard Heflebower, *Cooperatives and Mutuals in the Market System* (1980), p. 4.

44 Ibid., p. 124.

cause of the substantial economies in having a single organization assemble information about the texts to be assigned for courses and the projected class enrollments. The costs of ownership are also favorable: The amounts spent on books are a significant fraction of a student's budget; students typically continue to patronize the same store for four years or so; student demand is relatively homogeneous; and students can be easily organized through their common affiliation with the university.

B   Wholesale and supply firms

While consumer-owned retail stores are rare, wholesale and supply firms that are owned by the retailers or other businesses to which they sell are common. For example, although consumer cooperatives constitute less than .05 percent of the retail market for groceries,[45] retailer-owned wholesale cooperatives in 1985 accounted for 14 percent of all groceries distributed at the wholesale level, and 31 percent of the market if we exclude internal distribution within chains having integrated wholesale and retail operations.[46] Retailer-owned wholesale cooperatives are even more important in hardware, where they have 50 percent of the market.[47] Bakeries commonly obtain their supplies from firms that they own as cooperatives.[48] And the largest international news service, Associated Press, is cooperatively owned by the thousands of newspapers and broadcasting stations it serves.

Costs of market contracting. Market power appears to provide the principal incentive for customer ownership in many of these cases. The grocery business, for example, is highly competitive at the retail level. If independent stores are to compete with the large chains, which maintain their own wholesale distribution systems, they cannot afford to pay pure profits to a wholesaler. Yet economies of scale at the wholesale level generally leave room for at most a few firms to serve the independent retailers in a given area, so that the wholesalers have a degree of market power. Consequently, there is an incentive for retailers to avoid price exploitation by owning the wholesaler that serves them. The Associated Press is another obvious example: Economies of scale have led to a market occupied by only two substantial news services in the

45 Ibid., p. 4.
46 *Progressive Grocer* 65:8 (April 1986).
47 Wholesaling: A Leaner, Meaner Industry, *Hardware Age* (June 1984), pp. 36, 37.
48 See note 43, Heflebower, pp. 114–15.

United States, United Press International and Associated Press, the former investor-owned and the latter a cooperative.

Another source of the market power that provides the impetus for customer ownership derives from the use of a common brand name for marketing purposes. Retailers can achieve considerable economies in packaging and advertising through collective use of a single logo or insignia by which their stores and their products are identified. For example, most members of the largest bakery supply cooperative market bread under the common name "Sunbeam."[49] Similarly, independent hardware stores belonging to the same wholesale cooperative generally use a common store name and insignia, and also market products that bear that name; True Value and Ace Hardware are familiar examples.[50]

Of course, the mere existence of economies from use of a common brand name does not mean that cooperative ownership of the wholesaler possessing that brand name is efficient. An investor-owned wholesaler could also license a brand name to the retailers purchasing their supplies from it, as in the typical franchise arrangement, and this form of organization is in fact common in wholesaling.[51] But there is a lock-in problem, since the retailer can incur substantial costs from loss of the local goodwill it has built up if it changes its brand name affiliation.[52] Collective ownership of the franchiser by the retailers obviates this difficulty.

Costs of ownership. Costs of ownership are also strongly conducive to customer ownership here. A retail grocery or hardware store, for example, generally purchases a significant fraction of its goods from a single wholesaler with which it transacts continuously for years. Thus, the store is in a position to oversee the affairs of the wholesaler without incurring substantial costs beyond those it would incur under market contracting. Moreover, the supply business does not require large amounts of organization-specific capital: Warehouses are general-purpose structures, and inventory can usually be liquidated without

---

49 Ibid.

50 See James Cory, Dealer-Owned Wholesalers: What's Next?, *Hardware Age* (October 1983), p. 52.

51 IGA is an example in the grocery business. Interestingly, IGA is itself a *wholesaler's* cooperative owned by its twenty-two affiliated wholesalers. Ronald Tanner, Sixty Years of IGA: A Saga of American Independence, *Progressive Grocer* 65:25 (1986).

52 The economies of a common brand name presumably also help to explain the substantial economies of scale for wholesalers, and the consequent small number of competitors, that were noted above.

substantial losses. Consequently, risk bearing and liquidity constraints are not an important obstacle to customer ownership.

Finally, since retail hardware stores, or grocery stores, generally stock similar arrays of merchandise, their interests with respect to the wholesaler are reasonably homogeneous.

C   Farm supplies

Farm supply cooperatives are a particularly prominent form of customer-owned supply firm. In 1983 there were roughly 2,200 such firms, which together accounted for 27 percent of the overall market for farm supplies – up from 23 percent a decade earlier. The cooperatives are particularly important in supplying petroleum products (34% of the market), feed (23%), fertilizer (18%), and farm chemicals such as pesticides (8%).[53]

The large role of cooperatives in farm supplies can be explained by much the same considerations that are found in the case of retailer-owned wholesale cooperatives: The costs of market contracting are moderately high (owing to market power and, in some cases, asymmetric information about quality[54]), and the costs of organizing farmers for effective ownership are relatively low (owing to the homogeneity of the commodities involved, the geographic concentration of farmers, and the fact that farmers typically patronize the same firm continuously over many years).

Most farm supply cooperatives serve only a local area of one or several counties, and are controlled directly by their farmer–members. Often these local cooperatives are federated into much larger regional cooperatives, which have the local cooperatives as members and which supply many of the goods sold by the local cooperatives. And the regional cooperatives, in turn, are sometimes federated into national cooperatives, some of which are large enough to appear among the *Fortune* 500 listing of the largest U.S. industrial corporations. Through this federated structure, reasonably effective patron control is evidently maintained even in the national cooperatives.

The regional and national cooperatives have in many areas integrated upstream into manufacturing, and these operations sometimes require substantial capital. For example, farm petroleum cooperatives own, singly or jointly, refineries that provide roughly half their supplies, oil wells that produce close to 90 percent of the refineries' crude oil input, and

---

53 U.S. Department of Agriculture, Agricultural Cooperative Service, *Farmer Cooperative Statistics 1983*, pp. 10, 26.
54 Heflebower, note 43, Chapters 6 and 7.

pipelines that transport most of the oil from the cooperatives' wells to their refineries.[55] This indicates that, when conditions are favorable, relatively capital-intensive industries can be operated successfully as consumer cooperatives. Note, however, that when members of a co-operative have large capital investments in the firm, substantial conflicts of interest among groups of members can arise if one group supplies a disproportionate amount of the capital – since the apportionment of earnings between capital dividends and patronage dividends, which is necessarily a matter of judgment, can then be a subject of dispute. It is presumably for this reason that the more capital-intensive cooperatives have adopted elaborate schemes to keep members' capital investments proportional to their patronage.[56]

D   Costs of contracting versus costs of ownership

The large market share obtained by customer-owned firms in wholesale and supply industries provides important perspective on the relative importance of the cost factors outlined earlier.

What is most striking about these industries is that the degree of product market failure that characterizes them, and that provides the impetus for customer ownership, appears relatively small. Many other industries presumably exhibit similar degrees of imperfection in their product markets. The distinguishing feature that has led to widespread development of customer ownership in the industries at hand, rather, seems to be that the costs of customer ownership are uncommonly low. Evidently even modest degrees of product market imperfection make it efficient to abandon investor ownership in favor of customer ownership where the customers are in a good position to exercise effective control. To be sure, farm cooperatives have the benefit of favorable tax treatment, and this has presumably contributed to the cooperatives' market share. But farm cooperatives antedate these tax preferences, and the same preferences do not extend to the many wholesale and supply co-operatives found outside the agricultural sector.[57]

---

55 Heflebower, note 43, Chapter 7 (figures from 1969).
56 See Phillip F. Brown and David Volkin, *Equity Redemption Practices of Agricultural Cooperatives* (U.S.D.A. Farmer Cooperative Service Research Report No. 4, 1977), pp. 5, 8.
57 Nonfarm wholesale and supply cooperatives benefit from no subsidies or other special privileges other than the right to be taxed according to Subchapter T of the Internal Revenue Code, which essentially applies to them a single tax – rather than the over-lapping corporate and personal income taxes – somewhat along the lines of the tax treatment accorded partnerships and Subchapter S corporations. Since Subchapter T

V   Worker-owned firms

Worker-owned firms are the dominant form of organization in the service professions, such as law, accounting, investment banking, and management consulting. They are also relatively common in some other
service industries, such as taxicabs and trash collection.[58] Outside the
service sector, on the other hand, worker-owned firms are generally
isolated and often short-lived entities, competing in industries in which
investor-owned firms are clearly dominant. One of the few exceptions
is plywood manufacturing; roughly two dozen plywood firms in the
Pacific Northwest have long been operated, with considerable success,
as labor cooperatives.[59]

Much ink has been spilled in recent years on the subject of worker-
owned enterprise.[60] Nevertheless, a convincing explanation for the existing pattern of worker ownership has not been offered. That pattern,
and the strengths and weaknesses of worker ownership in general, become more understandable when viewed in terms of the framework
outlined in Section II.

A   Costs of contracting

Few firms have labor market power in the service industries in which
worker-owned firms are common. On the other hand, in many labor
markets there is some degree of lock-in; after an individual has worked
for a particular firm for a prolonged period of time, his or her skills are
often specialized to that firm. Moreover, workers and their families often
develop nonfungible personal ties to the community in which their workplace is located, thus enhancing the lock-in problem. This problem may

is available to producer and consumer cooperatives in all industries, it should not
directly affect the distribution of those forms across industries.

   Farm marketing and supply cooperatives have the further benefit of exemption
from the corporate-level tax on stock dividends and on certain forms of nonpatronage
income under I.R.C. sec. 521. Since, however, farm supply cooperatives rarely pay
stock dividends, it is not clear that this is an important reason why cooperatives are
unusually prominent in this industry.

58 On worker ownership in the latter two industries, see Raymond Russell, *Sharing
Ownership in the Workplace* (1985).
59 See Katrina Berman, *Worker-Owned Plywood Companies* (1967).
60 For surveys of the theoretical and empirical literature, see Avner Ben-Ner, Producer
Cooperatives: Why Do They Exist in Capitalist Economies?, in Walter Powell, ed.,
The Nonprofit Sector: A Research Handbook (1987), Chapter 24; Frederic Pryor, The
Economics of Production Cooperatives: A Reader's Guide, *Annals of Public and
Cooperative Economy* 54:133 (1983).

be a substantial cost of labor contracting in many industries, and the potential for its elimination presumably provides an important incentive for worker ownership in general. But in itself it fails to explain the existing pattern of worker ownership since, as workers go, service professionals are exceptionally mobile.

The third of the basic costs of market contracting – asymmetric information – could also provide an incentive for worker ownership. In this case, however, the information disadvantage runs in the opposite direction from the cases we have analyzed above: The principal problem is not that the individual patron cannot police the firm's behavior,[61] but rather the reverse. Where, as in the service professions, the employees are performing complex and highly skilled work that requires substantial autonomy and discretion, effective monitoring of employees may be difficult. Consequently, there is an incentive to integrate vertically to eliminate conflicts of interest between the firm and its workers, and thus give the workers stronger incentives for productivity. And since the firm cannot own the workers, the workers must own the firm.

An argument along these lines has been made before to explain the existence of worker-owned firms – most notably by Alchian and Demsetz.[62] Among other difficulties,[63] however, this theory is contradicted by the fact that workers appear much *less* difficult to monitor in those industries in which worker ownership is common than in other industries. Law firms, for example, routinely keep detailed accounts of each lawyer's individual productivity in terms of revenue to the firm – something that would be impossible for workers in most other types of firms.[64]

61 This is not to say that such problems do not exist. Indeed, as suggested in note 33, they may provide the best rationale for worker codetermination. As the codetermination example suggests, however, even minority worker representation on the board may be sufficient to eliminate the worst forms of opportunism from this source.

62 Alchian and Demsetz, Production, Information Costs, and Economic Organization, *American Economic Review* 62: 777 (1972). A similar argument appears, among other places, in Jensen and Meckling, note 3, and Russell, note 17.

63 In particular, where ownership of the firm is shared by a substantial number of workers, much of the incentive for opportunism would seem to remain: The individual worker will bear only a small fraction of the losses that the firm suffers from his or her shirking. On the other hand, the available evidence suggests that workers in worker-owned firms do not succumb much to this incentive to free-ride, and that worker ownership in fact has generally good consequences for productivity. See, e.g., note 59, Berman, chapter 12. This may be because mutual monitoring is fairly intense and effective under worker ownership, or because workers commonly respond more to the symbolism of ownership than to the actual incentives it creates.

64 As noted by Fred McChesney, Team Production, Monitoring, and Profit Sharing in Law Firms: An Alternative Hypothesis, *Journal of Legal Studies* 11:379 (1982).

In sum, there are probably substantial costs associated with labor contracting in nearly all industries, and these costs provide an incentive for worker ownership. Such costs seem unusually *low*, however, in industries where worker ownership is common. We must turn, therefore, to the costs of ownership to find an explanation for the existing pattern of worker ownership.

B Costs of ownership

Workers in nearly all industries are in a very good position, in comparison with other classes of patrons, to monitor the management of the firm. The majority of their income typically comes from their work relationship with the firm; they are in daily contact with the firm's operations, and knowledgeable about some aspects of them; and they are easily organized for collective decision making. This is not to imply, of course, that the typical shop-floor worker necessarily knows much about the firm's marketing problems or capital investment program. Rather, it is only to say that his or her opportunity and incentive to gain and use such information (or to locate, elect, and hold accountable representatives who will) is generally stronger than that of, say, the firm's customers or remote investors.

On the other hand, costs of risk bearing are often unfavorable to worker ownership. In discussing investor-owned firms, we noted that there are strong transaction-cost reasons for having the owners of the firm supply a substantial fraction of the capital needed to finance firm-specific assets. Yet if workers invest heavily in the firm for which they work, then their human capital and their savings, taken together, will be very poorly diversified – a problem with worker ownership that has frequently been noted.[65] It is not surprising, then, that those industries in which such firms are best established, such as law and accounting, are characterized by low amounts of organization-specific capital per worker.[66] Yet there are many service industries, such as retailing, hotel

McChesney's alternative hypothesis, that worker ownership provides a means for rewarding the promotional efforts of a firm's workers, is also unpersuasive, however.

65 See, e.g., James Meade, The Theory of Labour-Managed Firms and of Profit Sharing, *Economic Journal* 82:402 (1972); Jensen and Meckling, note 3.

66 Jensen and Meckling, note 3, argue that a major inefficiency of worker-managed firms lies in what they term "the horizon problem." By this they mean that when workers leave the firm they lose their share of the value of any capital that has been accumulated by the firm, and thus have insufficient incentive to invest in projects with long payback periods. Their analysis is confused by their assumption that it is, for unstated reasons, commonly impossible to arrange for the cooperators to redeem their equity share in

and restaurant services, and the construction trades, that are highly labor-intensive but are nevertheless populated largely with investor-owned firms.

To be sure, risk bearing might also appear to be a comparative liability for worker-managed firms even in labor-intensive industry. Since workers generally cannot diversify their source of income by working for more than one firm at a time, it would seem advantageous to have the firm owned by investors, who would provide workers with job security and a contractually fixed wage.[67] But, presumably because of the difficulty of writing workable long-term employment contracts, workers in fact generally bear substantial risk – in the form of layoffs – even in investor-owned firms.[68] Consequently, the risk-bearing features of worker ownership seem unlikely to be the reason it is so rare.

Rather, the truly striking feature that seems common to virtually all well-established worker-owned firms, and that seems most clearly to divide these firms from those that are investor-owned, is that there is strong homogeneity of interest among the workers involved. In particular, what seems to be important is homogeneity of jobs and homogeneity of skills: Labor cooperatives appear to work best where all of the workers who are also members of the cooperative perform essentially identical tasks within the firm.

Evidence for the importance of job homogeneity is impressive. For example, the partners in law firms all have similar skills and perform similar tasks. For the most part, the partners handle clients on their own or in small groups; there is relatively little vertical division of labor or hierarchy among the partners in the firm. Further, the trial periods

the firm upon leaving or to sell it to a new worker. (A similar analysis also appears in Eirik Furubotn, The Long-Run Analysis of the Labor-Managed Firm: An Alternative Interpretation, *American Economic Review* 66:104 (1976).) In fact, schemes of the latter sort are not only feasible but frequently employed; in the Pacific Coast plywood cooperatives, for example, departing workers sell their position in the firm to new workers at fair market value. Berman, note 59. (Fama and Jensen, note 4, themselves recognize such schemes in the context of partnerships of professionals.) Indeed, what is most interesting is that cooperatives do not employ such schemes more extensively even where they are clearly practicable. Thus, farm-supply cooperatives, which are relatively capital intensive, typically redeem capital investments only at book value. The absence of more generous redemption plans suggests that, even without them, the horizon problem may not in fact be particularly important in firms in which membership commonly extends over many years.

67 As emphasized in the implicit contracts literature. See Sherwin Rosen, Implicit Contracts: A Survey, *Journal of Economic Literature* 23:1144 (1985).

68 Unionization may also be a factor here. See James Medoff, Layoffs and Alternatives Under Trade Unions in U.S. Manufacturing, *American Economic Review* 69:380 (1979).

of roughly six years that young lawyers serve in law firms before being considered for partnership serve to permit the existing partners to select others to join them who are of like ability – and like temperament, for that matter. And much the same is true of other types of professional partnerships.

It is, in fact, striking that many large and highly successful law firms follow a practice of dividing income among partners strictly on the basis of number of years with the firm: All partners of a given length of tenure receive the same share.[69] Such a practice is presumably adopted in significant part because it reduces considerably the costs of decision making.[70] It is possible, however, only in a firm in which all owners make roughly equal contributions.

The plywood cooperatives, similarly, typically follow a rigid principle of equal pay for all worker–owners. The manager of the firm often is not a member of the cooperative, but rather is hired by the worker–owners. Worker–owners are generally capable of undertaking any job in the plant other than that of manager, since only semiskilled labor is involved. Job assignments are made according to a bid system, with more senior workers generally given preference, and there is much rotation among jobs.[71] Such a system reinforces the equal pay rule and reduces conflicts of interest among workers: Where all workers do, or will ultimately do, the same jobs, they will be affected similarly by any decision made by the firm.[72]

To the extent that workers in worker-owned firms perform different jobs, it seems to be important to the viability of the firm that the returns to those jobs be separable. The reason, evidently, is that this permits a differential division of the firm's earnings with a minimum of friction. Thus, some partners in law firms work longer hours, have greater skills, or bring in more new clients than others. Where such disparities are substantial, law firms sometimes use productivity-based formulas for dividing up earnings. Such formulas are feasible only where the returns

---

69 See Ronald Gilson and Robert Mnookin, Sharing Among the Human Capitalists: An Economic Inquiry Into the Corporate Law Firm and How Partners Split Profits, *Stanford Law Review* 37:313 (1985).
70 Ibid. Such a sharing rule may also serve important risk-sharing functions.
71 Berman, note 59, Chapter 10.
72 Egged, the large Israeli bus monopoly, is yet another example. It is a workers' cooperative in which the bus drivers, and only the bus drivers, are the owners. The administrators, ticket agents, interpreters, and mechanics are all just employees. Again, the reason is presumably that, whereas it is easy to secure consensus among the bus drivers, it would be much harder to secure consensus among the bus drivers, the interpreters, and the ticket agents.

to an individual worker's efforts are fairly easily observable, as they are in a law firm, in which such productivity devices as hours billed to individual clients are available. In contrast, it is hard to imagine how one would even design a productivity-based compensation formula for managers in most large business corporations, much less reach agreement on the terms of the formula among the different managers themselves.

Such considerations of homogeneity of interest are evidently an important reason why worker-owned firms appear, as remarked above, not where worker productivity is particularly difficult to monitor, but on the contrary in those industries in which worker output seems relatively easy to measure. Thus it is that trash-collection crews, taxicab drivers, and service professionals are the types of workers who form worker-owned firms, and not blue-collar or white-collar workers who work in large teams. It is, in fact, extremely difficult to find successful examples of worker-owned firms in which there is substantial hierarchy or division of labor among the worker–owners.

Indeed, worker-owned firms in the service professions, where they are most commonly found, are in many ways analogous to the wholesale supply cooperatives examined above. The partners in such firms are in considerable degree autonomous workers, servicing their own clients. In many cases they could do nearly as well practicing on their own, or in much smaller groups, affiliating in various combinations only when necessary to deal with large or complex matters. This very separability in their services, which makes their individual contribution to the firm relatively easy to monitor, is what makes the incentive pay system that accompanies worker ownership so effective; it is possible to assign to each worker roughly that portion of the firm's earnings that he or she contributes, and thus give the worker a strong incentive for maximum productivity.

There are, however, economies in sharing common services, such as a library, secretarial staff, receptionist, data processing, record-keeping, and so forth. Such services can be, and sometimes are, rented from a firm established to provide these services for multiple firms of professionals located in the same building. But there is at least some incentive for the professionals to own the provider of these common services collectively, to avoid the problem of lock-in and subsequent exploitation. More importantly, the professionals may find it efficient to advertise collectively, as it were, by adopting a common brand (firm) name. And, as in the case of the wholesale cooperatives that provide common brand names to their member retailers, there is some incentive to own the brand name collectively to deal with the additional lock-in problem that it creates.

It follows that worker-owned firms such as these can, alternatively, be viewed as consumer cooperatives rather than as producer cooperatives: In a sense, they are groups of independent firms that collectively purchase some common services.

VI   Mutual and nonprofit firms

Mutual insurance companies, mutual banks, and nonprofit firms have been examined elsewhere in transaction-cost terms similar to those employed here. Several observations, however, are worth making.

A   Mutual companies

Problems of asymmetric information were an important impetus to the formation of mutual (policyholder-owned) life insurance companies, while mutual property and liability insurance companies evidently arose in considerable part as a response to market power. In both cases, however, considerations of risk sharing also provided an important impetus for consumer ownership.

Life insurance contracts, for example, typically have a duration of decades and are written in terms of nominal dollars. Consequently, they involve a gamble on future interest rates and rates of inflation, and on the accuracy of mortality tables (which were quite crude in the nineteenth century, when the industry began). Stock insurance companies must charge substantial premiums for bearing these risks, which are largely nondiversifiable. Yet "insurance" for these matters is of little value to the insureds (and in fact constitutes a pure gamble so far as inflation is concerned). The mutual form eliminates these costs for policyholders, since, through adjustment in patronage dividends according to experience, only diversifiable risk is insured for. In short, mutuals permit pooling without creating the costs of risk bearing associated with long-term market contracts.

Similar considerations are operative in property and liability insurance. When the aggregate risk of loss for an industry as a whole is highly unpredictable – as it was in the early stages of the insurance industry, for example, and as it has become recently in medical malpractice owing to uncertainty about the legal standards of liability that will prevail when claims are litigated – the comparative advantage of the mutual form grows.

Other costs of ownership are less favorable to the mutual form. In particular, the policyholders in most mutuals are so numerous and so geographically dispersed as to make the exercise of collective control prohibitively costly. For example, the management of nearly all mutual life insurance companies has effectively been self-appointing and free of any direct control by policyholders whatever from the time the first such companies were established in the 1840s. Life insurance is thus a clear instance of an industry in which ownership has been assigned to a class of patrons in large part just to avoid the high costs of market contracting that those patrons would incur if ownership were assigned to anyone else.[73]

Similar considerations explain the large role that mutual companies played in the savings bank industry in its early stages.[74]

B   *Nonprofit firms*

Nonprofit firms typically arise in situations in which two circumstances are conjoined. First, there is a class of patrons for whom the costs of market contracting are so severe – typically as a result of the patrons' extreme informational disadvantage – that assigning ownership to anyone else who could exercise it effectively would be impracticable. But, second, those same patrons are so situated that the costs to them of exercising effective control over the firm are unacceptably large relative to the value of their transactions with the firm. The solution to this strong conflict between the costs of contracting and the costs of control is to create a firm without any owners at all – that is, without anyone who has the right to both net earnings and control.[75]

---

73 For more extended analysis see Henry Hansmann, The Organization of Insurance Companies: Mutual Versus Stock, *Journal of Law, Economics, and Organization* 1:125–53 (1985). See also David Mayers and Clifford Smith, Contractual Provisions, Organizational Structure, and Conflict Control in Insurance Markets, *Journal of Business* 54:407–34 (1981).

74 See Eric Rasmussen, Stock Banks and Mutual Banks, *Journal of Law and Economics* (forthcoming); Henry Hansmann, The Role of Commercial Nonprofits: The Evolution of Savings Banks, in Helmut Anheier and Wolfgang Seibel, eds., *The Nonprofit Sector: International and Comparative Perspectives* (forthcoming).

75 For a more detailed study of the nonprofit sector from a transaction-cost perspective similar to that developed here, including further observations on the respective roles of nonprofit and cooperative enterprise, see Henry Hansmann, The Role of Nonprofit Enterprise, *Yale Law Journal* 89:835 (1980). See also Henry Hansmann, Economic Theories of Nonprofit Organization, in Walter Powell, ed., *The Nonprofit Sector: A Research Handbook* (1987).

VII   Conclusion

The preceding survey points to several reasons for the dominance of investor-owned firms in market economies. One is that contracting costs for capital are often relatively high as compared to contracting costs for other inputs – including labor – and for most products. A second reason is that, however poorly situated investors may be to exercise effective control, there is seldom any other group of patrons who are in a better position to assert control. Where either of these conditions fails, other forms of ownership arise. Thus, when there are serious imperfections in the firm's product or factor markets, the firm is often organized as a consumer or producer cooperative or as a nonprofit. Similarly, when some group of patrons other than suppliers of capital is in a good position to exercise collective control, consumer or producer cooperatives often arise even when the patrons in question are faced with only modest problems of market failure. This suggests either that the effectiveness of the oversight exercised by shareholders – even with the assistance of the market for corporate control – is distinctly limited, or that other factors may be more important in constraining managerial opportunism.

In determining whether the costs of ownership are manageable for a given class of patrons, homogeneity of interest appears to be an especially important consideration. In particular, it is evidently a significant factor in the widespread success of the modern investor-owned business corporation, and it may be among the best explanations for the relative paucity of worker-owned firms, which otherwise have some significant efficiency advantages.

Index

acquisition gains
  breach of "implicit contacts," 33
  discount hypothesis, 35–9, 46–50
  division of, 207
  empirical literature on, 125
  joint-gains hypothesis, 60–2
  management buyouts and, 49–50
  market hypothesis, 35–9, 43, 53, 59, 63
  misinvestment hypothesis, 35–6, 53–4, 63
  monopoly power and, 33
  premia over share price, 31–2
  "private information" theory, 33
  recognition, timing of, 275
  takeover statutes and, 245
  target firms, created by, 125–6
  tax savings and, 34–5
  traditional gains hypothesis, 32–5
  trapped-equity theory, 34–5
acquisition premia, see acquisition gains
agency costs
  bonding against, 190 (see also mandatory terms)
  devices for controlling, 194 (see also mandatory terms)
  diversification and, 190–1, 207–8
  governance structure and, 187, 210–11
  mergers compared to takeovers, 146
  monitoring 190, 291–3
  no-resistance rule, 146
  optimal capital structure and, 261–9
  reincorporation and, 218
  state incorporation competition and, 219, 250
  takeover defenses and, 138–9, 146–8
  takeover threats and, 203
  tax law, 256, 266–8

American Stock Exchange, see stock exchanges
antitakeover statutes, see takeover statutes
Antitrust Merger Guidelines, economies of scale as defense to, 3
asset tax, 270–2
asymmetric information
  financing decisions and, 57
  see also market contracting, costs of
auctions in takeovers, 59, 65–8, 203–5

bankruptcy
  liquidation, 150–1
  reorganization, see reorganizations
Bankruptcy Code
  Chapter 7, 150
  Chapter 11, 150–1
bargaining in sale of assets, 122–4
breakup acquisitions, see discounted share price
bureaucracy, costs of, 6–7
  see also conglomerate structure
business judgment doctrine, 183

capital markets, failures of, 21–2
Chandler Act, 151
closed-end investment funds, see discounted share price
collective action problem
  corporate ownership and, 293–6
  reorganizations and, 172
  see also dual class recapitalization, shareholder approval of; ownership, costs of
conglomerate structure, 51
  see also bureaucracy, costs of

315

Connecticut fair price statute, 234–5, 248
  see also takeover statutes
consumer cooperatives, *see* customer-owned firms
contract-defeating doctrines
  contracting parties, protection of, 200–2
  corporate contracts and, 200–13
corporate bar, role in legislative process, 253–4
corporate charters
  amendments to, Delaware law on, 229
  market for, *see* state incorporation competition
  see also corporate contract; governance structures; mandatory terms
corporate codes, differentiation, 221
  see also state incorporation competition
corporate contract
  amendments, rules for, 210–11
  background terms, 212–13
  beneficial intervention and, 204
  breach of, 213
  generally, 192–6
  inefficient terms, 202–9
  latecomer terms, 209–11
  takeover defenses and, 204–6
  third parties, adverse effects on, 201–8
  see also, corporate charters; governance structures; mandatory terms
corporate form, *see* governance structures,
cost of capital
  proportion of debt and, 12–17
  state incorporation competition and, 218
CTS Corp. v. *Dynamics Corp. of America*, 108n35, 233
customer-owned firms
  cost of contracting vs. cost of ownership, 304
  farm supply cooperatives, 303–4
  retailers of consumer goods, 300–1
  wholesale and supply firms, 301–3

debt, substitution for equity, 14–16
  see also equity conversions
debt–equity ratios, effects of tax law on, 261
Delaware
  franchise taxes, 229
  legal capital, investment in, 229
  market share of corporate charters, 225
  "mutual reliance relationship" with firms, 232
  political equilibrium, 249

  see also Delaware corporate law
Delaware corporate law
  advantages to lawyers, 230–1
  commitment to responsiveness, 228–31
  court decisions, 241–5
  director liability statute, 251n85
  first-mover advantage, 227
  management discretion and, 218
  market for corporate charters and, 216
  state revenue and, 219
  takeover statutes, 238–9
  see also Delaware
disclosure, securities laws and, 203
discount hypothesis
  conversion behavior, 52–8
  takeover statutes, implications for, 64–71
  see also acquisition gains; discounted share price
discounted share price
  as acquisition motive, 59–64
  acquisition premia and, 46–50
  asset values and, 63
  breakup acquisitions and, 50–2
  closed-end mutual funds, 40–3
  holding companies, 44
  management reluctance to reduce, 59
  natural resource companies, 44–5
  see also acquisition gains, discount hypothesis
diversification, agency cost and, 190–1
dual class common stock
  American Stock Exchange rule, 75
  nonuniform rules, 111–12
  NYSE rule, 75, 142 (*see also* mandatory terms; New York Stock Exchange, single class common rule)
  OTC rule, 75
  uniform rules, 112–16 (*see also* SEC Proposed Rule 19c–4)
  see also dual class recapitalization
dual class recapitalization
  dilution of economic participation, 113–14
  dual class initial public offering, compared to, 79, 84–5
  justifications for, 70–86
  mechanisms to effect, 88–90
  shareholder approval of, 91–104
  shareholder wealth, empirical evidence of effects on, 86–8
  see also dual class common stock

equity conversions, 53
  see also debt, substitution for equity

fair price acts, ownership concentration
and, 237
see also Connecticut fair price statute;
takeover statutes
farm supply cooperatives
tax preferences, 304
see also customer-owned firms
federal system of corporate law, *see* state
incorporation competition
firm-specific human capital, investments in
takeover defenses and, 127–31
see also shareholder opportunism; specific capital
franchise taxes, *see* state incorporation
competition

golden parachutes, *see* managerial
compensation
governance structures
adaptations, 193
agency costs, 187
contractual terms of, 196
mandatory terms, 199–200
shaping of, 183–7
stock prices and, 197–200
valuation of terms, 198–9
see also corporate charters; corporate
contract
"greenmail," 80

holding companies, *see* discounted share
price
horizontal mergers, 3

information
asymmetries of, *see* market contracting,
costs of
investment in, 252
Indiana antitakeover statute, *see* takeover
statutes
institutional investors, 251–2
internal organization, costs of, *see*
bureaucracy
Internal Revenue Code
section 301, 264
section 305, 266
section 306, 266
section 338, 270–80
section 351, 266
investor-owned firms
market contracting, costs of, 297–8
ownership, costs of, 298–300
as producer cooperative, 284
irrelevance proposition, *see* Modigliani-
Miller irrelevance proposition

law firms, *see* worker-owned firms
leveraged buyouts
cash-flow vs. asset-based financing, 15
free cash-flow hypothesis, 16–17
innovators in, 20
major lenders, 15
management buyouts, 16
share prices, effects on, 55–6
tax law and, 257
transaction-cost theory, 12–17
liquidation reincorporation, tax treatment
of, 208
majority voting mechanisms, inefficiencies
of, 294
management buyouts, *see* leveraged
buyouts
management opportunism
dual class recapitalizations and, 80
see also agency costs
management resistance to takeovers, *see*
bargaining in sale of assets; takeover
defenses
managerial compensation
deferred compensation, 81–2
golden parachutes, 82
see also shareholder opportunism
mandatory terms
government, imposed by, 107–8 (*see also*
no-resistance rule; takeover statutes)
justifications for, 88–111, 200–11
stock exchanges, imposed by, 75–6,
111–16, 142–3, 108–9, 111
market contracting, costs of
asymmetric information, 289
investor-owned firms, 297–8
"lock-in," 288–9
market power, 288
wholesale and supply firms, 301–2
market power, *see* market contracting,
costs of
M-form structure
technology transfer, 19
U-form, advantages over, 10
see also multidivisionalization, innovators in; U-form structure
misinvestment hypothesis
acquisition premia, 35–6, 53–4, 63
auction debate and, 65–8
energy industry, applications to, 63
see also acquisition gains; discount hypothesis; discounted share price
Modigliani-Miller irrelevance proposition
generally, 12–13, 265
tax law and, 260–9
monitoring
corporate structure and, 185
division of interest and, 189–90

monitoring (*cont.*)
  generally, 136, 203
  profit sharing and, 189
  takeover defenses and, 143
  see also agency costs; ownership,
    costs of
Moran v. *Household Int'l. Inc.*, 134n39
multidivisionalization, innovators in, 19–
  20
  see also M-form structure
mutual companies, 311–12

NASD, *see* stock exchanges
national corporation law, advocates of,
  218–19
New York Stock Exchange
  delisting, cost of, 109
  rules discouraging defensive tactics,
    142–3 (*see also* takeover defenses)
  single class common rule, 75–6, 108–9,
    111
  see also stock exchanges
no-resistance rule
  disadvantages, 144–5
  see also mandatory terms; takeover de-
    fenses; takeover statutes
noise trading, 38
  see also acquisition gains; discount hy-
    pothesis; discounted share price
nonprofit firms
  generally, 284
  market contracting, costs of, 312
  ownership, costs of, 312
nonredeployable asset, 227–8
  see also specific capital
nonvoting stock, 182
  see also dual class common stock

organization-specific capital, 307
  see also specific capital
organizational innovation, antitrust and,
  21
ownership
  formal rights of, 283
  general theory of, 286–8
  market contracting, trade-off between,
    296–7
  transaction costs and, 287–8
ownership, costs of
  collective decision making, 293–6
  investor-owned firms, 283–300
  monitoring, 290–93
  risk bearing, 296
  wholesale and supply firms, 302–3
  see also agency costs

Pac Man defense, 80
  see also takeover defenses
place of business regulation, 246–7
poison pill defense, *see* takeover defenses
pooling capital, tax law effect on, 262
preferred stock, tax treatment of, 266–7
premia, *see* acquisition gains
producer cooperative, 285
proxy contests
  costs of, 8–10
  management control of, 252
  regulation of, 10

regulatory view of corporations, 184
reincorporation
  cheaper legal regimes and, 225–6
  merger-and-acquisition programs and,
    241
  stock prices and, 239–45, 249
  transaction costs of, 224–5
  transaction-type motivation, 223
  see also state incorporation competition
reorganizations
  Bankruptcy Code, Chapter 11, 150–1
  bargaining among participants, 154–5
  capital structure, choice of, 155–6
  collective action problems, 172
  division problem, 153–7
  entitlements of participants, 155, 164–
    74
  generally, 151–3
  information of participants, 171–2
  proposal for reform, 157–64
  reinstatement of contracts, 178
  valuation problem, 153–7, 165, 169–71
Revlon, Inc. v. *MacAndrews & Forbes
  Holdings, Inc.*, 134n39

"Saturday Night Specials," 67n124
search costs, *see* takeovers
SEC Proposed Rule 19c–4
  generally, 76–8, 112–16
  NASD and AMEX firms, application
    to, 115–16
  NYSE firms, application to, 113–15
SEC Schedule 13E–3, 49n63
separation of ownership and control, efficiency of, 291–2
share prices, *see* stock prices
shareholder distributions, 52–8
shareholder misinformation, 251, 253
shareholder opportunism
  firm-specific human capital and, 83–4
  management compensation and, 81–3
  takeover defenses and, 140–1

see also dual class recapitalization, justifications for
shark repellents
  ownership concentration and, 237
  predatory practices, solution to, 236–7
  welfare-enhancing properties of, 236–7
  see also takeover defenses
Singer v. *Magnavox Co.*, 243
Smith v. *Van Gorkom*, 244
specific capital
  asset specificity, vertical integration and, 5
  firm-specific human capital, 83–4, 127–31
  "lock-in, " *see* market contracting, costs of
  organization-specific capital, 307
  transaction-specific assets, 227
  see also firm-specific human capital
state incorporation competition
  agency costs, 219
  beneficiaries of, 239–45
  cost of capital and, 218
  differentiated codes, 321
  franchise taxes, 217
  literature on, 217–32
  policy implications, 248–54
  politics, local, 219
  "race for the bottom," 218
  self-selection thesis, 222–4, 227
  takeover statutes and, 232–9
  transaction-cost theory, 224–32
  uniformity, 220
  see also reincorporation
stock exchanges
  competition, 109–11
  migration between, 109, 114–15
  see also American Stock Exchange; mandatory terms; New York Stock Exchange
stock prices
  asset values and, 37
  mispricing, 37–9
  public information and, 197–8
strategic choice problems, *see* dual class recapitalization, shareholder approval of

takeover defenses
  agency costs of, 133–4
  bargaining rights and, 119–24
  corporate contract and, 204–6
  default options, 145
  disincentives to bidders, 133
  divergence between private and social optimality, 205

externalities from, 132–8
financial restructuring, 54–5
monitoring and, 143
NYSE rules discouraging resistance, 142–3
poison pills, 134n39
private solutions to the problem, 138–46
shareholder agreements and, 138–41
state laws barring resistance, 141–2 (*see also* takeover statutes)
tax liabilities, avoidance of, 275
waiting periods, 70
see also shark repellents
takeover gains, *see* acquisition gains
takeover statutes
  Delaware corporate law, 238–9
  fair price provisions, 237 (*see also* Connecticut fair price statute)
  Indiana law, 108n35
  opt-in provisions, 237, 250
  politics of, 234–5
  proportion of successful takeovers, effects on, 246
  second generation, 247–9
  shareholder sovereignty, effects on, 238
  shareholder wealth, effects on, 234–5
  state incorporation competition and, 232–9
  takeover premia, effects on, 245
  transaction-cost reduction, 238
takeovers
  auctions, 59, 65–8
  costs of, 11
  costs of ownership and, 299
  discount gains, *see* acquisition gains, discount hypothesis
  hostile, ban on, 69
  motives for, *see* acquisition gains
  no-resistance rule, 119
  recent wave of, 62
  search costs, 48, 131–2
  "stepping up" basis and, 269–80
  value creation by target firms, 124–31
tax-free reorganizations, 269–70
tax law
  agency costs and, 256
  capital assets, sale of, 259
  capital structure, influence on, 260–9
  disincentives to excessive debt financing, 265–9
  disincentives to financial fiddling, 265–9
  distributed bonds, treatment of, 262–9
  liquidation reincorporations, treatment of, 268
  positive effects of, 262–9

tax law (*cont.*)
  preferred stock, treatment of, 266–7
  stock and asset acquisitions, role in, 269–80
  see also tax law intrusions
tax law intrusions
  allocation of resources, 258
  capital structures, 256
  debt–equity ratios, 261
  disincentive to exchanges, 255
  disincentive to risky investments, 257
  dividend policy, 256
  economic explanation for, 259
  financial intermediaries, 256
  geographic location of capital, 258
  managerial compensation, 256
  mix of ownership forms, 257
  size of firms, 257
  tolerance of, 258–60
  see also tax law
Tax Reform Act of 1986, section 336, 270
Tobin's Q, 45
trapped-equity theory, *see* acquisition gains

U-form structure, 9
  see also M-form structure

Unocal Corp. v. *Mesa Petroleum Co.*, 134n39

venture capital, 186
vertical integration
  antitrust enforcement, 6
  applied-price theory, 4
  asset specificity, 5
  into final sales and service, 18–19
  innovators, 17–19
  inventory management, 17–18
  mistakes, 19 (*see also* bureaucracy, costs of)
  monopoly purpose, 4
  selective integration hypothesis, 17
  transaction-cost theory, 5–7, 17
vertical mergers, *see* vertical integration

Williams Act, 66–7, 69–70
worker-owned firms
  generally, 305
  law firms, 308–9
  market contracting, costs of, 305–7
  ownership, costs of, 307–11
  Pacific coast plywood cooperatives, 308n66